THE OFFICIAL
Formula 1™
SEASON REVIEW 2009
FOREWORD BY BERNIE ECCLESTONE

Published in November 2009

A catalogue record for this book is available
from the British Library

ISBN 978 1 84425 721 8

Library of Congress control no. 2009928032

Editor Bruce Jones
Managing Editor Steve Rendle

Design Lee Parsons, Richard Parsons, Dominic Stickland

Contributors Adam Cooper (race reports), Tony Dodgins
(round table, teams' technical review and race report panels),
Rob Aherne (season overview), Bradley Lord (race reports),
James Roberts (race reports)

Photographs All by LAT (Steven Tee, Lorenzo Bellanca,
Charles Coates, Glenn Dunbar, Steve Etherington,
Andrew Ferraro, Alastair Staley)
Group Operations Manager LAT Tim Wright
Digital Technicians LAT Steve Carpenter, Matt Smith,
Anna Boyce

Illustrations Alan Eldridge

Publishing Manager Sam Jempson
Publishing Directors Peter Higham, Mark Hughes

**Published by Haynes Publishing
in association with Haymarket Consumer Media**

Haynes Publishing, Sparkford, Yeovil,
Somerset BA22 7JJ, UK
Tel: +44 (0) 1963 442030
Fax: +44 (0) 1963 440001
E-mail: sales@haynes.co.uk
Website: www.haynes.co.uk

Haymarket Consumer Media, Teddington Studios,
Broom Road, Teddington, Middlesex TW11 9BE, UK
Tel: +44 (0) 208 267 5000
Fax: +44 (0) 208 267 5022
E-mail: F1Review@haymarket.com
Website: www.haymarket.com

Printed in the UK

CONTENTS

FOREWORD

People always ask me when we're going to have a quiet year and concentrate on the racing. This year, it was great on the track with Brawn and Red Bull out front. Jenson Button has always had the ability to be World Champion. After a great start to the year, he got a bit nervous and had a wobble, but that's normal: they've all done it. But he got the job done in style in Brazil, and that was a great drive. And once you're a champion, it's not just for one year – it's forever.

At Red Bull, Sebastian Vettel was a star. He was new to the team, but he just got the job done. There were some unfortunate incidents, which probably cost him the championship, but he's going to be World Champion one day, and I think that will happen sooner rather than later. He's a lovely person and a great character. It was also good to see Mark Webber winning a couple of races.

Changes keep everybody on their toes and sometimes even the big teams trip up – we saw that this year with McLaren and Ferrari. They did a super job to bounce back, especially Lewis Hamilton who was fantastic in the second half of the season.

We can concentrate on an even better season in 2010. There will be lots of new faces in new teams, so it's going to be more exciting than ever.

BERNIE ECCLESTONE

REFLECTING ON THE 2009 FORMULA ONE SEASON
A YEAR OF SURPRISES

THE SEASON

With new rules shuffling the pack, 2009 was an epic, producing a new champion, Jenson Button, for a new team, Brawn GP, as Red Bull Racing showed its credentials

As Jenson Button bounded down the Interlagos pitlane, beaming the mile-wide smile of a champion, and embracing all in his path, the irony of the moment was probably lost on him. A year earlier, at the 2008 Brazilian GP, the Formula 1 paddock had been feting a different British World Champion, while Button was wriggling free of his car in *parc fermé*. It had been an anonymous afternoon for Button, and nobody would have given him a second glance… had it not been for the fact that his Honda was on fire.

It seemed a symbolic moment. Button had hit rock bottom at Interlagos, yet things would get even worse soon afterwards, with the announcement that Honda was quitting F1. That both the 29-year-old and his team recovered from this hammer blow to clinch both world titles just 350 days later, ranks as one of the great sporting fairytales – one that encapsulated a year in which the sport was turned upside down on-track while seeming to lurch from crisis to crisis off it.

The politics can wait, because there was so much going on during the 2009 season's 17 grands prix that they never overshadowed the action. The

RULE CHANGES FOR 2009

When the covers were first lifted off the 2009-spec cars, there were a few gasps – were Formula 1 cars really going to look like that this year? Some of the biggest rule changes for years were implemented for this season, turning the formbook on its head from the opening race of the year.

The biggest visual difference was a tidying up of the cars, with a cut in the rear wing size and an increase in front wing size, plus the abolition of all the aerodynamic appendages, such as bargeboards, winglets and turning vanes. Front wings were now mounted lower and, at 1800mm, were 400mm wider than previously, while rear wings were narrower and taller compared to their 2008 counterparts. The intention was to reduce the aerodynamic wake in order to try and increase overtaking opportunities for cars following closely behind. To further help the cause, drivers could now adjust the angle of one

of the front-wing elements twice a lap, up to a limit of six degrees, by pushing a button on their steering wheel.

To compensate for the loss of downforce, Formula 1 reintroduced slick tyres for the first time in a decade, which increased grip by around 20 per cent over the grooved tyres used for the past few years, and kept lap times at similar levels to those achieved in 2008.

Another plan to help to improve overtaking was to provide teams with an engine power boost, obtainable through a kinetic energy recovery system (KERS). However, the controversial use of KERS probably did more to stifle overtaking, when used to fend off a passing move, than it did to improve matters. The new 'green' technology was optional, and only Ferrari and McLaren successfully used the system all year, the other teams finding the weight penalty wasn't worth the performance

advantage. The system worked by releasing energy recovered under braking and stored in a battery or a spinning flywheel, and was deployed via a 'boost button', providing around an extra 80 horsepower for up to seven seconds a lap.

Also in the engine department, rev limits were reduced from 19,000 to 18,000rpm, and each driver was limited to just eight engines for the season (receiving a 10-place grid penalty if they exceeded this limit). This was a cost-cutting measure, as was the ban on in-season testing, which put more emphasis on Friday practice for testing new parts and giving rookie drivers as much mileage as possible.

The last major rule change allowed cars to pit if the safety car was deployed, and all drivers were sent timing data to their cockpit display once the safety car was deployed, to ensure their speed was not excessive under caution, en route to the pits.

catalyst for much of the drama was the Brawn GP team, hastily assembled in the aftermath of Honda's exit, yet never bettered. The Brackley operation's survival was touch and go, but once technical chief Ross Brawn put his name above the door, the team had all the necessary ingredients in place: proven management; a new car finessed by months of development and some clever reading of the new F1 rules (see sidebar); the best engines in the field from Mercedes; and, in Button and Rubens Barrichello, experienced drivers with a point to prove.

The Brawn BGP 001 was launched only three weeks before the season-opening Australian GP, but its speed was immediately obvious. How much of this was down to controversial double-diffuser rear aerodynamics was a bone of contention that went all the way to the FIA Court of Appeal. However, by the time Brawn's rivals had caught up, Button had a stranglehold on the championship. Six of the first seven races fell to the Briton, who drove like a man sensing a career-defining opportunity.

The BGP 001 seemed tailor-made for Button's efficient style, but he piloted it with the confidence and aggression of a champion elect – to the extent that Ross Brawn was drawn into comparisons with Michael Schumacher. Equally at home in the monsoon conditions of Malaysia and the blistering heat of Bahrain, the only race that Button didn't win in the first half dozen, China, was the percentage drive of a man who already had the title in mind.

After a dominant performance in June's Turkish GP, his lead had stretched to 26 points, but it wasn't game over. In fact, he would grace the podium only twice in the remaining 10 grands prix. He never seemed at one with the Brawn again, frequently complaining that he couldn't generate tyre temperature, and an anxiety crept into his driving. Brawn himself likened it to being ahead in a football match and waiting for the whistle – and by the time it sounded, Button's team-mate Barrichello had positioned himself as a genuine challenger.

The oldest driver on the grid had made a relatively poor start, and railed against what he saw as attempts to cast him as Button's wingman. This culminated in a stinging attack on the management when race strategy went against him at the Spanish GP. His outburst cleared the air, and as Brawn's competitiveness faded, Barrichello gained the upper hand. He won at Valencia and Monza to almost halve his team-mate's lead and suggest that maybe, just maybe, the crown could be his. On home soil in

OPPOSITE Jenson Button and Ross Brawn started celebrating in Australia and still had reason to do so at the last race of the year

ABOVE Formula One is marching to an increasingly eastern beat as it broadens its global reach

BELOW McLaren reacted quickly to the double-diffuser ruling. Lewis Hamilton's can clearly be seen as he crests a rise at Suzuka

ABOVE Ron Dennis talks to Lewis Hamilton at the start of the year, before Dennis handed over the McLaren reins to Martin Whitmarsh

ABOVE RIGHT Brawn GP's Jenson Button and Rubens Barrichello controlled proceedings in the first half of the year, and they headed to their third 1–2 finish at Monaco

OPPOSITE Renault's Nelson Piquet Jr spins, but it was a spin in Singapore in 2008 for which he found himself under the spotlight

Brazil, Rubens finally ran out of road, but his tenacity did much to keep the season alive.

As did that of Red Bull Racing, which emerged to become Brawn's strongest rival over the balance of the season. The RB5 was easily the quickest car designed without a double diffuser, even though its Renault engines couldn't quite match the Mercedes V8s. The Milton Keynes team had another ace up its sleeve though: the pairing of Sebastian Vettel and Mark Webber. The duo were chalk and cheese away from the cockpit, but well matched in it; and although the hotly-tipped Vettel had the upper hand in qualifying, his more experienced team-mate often countered with greater aggression in races. Vettel gave the team its maiden win at a soaking Chinese GP in Shanghai, and both drivers scored stylish mid-season victories to make Button feel uncomfortable: Vettel at Silverstone, Webber (despite a drive-through penalty) in Germany.

Their challenge faltered over the summer, as neither found the consistency to press home their car advantage. In five races from Hungary to Singapore the pair amassed only 18 points, and team principal Christian Horner conceded that this

was not his team's year. However, there was still time for Red Bull to win the final three races, with Vettel victories in Japan and Abu Dhabi sandwiching a Webber win in Brazil. Vettel stole past Barrichello to rank second in the championship table, and both he and Webber emerged from the campaign with their reputations considerably enhanced.

For all this season's glorious unpredictability, that isn't necessarily something that you could say about F1 itself. Away from the track, the sport's stakeholders often seemed to be fumbling for the self-destruct button, and over the British GP weekend they actually seemed poised to press it, with the announcement from the Formula One Teams' Association (FOTA) of a breakaway race series.

The battle lines were familiar: namely, who stood to profit from F1's future commercial revenues, and who ultimately controlled its sporting and technical direction. What was different this time was the teams' united front and the intensely personal nature of their feud with Max Mosley, President of motorsport governing body the FIA, and architect of new rules that required teams to sign up to a swingeing budget cap from 2010 onwards.

OPPOSITE The teams formed a united front under FOTA, but scrapped talk of a breakaway series and signed the new Concorde Agreement before the year was out

RIGHT FIA President Max Mosley found himself the centre of attention at the Monaco GP when he held a meeting with the teams

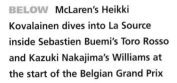

BELOW McLaren's Heikki Kovalainen dives into La Source inside Sebastien Buemi's Toro Rosso and Kazuki Nakajima's Williams at the start of the Belgian Grand Prix

Mosley's reasoning was sound, but his attempts to ride over the teams' objections met with such stubborn resistance that, for once, he was forced to back down. The breakaway threat dissipated, and a new Concorde Agreement was signed, paving the way for more teams to join the grid. By the time Mosley was replaced as FIA President by former Ferrari team chief Jean Todt, in the autumn, an uneasy peace had broken out.

It wasn't the season's only flashpoint. McLaren, hit with a $100m fine in 2007 following the 'Spygate' affair, was soon in the dock again: this time over 'Liegate', shorthand for its attempts to cover up some poorly-judged manoeuvring behind the safety car in the Australian GP. Its punishment amounted to a final warning, but more significant were changes to its management that included team principal Ron Dennis ceding control of the team.

Another of F1's 'big beasts' came a cropper in an even more unsavoury scandal, when Nelson Piquet Jr, recently fired by Renault, alleged that he had been told to crash at the 2008 Singapore GP. Piquet Jr's accident brought out the safety car that allowed team-mate Fernando Alonso to win, but it didn't look like anything other than outrageous fortune until an FIA investigation uncovered evidence that the Brazilian had deliberately taken a fall for the team. Crashgate dragged F1 through the mud once again, despite team chief Flavio Briatore and technical boss Pat Symonds falling on their swords. The colourful Briatore was effectively being banned from the paddock for good.

The nature of F1's inevitable feuds may take a different form in the post-Mosley era; and certainly, the economic climate gives its stakeholders the incentive to get along. It was reflected by Brawn GP's failure to land a title sponsor; in empty seats at high-profile races; and in the failure of Donington

Park to deliver on ambitious plans to host the British GP from 2010 onwards.

One race bucked the trend: the Abu Dhabi finale amid the jaw-dropping splendour of the new Yas Island marina circuit, but there are only so many Abu Dhabis left in the world. F1 has to economise, and even if cost-cutting is not of the order demanded by Mosley, the sport is poised for a relatively austere period.

Equally, 2009 underlined that money doesn't always equate to success. This was the first season in more than a decade that the wealthiest teams, McLaren and Ferrari, failed to mount a title challenge. For reigning champion Lewis Hamilton and McLaren, it was a game of two halves, and the first half was one to forget. The new MP4-24 proved woefully short of grip and, as the team tried to regroup in the aftermath of 'Liegate', it became clear that Hamilton's title defence was doomed to failure.

Hamilton cut a troubled figure in the races that followed, unhappy at the novelty of toiling in the midfield. Neither he nor the team gave up, however, and their persistence was rewarded by a mid-season aero upgrade that finally gave his car poise to match its power. Dominant wins followed in Hungary and Singapore, as Lewis left even critics in no doubt that he is one of the best in the business. Team-mate Heikki Kovalainen's uninspiring campaign, however, served only to multiply his doubters.

It was an authentic *annus horribilis* for last year's champion team too. Like its nemesis, McLaren, Ferrari had invested heavily in chasing the 2008 crown and developing KERS. Like the McLaren, the F60 lacked pace from the off, with Felipe Massa and Kimi Räikkönen struggling to master its tricky handling. However, its lacklustre performance paled into insignificance alongside the freak accident that befell Massa during qualifying in Hungary, when

he was hit by a suspension part from Barrichello's Brawn. F1 held its breath while the popular Brazilian underwent surgery on his fractured skull, and his full recovery was a tribute to the progress made in safety in recent years.

Thereafter, Ferrari prepared to write the season off, despite a stirring drive to victory from Räikkönen in Belgium. Elsewhere, the Finn looked jaded and unmotivated, a state of affairs that precipitated his departure from Maranello. His replacement, Alonso, looks like the tonic the Scuderia needs, but he must hope for better machinery: just ask Massa stand-ins Luca Badoer and Giancarlo Fisichella, whose travails underlined how far behind Ferrari had fallen.

Most teams seemed to take their lead, though, from the topsy-turvy form of the Big Two. How else do you explain Fisichella, for Force India, coming from nowhere to grab pole and a podium at Spa-Francorchamps? Or the BMW Sauber, in which Robert Kubica nearly won in Melbourne, being so disappointing almost everywhere else.

Toyota emerged as the best of the rest, although it was frustratingly inconsistent. Jarno Trulli and Timo Glock were capable of performing strongly,

but neither consistently captured the imagination – unlike Kamui Kobayashi, whose cameo deputising for the injured Glock caught the eye. By autumn there was change in the air, with talk of new drivers and a more streamlined approach – one that might finally yield a dividend on the company's substantial investment. However, this counted for naught when Toyota pulled the plug on its F1 programme in the week after the final race.

Williams provided Toyota with a few highlights, often dominating practice with Nico Rosberg, even if the German flattered to deceive when it truly mattered in qualifying. Rosberg still enjoyed the best points finish of his F1 career, but the 24-year-old now seems to be at something of a crossroads. Kazuki Nakajima starred at Silverstone, but disappointed elsewhere; and the Grove team, running its customary tight ship, is changing both pilots and powerplant for 2010.

Last year's surprise package, BMW Sauber, suffered a shocker, to the extent that the German car maker's board called time on the team in July. The F1.09 generally looked dismal in Kubica's and Nick Heidfeld's hands, even though the team had

OPPOSITE TOP Giancarlo Fisichella celebrates after taking a suprise pole position for Force India at the Belgian GP at Spa

OPPOSITE BOTTOM Ferrari's crew send a message to Felipe Massa after he suffered a serious head injury in qualifying in Hungary

ABOVE Sebastian Vettel scored four wins for Red Bull as he raced to second place in the championship

stopped chasing the 2008 title to focus efforts on its 2009 car. However, there was the odd gritty drive – notably Kubica's to second place in Brazil – that helped it to pick off Williams and Renault.

A miserable season on the track was probably the least of Renault's problems between 'Crashgate', the loss of major sponsors and the impending departure of its star driver. The errant wheel that cost Alonso the lead in Hungary, and almost led to a race ban, summed things up, while the pace of both Piquet Jr and Romain Grosjean put into perspective what the double champion brought to the party.

The mood at Force India was buoyant, by contrast, as Vijay Mallya's team finally rose above the station of tail-end Charlie. The Silverstone outfit reaped the benefits of a new technical partnership with McLaren-Mercedes that made the VJM02 fly on fast tracks. It failed to score prior to Fisichella's weird weekend in Belgium, but this, and a couple of decent drives from the mercurial Adrian Sutil, allowed it to usurp Scuderia Toro Rosso in the points table. STR's was a low-key campaign following the recruitment of the relatively unheralded Sebastian Buemi to replace Vettel. Buemi applied himself well, however, scoring the lion's share of the points and showing up the more experienced Sebastien Bourdais. The latter was ditched for British F3 champion Jaime Alguersuari, who in Hungary became the youngest GP starter at 19 years and 125 days. The Spaniard's level-headed approach laid to rest fears over his lack of experience, but he never troubled the scorers.

The strugglers have plenty to chew on this winter, not least because of changes in store for 2010. The competition will be more intense, with new teams, drivers, races and (no doubt) political battles to be joined. But one thing is for sure: next season will have to go some to beat 2009.

BELOW Robert Kubica felt his BMW Sauber was competitive in Malasyia, but its engine failed

ABOVE Abu Dhabi's all-new Yas Island circuit is like no other circuit in the world, dipping under a foot bridge between two parts of a hotel

RIGHT Brawn GP had two reasons – two World Championship titles – to celebrate at the Brazilian GP, after an extraordinary year that saw the new team rise from the ashes of Honda after the Japanese manufacturer pulled out at the end of 2008

THE PANEL

MARTIN BRUNDLE
TV COMMENTATOR, *BBC*

CHRISTIAN HORNER
TEAM PRINCIPAL, RED BULL RACING

MARK HUGHES
JOURNALIST, *AUTOSPORT*

MARTIN WHITMARSH
TEAM PRINCIPAL, McLAREN

CHAIRED BY
TONY DODGINS
JOURNALIST, *AUTOSPORT*

ROUND TABLE

With Formula 1's established order turned on its head by new regulations, there was plenty to discuss when we got some of F1's leading players together in Abu Dhabi

There can be no question that 2009 was an incredibly busy year for everyone involved in Formula 1. There were new technical regulations to cope with, the introduction of new technology in KERS, considerable debate about F1's future, more than the usual amount of political wrangling, and a couple of scandals too. Small wonder then that organising this Round Table feature was a Herculean feat, as it was scuppered time and again by the sudden calling of yet another meeting of F1's big wigs. At the end of a fascinating season, though, F1 is now being talked about again, its popularity has been boosted, and a far more positive future secured. However, nothing is ever straightforward in this most complicated of sports, so our knowledgeable panel tackled the influence of the double diffuser, of KERS, of the lack of testing and, sadly, the lack of overtaking. Looking to the future, and they all do, they produced lively debate about how to improve the show and, of course, not all are in agreement about some of the more radical plans.

TD: *Was the double-diffuser controversy and its ultimate acceptance the biggest influence on the season?*

CH: Well, it screwed our season completely! In reality, there was a big performance advantage from the double diffuser. Brawn managed to exploit it very well, with Jenson Button in particular in the first third of the championship, then made it stick.

MW: The double diffuser gave some teams a flying start. A number of teams spent a lot of time on it and were ahead with development. At the beginning of the year, we were nowhere and that was a combination of an average job we did, the lack of a double diffuser, and being behind the others in terms of development.

MB: It seemed to me that the big teams focused on KERS, and so much resource went on something that didn't give the payback expected, whereas the smaller teams didn't have that option and were tidying up other areas. Normally, when you get such a big 'reset' it's the big teams that get there first because they've got three different potential solutions to every problem. So KERS clouded it and then the lack of testing to sort the cars out compounded it. For me, the diffuser affair wasn't the defining point of the year.

TD: *Was the fact that KERS was politically important to [FIA President] Max Mosley a factor in pushing the big teams so earnestly down that road?*

MW: I think KERS had some advantage, but when you looked at non-KERS cars they had more freedom in the undercutting of the sidepods, which became more critical this year because we lost all the 'furniture' forward of the pods. We decided to commit to KERS and ultimately I don't regret that. It was a great technical challenge, although undoubtedly a distraction.

BELOW In his role as chairman, Tony Dodgins listens as Martin Brundle answers one of his questions

MH: It's difficult not to conclude that there might have been a political element in not settling the diffuser issue before the season started, in terms of what was going on in the background between FOTA and the FIA.

MW: Yes, I think it could have divided the teams. It did for a while, but fortunately FOTA managed to pull through that. On the other hand, it was good for the sport, because in reality people enjoyed seeing Ferrari and McLaren having their arses kicked at the beginning of the year. Can't imagine why, but they did…

MB: Ross Brawn says, and for me it's pivotal to the whole double-diffuser thing, that he tried to give everyone a heads-up (see p60), without giving the game away, that there was going to be a lot more downforce than expected. Do you accept that?

MW: I think what Ross said was that we can get more performance, but it certainly wasn't giving the game away, and that's just normal banter throughout the winter in any case. I think it had long been accepted that you couldn't have holes in a diffuser and in the floor. I personally believe it was a mistake. At the time, McLaren didn't make any protest and we didn't say anything against it publicly. We had our own issues, like a slow car, but privately I told Ross that I thought it was wrong. I also think that perhaps some of the leading teams wouldn't have got away with such an interpretation. The other sad thing is that people will judge that the Overtaking Working Group (OWG) project was a failure. To some extent it was, because it didn't anticipate the amount of downforce from a double diffuser, and quite a lot of the OWG efforts were therefore negated, which was a shame. Having said that, we, like everyone else, have got an even more extreme version for 2010, because obviously we've been able to redesign the back of the engine, the transmission, the suspension and we're going more extreme because we've got no choice.

MB: So, if we went and tank-taped up the slots and the concept, the cars would overtake more, would they? I'm not convinced.

MW: I think the primary thing that will help overtaking is circuit design, not car.

MB: I agree.

MW: You only need to do a simple bit of statistical analysis and look at where the passing moves are. If, say, we race on 18 circuits and there are 350 corners, then 90% of passing moves in a year would happen at probably just 10 corners. The other mistake is, it's not just the corner itself, but you have to look at the preceding corner. The fact that overtaking is focused on such a small number of corners clearly demonstrates that it's circuit dependent. However, the OWG conclusion was a 50% reduction in downforce and we haven't got it. If you reduce the downforce and the sensitivity and the weight generated at the back of the car, then I think you will be able to get a bit closer to the target.

TD: *Although Yas Marina is fabulous, is Turn 7 onto the back straight a case in point? Everyone files through T5 and T6, then around T7, whereas if they'd elevated the grandstand at T7 and had more run-off, as they've done at T8, the circuit could have continued straight into T7, without the slow T5/6, forcing people to defend the inside and creating varying speeds and lines onto the back straight?*

MW: Actually, do you remember Nigel Bennett? (ex-Lotus/ Hesketh/Theodore/Lola/Penske/G-Force). I probably hadn't spoken to him for 10 years, but he rang me and told me that he'd been invited, as an expert, to an FIA overtaking seminar. None of the F1 teams were invited incidentally, but Nigel asked if I would help. We've basically pointed out the statistical analysis on corners, and we are devoting simulation stuff and simulator staff to the seminar (on 10 November) to demonstrate at which circuits we can improve overtaking. Everyone has been crying about overtaking for a long time and we, the industry, collectively, haven't really squeezed our brains. Even now, I've probably put about 10–15 man days of work into it, and inevitably people in our organisation will ask why we're doing it. How does it help us next year? Why are

you doing that, Whitmarsh? And I'm glad they are, I'd be worried if they weren't challenging it, but that's the problem. We all go from one grand prix to the next and we don't want to give that time, and there isn't proper engagement of all parties to solve the problem. We know that it can be a lot better.

MH: You say that the circuits are the major problem, but I wonder do we need to revise the understanding of the overtaking etiquette, because at the moment you can make one move to defend and then you're allowed to go back to the outside to take your place before the corner. We saw Mark Webber take it to the extreme in Brazil with Kimi Räikkönen's nose. Aside from the safety aspect, would you think about revising it so that you can only make one move before the corner? There would be more overtaking then, by definition.

MB: I think it needs heavily policing. The Indycar system is too extreme, where you're not allowed to defend at all – you take your one position down the straight and if the guy comes up the inside you sort of have to let him through. That all looks a little bit forced. I do think you should be allowed to move just once, because when you

ABOVE TV man Martin Brundle is sandwiched by team principals Christian Horner and Martin Whitmarsh as he answers a question

ABOVE Red Bull Racing chief Christian Horner warms to a theme, as the other members of the panel listen intently against the backdrop of the impressive Yas Island marina

saw Nakajima's Williams nose, presumably with a chunk of ballast in for good measure, flying down the race track at Interlagos, that's just crazy. And Kobayashi didn't even get a penalty for it. Not even a mention in despatches on the computer screen. I think that's a good idea Mark, but assuming that the cars are close enough in the first place to only have to defend like that. And that's the problem really. For some reason, Button seems to have been able to overtake this year but, apart from that, the cars haven't really been in a position to, KERS and non-KERS cars apart, and my great fear is that with today's levels of aerodynamics and general grip, and the tyres the way they are, a lot of overtaking has gone forever.

TD: *Going back to the start of the season, which was all upside down with the World Champion at the back…*

CH: It was all bloody Ross's fault!

TD: *But it proved that the car is more important than the driver. Not all of the public grasps that, so is there a case for rotating drivers, something that Max suggested some time ago?*

MB: It's utterly impractical and impossible from a commercial point of view and also bearing in mind how the cars are designed.

MH: That would be solvable with a will though, surely?

MB: But why would you want to do that? I don't agree that it's all about the car and not the driver.

CH: Chelsea and Manchester United don't suddenly swap players, so I just don't see it being a part of what F1 is all about. It's a team sport: you nominate your team before the start of the season, you nominate your drivers and you do the best job you can.

MW: Would it create interest? Yes it would. We can't deny that. But it isn't going to happen.

MB: Every time you see a global advertising campaign for cars, oil or brands, how are you going to do that if you are swapping your drivers around in different overalls and so on?

TD: *Alright, but if marketing is leading everything, is that not tail wagging dog?*

MB: Big tail, little dog then!

TD: *If the team didn't have to pay the driver, though, and instead he received a nominal FIA salary and won big prize money, the best team would still win over a season, but so would the best driver, which isn't necessarily the case now. The marketing men would have access to a bigger pool of drivers and could pay for the most appealing, hardest working ones. What is the downside?*

CH: I struggle to see the upside as well, though, because part of the sport and the theory of it is teams competing against each other, and if you keep moving the key players around…

TD: *The teams still would be competing against each other, wouldn't they?*

MW: What you're suggesting is right, but there is no will to do it because the current business model of F1 doesn't support that. Brands want to be associated with personalities. Sebastian Vettel is a personality who has been invested in by Red Bull, it's a fantastic story, they've developed him, they've made him a star and I'm sure… well, I asked them, and they didn't want to give him to me!

MB: Golden rule number one of selling anything, speaking as a car dealer, is never confuse the customer. And that would. Ladies and gentleman, this week Sebastian Vettel is in the white car with the Mercedes Benz engine, and next week he's in the red car… It just wouldn't work.

CH: How hard would Lewis Hamilton or Sebastian Vettel push when they're in a car at the back of the grid?

MH: Well they'd have to.

TD: *Lewis Hamilton would push 100% if he was driving a dust cart.*

CH: Their motivational incentive would be way less and you'd have all kinds of factors that would come into play that we wouldn't even think about around this table.

MW: Imagine, Sebastian Vettel, you're in USF1 this week!

TD: *It leads on to the next question. In the past, we've had dominant drivers – Juan Manuel Fangio, Jim Clark, Ayrton Senna, Michael Schumacher. Do we have a stand-out driver in the current era?*

MH: I think we've got an excellent elite of drivers at the moment: Lewis obviously, Sebastian, Fernando Alonso and Robert Kubica.

MB: You haven't mentioned the World Champion…

MH: Yeah, Jenson as well, absolutely. But whether one stands out, I don't know.

MB: I think we've got the quality, but not the depth if I think back to the 1980s and the pre-Michael Schumacher days. He really did stand out. The only one who could beat him was Mika Häkkinen and then finally Alonso knocked him off his perch. But, if I think back to the household names from the 1980s, you could name 14 or 15 of them, which is interesting when you consider that the media and the TV coverage was a small percentage of what it is now. There was no internet, no press officers, and yet these guys were household names. Go back even to the 1960s with Jackie Stewart and Stirling Moss or Jim Clark. There used to be more legends somehow. So, for me, you've got the quality, but you just haven't got the depth. Alonso would stand up against any of those eras, though.

TD: *So you would identify Alonso as the stand-out driver?*

MB: And Hamilton. And potentially Vettel. Kubica I'm not quite so convinced about, Jenson if he can raise his game and win again next year, potentially on more equal terms, then I'd put him in that bracket. I just don't think that there's as many as when you had Senna, Alain Prost, Niki Lauda, Nelson Piquet, Keke Rosberg, and on and on.

MW: And don't forget Nige!

MB: And Noige…

CH: I totally agree with Martin. I think you have an elite group and I agree with the drivers Martin identified. I think Alonso as a package is phenomenal. Lewis too. I think Kimi was in that club and perhaps isn't quite at the moment.

MB: Obviously, if you could, you'd have Hamilton and Alonso in the same team wouldn't you?

MH: That would be a good idea!

BELOW Martin Brundle turns to listen as McLaren chief Martin Whitmarsh offers his point of view

ABOVE The Round Table topics raised a good deal of laughter, as Mark Hughes demonstrates

[Agreement] signature to split it up. It's good that it has been reunified and I think we now have the opportunity, I hope, for FOTA, the CRH and the governing body to work together and increase competition in the sport, make it more accessible, more interesting, a better show, keep costs down, make sure the teams that we've got are sustainable and that the new teams survive. If we can continue to develop the spirit – and it's difficult for competing organisations with self-interest – I think what FOTA has achieved has been quite remarkable. It ain't perfect, we've fallen out over a variety of things and we can do a better job, and that will come with trust, respect and co-operation in the future.

CH: FOTA has achieved a great deal in its first year. It's helped reduce costs significantly for an independent team such as ourselves, and has reacted responsibly to the credit crisis and with the proposals that it put to the FIA and which were signed off by them. FOTA wasn't formed to deal with those issues, but to deal with some of the commercial aspects going forward for 2012 and beyond. It was sort of thrown into a load of crucial and critical items, and I think that the harmony that has been achieved and the progress made is quite remarkable. I think now is an important time, with Concorde signed off and changes in the FIA. It's time for all the parties to work together for the benefit of the sport and to improve the show.

TD: *A breakaway was threatened at one point. Is the foundation there for a solid future, or do you see more problems in 2012?*

CH: I think the groundwork is in place. Obviously, it's going to potentially become a bigger club with more members as the new teams come in, but I think the principles of what FOTA is trying to achieve are in many ways aligned with the CRH and the FIA, it's just a matter of the parties all working together to achieve a common goal.

MB: I'm intrigued to know why FOTA got it together while GPMA [Grand Prix Manufacturers' Association] and all the previous iterations failed?

MW: Ferrari.

CH: Ferrari.

MB: Was that the only key?

CH: I think there are two things. Firstly, Ferrari and Luca di Montezemolo's leadership. Secondly, we just had to get it together. With the financial crisis and teams disappearing… Let's face it, unless Martin had given Brawn an engine this year – bastard! – they wouldn't be here.

MW: Don't worry, they're not getting one next year. We've learned our lesson!

MB: The other thing I'm interested to know is, has FOTA truly got a seat at the table?

MW: There's an idea!

MH: Might be a bit sparky…

CH: If we had available seats, that's what we'd do…

MB: Sorry if I interrupted your flow Christian, I couldn't resist that…

TD: *Moving on, how big an influence has FOTA had on and off the track, and what's its future?*

MW: I think it's had an enormous influence, looking at what it did in the first few months, when F1 went through a real crisis – the low-cost engines, low-cost transmissions, the testing restrictions, the aerodynamic restrictions. The spirit of camaraderie it created meant people have been more willing to compromise. The resource restriction is a good thing and will progressively bring down costs further. What we've got to do is make sure that FOTA isn't seen as an organisation against the commercial rights holder (CRH) or the governing body. That's the challenge now. It's been a fire-fighting operation, and there was a lot of effort pre-Concorde

CH: I think it has. I think it's recognised by the FIA now.

MW: I think there has been a reluctance to acknowledge and accept it, and a desire to deal with the teams independently. I think there are still some people who would like to do that, but progressively people have to accept it. Having the traditional model, which was the teams divided, was a great opportunity for some people to make hay, and I understand that, but it's to the detriment of the sport. The teams working together bring some advantage if they engage uniformly with the CRH and the governing body. There's lots of opportunity to be better as a sport.

MH: Do you see it as the first stage of a more managerial rather than entrepreneurial approach?

MW: I don't, as I think there's a maturing of the industry and a recognition that we're all in it together. I think Red Bull have made a fantastic commitment and clearly want to be in F1 for a long time and be a top team. McLaren is committed to being here in 10, 20 years time. The old approach, which was 'stuff everyone else and let's fight for what suits us', was going to be damaging and reduce the prospects of us actually having competitors in five or 10 years time. You need strong competitors. You do want to go out and dominate every race but, if anyone was to do that, I think that it would destroy the sport.

CH: The main thing is that it has required compromise from all parties, and what we've actually ended up with is a set of regulations that has enabled an independent team such as ourselves to compete. When you look at some of the sacrifices that some of the big teams like McLaren have made – giving away the testing, five-million Euro engines… that's something that, when we came into F1, was a pipe dream. It's enabled the cost of being competitive in F1 to be affordable and, through the resource-restriction agreements going forward, that level becomes even further diminished. There are some significant cost savings that all of us will realise from FOTA initiatives.

TD: *As a result of the scandals we've had –*
'Liegate' and 'Crashgate' for want of better
descriptions – people like Davey Ryan, Pat
Symonds and even Ron Dennis are no longer
in the paddock. What are your thoughts?

CH: When I came into F1, Ron Dennis, Flavio Briatore and even Eddie Jordan were sitting around a table and they were big characters. The sport has recently lost some of those big hitters and there's a new generation coming through, but I think the sport has still shone above the politics, I think we've had a great championship this year with different winners and different teams running at the front and showing form at different times of the season. We've even had a Force India on the podium. On the whole, I think it's been a really positive year.

MH: I think the way that controversies were

personalised and politicised was very much a characteristic of Max Mosley's regime. Hopefully it's a thing of the past.

MB: Whether you do a piece for TV, a *Sunday Times* column or whatever, it's nice to have the skulduggery, otherwise you'd have nothing. This season has been so interesting that hasn't been the case, but I don't subscribe to the 'all publicity is good publicity' theory. I think the fans finally got fed up with the grubby political and personal nature of F1 this year, and I'm not talking about those who have left. I think characters like Ron and Flavio are a great loss to the sport and if we see them replaced by managerial-style people from manufacturers, not wanting to beat-up on anyone in particular, they are not racers. They are a different type of character and F1 is the cutting edge of motor racing and needs to be driven by people who take the pain beyond belief on a Monday morning.

MW: There are some really sad personal stories. You mentioned Davey and Pat, and they are guys who put in a huge amount of time and effort and toil over 30 years with their respective teams and it's very sad. I don't personally believe that either of those people set out to cheat or act in a manner that destroyed their careers and lives in the way that it did. I don't believe that Pat got up after all those years and decided to organise a crash to the advantage of his team. He may have been aware of it, or could have been stronger in preventing it from happening, but I don't think that he was the initiator or the catalyst. Sadly, there have been a few human victims of the politics of F1 and I think that's very sad.

MB: Yeah, two of the best guys in the paddock got caught in the crossfire. They were part of the problem, but it's a real shame. We all know of things that have gone on in the world of motor racing, some that I daren't even think about let alone talk about, and these guys just literally got caught in the crossfire.

TD: How do we look at 'Crashgate'? Do we see it as the most heinous crime in sporting history, or was it someone taking advantage of a particularly poor safety-car rule?

MW: We've got to be careful in that we don't know everything that led to it, but it was very bad. However, as I've said, some of those who have paid the price probably weren't the instigators.

MH: I think it should have been penalised with a disqualification and possibly some heavy fine, but I don't think it was anything like it was made out to be.

MB: I do. I think it was crazy and I still can't believe that they did it and how they did it. We all push the boundaries, but that was so far beyond them. Once the fans stops believing what they're seeing, the sport's over. If he thinks the goalkeeper is letting in goals, or the snooker player is throwing games because he's in a betting ring, you've got a problem. If someone is going to give up two or three hours of his precious free time on a Sunday afternoon to watch a sport and sees a crash and then has to consider 'did he do it on purpose,' then that's terrible.

TD: But Renault was actually trying to win, not lose – they weren't throwing the race, so it wasn't match-fixing as we know it.

MH: There wasn't a collusion of competitors, and so I think there's a distinction between what happened in Singapore and a goalkeeper letting in goals. It wasn't someone trying to make personal gain and thus letting his team down.

CH: It's still wrong if it's done deliberately, because you're putting people's lives – spectators and marshals –

in danger. But then I remember seeing a race shown not so long ago when Mansell was black-flagged at Estoril and then drove into the back of Senna in frustration and annoyance to take him out of the race. I also remember Michael turning-in on Damon Hill…

MW: Michael turning-in on lots of people… and parking it at Rascasse. That's one of the things you think: has it been fair and equitable? Or has the opportunity been taken, for other political means, when an issue has arisen? Really, I do think it's extremely sad for those people who gave so much. Pat in particular, and Davey, had their careers destroyed.

MB: I know that Michael can't understand why he was castigated for some of the things he did, when Senna was almost revered for what he did to Prost at Suzuka in 1990, because I've had that discussion with Michael. I guess that what's happened is that sooner or later it's had to come to a stop. I'm sure when Renault stop, turn around and look back at what they did, they've got to ask themselves, why? But then with the way the sport has evolved, it probably didn't seem that unreasonable when they were going through the thought process at the time.

MW: I think you're right. Ayrton at Suzuka was a shocking one and I have to say that I remember what a weird feeling it was for the team at the time. I've been fortunate enough to have been around one or two World Championship successes and that was my least favourite, even though Ayrton said afterwards: 'Well, I only did what he did to me last year…'

MB: He was angry because of the pole position switch [to the right side of the track] favouring Prost. He felt personally slighted and, when you look at that again, he was quite a long way up the inside of Prost when he ran into him, even though I'm not trying to defend it.

MW: The wheels were still turning when it all came to a halt 50 metres into the sand traps. He knew it was going to happen!

TD: Significant rule changes this year, not so significant ones for 2010, but still differences. What will be the key?

MW: I think tyres and drivers dealing with fuel load will be issues. I think KERS disappearing too, but you've got to say Red Bull this year without the double diffuser would have won, and they've not had KERS either, so I think you have to expect Adrian Newey's car to be very strong. It will be about who can get that 160 kilos of fuel into the car with minimum impact on packaging, aerodynamics, handling and balance change. Who is going to make a car kind enough on tyres, and get their drivers to be kind enough barrelling into the first corner with 160 kilos of fuel. I'm not sure prohibition of refuelling is a good thing, and you can argue both ways. Much of the overtaking that we enjoy doesn't get seen on TV because it doesn't happen on the track, and you get situations where you tell your guy, take it easy, don't take a risk, so-and-so is pitting in three laps time.

BELOW Christian Horner agreed that race-fixing was wrong, but recalled some 'interesting' racing moments in years gone by

MH: As long as it's replaced by genuine overtaking, then that's fine.

CH: The cars are going to have to be very versatile in 2010, because qualifying will be at a premium, and it depends on what the qualifying format will be, because if you put the quickest cars at the front they are going to disappear. A lot depends on what the regulations are going to be over tyre stops. The worst-case scenario is that we find everyone gets their pit stop out of the way in the first 10 laps and you've then got an hour and 15 minutes of formation driving. I don't believe that will happen, though, as I think there will be other issues to deal with. The weights of the cars are going to be significantly different, you are going to have brake issues, fuel economy is going to be crucial, and you are going to have to manage a whole lot of different parameters that we haven't had to think about this year.

MB: I'm slightly concerned about it, because it takes a level of interest away in the pits, and I remember the long afternoons in the 1980s when 'you run what you brung', and if your car wasn't economical or was just

difficult, it turned into an endurance event. The cars are somewhat better now in that respect, but are you saying that the qualifying format and tyre usage are still up for change?

CH: There's still debate about what that format should be. For me, the first two elements of qualifying work very well at the moment. The crucial factor is what we do in Q3, because if you end up with the fastest cars at the front, then they will run in clean air and disappear. Introducing a degree of randomness, or a reward for qualifying, is something that we need to consider. And the tyre will have a big effect as well. If you have a tyre that needs managing, that will create opportunities.

With the lights of Abu Dhabi's unbelieveably spectacular Yas Island hotel and marina twinkling behind them, this group of committed and passionate Formula 1 insiders ended their 2009 campaigns in an upbeat mood, and that's a considerable triumph at a time of global economic difficulty. Sense has prevailed, cost-cutting embraced and, through it all, we have just enjoyed a wonderful season of racing ,full of surprises, and are all set for another exciting chapter of F1 history in 2010.

ABOVE The removal of refuelling for 2010 was met with mixed reaction, and Martin Whitmarsh was one who of those wasn't sure that it was a good thing

THE DRIVERS

All 25 drivers who competed in F1 in 2009 tell us of their campaigns, led by new World Champion Jenson Button, as we list them in their World Championship order

1 JENSON BUTTON
BRAWN GP

"It's been a rollercoaster of emotions this year, and it's been extremely stressful, especially in the middle of the season, but it wouldn't be the World Championship if it was easy. I've spoken to a few people about it, one being Ross [Brawn], and he assures me that this is pretty normal. You have your ups and your downs.

It was great to finish with a podium. I don't think we could have ever dreamed about a season like this, so everyone in the team should be very proud of themselves, and I must say a thank you to all of them for the hard work through the difficult times of the winter. We've won the World Championship, so we should be very proud.

I think you're always going to have difficult moments when you're fighting for the championship. It's mentally very draining. The middle part of the season was tough for me, but we fought back. I spent quite a bit of time with Ross. He's been in every situation before, he's fought for world titles before in F1 and I haven't, so it was very useful. We've been quite close this year.

I think for anyone winning the World Championship in any sport it's a very special feeling, because you're the best in the world at that moment in time. It's something you dream about when you're a kid, something you think about when you're eight years old, about how you would love to win an F1 World Championship.

You don't actually mean it, though, as you don't think about tomorrow when you're eight years old. But in reality even though I didn't know it I've been driving cars and karts since I was eight years old basically to make sure that I'm ready for this moment. Twenty-one years later I've won the World Championship. It's a very strange feeling, and I've spoken to a few other people about it.

I've achieved what I set out to do in racing, so where do I go from here? That's the question I'm going to be asking myself. I know the answer really. It's about challenging yourself, and there's a lot more challenges out there for me in F1, and that's exciting. However, I'm not going to think about that too much right now, because it's a very special time for me. I'm just going to enjoy the moment, and I'm going to be ready 100% for next year.

The one race that stands out was the first race of the year. That was a special race because we didn't even think we'd be in Australia, so getting pole position there and winning that race was very special. That was a race where I think we had an advantage as a team with the car.

From then on, it was a lot closer. We won in Bahrain and Spain because we did the best job on the day. We maybe didn't have a quicker car than anyone else, but we did the best job on the day. In reality, Toyota should have won Bahrain. Then the Red Bulls were quicker than us in Barcelona, but it didn't go their way, and their strategy didn't work. Ferrari were very quick in Spain too. So there were lots of races where we really had to fight for it, and we came away with the victory because we did everything right, not just because we had a quick car.

"I SPENT QUITE A BIT OF TIME WITH ROSS. HE'S BEEN IN EVERY SITUATION BEFORE, HE'S FOUGHT FOR WORLD TITLES BEFORE IN F1 AND I HAVEN'T"

Monaco was very special, because that's where I live to start with, I drive those streets when I'm at home. But it's a special race. It's a different circuit to any other, as it's very technical and it's unforgiving. So winning on that circuit is probably the one that will stay with me most when I look back at the victories this season, along with Australia.

And for me, winning Monaco and parking in the wrong place was the best thing I could have done. I think things happen for a reason, and running down the pit straight, seeing all the fans waving and all the teams was spectacular, and I think every person who wins Monaco from now on should stop there and run down to the podium..."

NATIONALITY British
DATE OF BIRTH 19/1/80
PLACE OF BIRTH Frome, England
GRANDS PRIX 171
WINS 7
POLES 7
FASTEST LAPS 2
POINTS 327
HONOURS F1 World Champion 2009, Formula Ford Festival winner 1998, European Super A Kart Champion 1997

"WE WERE STRONG ENOUGH IN EVERY RACE THIS YEAR TO FINISH IN THE TOP FIVE, WHICH NOBODY ELSE WAS, EXCEPT MAYBE IN MONZA"

that the guy who wins the championship is the guy with more points than anyone else. And you don't score points for first only, also for second place down to eighth. Sometimes you find yourself in a situation where you're not strong enough to win, but it's still important to bring the car home in third, fourth or fifth and collect points.

We were strong enough in every race this year to finish in the top five, which nobody else was – except maybe in Monza. Sometimes you may call it bad luck or whatever, other times we made mistakes with the strategy and other things, sometimes mistakes from myself. We had five races we didn't finish and score any points.

Australia was one of those, but I think Australia was a racing incident, and it happens if you race. I'm not on the circuit to wave everybody past as soon as someone appears in my mirrors. I would say these kinds of things just happen, but there were too many other things happening and costing us important points.

After Australia I got a penalty I didn't deserve. In Malaysia I spun, I aquaplaned off, but the problem was that the car stalled because of an electronic issue and I couldn't continue. If I had managed to come back, we would have collected points. Looking back at Monaco, we had a strong strategy, but in Monaco, Hungary and Valencia we didn't have the pace to win, although it was enough to finish on the podium, or at least in the top five. So, another four or five points per race.

In the end, we are a team, and at the time make your decisions because you think it's best. After the race you learn, OK, was it a good decision or not? Some of our decisions were not the smartest. This is something we can certainly improve for 2010. We were obviously also handicapped a little bit with the engines, but I have to say that everyone was expecting us to change at least one engine before the last race, but we didn't have to, so thanks to Renault we made it.

It's pretty simple in the end. Looking back, I think that there are things we could have done better, but the most important thing is to learn from those situations, and not do those things again.

If it's a normal kind of race, you can't be magical on the strategy. It's pretty easy and pretty straightforward. You can only mess it up. Some of our strategies were not the best probably. Looking back at races like Turkey, we tried to put Jenson under pressure, but we just didn't have the pace, so it didn't work. Then because of the strategy, I lost a position to Mark. In Monaco we were just too aggressive. But all these decisions we took as a team, so there's not one person from a group of people to blame.

I'm enjoying myself, so I'm looking forward to the future. We have a good team, we are getting stronger. We are still very young, and this was the first proper season we had – a kind of a breakthrough."

2 SEBASTIAN VETTEL
RED BULL

NATIONALITY German
DATE OF BIRTH 3/7/87
PLACE OF BIRTH Heppenheim, Germany
GRANDS PRIX 43
WINS 5
POLES 5
FASTEST LAPS 3
POINTS 125
HONOURS German Formula BMW Champion 2004, European Junior Kart Champion 2001

"I think it's normal to be disappointed, and for sure it took some time to get over Brazil. It was a big disappointment. In the end, you have to see the positives. I think it was a very good season for us. A lot of things happened, a lot of things we learned. All in all, there are a lot of things we can do better next year.

I think this year was special because the rules changed so much. We didn't know what to expect. Straight away at the first test we had a very good feeling with the car, we were very happy, but we didn't really know until going to Australia how competitive we were. I think it was very important to be competitive from the start to the end. On top of that, this year was very up and down anyway, with different teams at the top.

Looking back, I don't think there's only one race where things went wrong. In the end, it's not a secret

"FROM SILVERSTONE, I STARTED TO BE ON TOP FORM: I HAD BETTER BRAKES, AND I STARTED TO OUTQUALIFY JENSON. IT JUST FELT GOOD"

"It's been a great season. People put flowers on my coffin at the beginning of the year, but I was back driving a fantastic car, and I was so up for it. I've got to really thank God for the year we had. It was altogether a great car to drive all year.

Jenson won the title, and he deserved to, but he won it in the first seven races. I think the second half of the championship was mine. It was a true fight and I fought really hard, but at a time of the championship when we didn't have that great a performance any more.

Jenson didn't have to do much in all honesty, and I had to fight really hard. Not that I'm the hero, he was the hero the whole time, but I just kept on fighting, and kept it very alive. For me, Valencia and Monza were great, as was Brazil, but we didn't have the performance there to win the race. It was frustrating not to be able to win, but I consider myself a big winner and a big loser. I know how to win and lose.

So it was a big fight, and I kept on going, kept myself alive, and I'm really pleased. I'm pleased for Jenson as a friend and a great champion and, if I didn't win, he should have won it. So, well done to him.

At the end of the day, we all know that if you deserve something you get it. Destiny is there for you to catch, and for you to prove you're right or wrong. I've tried really hard the whole season, against my problems at the beginning year with brakes, I've fought some difficult situations during the year.

But I won races, and I kept things very much alive in the championship, and I kept it going. You need to be a big winner, but you need to know how to lose as well. I think it's been a great championship and Jenson won because he deserved to win. I'm disappointed that it didn't go my way, because I tried hard, and I've been here for longer, but I'll keep on trying.

The team has been superb, and Ross [Brawn] was able to get everyone together, to prepare them. And they were really well prepared. It's a helluva team, it deserves to win. It's been fantastic trying to find the problems without testing and, for me, it's been a challenging year and even more fascinating because, without the tests, in two laps you need to feel whether the package is better or not. I've enjoyed it very much.

Of course, when you're looking back, you always think that you could have done better. We can't forget, though, that something could have gone worse. I could say that I could have won all the races, which is bullshit, but I should have won Malaysia in the rain, and I could have finished better in China, but I had a glazed disc that only came alive after my first pit stop, when everything came hot. I could have won in Spain if it wasn't for the strategy. I had a terrible start in Turkey, but my worst enemy was a wrong second gear. We were so short

3 RUBENS BARRICHELLO
BRAWN GP

that I couldn't use the slipstream to overtake people. So I really had to force it. I was having fun, and I tried to overtake Kovalainen on the inside, and we touched. There was no way to overtake, because I was on the limiter almost every straight. Then, from Silverstone, I started to be on top form: I had better brakes, and I started to outqualify Jenson. It just felt good.

Germany was where I said everything I said. I was so damn disappointed with the final result. People seemed to think that I said I could have won the race. I knew that I couldn't have won, but the fact is that I said it was a good demonstration of how it was to lose a race because I thought that the team should have changed strategy in the middle. You're leading by 16s, you have 30s to the third guy, and you finish sixth! So, for me, it was more of a loss than anything else."

NATIONALITY Brazilian
DATE OF BIRTH 23/5/72
PLACE OF BIRTH São Paulo, Brazil
GRANDS PRIX 287
WINS 11
POLES 14
FASTEST LAPS 17
POINTS 607
HONOURS British F3 Champion 1991, European Formula Opel Champion 1990

4 MARK WEBBER

RED BULL

NATIONALITY Australian
DATE OF BIRTH 27/8/76
PLACE OF BIRTH
Queanbeyan, Australia
GRANDS PRIX 139
WINS 2
POLES 1
FASTEST LAPS 3
POINTS 169.5
HONOURS Formula Ford
Festival winner 1996

"If at the start of the year you had said seven podiums, a couple of wins, several fastest laps and lots of trimmings to go with it, given that it was the worst preparation of my career coming into the start of the season, it would be something that in the end I would have taken.

You know that Jenson [Button] is consistent, and I've always said that. Unfortunately, he was blisteringly quick at the start of the year as well, with the consistency. A lot of drivers, particularly Sebastian [Vettel] and I, and Rubens [Barrichello] and other guys he was fighting, had a shopping list of excuses as to why they weren't getting the results. At the end of the day, you're not, and he was, and that's where he put a big hit into the championship. Other teams arrived in the back

part of the year, particularly McLaren with Lewis [Hamilton], and that made it hard for him to close the deal out. But he's a deserving champion.

Where did we lose the championship? I think the double diffuser played a huge role. It affects your attitude towards races, how you go racing, what you do if you aren't quite the pace. If you are totally the pace, we saw several times this year where Sebastian and I did get one–twos, where you can control a lot more of the weekend. So there was a lot of damage done early on with the interpretation of that [diffuser] rule.

With the packaging on these cars, everything is a disaster when you have to go to a different set of rules mid-season. It was a huge and expensive challenge for us to do. And, with no testing, you've got to look at reliability, with driveshafts and suspension. That was a big recovery from us. Obviously, Brawn had it in the design concept from eight months away from Melbourne.

For a few races from Turkey to Hungary I had such a phenomenal run, scoring more points than any other driver. Then in Valencia, Monza, that sort of window, we basically didn't get any points. Seb got a point when Lewis crashed on the last lap in Italy, but it was a tough race for us there.

I still to this day don't understand how Force India did what they did in Spa, and we were in the middle of the pack. That one hour on Saturday in Spa was bizarre. In the race, obviously I was given a drivethrough penalty for an illegal release, but Seb still got some points there. Monza was as good as we could have done. We could have driven round there for two weeks and still been nowhere! In low-downforce trim we were still learning a lot about the car, but we certainly improved it for Singapore.

I really needed to get Brazil under my belt. We'd had a few 50:50s go against us, although the crash in practice at Suzuka was my fault, a big missed opportunity to score points. But I was very, very determined to go to Brazil and focus on winning. I was nearly out in Q1, and in the break I said to my engineer: 'we can get something out of this now, we really have to capitalise'. In the end, after the first pit stop, it was a case of trying to control the race from there to the chequered flag.

There were some tracks where we weren't far off unbeatable, and there were some tracks where we were struggling to close that 10–15s difference to the race leader. It's been more like 25–30s at some races, and that makes a big difference to the points that you collect.

Looking ahead to next year, we've got awesome continuity in this team. Clearly, a lot of good guys have done a good job with the regulations, and that's why we've been a force this year. Not the force, but a very, very strong force. Going into 2010 is going to be quite exciting really. It's not like the Jaguar days, that real big hope of being able to pull something out. Next year, it's like we've done the main part of that, and we've got to build on what we did this year. And that's exciting."

"I think we just did a better job than everyone else apart from Brawn in the first race. Everyone fell off and made mistakes. The cars weren't reliable. At the second race, the cars still weren't reliable, then the weather intervened. In the third race, people starting to pick up the pace, like the Toyotas, and then bit by bit people made fewer mistakes and it became more of a reality just how bad our car was. Simple as.

You do everything you can to prepare for the season better than you did the previous year when you were leading the points table, and you had the package to challenge for the World Championship. Then you arrive and there's nothing you can do. You can't get out and push the car any faster. There's nothing you can do but try to will your team on and encourage improvement and try to inspire people.

When you're starting a race dead last, you have to find the inspiration for yourself, pull yourself back up somehow, do some overtaking manoeuvres that people enjoy, make your way up the order in some way, that's what I just try to do. In fact, that's what I tried to do all year.

I think we all had our doubts at some stage or another. At the end of the day, no one got to drive what I was driving, apart from Heikki [Kovalainen]. We were very polite in how we commented on just how bad it was. It was very tough to drive something so drastically different to the previous year, and also to see where we had gone wrong, because other people had done it right. We knew that if anyone could correct it, we could correct it. But our improvement arrived just too late, unfortunately.

We were at the back for a solid period of time, because more people were finishing races, more people were getting the performance out of their cars and we had no more to give. Eventually, we got the update package that mattered and we were back up competing at the front. But, even being there, it's been hard to stay at the front.

The Hungarian GP was a great weekend. I'm still living off that grand prix! It was a great weekend, a great experience, to be able to overtake one of the leading cars... Again on that weekend, though, I don't feel that we were the fastest, I just feel that we did a better job than the others.

The Red Bull all of a sudden dropped off the pace through the weekend, the Brawn couldn't get its tyres warm supposedly, which I find hard to understand, because there's heat all over the place so I'm sure there was heat on those tyres! But we were a little bit better than we were in the previous race, and nobody else did as good a job.

I have learned a huge amount through the 2009 season, and as a team, how we work together, I think we've learned quite a lot. There's still going to be many things we're going to learn next year, and I have no doubt there will be mistakes next year, but I've got to try and do everything I can to minimise them.

I've noticed how much support I have this year from my fans, regardless of where I'm finishing. It has really just shown the loyalty of my supporters – which is incredible for me. Especially at the British GP, when I

was at the back of the field and yet the fans were still rooting for me all the way, even though I wasn't at the front of the field.

Just bit-by-bit, you learn how to balance your life a little bit better. Sometimes you unbalance it, making changes. Sometimes you correct it.

On track, I learned in 2009 how hard I can push and also how hard I can't push. At Monza I learned not to push 110% on the last lap of the race! Bit by bit, you just keep on learning and keep putting that knowledge into a jar and, at some stage, you can use it all together.

My dream is to have a competitive car each year, with which I can build on myself and become a better racing driver year by year, and win more and more races and more and more championships."

5 LEWIS HAMILTON
McLAREN

NATIONALITY British
DATE OF BIRTH 7/1/85
PLACE OF BIRTH
Stevenage, England
GRANDS PRIX 52
WINS 11
POLES 17
FASTEST LAPS 3
POINTS 256
HONOURS F1 World
Champion 2008, GP2
Champion 2006, European F3
Champion 2005, British Formula
Renault Champion 2003, World
Kart Champion 2000

6 KIMI RÄIKKÖNEN
FERRARI

NATIONALITY Finnish
DATE OF BIRTH 17/10/79
PLACE OF BIRTH Espoo, Finland
GRANDS PRIX 157
WINS 18
POLES 16
FASTEST LAPS 35
POINTS 578
HONOURS F1 World Champion 2007,
British Formula Renault Champion 2000,
Finnish & Nordic Kart Champion 1998

"I think I've been driving well this year. We got some good results in the end, but unfortunately we never really had a car to fight for the World Championship, or even for regular front rows, podiums and wins.

The car was the biggest problem for us this year. I guess everybody saw when we went to the pre-season Barcelona test and Brawn came, that it was quite clear that everybody else was behind. If you are 1s behind at that time, it's hard to catch up. We were losing out in every area. For sure, I should have finished second or third in the opening race in Australia, but I hit the wall. Apart from that, I don't think we had the speed. We did the best that we could.

We got the first improvements for the Spanish GP, and the car was much faster, but something happened on the car and I stopped. Then, after that, it improved a bit, but everybody else was improving too. Monaco was good for us, and we should have fought for a win, but you have to start in first place there. After that, it continued

to get better, although I would say that at this point of the season the circuits probably weren't the best for our car. The German GP was OK, but then I had a hole in the radiator.

Most of the time we were around sixth in qualifying, although in Italy we were surprisingly third. We found quite a good way of working with the car, and got it a little bit more right. I think the people who were at the front should have done a better job with the car that they had, compared to us.

If the top teams like Brawn and Red Bull had qualified in front of us at Spa, it would have been more difficult. After this kind of season it was nice to win, and with a car that's not the fastest. It definitely gives you more of a good feeling than if you have the best car and you win. Then it's 10 times easier.

Even without the win, though, the last part of the season has been good. We have done the best that we could, and we can be happy. If we'd been pushing ahead with the 2009 car, we could have won more races, but that was the decision."

7 NICO ROSBERG
WILLIAMS

NATIONALITY German
DATE OF BIRTH 27/6/85
PLACE OF BIRTH Wiesbaden, Germany
GRANDS PRIX 70
WINS 0
POLES 0
FASTEST LAPS 2
POINTS 75.5
HONOURS GP2 Champion 2005,
German Formula BMW Champion 2002

"I've been pleased with my season. The 2008 World Championship was very difficult, and to be honest I had no idea what to expect from this season, because we did so badly last year.

This year, the team gave me a very solid car. Of course I would have wanted to get podiums and wins, but Williams gave me a solid car that could finish in the points all the time.

We always knew going to a race where we would be relative to the others, as it was very consistent going from one track to another, always up there. That was nice, and it really gave me a chance to score a lot of points, decent points, and I had my best season in terms of consistency. Most importantly, the season was in my head a stepping stone to better things in terms of results. I needed to use this season to get this chance to get a winning car for 2010.

I ranked seventh in the World Championship. I couldn't have beaten [Lewis] Hamilton and [Kimi] Räikkönen, because their cars were just superior, so I think we got the best out of it.

Our straightline speed has been terrible all year. I didn't say our engine power was weak –

it was straightline speed, so that's engine and car. And that was our main problem from the Bahrain GP on. We also had problems with tyre warm-up in quite a few races.

The middle of the season was very consistent, always finishing sixth, fifth, fourth, always in the points. We could have brought that all the way to Abu Dhabi, but in Belgium and Italy our car was a disaster, and then there was my mistake on the pit exit in Singapore, and a car failure in Brazil.

Singapore was quite frustrating, because I would have finished second there. The rain in Malaysia was another disappointment, because otherwise I could have finished second there. There wasn't really an absolute highlight, but maybe it was fourth place in Germany, starting 15th and taking six places at the start, and then another five through the race.

It was unfortunate that we made such a big announcement about KERS, and then didn't come close to using it. Racing against the KERS cars was a challenge, especially at the start, as the cars using KERS would just storm past, and that would definitely hamper your race."

8 JARNO TRULLI

TOYOTA

"To be honest, we were all expecting more from this season. Especially after such a very good start, I expected good progress from the team. The problem is this has been a weird season for everyone, not only for us. You can see how sometimes you are very competitive, and sometimes you are not competitive at all, without knowing why.

We started off very well and, yet after a front-row lock-out for Toyota in Bahrain, we were on the last row in Monaco! I can't find a way to explain it, honestly. You can't imagine that winning car, or at least a car that was on pole position can be at the back of the grid just two races later. For me, it all sounds a bit strange and weird. I can't find an explanation that I can tell you, but definitely it has been a crazy season, both up and down.

We had some times when we were very good, and sometimes when we were not. We had some times where we were unlucky, I had some times where I made a mistake. But, in general, when I had the chance, I more or less took it.

There was one race which was very unfortunate for me, which was the Belgian GP, where I qualified second. It was one of those races where I was really hoping to fight. There was a problem with Nick Heidfeld at the start, he was stuck in the middle of the road, and I damaged my car's nose. That was bad, but the worst thing is I wouldn't have finished anyway, because I had a problem with the brakes. It was really an unfortunate grand prix. Apart from that, when it was the time to be in the front, I was in front.

Australia was a big drama for us, the disqualification on Saturday. If we had started where we should have been, it would have been a different race for us. It was a big chance maybe to win a race, even though Brawn was very competitive there.

We were basically the second quickest car at the beginning of the season. You can argue that maybe in Bahrain we could fight for the win, but at the end of the day to win you need to get everything right, and you need to be very competitive in all areas."

NATIONALITY Italian
DATE OF BIRTH 13/7/74
PLACE OF BIRTH Pescara, Italy
GRANDS PRIX 219
WINS 1
POLES 4
FASTEST LAPS 1
POINTS 246.5
HONOURS German F3 Champion 1996, World Kart Champion 1995, European Kart Champion 1994

9 FERNANDO ALONSO

RENAULT

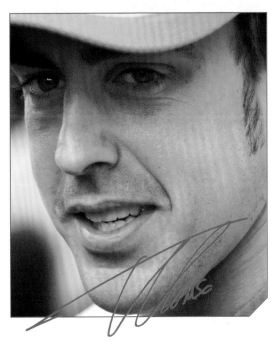

"The disappointment came in the third or fourth race of the year, when we realised that we were not able to fight for the World Championship. We'd finished the 2008 season very strongly, and our expectations in the winter tests were very high, as the car was running very quickly with no problems. The KERS was working very well for us, and in the first race we realised that, against the double-diffuser cars, the KERS wasn't doing what it should do. It was a disappointing part of the championship.

Like I said, from race three or race four, it was the same as last year when you realise that you won't fight for the World Championship. So, in that sense, it hasn't been a disappointing season. You just miss some opportunities, like in the Hungarian GP, where the car was competitive and we didn't finish the race.

Overall, it's more of a preparation for the year after. Once you realise you aren't fighting for the World Championship, you start working on next year, when you can attack again.

There have been some good races. I remember the Spanish GP as a good race,

finishing fifth and overtaking Massa on the last lap when he had some fuel problems. We had a good race too in Valencia. We were in the middle of nowhere between fifth and seventh positions. In the Belgian GP, the race was going well until the pit stop. So, for sure, we had some positive feelings and some good Sundays, but we don't have enough points.

Obviously, it's easy now to say after knowing everything, but I think the key to success this year was stopping development on the 2008 car early, and preparing for this year's new rules as early as you could, and understanding the new rules a bit better, as the double-diffuser teams did. That was quite an advantage at the beginning of the season.

At the top teams, we developed our cars around the KERS, and the design of the car was already behind the others because of that. However, it's easy to say that now, and if it had been the opposite way we would maybe have been winning races. KERS was a new device in F1, and it was difficult to predict just what was going to happen."

NATIONALITY Spanish
DATE OF BIRTH 29/7/81
PLACE OF BIRTH Oviedo, Spain
GRANDS PRIX 140
WINS 21
POLES 18
FASTEST LAPS 13
POINTS 577
HONOURS F1 World Champion 2005 & 2006, Formula Nissan Champion 1999, Italian & Spanish Kart Champion 1997, World Kart Champion 1996

10 TIMO GLOCK
TOYOTA

"We had a strong winter testing season, and we were hoping for a strong start to the season. And that's what happened, as we had a good race in Australia, and a good race in Malaysia, getting to the podium. We also had, on a couple of occasions, strong races from the pitlane, like in China and at the Nürburgring, where I had to start from the pitlane and had a good, solid result.

Bahrain was a big disappointment. We started at the front, but made a little mistake with the strategy and both went a bit too short. In the end, though, it's like it is. I came out on the wrong side of the traffic.

The positive races were Malaysia, where I made the right strategy call for myself in terms of tyre choice. I went the opposite way to the others, and it worked. It was a shame because, with one or two laps more, I think we would have had a chance to be fighting for the win. In the wet conditions in China, we were quick in the race. I started from the back and made my way up to seventh. Obviously, second in Singapore was a great result for us.

At the end of the year, though, it's a bit disappointing that we couldn't score more points. There were a lot of races where we had good possibilities in qualifying, but messed it up in the race itself, or the other way around, where we had trouble in qualifying and started from the back and came through to score points. There were too many ups and downs. At Spa for example, I had a chance to be in the top five, but I had a problem at the pit stop.

In some races we didn't really know what was going on. There were a couple of races where we didn't understand why we were so quick in the race, and not so quick in qualifying. I liked the slick tyres, but sometimes this year it was a bit difficult to understand the reaction of tyres at some tracks.

Toyota has had a couple of strong years, especially at the beginning of the season, and then dropped down a bit, so I was pushing hard to be focused on stronger development through 2009, so that the team could develop at a faster rate than the other teams."

NATIONALITY German
DATE OF BIRTH 13/3/82
PLACE OF BIRTH Lindenfels, Germany
GRANDS PRIX 36
WINS 0
POLES 0
FASTEST LAPS 1
POINTS 51
HONOURS GP2 Champion 2007, German Formula BMW Champion 2001, German Formula BMW Junior Champion 2000

11 FELIPE MASSA
FERRARI

"I think I had a very good season. Looking at the car we had, how difficult it was to drive, I think the season was really good. We had many good results, but I had some problems at the beginning of the season in races that could have given me a podium finish. I definitely feel that for myself everything was going in the right direction. I had the possibility to keep doing a good job, but the accident in Hungary changed many things.

I think we were very strong at the Hungaroring, and I could have fought for a podium or even for victory. I have no memory of the accident. I remember the previous qualifying run, when I was on a scrubbed set of tyres, but I don't remember the run I crashed. I knew I was 10th, and I moved to Q3, but then I was coming back to the pit and I crashed. It's amazing that things take away the memory of the accident, but I remember everything before the accident, my whole life, so it's very strange. I suppose it's a good thing, not having the accident left in your mind.

When I came out of the car after my test at Maranello, everybody was shaking hands and was very happy. It was a great feeling, that we are a big family at Ferrari, and everybody likes each other. I felt very emotional. It was fantastic: this is our job, what we love to do is to drive the car at the quickest speeds possible.

And that is exactly what I did, pushing hard straight away and trying to do good lap times, consistent lap times, and I have to say everything was great. Even the result was very good. The result on my body was normal, as I didn't feel anything strange with the acceleration, braking, vibration.

When I went to the Brazilian GP, I was thinking all weekend that maybe I would race. The feeling was similar to a normal race weekend, and then when you go there you feel that something is missing. OK, I was together with the team, trying to push the team, but I wanted to be in the car. I can tell you that it wasn't a fantastic feeling! Anyway, the most important thing is that I'm fine, and now I have to prepare thoroughly for the 2010 championship."

NATIONALITY Brazilian
DATE OF BIRTH 25/4/81
PLACE OF BIRTH São Paulo, Brazil
GRANDS PRIX 115
WINS 11
POLES 14
FASTEST LAPS 13
POINTS 320
HONOURS Euro F3000 Champion 2001, European Formula Renault Champion 2000

12 HEIKKI KOVALAINEN
McLAREN

"I obviously had high hopes for this season, but as soon as we began testing the new car it was clear we weren't quick enough. Then it was a matter of trying to catch up and come back as quickly as possible.

The team worked very hard, but I haven't been able to get good enough results. There were a lot of different incidents, and I made a few mistakes at the beginning of the season. It's probably been my most difficult F1 season, although my first one with Renault in 2007 was quite tough as well. That's the way it is sometimes.

Going to Australia, we thought that potentially we could be the two slowest cars. We weren't expecting much, and of course to get to Q2 was a bonus. But it wasn't great, and the gap to the leaders was so big all weekend, so it was tough.

I didn't manage to complete the opening lap in either of the first two grands prix: I was out at the first corner in Australia, and then at the fourth corner in Malaysia. In both cases, I'd had a good qualifying run, as I'd outqualified Lewis in Australia, and was just behind him in Malaysia.

It was very tough, making corrections all the time, because the rear of the car was so poor. In Monaco it was quite warm, and there are a lot of corners, and I had to fight all the time to keep it on the track. I couldn't relax at any point, and it was physically very tough.

After we got the new package for the German GP, I started to score points every race. It was like night and day, and suddenly the tyres started to work. I was able to brake later, and the car had good stability under braking. It still didn't have the grip in the high-speed corners, but it was a big difference.

Obviously, I didn't win a race like Lewis did. I was in a position potentially to win at Valencia, and definitely at Monza. In Singapore, I felt I had the pace to be at the front, but something came up in each of the stints. Likewise, in qualifying in Singapore, I didn't really get a chance to have a go at it. I'd say this is the story of the year."

NATIONALITY Finnish
DATE OF BIRTH 19/10/81
PLACE OF BIRTH Suomussalmi, Finland
GRANDS PRIX 52
WINS 1
POLES 1
FASTEST LAPS 2
POINTS 105
HONOURS World Series by Nissan Champion 2004

13 NICK HEIDFELD
BMW SAUBER

"I expected more from this year. Our target was to fight for the World Championship, and we were very outspoken about that after we had made good progress in the previous years. In the winter I also thought we had a good car. I still believe we had a reasonable car, but probably not as good as we thought.

The big problem was that up to the first race and then through the next three races we introduced no new parts, and everybody stuck a lot of downforce on their cars. That's when we fell back even more. After that, we were playing catch up. It worked, but it took its time. We didn't have a double diffuser, and we were one of the last teams to introduce one, and that was the biggest downside.

KERS was also a downside, because at the beginning of the year when I used it, it was a disadvantage rather than an advantage. That's why we took it off. I still believe that at the time the decision was made it was right, but we didn't develop it well enough. The fact that McLaren and Ferrari were using it, and Renault from time to time, showed there was some potential there. I wasn't always the happiest guy, having to use it...

Malaysia was good. It was great to be on the podium, but in hindsight you always think it could have been better if you'd done this or made that decision. If I had put inters on, I would have won it. It was a good choice that I stayed on wets, but on inters it would have been even better. But that's the way it was.

The Spanish GP was a good one, because it's very unlikely to overtake at Barcelona. Starting from 13th, I had a good start, passing four cars at least, and then finishing in the points. Up to then, apart from Malaysia, we had scored no championship points.

There were races that were disappointing because you didn't get what you thought was possible. At the beginning of the year the car wasn't good enough anyway, but the Italian GP was disappointing because I had the engine failure there in qualifying after being quite strong in practice and the early stages of qualifying. I scored points in the race, but it could have been a whole lot better."

NATIONALITY German
DATE OF BIRTH 10/5/77
PLACE OF BIRTH Mönchengladbach, Germany
GRANDS PRIX 169
WINS 0
POLES 1
FASTEST LAPS 2
POINTS 219
HONOURS Formula 3000 Champion 1999, German F3 Champion 1997

14 ROBERT KUBICA
BMW SAUBER

"The season started pretty well in Australia, better than we expected and better than the performance of the car was in reality. Unfortunately, the accident with Sebastian [Vettel] cost us quite a lot of points, important points, because in the end I knew more or less that it would be really difficult in the remaining races, or at least in the early-season races, to jump on to the podium.

We also had a not bad performance in Malaysia, where we were quite competitive, but not quite as good as in Australia, not fighting for a podium. But then I had an engine failure before the start of the race… So, the beginning of the season was quite negative for us. Also, we didn't have anything new on the car in the first four overseas races, and we lost ground. At that point, there was also the double-diffuser story. The teams that didn't have one brought it in quite quickly, and they jumped in front of us. We started the season in front of McLaren and Ferrari, and clearly in front of McLaren, but after five or six races they were already a lot in front of us.

So we lost it in the beginning of the season, let's say. Once we started working and pushing, we slowly caught up, but it was too late, and we had too big a gap to the front. You saw that the cars were very close together, so two- or three-tenths of a second made a huge difference. In the past, with two- or three-tenths you maybe gained one position. In 2009, you could gain anything from five to eight positions.

Once you fall behind too far, it's very hard to catch up, unless you have a really big package. We had a few upgrades coming that we thought were very big, but in reality they were never so big. Sometimes they were never even half of what we were expecting them to be on the track. So this didn't help us to catch up.

Second in Brazil was a good surprise. We had good pace, but it wasn't easy, as we had a small problem with high water temperature, so we dropped the revs in the first stint, meaning that I wasn't using 100% of my revs. Because of that, I was surprised about being able to match the pace of Brawn and Red Bull."

NATIONALITY Polish
DATE OF BIRTH 7/12/84
PLACE OF BIRTH Krakow, Poland
GRANDS PRIX 57
WINS 1
POLES 1
FASTEST LAPS 0
POINTS 137
HONOURS World Series by Renault Champion 2005, German & Italian Junior Kart Champion 2000, Polish Junior Kart Champion 1997

15 GIANCARLO FISICHELLA
FORCE INDIA & FERRARI

"At the beginning of the year, it looked like another tough and difficult season, as we received the car quite late. Then, as soon as we put the car on the ground, I wasn't happy at all, because we were about two seconds slower than the leaders. I already realised that it was going to be another difficult season, being at the back of the grid again and maybe struggling to score a point.

However, I have to say the Force India team did a fantastic job. Already in Bahrain they made a step forward with the double diffuser. We made another step at Silverstone, a big one, about 0.6s, but still not enough to score points there. In Valencia, we made another big step, another 0.6s.

Then we went to the Belgian GP, and when we put the wing from Valencia with the new package for Spa-Francorchamps, the car was so good. I was quite sure that I'd be in the top 10, I was so confident. I did a fantastic lap in Q3. The strategy was fairly aggressive, but the fuel load was quite similar to the other teams, and I was on pole…

I was confident of scoring good points in the race, but I really didn't expect to be that quick. I was even quicker than Kimi [Räikkönen] and I could have won the race. But for us even second place was amazing, it was a brilliant result.

Then, as you know, I moved to Ferrari. It was fantastic, it was the dream of my life. It happened very quickly. I went to the factory for three days, I did the seat fitting, I did the simulator and then I went to Monza. I was so excited that first day, so nervous.

It was tougher than I had reckoned, as the car was completely different from what I expected, completely different to the Force India. You need to drive differently with the KERS system, and it's not easy because I haven't done this kind of driving for 15 years. You have to concentrate on braking and do different things because of the KERS, especially on the downshift you have to be later on that or there is a lot of rear locking. The car was quite inconsistent, and the fact that there was no testing at all didn't help me."

NATIONALITY Italian
DATE OF BIRTH 14/1/73
PLACE OF BIRTH Rome, Italy
GRANDS PRIX 231
WINS 3
POLES 4
FASTEST LAPS 2
POINTS 275
HONOURS Italian F3 Champion & Monaco F3 GP winner 1994

16 SEBASTIEN BUEMI
TORO ROSSO

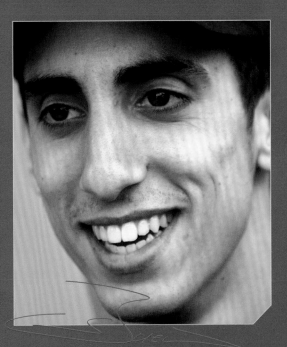

"If I start from the beginning of the season, I wasn't honestly expecting to score points in my first grand prix, but you never know what might happen, if there are a lot of crashes and everything. I finished in seventh place in Melbourne, and then in China I went into Q3 after just three races. So I would say the start of the season was very good for me, certainly better than I had expected.

Then, for sure I was expecting a little bit more from the next races, because you get used to the car, to the team, to the races and everything, and you expect to be better. In reality, though, we were slower, so it was I would say a little bit difficult to accept. You see, you feel, you try harder, and in the end you just don't get the same results.

There is a lot of explanation about that, but I won't go through everything. For sure the fact that there were big developments, and we were the last team to get the double-deck diffuser, didn't help. There are a few points that can explain why we struggled, along with the fact that the field was so close to each

other. I was 19th in qualifying at Monza, but was just 0.9s of a second off pole position! It wasn't easy, but then we received a new update for the Japanese GP.

The Chinese GP was one of the best races. We were fifth and then I broke the front wing hitting Vettel. I was still eighth, but we lost what would have been a fantastic result for us. In Monaco I qualified 11th. [My team-mate Sebastien] Bourdais, who was far behind me on the grid, scored a point. It would have been possible to score, but I crashed into Piquet.

It was important to score points early in the season, because they need to see that you can do it, and also for me, because if you chase after your first points it's not so easy. At least we did it straight away. However, you always do your maximum. You don't think: 'I didn't score points, I need to do this or that', you just push as hard as you can.

In the end, I'm quite happy with my season, because compared to Bourdais at the start of the season I was quite competitive, and he was the only guy you can really compare me with."

NATIONALITY Swiss
DATE OF BIRTH 13/10/88
PLACE OF BIRTH Aigle, Switzerland
GRANDS PRIX 17
WINS 0
POLES 0
FASTEST LAPS 0
POINTS 6
HONOURS Italian Kart Champion 2003, European & Swiss Junior Kart Champion 2002, Swiss Super Mini Kart Champion 2000

17 ADRIAN SUTIL
FORCE INDIA

"It looked very hard and difficult at the beginning of the season, because we had a good baseline with the car, but no downforce. You don't really believe that suddenly you can move up the whole grid within half of the season. I was so impressed that what Vijay [Mallya] promised actually happened!

I thought the change to Mercedes engines was the right thing to do. There was just not the right offer from Ferrari, and Mercedes looked much better, with the gearbox and the whole hardware package. I was quite sure that we were going to do well.

We built the car in I think two months, and it was a really good job. As I said, the baseline was very good and I never really had trouble setting up my car. But I was at the back in qualifying in Australia, as grip was missing at every corner. The Chinese GP was a really difficult race in the rain, as we were all on the edge everywhere. I had a whole train behind me, pushing quite a lot. I was sixth when I crashed with six laps to go. I was nearly crying in my car, I couldn't believe it...

In Bahrain, we put on the first update, and it went quite well, and I nearly made it into Q2. The next big step came at Silverstone, and it went really well, except I had a brake failure in qualifying.

We could see it was going in the right direction, though, but somehow luck was not on our side. I had a very good qualifying run in Germany, and made it to Q3. I was the heaviest car in Q3, and qualified seventh. I went up to second place in the race, then I went into the pits, and on the way out I had the accident with Kimi. I still think the same thing, that there was enough space for him to go a little bit wider...

Finally the next package in Valencia put us really close to Q3 again. And then suddenly from Spa onwards we were always near the front. In Italy, it was quite scary – Friday P1, Saturday morning, P1. I thought I was really going for pole! And that's what I did in qualifying. I got it, but then Lewis beat me by a little bit. Still, it was one of the best moments of my life."

NATIONALITY German
DATE OF BIRTH 11/1/83
PLACE OF BIRTH Graefeling, Germany
GRANDS PRIX 52
WINS 0
POLES 0
FASTEST LAPS 1
POINTS 6
HONOURS Swiss Formula Ford Champion 2002

18 KAMUI KOBAYASHI
TOYOTA

"Before Interlagos I drove one or maybe two tests with slick tyres at Jerez, because in Portimao I only drove with treaded rain tyres. So there were a lot of new things, especially with the tyres... I drove on Friday in Suzuka, but it was wet.

It was easy for me to get into Q3 in Brazil, but I had a spin. I was really surprised at the start, because normally in F1 it's quiet at the beginning, because they know the race is long. At Interlagos, it wasn't! People were quite aggressive. I just did my race, and with my situation I just wanted to finish, so I didn't want to take risks, but it seemed that everybody was pushing quite hard...

The safety car restart was quite hard, especially with the tyres. It's important to keep the temperature, and for me that was really new. With GP2 tyres, the working range is really low, but with F1 it's really high, so it's difficult to warm them up. I tried to warm them as much as possible, and it wasn't such a big problem. I overtook Kazuki [Nakajima] after the restart, so that was really good for me.

I had Jenson [Button] behind me, but I really didn't care about his championship, because it was my first race and I wanted to do my own race, so I tried to defend my position.

In the incident with Kazuki, I exited the pitlane and was in the middle of the track. I didn't know what he was going to do. I tried to move to the left, and he was immediately behind me. Afterwards he disappeared. I couldn't find him in the mirrors, and a few seconds later he overtook me really fast!

Overall, the race was a little bit hard, because I didn't expect such a long race – 71 laps is really long.

Abu Dhabi was definitely a fantastic race. I didn't expect to finish sixth there. I thought maybe I can score one or two points. I overtook Jenson but he was on cold tyres after a pitstop, so it's difficult to compare. I had to overtake at that moment, or it would have been difficult to improve my pace later.

F1 is fantastic. We go all over the world, and I can gain experience of a lot of things, not only racing. This for me is really nice..."

NATIONALITY Japanese
DATE OF BIRTH 13/9/86
PLACE OF BIRTH Hyogo, Japan
GRANDS PRIX 2
WINS 0
POLES 0
FASTEST LAPS 0
POINTS 3
HONOURS European & Italian Formula Renault Champion 2005, Japanese Kart Champion 2001, Suzuka Kart Champion 2000, Japanese Cadet Kart Champion 1997

19 SEBASTIEN BOURDAIS
TORO ROSSO

"This season obviously didn't go the way that any of the two parties wanted. I wish I could say that I felt great in the car and the car was fast and it was all rosy, but it wasn't!

We struggled for grip most of the time. We did the best we could with the car, but ultimately to make it driveable you had to drive with a loose car on entry. It was pretty much the same as last year, except we struggled a lot more for grip because there was a bit less aero on the car, and we couldn't get the tyres started most of the time. When the track was getting grippy, it wasn't so bad. When the track was low grip, though, we were just massively struggling.

At Monaco, the car was really, really tough to drive and was sliding around a lot, with no stability. I was pushing the best I could with what I had, but it was a very stressful race, because there was a point at stake and the race wasn't going so badly. We started 14th and made up good ground, but it was a nerve-wracking race! I just missed stuffing the car about 50 times, but

in the end the result was very satisfying because obviously to score a point is always a good thing, and there was not so much attrition in the race.

The best feeling I had all year was probably in Bahrain. We were pretty competitive in terms of lap time during the race and, had we started higher up, we would have done something pretty good I think. But it never quite materialised. For most of the first part of the season we were always one or two steps behind Red Bull Racing, and with the rate of development it made things very, very difficult to be competitive. Even when the car felt alright, it just wasn't quite quick enough to make the step up.

It's just not been a lot of fun, and then the way it ended was the nadir, I guess. To hear it from the press pretty much is never a fun thing to go through, but in the end the most important thing for me is to find the next chapter and to enjoy myself behind the steering wheel again."

NATIONALITY French
DATE OF BIRTH 28/2/79
PLACE OF BIRTH Le Mans, France
GRANDS PRIX 27
WINS 0
POLES 0
FASTEST LAPS 0
POINTS 6
HONOURS ChampCar Champion 2004–2007, Formula 3000 Champion 2002, French F3 Champion 1999, French FRenault Champion 1997

20 KAZUKI NAKAJIMA
WILLIAMS

"If I see the results, it was a very disappointing season! I didn't score any points, which was pretty bad I would say. However, compared to 2008, in terms of my performance I would say it's much better. My qualifying, race pace and consistency have all been better than last year. I feel quite positive with myself, but the results haven't come. So it's a little bit of a complicated feeling!

Things didn't really work out for me at the start of the season. Especially in Australia where I had quite a big chance because I was just outside the top 10 in qualifying. There was an incident at the first corner which made it easy for me to move up to the front with quite a heavy fuel load. With my mistake and crash though, it didn't work out.

After that race it was very difficult for me, because every time there were cars around me that had KERS, and every time I was losing my position at the start...

There were a lot of races from Monaco up until Valencia where I had a chance to score points, but I had problems with traffic or problems with a pit stop. At Silverstone, I qualified fifth and I had traffic. But I could have done better with the in-lap and out-lap as well. All these small things were very costly every time, because the difference between the cars is very small.

Turkey was a good race. The grid position wasn't that good, but we had a very good pace in the race. If we hadn't had a problem in the pit stop, I am sure we could have scored a couple of points.

It was very frustrating to sit 11th in qualifying so many times... At the same time, it's not too bad, because you can play with the race fuel load. For qualifying I think there's still room to improve, and of course nowadays only 0.2s makes quite a big difference around that position. Especially compared to last year, I could be consistently closer to Nico [Rosberg], but if you see the results it was clear that he was always doing a pretty good job in the races, and even when I was ahead of him at the start he managed to have a really good first lap!"

NATIONALITY Japanese
DATE OF BIRTH 11/1/85
PLACE OF BIRTH Aichi, Japan
GRANDS PRIX 36
WINS 0
POLES 0
FASTEST LAPS 0
POINTS 9
HONOURS Japanese Formula Toyota Champion 2003

21 NELSON PIQUET JR
RENAULT

"The year was extremely difficult for me, because the car was so different, the tyres were so different, and there was KERS as well. Plus I had no testing at the beginning of the year. I had maybe two days in the dry or something ridiculous like that. Fernando [Alonso] wanted to test more because the car was completely new.

So it was like it was a first year of F1 for me. Every session I was learning something new, like new buttons on the steering wheel, new feelings on the car. It was quite tough at the beginning of the year because it had been such a hard pre-season for me. The difference between Fernando and me was more than in the 2008. Then there were also a lot of issues of everybody having upgrades on their cars at the beginning of the year.

We had them on only one car all the time, and that really pissed me off a little bit. Plus there's Fernando's other few tenths of a second over me because he's bloody quick, plus all the extra mileage he had at the beginning of the year to get used to the car. It all starts adding up, and the harder you try, the worse it gets. There was nothing my engineers could do. At the same time, I was getting bollocked by the boss [Flavio Briatore], so it was a tough beginning of the year.

When somebody wants to kick you out, they want to kick you out. It was a decision that was probably taken earlier on in the year. To put me in a situation at the beginning of the year where I wasn't testing, and then putting on the pressure and questioning me all the time, then no upgrades during the races, and then still blaming me... There was no reason really to keep barking at me, and if that was happening it's because they knew they were going to do it.

What happened afterwards was a lesson for life, a big lesson that I learned. Even in a weak position, never be convinced or persuaded to do something. Take your time to make decisions and don't feel obliged. I think it was a big mistake on my part as well. But, anyway, it has passed. What happened happened, and that was it."

NATIONALITY Brazilian
DATE OF BIRTH 25/7/85
PLACE OF BIRTH Heidelberg, Germany
GRANDS PRIX 28
WINS 0
POLES 0
FASTEST LAPS 0
POINTS 19
HONOURS British F3 Champion 2004, South American F3 Champion 2002

22 VITANTONIO LIUZZI

FORCE INDIA

"Of course I was really happy when my chance came to race for Force India, because I was really dying being a third driver and watching the grands prix on TV... I think I'm born for racing and I was suffering in that position.

I got the chance, and I think I used it the maximum I could, because I had just five races to show my speed again. I was pretty confident that I would race in 2010, but you know how F1 changes, so I had to maximise my five events.

I think we always had strong races. It was a shame at Monza, because the car was really strong there, and we could have finished between third and fifth in the race, which would have been a really beautiful comeback. But the car broke a driveshaft. However, that's part of the game. Sometimes when luck is not with you, you cannot get more. Points would have been fantastic at my home race.

After Luca Badoer went back to Ferrari, and the other times a third driver drove, nobody could believe that we could be so strong, but in fact it was the opposite thing for me, as I was feeling really confident about everything there.

I could have been even faster, because I was not 100% myself.

We were pretty unlucky in several events. Singapore was the only race where we weren't actually too quick, but both in Japan and Brazil we had really strong pace but were unlucky in qualifying. In Japan, we broke the gearbox in third practice, and when we rebuilt it we had no time to put it on the scale, and the car was sliding on the ground in qualifying. That's why I was losing 0.5s on the straights. In Brazil, I had a lot of aquaplaning when I was pretty strong in the rain, and I was pretty sure I would reach Q3. In the races, though, we always had really strong race pace, and we showed really aggressive races and good performances, so I'm pretty happy overall.

Without testing, it has been pretty difficult, because it's quite different from other categories that I competed in this year, like A1GP. F1 is the cream of motor racing and, apart from the speed of the car, you are competing with drivers that are mostly 100% at the top. So it's pretty challenging."

NATIONALITY Italian
DATE OF BIRTH 6/8/81
PLACE OF BIRTH Locorotondo, Italy
GRANDS PRIX 44
WINS 0
POLES 0
FASTEST LAPS 0
POINTS 5
HONOURS Formula 3000 Champion 2004, World Kart Champion 2001, Italian Kart Champion 1996

23 ROMAIN GROSJEAN

RENAULT

"When someone telephones you and says that you are going to Formula 1, you just say 'Yes! Yes, I want it, I'll come, I'll run, whatever you want.' It was a dream coming true.

For sure it was a tough experience, with no testing in the R29 and only three days in F1, and a new circuit for half of the races I contested. On the flip side, I think it was the best chance of my career to get to F1.

The first weekend in Valencia went pretty well. In the second one, at Spa, unfortunately I got traffic in qualifying, and then had a crash on the first lap. But it could have been a good race. The Italian GP was my best qualifying, and I was quite happy with that until somebody hit me at the first chicane. It happens sometimes. Singapore was a disaster, as I had no brakes all weekend.

At Suzuka, the conditions were just very difficult, raining, raining, raining and then suddenly you get dry for qualifying. When you don't know the track, it's really quite difficult. In Brazil, I was very happy with my race, as I made no mistakes and had a very consistent

race. We weren't performing very well I have to say, but in the end the race was very good. I did my best but we were just missing performance. In Q1, I had been eighth when everybody had the same conditions.

Every time I got in the car I felt that I was improving, I worked hard with the engineers and they tried to get the car more around me, and it was getting better and better.

Fernando [Alonso] is the best driver on the grid for me, and in qualifying he was always finding something new and impressive. So, every time I checked the data after qualifying and thought 'OK, we can do this with the car. But it's too late for this qualifying, so I'll bring it to the next one.'

People just watched the gap between us, and for sure the gap was bigger than with another driver who is maybe not as good as him. But he's a two-time World Champion, and he brought me so much experience outside the car. In the car, it's everybody for himself, but outside the car he was trying to help me as much as he could."

NATIONALITY French/Swiss
DATE OF BIRTH 17/4/86
PLACE OF BIRTH Geneva, Switzerland
GRANDS PRIX 7
WINS 0
POLES 0
FASTEST LAPS 0
POINTS 0
HONOURS European F3 Champion 2007, French Formula Renault Champion 2005, Swiss Formula Renault 1600 Champion 2003

24 JAIME ALGUERSUARI
TORO ROSSO

"I was definitely not thinking of upgrading to F1 for 2009. If you review the season, how it went for me in World Series by Renault and F1, if I'd had that on paper at the start of the year, for sure I would have signed for it! I'm quite happy with how everything went.

It's difficult to expect anything better than I achieved in F1, because the step up is huge, it's so different. With no testing, it was so hard, and even with testing I would say it was going to be hard halfway through the season to take the rhythm of the championship and everything. As I had no testing, though, I think I have to be quite proud.

To mix World Series and F1 was very tough, because you use different tyre compounds, the car is completely different, as is the seat. Everything changes. So, like I said, I am proud of the way it went, and I'm really looking forward to my future in F1. I've already advanced to Q2, so I'm in the top 15 drivers, and I know there's a lot more to come. As a result, I'm really motivated and really satisfied.

One of the main reasons I think Red Bull put me in the car was because of my age and experience. I guess this is very important. If you are five out of 10 when you are 18, you will be six out of 10 when you are 19, and it's like this going through the years. Every year you grow up and get more mature, and you learn from a lot of situations. I think that's the story, really.

Hungary was quite tough. OK, I had the 'no pressure' effect from Franz Tost, from Giorgio Ascanelli, from Mr Mateschitz, from everyone. Because, in the end, you know you can't judge a guy who hasn't driven the car before. I'd only driven it in a straight line. When I joined the team, I was completely sure I was going to be 3–4s off the lead, even though I'd been at 100%. Then, when I saw I was just 0.3–0.4s behind Buemi, I was really very impressed with myself...

On the physical side, the toughest circuit was Singapore, because it was the longest and hottest race I've ever done in my life. It was a great experience for me, and we saw good progress in Japan."

NATIONALITY Spanish
DATE OF BIRTH 23/3/90
PLACE OF BIRTH Barcelona, Spain
GRANDS PRIX 8
WINS 0
POLES 0
FASTEST LAPS 0
POINTS 0
HONOURS British F3 Champion 2008, Italian Formula Renault Winter Series Champion 2006

25 LUCA BADOER
FERRARI

"I think for any driver to drive a Ferrari in a grand prix is a dream. It's something really special. After Felipe Massa's accident in Hungary, the situation was immediately very clear: I was the third driver at Ferrari, but I stepped aside of course for Michael Schumacher to be Felipe's replacement. The team told me if Michael can drive, he's the best choice. I agreed obviously, and I was happy for him. But, if Michael could not drive, I would drive. This was all very clear immediately after the Hungarian GP.

Then I kept increasing my training, and I was ready in case. Then Ferrari chose me, and the reason was very simple, because first of all I was the third driver, and all the teams have a third driver and test driver for some reason. When I was driving regularly, driving in tests until last year, I was quick enough to match the official drivers. Over the 10 years that I have held this position, these drivers were Felipe, Kimi [Räikkönen], Rubens [Barrichello]. So it was the right choice, from my point of view.

The thing is, I needed more time in the car. Unfortunately, I started in Valencia and I didn't know the track. It was 10 months since I had driven an F1 car, and this car was very different. So Valencia was a disaster, I'm the first to admit. I then made a step forward at Spa, and I'm sure if I had had a bit more time I would have been able to do better, able to do a normal performance.

Unfortunately, for a lot of reasons, Ferrari decided they didn't have time to wait for my development or my improvement. They were fighting for third place in the World Championship and they told me they needed a driver who didn't need time and could immediately score points. So they decided to take Giancarlo [Fisichella] for this reason.

I have to say thanks to Ferrari, because they trusted me when they took me. I just think that from my point of view, looking at my past record, I'm sure I would have been able to do a reasonable job if I'd been given a few more races. Anyway, I'm happy that I did two races for Ferrari, and if I could go back, and had the chance, I'd do the same. Driving for Ferrari is something special."

NATIONALITY Italian
DATE OF BIRTH 25/1/71
PLACE OF BIRTH Montebelluna, Italy
GRANDS PRIX 53
WINS 0
POLES 0
FASTEST LAPS 0
POINTS 0
HONOURS Formula 3000 Champion 1992, Italian Kart Champion 1990

THE TEAMS

A new set of rules shook up Formula 1's order and it led to a year of intrigue and ever-changing positions, as the established teams fought back against the challengers

BRAWN GP

TOYOTA

BRAWN GP

THE TEAM

PERSONNEL

TEAM PRINCIPAL Ross Brawn (above)
CHIEF EXECUTIVE OFFICER Nick Fry
HEAD OF RACE AND TEST ENGINEERING Steve Clark
HEAD OF VEHICLE ENGINEERING AND DYNAMICS
Craig Wilson
OPERATIONS DIRECTOR Gary Savage
SPORTING DIRECTOR Ron Meadows
CHIEF RACE ENGINEER Simon Cole
DRIVERS Rubens Barrichello, Jenson Button
TEST/THIRD DRIVERS Alex Wurz, Anthony Davidson
SENIOR RACE ENGINEER (Barrichello) Jock Clear
SENIOR RACE ENGINEER (Button) Andrew Shovlin
CHIEF MECHANIC Matthew Deane
TEST TEAM MANAGER Andrew Alsworth
TOTAL NUMBER OF EMPLOYEES 450
NUMBER IN RACE TEAM 45
TEAM BASE Brackley, England
TELEPHONE +44 (0)1280 844000
WEBSITE www.brawngp.com

TEAM STATS

IN F1 SINCE 1999, as BAR then Honda Racing
FIRST GRAND PRIX Australia 1999
STARTS 188 **WINS** 9 **POLE POSITIONS** 8
FASTEST LAPS 4 **PODIUMS** 30 **POINTS** 496
CONSTRUCTORS' TITLES 1 **DRIVERS' TITLES** 1

SPONSORS

Virgin, Bridgestone, MIG, Henri Lloyd

22 JENSON BUTTON   **23 RUBENS BARRICHELLO**

FROM FACING OBLIVION TO THE HIGHEST PEAK

By Ross Brawn
(Team Principal)
"The regulations were obviously quite different for 2009, and because we started our project early it became clear that the target downforce levels were going to be exceeded. The whole purpose of the Overtaking Working Group (OWG) was to decrease aerodynamic performance and increase tyre grip, but the numbers I was seeing made me think we were going to exceed those targets, even without any knowledge of the double diffuser. I told the working groups that we weren't draconian enough in the changes, and I remember Patrick Head making a very impassioned speech about how I was scaremongering. Several others pooh-poohed the idea too, but I think they now see that it was fact.

When Honda announced its withdrawal, I got fully engrossed. It was sometime during January that I got a 'phone call from Ferrari, asking 'had I seen the Toyota diffuser? It was a disgrace and shouldn't be allowed.' I asked our guys what it was all about and they said 'Ooh, we've got one the same as that!' I realised that there was going to be a fuss, but went through the detail and was comfortable that the interpretation was lateral yet within the wording of the regulations.

We put a lot into the 2009 car. A pilot group looked at the concept and by the middle of 2008 all our staff were working on it, but I think the amount of wind tunnels has been rather overstated! I've seen four mentioned, but the reality is that we have two tunnels at Brackley – one is new and full-size, the other a very old, open-jet tunnel.

We also absorbed Ben Wood and his group from Super Aguri when they ran out of money. They were the ones able to do the pilot project and their aero group had a contract to use a tunnel in Bedford, which ran out in August 2008, so we used up that time since Honda was paying for it. There is a tunnel in Japan, but it's not a particularly good one, so it was two and a half tunnels really.

DIFFUSER PROVIDES A SMOKESCREEN

The front wing was key to these cars, and some who struggled at the start of the year didn't have that sorted. The fact that they hadn't worked out the fundamentals may be why people were so sceptical about some of the comments I was making.

I was happy people were obsessed with the diffuser, as they missed a lot of the other stuff. With a conventional diffuser we lost several per cent, but it wasn't the second-a-lap claimed. In a way, it was a nice smokescreen, as we had other important parts of the package: the front bib treatment and brake ducts were important, as well as the front wing.

MERCEDES NEEDED FEWEST CHASSIS MODS

Our late adaptation to the Mercedes engine was a bit crude. We cut the back of the chassis off and bonded on a new rear bulkhead with different engine mounts. We decided to go the Mercedes route because it was very close to the Honda. The Ferrari had a very low front-top engine mount which would really have been in the middle of nowhere, so the Mercedes was the closest, but both the front of the gearbox and back of the chassis were cut off and had pieces grafted on.

We didn't have a lot of time to deal with the cooling package. The Mercedes has two oil coolers and we had to add a cooler just behind the roll hoop, although it wasn't run at all races. Probably the biggest deficiency was lifting up the rear suspension and gearbox by about 6mm because the output shaft of the engine and input shaft of the gearbox were different heights. The Honda crankshaft was lower, so we've lived with an assembly that's 6mm too high all year. The chassis weight also went up with all the bits we put on. We just about had the capacity to cope with a KERS system with the car as designed, but not on what we ended up with if we were going to achieve the weight distribution that we wanted.

While the car was born with quite a big team, it was developed with a much smaller one – around 450 people. We put our effort into aerodynamics and did work on suspension too: dampers, springs and ride quality with inertia dampers.

TYRE WARM-UP PROVED A PROBLEM

We had a fine start, but beginning at Silverstone we had tyre warm-up issues. There was a narrow window in which they worked and I think that's why you saw cars going forward and backward at different tracks, as the energy going into the tyre is dependent on the track and ambient temperatures.

The first indication that we might have issues was the wet race in China when [Mark]

TECHNICAL SPECIFICATIONS

ENGINE
MAKE/MODEL Mercedez-Benz FO108W
CONFIGURATION 2400cc V8 (90 degree)
SPARK PLUGS NGK
ECU FIA standard issue
KERS n/a
FUEL Mobil 1
OIL Mobil 1
BATTERY Not disclosed

TRANSMISSION
GEARBOX Not disclosed
FORWARD GEARS Seven
CLUTCH Not disclosed

CHASSIS
CHASSIS MODEL Brawn BGP 001
FRONT SUSPENSION LAYOUT
Wishbones and pushrod-activated
torsion springs and rockers
REAR SUSPENSION LAYOUT
Wishbones and pushrod-activated
torsion springs and rockers
DAMPERS Sachs

TYRES Bridgestone
WHEELS BBS
BRAKE DISCS
Brembo & Hitco
BRAKE PADS
Brembo & Hitco
BRAKE CALIPERS
Brembo
FUEL TANK ATL
INSTRUMENTS
Not disclosed

DIMENSIONS
LENGTH 4700mm
WIDTH 1800mm
HEIGHT 950mm
WHEELBASE
Not disclosed
TRACK
front Not disclosed
rear Not disclosed
WEIGHT 605kg (including
driver and camera)

Webber, with a lot of grip, just drove around the outside of Jenson [Button]. Also, to get a balance on the car there, we'd had to drop a lot of front wing angle and that's when we discovered that with a flat flap angle we lost a huge amount of performance. So we developed a different family of wings that worked over a much wider range of angles.

We were confident we could sort out our issues, but where it got complicated was with some of the suspension changes we made, as they definitely influenced tyre temperature. Changes we made around the Turkish GP helped us win there, where the tyres run at the top end of the scale, but also hurt us at places like Silverstone and the Nürburgring where we wanted to generate tyre temperature. We didn't understand how to manage that as well as we should have done.

Rubens [Barrichello's] style sometimes generated more temperature than Jenson's: we could see it and measure it. But Jenson learned from that and it didn't occur at the later races. It's difficult and you have your inherent style, but Jenson did force the car more when he thought that tyre temperature was an issue.

THE DRIVERS HAD TO ADAPT THEIR STYLE
Sometimes it's keeping the tyres hot after leaving the pits that's just as important, as if they drop off and you've got no grip you can't get them back again. Both drivers became more conscientious about keeping the temperature in the tyre. Our first laps after the start became good and a lot of other guys struggled. Our drivers learned to get the tyres hot and do more on the formation lap. The rears you can heat with the throttle, but the fronts are much more difficult, and if you watched Alonso, for example, he induced huge understeer and our guys did the same.

Whether a car is kind to its tyres or not is down to its culture and philosophy, and mine is born of Ferrari, which also struggled to generate temperature. The teams that can find a way to deal with all scenarios will gain an advantage and that's what we've got to try to do.

The drivers did an excellent job. Jenson's start to the year was extraordinary and there were very few mistakes. And Rubens is very good at feeling through what the car is doing and looking at the second level of analysis. When we did front wing comparisons, he was sensitive and able to analyse them, a little more so than Jenson, who is more like Michael and tends to cope with what's there. Rubens has always been technically astute and, with no testing, that helped."

RED BULL

THE TEAM

PERSONNEL

CHAIRMAN Dietrich Mateschitz
TEAM PRINCIPAL Christian Horner
CHIEF TECHNICAL OFFICER Adrian Newey (above)
HEAD OF RACE ENGINEERING Ian Morgan
CHIEF DESIGNER Rob Marshall
HEAD OF AERODYNAMICS Peter Prodromou
TEAM MANAGER Jonathan Wheatley
TEAM CO-ORDINATOR Gerrard O'Reilly
CHIEF ENGINEER ENGINES Fabrice Lom
DRIVERS Sebastian Vettel, Mark Webber
RACE ENGINEER (Vettel) Giullaume Rocquelin
RACE ENGINEER (Webber) Ciaron Pilbeam
SUPPORT TEAM MANAGER Tony Burrows
TEST/THIRD DRIVERS David Coulthard,
Jaime Alguersuari, Brendon Hartley
CHIEF MECHANIC Kenny Handkammer
TOTAL NUMBER OF EMPLOYEES 534
NUMBER IN RACE TEAM 54
TEAM BASE Milton Keynes, England
TELEPHONE +44 (0)1908 279700
WEBSITE www.redbullracing.com

TEAM STATS

IN F1 SINCE 1997 as Stewart Grand Prix then Jaguar Racing
FIRST GRAND PRIX Australia 1997 **STARTS** 223
WINS 6 **POLE POSITIONS** 6 **FASTEST LAPS** 6
PODIUMS 20 **POINTS** 344.5 **CONSTRUCTORS' TITLES**
0 **DRIVERS' TITLES** 0

SPONSORS

Red Bull, Red Bull Cola, Bridgestone, Total, Magneti Marelli,
Rauch, Siemens

14 MARK WEBBER **15** SEBASTIAN VETTEL

LACK OF DOUBLE-DECK DIFFUSER HURT EARLY ON

**By Adrian Newey
(Chief Technical Officer)**

"We got a relatively early start on the Red Bull RB5 for 2009, looked at the technical regulations in April of 2008 and had a model in the wind tunnel around June if my memory serves me correctly.

We started at around 50% of the 2008 downforce level and began the painful process of trying to get as much back as possible.

We had a little look in the double-deck diffuser direction, albeit not in exactly the same way as other people did, but we didn't pursue it because, to be perfectly honest, we were extremely surprised that it was eventually deemed to be legal.

ADAPTING FOR A DOUBLE-DECK DIFFUSER

It took us a while to adapt the car to a double-deck diffuser, simply because it wasn't designed for it. And then it took a while to understand within the hardware constraints that we had how best to fit the double-deck diffuser to the car.

We didn't really have the time or resources to change the gearbox and the rear suspension to accommodate it, so we had our first attempt at a double-deck diffuser on the car at the Monaco Grand Prix. It produced a small improvement, but we weren't very happy with it and the more definitive attempt was a month later for the British Grand Prix at Silverstone. There was a further diffuser update for the Singapore Grand Prix.

Had the World Championship started at the stage we were at with the car by Silverstone, we would have been looking good, but the ground that the Brawn team had made on us between the start of the season and then meant that it was really asking an awful lot of the team to close the gap in the second half of the season. It was a bit of a frustration to be tripped up by the technical regulations, but that's the very nature of F1 and there's no point in lamenting it.

REDUCING THE CAR'S APPETITE FOR TYRES

We were the only team to use pull-rod suspension. The intention of the 2009 technical regulations was to move the point at which the diffuser starts from the front edge of the rear tyre, where it had been since 1993, to be level with the rear axle. This meant that everything was carried lower on the car, giving you more room, and the thinking behind the pull-rod layout was to use the change in bodywork regulations to best effect. It was a very good solution of which we were quite proud.

The RB5 proved to be quite hard on its tyres initially and we worked extremely hard to counter that. I think some of the changes that we made, both mechanical as well as aerodynamic, certainly bore fruit.

In terms of development, front wings and diffusers were the key areas on the car. They have always been the biggest performance areas on a car and, especially when you have a new set of technical regulations, yield the biggest benefits.

LACK OF TESTING AFFECTS KNOWLEDGE

Our revisions for the British Grand Prix involved a lot of work but, because you are no longer allowed to do back-to-back testing, it's quite difficult to assess your progress exactly and you are relying purely on the team's simulation results. I'd say that the gain we made at the British Grand Prix was around half a second.

What the testing restrictions really meant was that compared to a 2008 race weekend we did a lot more testing on a grand prix Friday in 2009 than we had before, and so were more reliant on simply believing our wind tunnel and simulation tools. You'd put things on the car and hope that you had gone forward, but you really didn't know with complete confidence if you had. Short of going back through the changes again once the season is over, we probably never will know.

NOT ALL ENGINES WERE EQUAL...

I think that it became very clear that one of the engines in particular was very strong and the rest of us were all a little behind. Bearing in mind that 1% power, thus equating to roughly seven horsepower, is somewhere around 0.13s per lap, engine power remains an extremely major factor. There is always considerable conjecture on the power of different engines and also a fair bit of evidence that one manufacturer is ahead of the rest of us. Significantly ahead, I should say.

Having said that, our relationship with Renault was really very good from a logistics and operational point of view. We were very happy with their service and the way that they treated us.

Our general reliability was very good. We failed to finish in Hungary with Sebastian

TECHNICAL SPECIFICATIONS

ENGINE
MAKE/MODEL Renault RS27
CONFIGURATION 2400cc V8 (90 degree)
SPARK PLUGS Champion
ECU FIA standard issue
KERS n/a
FUEL Total
OIL Total Group
BATTERY Not disclosed

TRANSMISSION
GEARBOX Red Bull Technology
FORWARD GEARS Seven
CLUTCH AP Racing

CHASSIS
CHASSIS MODEL Red Bull RB5
FRONT SUSPENSION LAYOUT
Aluminium alloy uprights, carbon-composite double wishbones with torsion bar springs and anti-roll bars

REAR SUSPENSION LAYOUT
Aluminium alloy uprights, carbon-composite double wishbones with torsion bar springs and anti-roll bars
DAMPERS Multimatic
TYRES Bridgestone
WHEELS OZ Racing
BRAKE DISCS Brembo
BRAKE PADS Brembo
BRAKE CALIPERS Brembo
FUEL TANK ATL
INSTRUMENTS Red Bull Technology

DIMENSIONS
LENGTH Not disclosed
WIDTH 1800mm
HEIGHT 950mm
WHEELBASE Not disclosed
TRACK front 1800mm maximum
rear 1800mm maximum
WEIGHT 605kg (including driver and camera)

Red Bull racing
FORMULA ONE TEAM

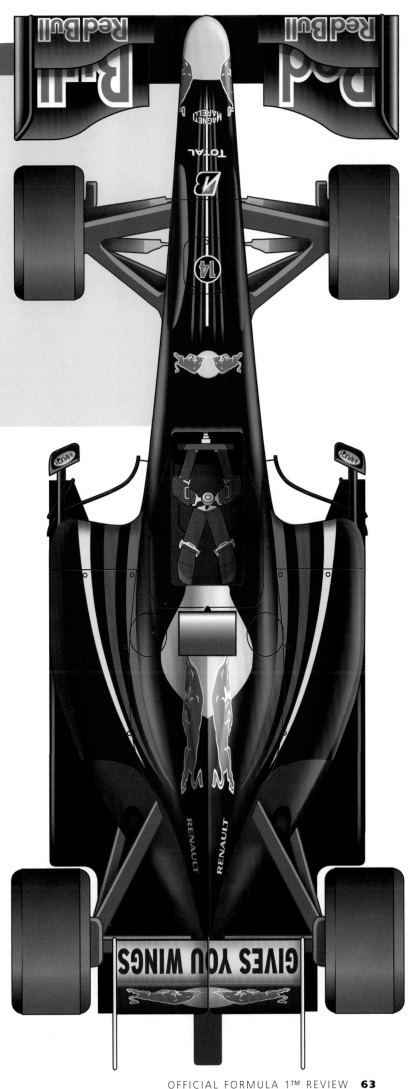

[Vettel] through a problem in the front suspension. He did bang wheels with Kimi [Räikkönen] at the start of the grand prix, which might have accentuated it, but I'm not happy with what was probably a problem of our own making.

Mark [Webber], of course, started the 2009 season not long after he had sustained both leg and shoulder injuries in his cycling accident. He coped, but I'm convinced that it did impact on his early season form in truth. He typically put on a very brave face and got on with the job and I think that he had an extremely strong season. As, of course, did Sebastian.

Sebastian possibly made a mistake in Melbourne, but I think the decision to then penalise him 10 positions at the Malaysian Grand Prix was very harsh.

RED BULL MUST BOX CLEVER IN 2010
The regulation changes for 2010 are reasonably significant by normal standards in as much as the ban on refuelling and the fitment of a smaller front tyre. However, in comparison to what we faced this year, they are relatively trifling. It means that our car for 2010 will be evolving, whereas the RB5 gave us a clean-sheet-of-paper car.

I think what may happen in 2010 is that the teams with a lot of resource will now be able to do their usual thing of trying lots of iterations on a theme and so perhaps size will count more. It's up to us, as one of the slightly smaller teams, to be reasonably inventive and clever in the way that we operate.

TEAM INFRASTRUCTURE IS STILL DEVELOPING
I would say that in terms of the total number of people we have a decent-size team now. However, our infrastructure, by which I mean not just the straightforward managerial side but also all the simulation tools that you can't simply buy off the shelf and actually take time to develop, is still relatively young.

Depending on whether you view Red Bull Racing simply as a reincarnation of Jaguar Racing or as an entirely new team – and in truth I think that we're halfway in between these extremes – then we are clearly much less established than some of the other teams. But we're getting there, and that was proven by our multiple race wins."

McLAREN

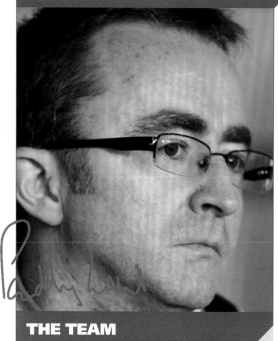

THE TEAM

PERSONNEL
TEAM PRINCIPAL, VODAFONE McLAREN MERCEDES Martin Whitmarsh
VICE-PRESIDENT MERCEDES-BENZ MOTORSPORT Norbert Haug
MANAGING DIRECTOR, McLAREN RACING Jonathan Neale
MANAGING DIRECTOR, MERCEDES-BENZ HIGH PERFORMANCE ENGINES Thomas Fuhr
ENGINEERING DIRECTOR, McLAREN Paddy Lowe (above)
ENGINEERING DIRECTOR, MERCEDES Andy Cowell
DESIGN & DEVELOPMENT DIRECTOR Neil Oatley
HEAD OF AERODYNAMICS Simon Lacey
HEAD OF VEHICLE ENGINEERING Mark Williams
CHIEF ENGINEER MP4-24 Pat Fry
CHIEF ENGINEER MP4-25 Tim Goss
TEAM MANAGER David Redding
DRIVERS Lewis Hamilton, Heikki Kovalainen
RACE ENGINEER (Hamilton) Phil Prew
RACE ENGINEER (Kovalainen) Mark Slade
TEST TEAM MANAGER Indy Lall
TEST/THIRD DRIVERS Pedro de la Rosa, Gary Paffett
CHIEF MECHANIC Pete Vale
TOTAL NUMBER OF EMPLOYEES 550 (McLaren Racing)
TEAM BASE Woking, England
TELEPHONE +44 (0)1483 261000
WEBSITE www.mclaren.com

TEAM STATS
IN F1 SINCE 1966 **FIRST GRAND PRIX** Monaco 1966
STARTS 665 **WINS** 163 **POLE POSITIONS** 144
FASTEST LAPS 136 **PODIUMS** 436 **POINTS** 3362.5
CONSTRUCTORS' TITLES 8 **DRIVERS' TITLES** 12

SPONSORS
Vodafone, Santander, Mobil 1, Johnnie Walker, Aigo, Boss, SAP, Hilton, Bridgestone

1 LEWIS HAMILTON **2 HEIKKI KOVALAINEN**

A TOUGH YEAR FIGHTING A LACK OF DOWNFORCE

By Paddy Lowe
(Engineering Director, McLaren)

"The grid has never been so tight. In the past five years the difference spread, first to last, has halved. Historically, ours may have been a great recovery this year, but in absolute lap time it's not the biggest-ever gain.

At the pre-season Barcelona test we had the worst car, almost 3s slower than the fastest. There were some simulation versus reality issues. We had a bit of hopping and three-wheeling which was a function of the slick tyres, but we had roughly the downforce predicted in the tunnel. The main miss was not having the right downforce in the tunnel.

The original Overtaking Working Group (OWG) target was to halve the downforce of the 2006 car. If a 2008 car had a coefficient of lift of about 3.5–3.6, when we first put our 2009 car in the tunnel it was 1.5, more than meeting the OWG expectation. Having set a target around the 2.5 mark, the worrying thing was that at the Technical Working Group meetings in February/March 2008, Honda warned the group – I'm not sure why – that performance was going to be much greater than expected. Ross [Brawn] was claiming that he was already well in excess of 2.5.

We said either 'Ross, we don't believe you, you've got the numbers wrong' or, 'if it's true, well done, good luck!' We were thinking his calibration must be wrong. The rest is history. We just didn't have enough downforce, but we had a great team and there was no picking on any one group. All credit to everybody, specifically Martin Whitmarsh, because it was quite a difficult period for him and became even more difficult in Australia and Malaysia…

TACKLING THE DOWNFORCE PROBLEM
We tackled the problem on two fronts. First, we rushed out all we could to save face and not be last at the Australian GP. For the Jerez test the next week, we took so many mods from the tunnel to the car in six days – we'd never before done anything even close to that speed. We took the first four races with that approach. It was relentless.

While we were bringing things to the circuit earlier, our competitors did it in one lump later on, which was why we looked relatively good in the Bahrain GP– we'd gone from the back to halfway up the grid – then went back down to Q1 level by Spain.

Because we'd been so wrapped up getting through those first four races, we probably didn't pay enough attention to developing the shadow [double-deck] diffuser. We were reasonably early adopters (by Spain) among the reaction teams, but our solution wasn't well thought out. It wasn't really until we got to Germany that we got it done properly.

When we saw that teams had seen the flat-bottom rules differently, it was quite a shock. Bear in mind that the regulation was 26 years old, written in 1983 for non-ground-effect cars, and in 1994 they brought in a stepped plane. If, another 15 years later, that same wording suddenly allowed holes, it was extraordinary. It was wrong, but you had to go with it.

KERS OFFSET DOWNFORCE DEFICITS
The square-law effect of downforce always exaggerates any deficiencies at high speed. Our car had some good attributes mechanically, and in slow corners there's more emphasis on that and less aerodynamic influence. We also had some help from KERS to offset aero losses in certain sectors. Essentially, it was just downforce and not a speed-related issue. The low point was Silverstone: it felt extra bad that Lewis was there with No1 on his car in front of his home crowd and we hadn't given him the equipment.

There were two philosophies on front-wing endplates: more air going inside the front tyres or more outside. We were in a minority of one in pursuing the former. At the Nürburgring, we introduced a wing that was following the consensual direction and it complemented the step we'd made on the floor.

The KERS packaging was not as difficult as we first thought. We put the motor at the front of the engine and made a recess in the rear bulkhead, which was really quite straightforward but we lost fuel volume.

The battery pack was the biggest challenge, but we honed it down to a size that would fit beneath the radiator. There is a slight cost in terms of the size you can have and it restricted what you could do with aero development in the lower lip area of the sidepod.

WEIGHT DISTRIBUTION WAS A HEADACHE
Weight distribution proved the biggest difference. KERS is always going to be a battle on two fronts, as the system needs to work safely, and a 600-volt system is a pretty daunting idea in covering all the hazards. The

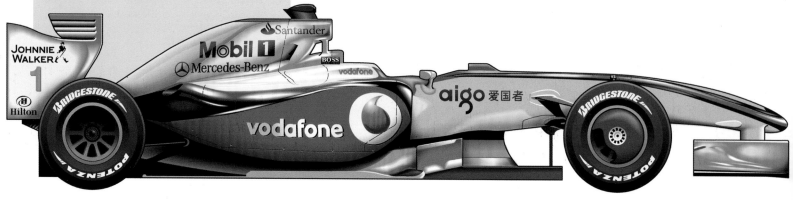

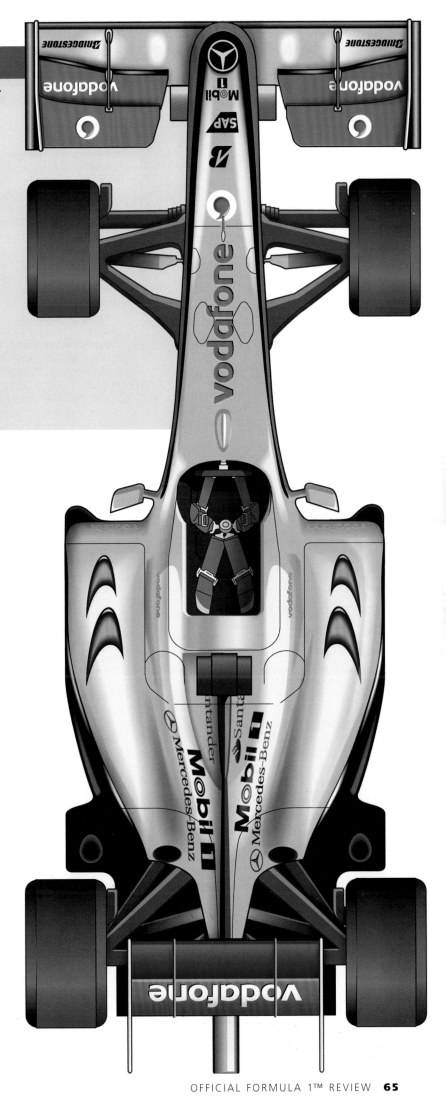

TECHNICAL SPECIFICATIONS

ENGINE
MAKE/MODEL Mercedes-Ilmor FO 108W
CONFIGURATION 2400cc V8 (90 degree)
SPARK PLUGS Not disclosed
ECU FIA standard issue
KERS McLaren Electronic Systems
FUEL Mobil 1
OIL Mobil 1
BATTERY GS Yuasa

TRANSMISSION
GEARBOX McLaren
FORWARD GEARS Seven
CLUTCH Not disclosed

CHASSIS
CHASSIS MODEL
McLaren MP4-24
FRONT SUSPENSION LAYOUT
Inboard torsion bar/damper system, operated by pushrod and bellcrank with a double-wishbone arrangement

REAR SUSPENSION LAYOUT
Inboard torsion bar/damper system, operated by pushrod and bellcrank, with a double-wishbone arrangement
DAMPERS Koni
TYRES Bridgestone
WHEELS Enkei
BRAKE DISCS Not disclosed
BRAKE PADS Not disclosed
BRAKE CALIPERS Akebono
FUEL TANK Not disclosed
INSTRUMENTS
McLaren Electronic Systems

DIMENSIONS
LENGTH Not disclosed
WIDTH Not disclosed
HEIGHT Not disclosed
WHEELBASE Not disclosed
TRACK front Not disclosed
rear Not disclosed
WEIGHT Not disclosed

Team McLaren Mercedes

second part of this project is how you get the car down to the corresponding weight that matches what you need in the allowed spend you've allocated to KERS.

Go back to 2008 and there were a number of teams wanting to raise the weight limit. We played hard to get. You could position the teams on how good they thought they'd be on KERS as to whether they wanted more weight or not. We were one of the teams who didn't support weight increase. I think that we overcooked it slightly and 5kg extra would certainly have been nice to have to play with!

We were right up against the wire. We had literally no ballast on the cars and the weight distribution was what it was. We did a lot of weight saving through the season on the KERS and the car, ending up with enough weight distribution freedom to do the job we needed to do, whereas in the first half of the season we weren't able to run the right weight distribution for the tyres. That was a big deficiency with the MP4-24.

The shorter wheelbase was intended to give us a further step in freedom of weight distribution and we knew we were a fair way off where we needed to be. The weight distribution without the axle move got us near enough into the working area, but we had to adapt around it with set up. Knowing we would have very little freedom, we had to take a punt on where the window was and, moving to slicks and new aero rules, it took a lot of guesswork. We did our best, but didn't get it right.

LIMITED AERO TWEAKING IS NOW AVAILABLE
Previously, there were many more aero components that could be played with. Now, though, you are down to front and rear wings and floor, a bit of messing about with the sidepods and deflectors and that's it. On the mechanical side, the testing ban certainly had an effect, and that was given a lower priority because a lot of it is trial and error and you need track time.

Everything was so closely matched this year that if you had a particular strength it translated in the order. Mercedes did a fantastic job with the KERS and I think it was the best system, although Ferrari's KERS seemed to work well. It took a while to tune the car to get the most out of it, but Lewis's Hungary win was a highlight – with a classic KERS overtaking move that was really nice to see. Overall though, it was a tough year."

FERRARI

THE TEAM

PERSONNEL
PRESIDENT Luca di Montezemolo
TEAM PRINCIPAL Amedeo Felisa
TEAM PRINCIPAL Stefano Domenicali
TECHNICAL DIRECTOR Aldo Costa
TEAM MANAGER Chris Dyer (above)
ENGINE DIRECTOR Gilles Simon
OPERATIONS DIRECTOR Massimo Rivola
CAR DESIGN & DEVELOPMENT CONSULTANTS
Rory Byrne & Michael Schumacher
CHIEF DESIGNER Nikolas Tombazis
CHIEF AERODYNAMICIST John Iley
HEAD OF CAR PERFORMANCE Marco Fainello
HEAD OF STRUCTURES DEPARTMENT Davide Terletti
HEAD OF ENGINE ASSEMBLY Mattia Binotto
RACE ENGINE MANAGER Luigi Fraboni
DRIVERS Felipe Massa, Kimi Räikkönen, Luca Badoer,
Giancarlo Fisichella
RACE ENGINEER (Massa, Badoer, Fisichella) Rob Smedley
RACE ENGINEER (Räikkönen) Andrea Stella
TEST DRIVERS Luca Badoer, Marc Gené
PERFORMANCE DEVELOPMENT Luigi Mazzola
CHIEF MECHANICS (Massa) Salvatore Vargetto (Räikkönen)
Giuseppe Rizzo
TOTAL NUMBER OF EMPLOYEES 900+
NUMBER IN RACE TEAM 90
TEAM BASE Maranello, Italy
TELEPHONE +39 0536 949450
WEBSITE www.ferrariworld.com

TEAM STATS
IN F1 SINCE 1950 **FIRST GRAND PRIX** Britain 1950
STARTS 793 **WINS** 210 **POLE POSITIONS** 203
FASTEST LAPS 218 **PODIUMS** 621 **POINTS** 4077.5
CONSTRUCTORS' TITLES 16 **DRIVERS' TITLES** 15

SPONSORS
FIAT, Marlboro, Shell, Etihad Airways, Alice, Bridgestone,
AMD, Acer, TATA, Mubadala Abu Dhabi

3 FELIPE MASSA   **3 LUCA BADOER**   **3 GIANCARLO FISICHELLA**   **4 KIMI RÄIKKÖNEN**

KERS PROVED TO BE BOTH GOOD AND BAD

**By Chris Dyer
(Team Manager)**

"The story was dominated by the double diffuser and although I'd like to be able to say that at the start of the year we had the fastest car without a double diffuser, we didn't. Even as a conventional car, it could have been better. We didn't have enough downforce or efficiency and the rest is window dressing.

I don't want to go right through the saga, but we were of the opinion that the double diffuser concept wasn't legal, so we didn't devote any resources to it. When we did have to go down that road, we were compromised because, for sure, if you design a car from scratch, you design a different gearbox, a different rear suspension, a different rear crash structure and so the whole back half of the car is different. Not just in terms of bodywork, but in terms of mechanical layout as well.

We evaluated doing a new gearbox, but chose not to. With no testing, homologating a gearbox for four races meant that you needed to test for eight Fridays, so it made it extremely difficult. In previous years, the reaction would probably have been different.

BRINGING UNTESTED PARTS TO RACES
We brought the first version of the double diffuser to the Spanish GP at Barcelona and it was a huge change for us. Certainly in my history at Ferrari, we have never brought such a huge mechanical update to the track so quickly. There was an awful lot of resource involved in designing and making the pieces, and then they went to the track untested and ran for a race.

We're also talking about new hydraulic and electrical systems, and they are not always easy things to get right straight out of the box. They are the kind of things that give problems in winter testing, so it was a pretty huge achievement to get those pieces on the car and to get the car running reliably. I think if the season had panned out differently, we would have been considering even bigger steps later in the year.

Aerodynamically, there were no dramatic changes in the way that we developed the car and the objectives that we had. Obviously the rules were completely different, but I don't think that it changed the way we worked. We did have to incorporate the KERS, though.

KERS FORCED A CHANGE OF WHEELBASE
I don't think that KERS really compromised us too much in other areas of car development. In low-fuel trim, our centre of gravity was actually lower than in the past, even with the KERS. However, in high-fuel configuration, the centre of gravity was higher, so it was a compromise. Probably the biggest penalty we had with the KERS was weight distribution. I don't think that we started the season where we wanted to be in terms of having the options on that, and it was the biggest single issue for us.

That hurt us more on tracks with faster corners, where you tend to be running a bit more forward on the weight distribution, so it affected us at places like Silverstone and Spa and not so much at tracks like Monaco and Hungary. That was the thinking behind the change of wheelbase at the British GP and it was obviously a step in the right direction, although it's always difficult to put accurate lap-time numbers on those things. It's not like being able to say that 10 points of downforce is worth precisely 'X' lap time. It's always a bit more of a grey area and related to car set-up.

We had a couple of reliability issues early in the year, but got on top of them pretty quickly and saw that the KERS, for us, was a very positive performance item. We've had some good results this year and a lot of it has been down to the KERS. It wasn't just about pure lap time either, it was about being able to make another place or two at the start, or being able to jump a car on a safety car restart such as when Kimi won at Spa. From a technical viewpoint though, it would have been much less interesting if we'd had 20 cars out there all with it.

THREE MAIN WEIGHT-SAVING UPDATES
The main KERS development focus was reducing weight. It was pretty much there straight out of the box in terms of performance potential and the gains to be had were with weight, so we introduced three significant updates throughout the year, all targeting that.

The front wing was a major area of development for everyone and it was the same with us. As the year went on, the front wing became more and more complicated, which is a sure sign that it's having a lot of effort put into it.

Overall, if you look at the swings and roundabouts, it was more about tyres than anything else for us. At circuits where the tyres

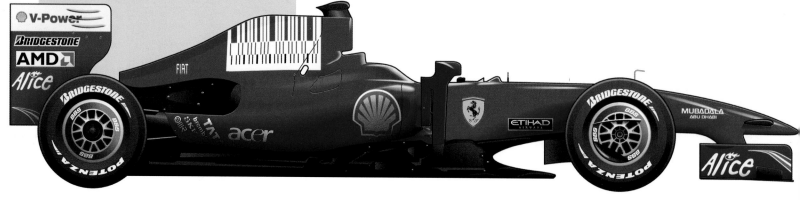

TECHNICAL SPECIFICATIONS

ENGINE
MAKE/MODEL Ferrari 056
CONFIGURATION 2398cc V8
(90 degree)
SPARK PLUGS Not disclosed
ECU FIA standard issue
KERS Ferrari/Magneti Marelli
FUEL Shell
OIL Shell
BATTERY Not disclosed

TRANSMISSION
GEARBOX Ferrari
FORWARD GEARS Seven
CLUTCH Not disclosed

CHASSIS
CHASSIS MODEL Ferrari F60
FRONT SUSPENSION LAYOUT
Independent pushrod-activated
torsion springs
REAR SUSPENSION LAYOUT
Independent pushrod-activated
torsion springs
DAMPERS Not disclosed
TYRES Bridgestone
WHEELS BBS
BRAKE DISCS Brembo
BRAKE PADS Not disclosed
BRAKE CALIPERS Not disclosed
FUEL TANK Not disclosed
INSTRUMENTS
Ferrari/Magneti Marelli

DIMENSIONS
LENGTH Not disclosed
WIDTH Not disclosed
HEIGHT Not disclosed
WHEELBASE Not disclosed
TRACK front Not disclosed
rear Not disclosed
WEIGHT 605kg (including
driver and camera)

were working well, the car was competitive, and at tracks where we were struggling to get the best out of the tyres we were less competitive. We've seen generally that we can survive on the soft tyre a bit better than other people, and at some circuits that gave us an advantage.

For sure, that trait hasn't happened by accident: it's the culmination of many years of car development. One of the problems with that is that it's difficult when you want to switch it off, say when you want to get the tyre temperatures up on a particular day. It's fundamental to the DNA of the car, and for sure it would be nice to understand it to such a level that we could have a nice switch on the dashboard that changed it. However, it's not like that, as it's much more tied into the whole concept of the car, the suspension geometry, etcetera.

The field was very close this year, but amazingly volatile. The spread of times from pole to the Q1 cut was tight. I think we have had a consistent level of performance, always somewhere around the top 10, but the really strange thing is that it was always different people in front and behind.

MASSA'S ACCIDENT WAS A BLOW
Felipe's accident was a blow and people have suggested that Kimi seemed to thrive more in the aftermath, but there was no noticeable change in his attitude to the weekend, his level of concentration or any of those things. I think what happened was that we were into the window where we were more competitive and Kimi collected the fruits. Remember that Felipe finished fourth at Silverstone and was on the podium at the next race at the Nürburgring, so it was coming.

Obviously, Luca and Giancarlo had a tougher time. Both found the car hard to balance under braking with KERS, and that was one of its negative points, but not a big issue for either Kimi or Felipe, who had more experience with it. It was something that was part of setting up the car for the weekend, though, rather than something that you put on the car and forgot about. It required constant effort every weekend."

TOYOTA

THE TEAM

PERSONNEL

CHAIRMAN & TEAM PRINCIPAL Tadashi Yamashina
PRESIDENT John Howett
EXECUTIVE VICE-PRESIDENT Yoshiaki Kinoshita
SENIOR GENERAL MANAGER, CHASSIS
Pascal Vasselon (above)
SENIOR GENERAL MANAGER, ENGINE
Kazuo Takeuchi
DIRECTOR TECHNICAL CO-ORDINATION, CHASSIS
Noritoshi Arai
HEAD OF AERODYNAMICS Mark Gillan
TEAM MANAGER Jens Marquardt
DRIVERS Timo Glock, Jarno Trulli, Kamui Kobayashi
CHIEF RACE & TEST ENGINEER Dieter Gass
RACE ENGINEER (Glock, Kobayashi) Juan Pablo Ramirez
RACE ENGINEER (Trulli) Gianluca Pisanello
TEST/THIRD DRIVER Kamui Kobayashi
CHIEF MECHANIC Gerard Lecoq
TOTAL NUMBER OF EMPLOYEES 650
NUMBER IN RACE TEAM 80
TEAM BASE Cologne, Germany
TELEPHONE +49 (0)223 4182 3444
WEBSITE www.toyota-f1.com

TEAM STATS

IN F1 SINCE 2002 **FIRST GRAND PRIX** Australia 2002
STARTS 140 **WINS** 0 **POLE POSITIONS** 3
FASTEST LAPS 3 **PODIUMS** 13 **POINTS** 276.5
CONSTRUCTORS' TITLES 0 **DRIVERS' TITLES** 0

SPONSORS

Panasonic, Denso

9 JARNO TRULLI   **10** TIMO GLOCK   **10** KAMUI KOBAYASHI

A YEAR OF STRONG FORM BUT INCONSISTENCY

By Pascal Vasselon
(Senior General Manager, Chassis)
"Judging from what we learned in preparation for the World Motor Sport Council diffuser court case at the start of the year, it seems that we were the first to go to the FIA to validate the concept of the double-deck diffuser.

We knew when the double-deck diffuser was being proposed and designed within our aero group that it was extremely innovative, but also strictly within the regulations. That said, we still wanted to validate it with [FIA Safety Delegate] Charlie Whiting and his team, simply because we didn't want to waste time on developing something that might not be considered legal. After several exchanges of information, we got the FIA's approval. It was one of the features you needed for 2009, but it certainly was not the only requirement.

Some people thought that because we have an engine deal with Williams that there may have been some cross-pollination of ideas, if you like, but we were very surprised to see Williams also using a similar double-deck diffuser at the first test session. It was not exactly the same as ours, but it was similar.

LEADING THE WAY IN FRONT WING DESIGN

Apart from the double-deck diffuser, the front wing treatment was also very important, and it was quite obvious that only two teams, ourselves and Brawn, had a certain type of front wing from early in the season. We had been very pleased with the results we were seeing in the wind tunnel but, with a new set of regulations such as we had for 2009, it's very difficult to know what is normal or good.

Obviously, we were surprised by how steep a progress curve we had with our headline figures, but straight away we told ourselves, 'okay, maybe it will be the same for the other teams, or perhaps even steeper'. Starting from half the previous downforce efficiency, we very quickly recovered a big part of it.

A FLYING START TO THE SEASON

We started the campaign well, with Jarno [Trulli] finishing third and Timo [Glock] fourth in Melbourne, and then the reverse, Timo third and Jarno fourth, in Malaysia after Jarno had qualified on the front row. Then, at the fourth round in Bahrain, we had an all-Toyota front row. Bahrain is a higher-downforce track and if we didn't win, it was because we were slightly slower than [Jenson] Button. At the time, there were questionmarks about our race strategy, querying our decision to run the harder tyre in the long second stint, but I can say absolutely 'no', as we did this race simulation several times and there was nothing wrong with it. We just weren't quite fast enough.

After that, we had races where if we'd qualified in front we would have won. And, strangely, races where we didn't qualify so well, like Hungary and the European GP at Valencia, where our race pace was better than it had been in Bahrain. It's a paradox that we didn't really understand.

RACE PACE CAME LATER IN THE YEAR

Later in the season, we achieved much better race pace. At the Belgian GP, Jarno qualified on the front row with the best fuel-adjusted time, and we'll never know where that might have led, because it all went wrong at the start when Jarno's front wing was damaged against [Nick] Heidfeld's BMW. Whereas in Bahrain we had been scratching our heads about strategy on Saturday evening knowing that we were fuelled light, at Spa we didn't spend more than five minutes on strategy. The plan was simple, Jarno would start from the front row, pass [Giancarlo] Fisichella at the first stops and win, as the tyre degradation wasn't reckoned to be a problem. So that was very disappointing.

I think everyone was much closer than you might have expected in a season with such major regulation changes. As soon as you made the slightest mistake in a weekend, you were down five to seven places. But the TF109's potential was there and our race pace at Valencia, Budapest and Spa was really good.

Monaco was a strange one for us and we were never 100% clear about what happened. Our Monaco package appeared relatively weak at low speed. We didn't treat it as a special race as such, but a small gap becomes a big one at Monaco, drivers lose confidence, don't get the tyre temperatures they need and what should be a deficit of 0.2s suddenly becomes a full second. We were in trouble, no doubt, with Jarno, who won the race there in 2004 remember, qualifying 18th and Timo 19th.

Yet, in terms of race pace, we were back to normal. Timo was with the top three cars and faster than Ferrari and [Rubens] Barrichello. A small detail makes a big difference, and we suspect all our problems there were derived

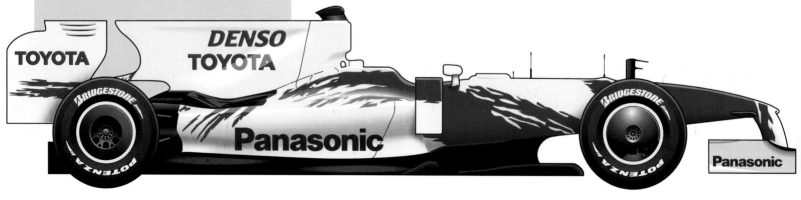

TECHNICAL SPECIFICATIONS

ENGINE
MAKE/MODEL Toyota RVX-09
CONFIGURATION 2398cc V8
(90 degree)
SPARK PLUGS Denso
ECU FIA standard issue
KERS n/a
FUEL Esso
OIL Esso
BATTERY Panasonic

TRANSMISSION
GEARBOX Toyota
FORWARD GEARS Seven
CLUTCH Sachs

CHASSIS
CHASSIS MODEL Toyota TF109
FRONT SUSPENSION LAYOUT
Carbon-fibre double wishbones with
carbon-fibre trackrod and pushrod

REAR SUSPENSION LAYOUT
Carbon-fibre double wishbones with
carbon-fibre trackrod and pushrod
DAMPERS Penske
TYRES Bridgestone
WHEELS BBS
BRAKE DISCS Hitco
BRAKE PADS Hitco
BRAKE CALIPERS Toyota/Brembo
FUEL TANK ATL
INSTRUMENTS Not disclosed

DIMENSIONS
LENGTH 4636mm
WIDTH 1800mm
HEIGHT 950mm
WHEELBASE 3090mm
TRACK front 1420mm
rear 1405mm
WEIGHT 605kg (including
driver and camera)

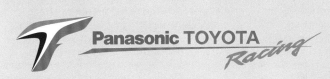

Panasonic TOYOTA Racing

from not turning the tyres on in qualifying. Then, in the race,
with grip, the spiral turned around and at the following race
in Turkey we were straight back into the top four with Jarno.

A VERY STEEP RATE OF DEVELOPMENT
In terms of car development, we had an evolution at almost
every race. One of the biggest packages was for the Turkish
GP, but there was something at every single race. We had an
upgrade in Barcelona that wasn't bad, but also not as good
as we'd hoped. Monaco obviously wasn't a good one! Turkey
was a nice gain. Then we had a range of one-offs – Budapest
high downforce, then Spa and Monza packages. You needed
a few must-have features this year and, as soon as everyone
finally got proper front wings and proper diffusers, they were
all very close together.

It was good for us to see that starting from scratch our
team was able to put together exactly what was required.
Then the rate of development was extremely steep and the
other teams caught up, but not completely.

I still feel that when everything went right we were in
the top three or four cars but, for sure, everything was much
tighter at the end of the year.

The testing ban certainly didn't help, but it's not an excuse,
as it was the same for everyone. It can't prevent a good aero
package being a good aero package, but it was very difficult
to bring on items like new suspension or gearbox, things that
need high-mileage testing.

A STRUGGLE TO FIND CONSISTENCY
The drivers did pretty well at times, but we were struggling
with inconsistency as a team. The first races were much easier
from that point-of-view but, even at the end of the season,
almost everywhere we went we still had a chance to be on the
podium or even win, but we had to put it all together. Jarno
was very strong in Japan for example, and Timo produced
some fighting drives, finishing second in Singapore. I think
it's true that Timo could handle any type of grip or change
of grip, whereas Jarno was more sensitive.

With refuelling banned for 2010, the tyre change will be a
key item and the only thing that we can play with. Tyre usage
will ultimately determine pace, and the race strategy will be
all about when to change from one type of tyre to the other.
Globally, though, the rule changes are less significant than
what we had to contend with this year. The tyre sizes have
aerodynamic implications, but the rest will be pretty similar."

BMW SAUBER

THE TEAM

PERSONNEL

BMW MOTORSPORT DIRECTOR Mario Theissen
MANAGING DIRECTOR Walter Riedl
HEAD OF ENGINEERING Willy Rampf (above)
DIRECTOR OF POWERTRAIN Markus Duesmann
CHIEF DESIGNER Christoph Zimmermann
HEAD OF AERODYNAMICS Willem Toet
TEAM MANAGER Beat Zehnder
HEAD OF TRACK ENGINEERING Giampaolo Dall'Ara
DRIVERS Nick Heidfeld, Robert Kubica
RACE ENGINEER (Heidfeld) Paul Russell
RACE ENGINEER (Kubica) Antonio Cuquerella
CHIEF ENGINE ENGINEER Tomas Andor
TEST/THIRD DRIVER Christian Klien
CHIEF MECHANIC Amiel Lindesay
TOTAL NUMBER OF EMPLOYEES 680
NUMBER IN RACE TEAM 80
TEAM BASE Hinwil, Switzerland & Munich, Germany
TELEPHONE +41 44 937 9000
WEBSITE www.bmw-sauber-f1.com

TEAM STATS

IN F1 SINCE 1993, as Sauber until 2005 **FIRST GRAND PRIX** South Africa 1993 **STARTS** 287 **WINS** 1 **POLE POSITIONS** 1 **FASTEST LAPS** 2 **PODIUMS** 22 **POINTS** 497 **CONSTRUCTORS' TITLES** 0 **DRIVERS' TITLES** 0

SPONSORS

Petronas Malaysia, Intel, T-Systems, GO-GP.ORG, ExPro

5 ROBERT KUBICA   **6 NICK HEIDFELD**

A YEAR OF REACTING TO UNEXPECTED CHANGES

By Willy Rampf
(Head of Engineering)

"I'd done the car concept in close collaboration with Walter Riedl, then was away for three months after the last race of 2008 in Brazil. I came back to the team as head of engineering, then, after the overseas grands prix, went back to the original position I had in 2008, that's to say leading the technical side.

The main issues driving the concept of the car were much reduced aerodynamic performance, slick tyres, and the need to get the weight distribution much further forward in the car. There was also the need to find enough space in the car for fitting the new Kinetic Energy Recovery System (KERS).

On the weight-distribution side, installing a KERS system was a problem with Robert [Kubica] but not with Nick [Heidfeld], who is obviously smaller. We had air-cooled batteries for the KERS, that required them to be located somewhere outside the car in the airstream, which affected the packaging more than we had thought it would in the beginning. It's definitely fair to say that we underestimated the complications and the impact that they would have on the car.

CAUGHT OUT BY DOUBLE-DECK DIFFUSER

I had been on a three-month sabbatical and came back when we tested the F1.09 in Bahrain at the start of the year. There was no initial sign that we were lacking performance, as we were very close on lap times to Toyota and Ferrari at that test. It was a bit of an eye-opener when we tested in Barcelona when the Brawn BGP 001 arrived with this different aero concept – the double-deck diffuser – and started going so quickly. Well, it showed us what was possible.

When we saw the double-deck diffuser on the Williams as well, we assumed that it wasn't a legal interpretation. It certainly wasn't according to the spirit of the regulations, so we didn't immediately jump on it which, with hindsight, was the wrong conclusion... We should have put a lot of resource onto designing and implementing a double-deck diffuser immediately, but we only started in the wind tunnel with one four weeks later.

The way the season goes, starting with a run of flyaway races, what you don't have on a car for the Australian Grand Prix, you can't put on for the next races either. But, sure, we underestimated it.

FRONT WING KEY AREA OF DEVELOPMENT

The new aerodynamic requirements for the 2009 World Championship needed a lot of work, and we tried a number of different front-wing endplates, but our car was still underperforming. At the beginning of May, we started with what would become a significant update for the European Grand Prix at Valencia at the end of August. We concentrated on aerodynamics, took out the KERS and started further development on the F1.09's front wing. We then had another completely different wing concept for the package of changes that we introduced for the Singapore GP at the end of September.

The car's front wing is obviously important, but it always goes with the rest of the car. We tried various front wings, but somehow they never worked with the F1.09 and only really started to do so properly when we went to much tighter sidepods. That got the air to flow around the side of the pods to the upper surface of the diffuser and that's when these different concepts of front wing really began to work. Before that, we were really locked into our situation with all this endplate development unfortunately showing no real positive effect.

MONACO PERFORMANCE A PUZZLE

At the Monaco Grand Prix, like Toyota, we were very slow in qualifying and we weren't 100% sure why. In practice and qualifying we had been dreadful, but in the race the performance was acceptable, which was extremely puzzling. Our theory was that we didn't utilise the tyre performance and never got [the tyre] up to the correct temperature except in the race with the higher fuel load and heavier car. There was no other reason that we could manage to identify.

If we had had a car that possessed more downforce, I feel that the tyre issue would have been much less. It all added up to not putting enough load onto the tyres, which was the opposite problem to what Red Bull experienced in Monaco.

KERS PROVED DIFFICULT TO DEVELOP

In between the original car and the Valencia specification F1.09, we still had KERS potential but it was different, a reduced system with a smaller capacity and a smaller battery. The components were still mounted in the sidepod

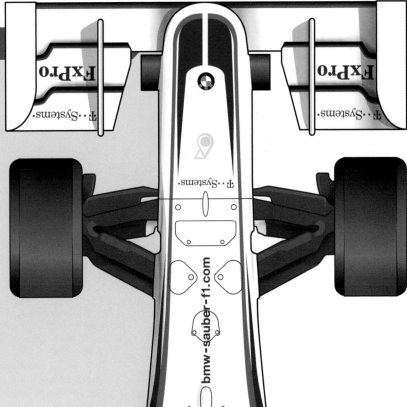

ENGINE

MAKE/MODEL BMW P86/9
CONFIGURATION 2400cc V8
(90 degree)
SPARK PLUGS NGK
ECU FIA standard issue
KERS BMW Sauber
FUEL Petronas
OIL Petronas
BATTERY Not disclosed

TRANSMISSION

GEARBOX BMW Sauber
FORWARD GEARS Seven
CLUTCH AP Racing

CHASSIS

CHASSIS MODEL
BMW Sauber F1.09
FRONT SUSPENSION LAYOUT
Upper and lower wishbones,
inboard springs and dampers
activated by pushrods

REAR SUSPENSION LAYOUT
Upper and lower wishbones,
inboard springs and dampers
activated by pushrods
DAMPERS Sachs
TYRES Bridgestone
WHEELS OZ Racing
BRAKE DISCS Carbone Industrie
BRAKE PADS Brembo
BRAKE CALIPERS Brembo
FUEL TANK Not disclosed
INSTRUMENTS MES

DIMENSIONS

LENGTH 4690mm
WIDTH 1800mm
HEIGHT 1000mm
WHEELBASE Not disclosed
TRACK front 1470mm
rear 1410mm
WEIGHT 605kg (including
driver and camera)

BMW Sauber F1 Team

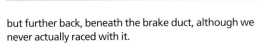

but further back, beneath the brake duct, although we never actually raced with it.

In testing, we did see the lap time that the simulation programme indicated, but the key KERS issue was always braking stability. We could never sort this out 100% and then, when the season started, there was no track testing and so we didn't really want to be using Fridays at the grands prix to sort out braking stability problems on top of everything else. That's why we told ourselves that we couldn't concentrate on three things, so we prioritised the aerodynamic work because it had more potential, especially after we saw what was possible with the double-deck diffuser.

BMW PULL-OUT RESTRICTS DEVELOPMENT
We first used a double-deck diffuser at the Turkish Grand Prix, and I think the lap time gain was maybe three-tenths of a second. The rear-end components were a limitation, but the bigger part was we had to understand how it worked. You can't just make an opening in the floor of the car and expect the air to know where to go. It took time to get it working. We developed it, made it larger and the biggest step of all was for the Singapore Grand Prix.

We did a new gearbox casing that was a bit narrower and lower for aerodynamic reasons. The guys working at BMW in Munich developed it for our revised aero package, and there was also slightly revised rear suspension. However, for the last iteration, the gearbox and rear suspension would have looked different again if it had not been for cost considerations.

Not surprisingly, the announcement that BMW was pulling out of Formula 1 at the end of the season arrested development at the back end of the car because, although we obviously had a development budget, the decision was that there would be no BMW engine or gearbox for next year.

The gearbox and rear suspension had a much bigger influence on the aerodynamics of the car than they had two years ago, but we had no real final evolution of the rear suspension, even at the end of the year. It also had to be done in aluminium rather than titanium, because that was quicker to make.

So, in many respects, after our 2008 season it was a far from ideal year reacting to unexpected developments."

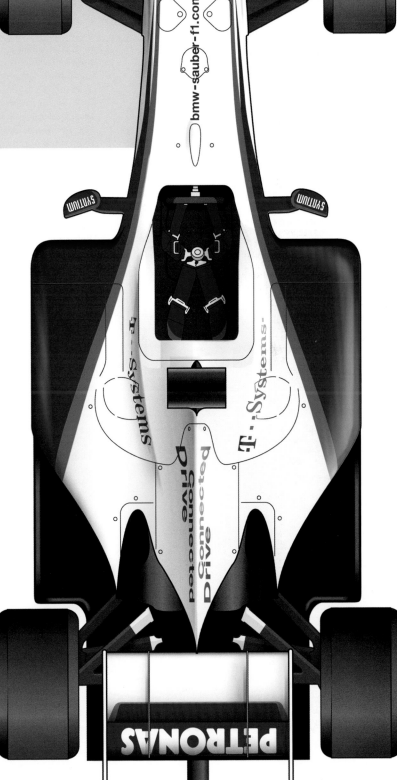

WILLIAMS

THE TEAM

PERSONNEL

TEAM PRINCIPAL Sir Frank Williams
DIRECTOR OF ENGINEERING Patrick Head
CHIEF EXECUTIVE OFFICER Adam Parr
TECHNICAL DIRECTOR Sam Michael (above)
CHIEF OPERATING OFFICER Alex Burns
CHIEF DESIGNER Ed Wood
HEAD OF AERODYNAMICS Jon Tomlinson
SENIOR SYSTEMS ENGINEER John Russell
CHIEF OPERATIONS ENGINEER Rod Nelson
TEAM MANAGER Tim Newton
DRIVERS Kazuki Nakajima, Nico Rosberg
RACE ENGINEER (Rosberg) Tony Ross
RACE ENGINEER (Nakajima) Xevi Pujolar
TEST TEAM MANAGER Dickie Stanford
TEST DRIVER Nico Hulkenberg
CHIEF MECHANIC Carl Gaden
TOTAL NUMBER OF EMPLOYEES 520
NUMBER IN RACE TEAM 70
TEAM BASE Grove, England
TELEPHONE +44 (0)1235 777700
WEBSITE www.attwilliams.com

TEAM STATS

IN F1 SINCE 1973 **FIRST GRAND PRIX** Argentina 1973
STARTS 585 **WINS** 113 **POLE POSITIONS** 125
FASTEST LAPS 130 **PODIUMS** 296 **POINTS** 2606
CONSTRUCTORS' TITLES 9 **DRIVERS' TITLES** 7

SPONSORS

AT&T, RBS, Philips, Oris Swiss Watches, Randstand, Thomson Reuters, Air Asia, Green Flag

16 NICO ROSBERG   **17** KAZUKI NAKAJIMA

A CONSISTENT YEAR AND THE MODS ALL WORKED

By Sam Michael
(Technical Director)

"I was surprised that more teams didn't do the double diffuser. We thought that most teams would and maybe there'd be one or two who didn't. We didn't even talk to Charlie Whiting until after the first test in Portugal. He said straight away that it was fine.

The diffuser itself is actually quite simple, it's just a ramp and, that apart, front wing endplates have been the biggest story of development. We did 17 different wings, while in 2008 we did just five.

The wing is now 400mm wider and in ground effect. It's changed so much that you need to re-optimise everything around it. Slick tyres had a bit of an effect, but really it was about the position of the endplate. Basically, you're trying to control the tyre vortex.

There was more work underneath the nose and chassis because it was one of the few boxes left, whereas before there were bigger gains to be made elsewhere. Underneath, there are even more devices than in 2008, certainly in terms of the front wing strakes and endplates. Developments were where the freedoms were and brake ducts were another one.

WEIGHT DISTRIBUTION MOVED FORWARD

The weight distribution went forward this year because so did the percentage of tyre contact patch. Without KERS that wasn't difficult to achieve, but with KERS on the car it would have been. We had a flywheel and a battery programme going for 18 months, so we could have brought either to the car but didn't think it was worth the expense. Because of WHP (Williams Hybrid Power), we have a lot of non-F1 related projects that benefited so, regardless of whether we continue with KERS in F1, WHP will continue as a commercial entity.

The lack of testing and wind tunnel restrictions were the same for everyone, but in the past I quite liked testing like that anyhow, as chucking stuff on the car is quite exciting! One thing that's been really good about the FW31 is that every single aero part we put on the car worked and produced the lap time gains that it should have.

GAINS WERE EXACTLY AS EXPECTED

We expected a 0.25s gain in Singapore and it translated exactly: you can measure the downforce with data and diffuser pressure tappings. Maybe it's because the cars were so much simpler because of less complicated flip-ups and vanes, and were less sensitive to wind and weight changes.

There are things we can do a much better job on – aerodynamically and mechanically – either because we've measured things or we've seen how others have done it. Everyone does that process with new regulations and after a year or two everyone comes together. But, saying that, one of the surprises was that the absolute level of everyone's performance was so close. The level between first on the grid and 20th was 1–1.2s. Then you also have the spread – how it spreads over 10 laps. It'll now typically be 15s, whereas a year ago it would have been 25s. I think next year will be incredibly tight.

Spa and Monza were weak, but we consciously didn't put a lot of development into them. We took our 2008 rear wing, adapted it as well as we could and did only a couple of tests on those downforce levels. Go back three or four years and there were 16 races, four of them low drag – Monza, Spa, Indy and Montréal. Now there are 17, with only two low drag, so the percentage shifts massively.

Every race is important, but we had the choice of doing another iteration of the Spa and Monza package, or doing everything for Singapore, and we concluded that whatever we did for Singapore would work for four races, so we took the decision to put everything into that package. Take Spa and Monza out, and our performance has been really consistent. We also had bad races in Shanghai and Bahrain where it wasn't a disaster, but we weren't as competitive as we think we should have been.

IMPROVED FORM ON HIGH-SPEED CIRCUITS

Relative performance did seem very circuit dependent this year. We had been pretty poor on high-speed tracks before this year, whereas in 2009 we were good on them – and stayed good on street circuits.

Street circuits come down to two or three things that are completely mechanical, and whatever we're doing, the other guys aren't. When you analyse things like that, it's extremely difficult to work out why other people are strong and weak. I remember in 2003 when we were fighting Ferrari. You'd go to some tracks knowing Ferrari were going to be better, and we'd go to others and know that we were going to be stronger than them.

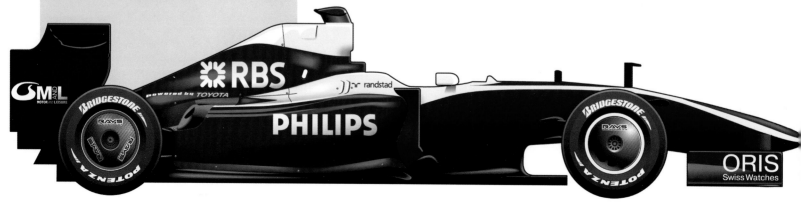

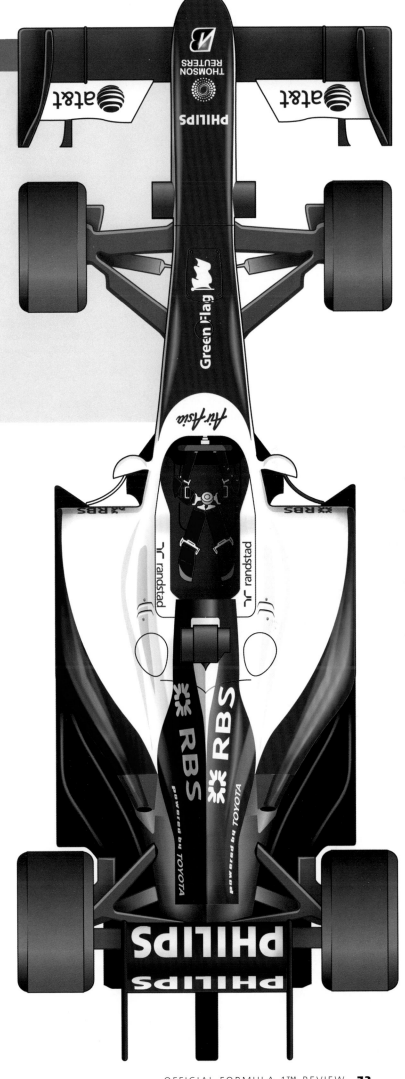

TECHNICAL SPECIFICATIONS

ENGINE
MAKE/MODEL Toyota RVX-09
CONFIGURATION 2398cc V8
(90 degree)
SPARK PLUGS Denso
ECU FIA standard issue
KERS Williams F1
FUEL Not disclosed
OIL Not disclosed
BATTERY Not disclosed

TRANSMISSION
GEARBOX WilliamsF1
FORWARD GEARS Seven
CLUTCH Not disclosed

CHASSIS
CHASSIS MODEL Williams FW31
FRONT SUSPENSION LAYOUT
Carbon-fibre double wishbones with
composite toelink and pushrod-activated
springs and anti-roll bar

REAR SUSPENSION LAYOUT
Double wishbones and
pushrod-activated springs
and anti-roll bar
DAMPERS WilliamsF1
TYRES Bridgestone
WHEELS RAYS
BRAKE DISCS Not disclosed
BRAKE PADS Not disclosed
BRAKE CALIPERS Not disclosed
FUEL TANK Not disclosed
INSTRUMENTS Not disclosed

DIMENSIONS
LENGTH 4500mm
WIDTH 1800mm
HEIGHT 950mm
WHEELBASE 3100mm
TRACK front Not disclosed
rear Not disclosed
WEIGHT 605kg (including
driver and camera)

We've had people join Williams from Ferrari and we'd ask them how they did 'x' and it would be exactly the opposite to us. And they'll pull themselves to bits trying to work out why they were so bad on other tracks. It's been like that ever since I've been in racing. For example, Red Bull were not great on street tracks but thrashed us at Silverstone.

TYRE MANAGEMENT WAS CRITICAL
Despite the move to slick tyres, the working window was narrow, and a lot came down to how the driver did the warm-up lap, especially in qualifying. There are certain ways of warming tyres up without overstressing them. You can go flat-out, destroy a tyre and then by the time you do your fast lap there's no grip left. Tyre management was a big part of it. We had the least problems ever with tyre warm up. We saw problems a few times but, whenever we did, others had them worse.

We had good performance steps at Barcelona and Silverstone – 0.4–0.5s. Whatever Red Bull did at Silverstone was impressive because we know we found 0.5s and they moved 0.2s further away from us! Each package was diffuser, front wing and occasionally rear wing. We made seven or eight rear wings as well as all the fronts, but most of the gains came from diffuser and brake ducts.

THE TESTING BAN DID SAVE MONEY
The testing ban certainly cut parts usage. You would turn up with two sets of parts and when you were updating so much you didn't ever make more than that, whereas in the past we'd have five or six sets plus one for the test team. So your quantities have come down a lot and your consumption has come down, although the budget might not be hugely different because things like front wings, brake ducts and flaps, while not very expensive, still involve five or six guys in the composites department working only on those parts.

I'd say that the testing ban saved 7–8 million Euros. There was the engine saving and we had 30 people on our test team at the start of the year. Now we have about eight, to do the aero test days and PR stuff.

As far as the drivers are concerned, I feel a bit sorry for Kaz not scoring any points, because his delta [gap] to Nico – who did a very good job – and his contribution were much better than in 2008 when he did score. I can only put that down to the field being so much closer."

RENAULT

A SEASON CONSTANTLY SPENT PLAYING CATCH-UP

By Bob Bell
(Technical Director)

"Pre-season, the big talk was the double deck diffuser. We had heard rumours creeping out of Toyota that they were abnormally bullish. We didn't have a clue why and in some ways it was a relief to discover it was this exploitation of rules that not everyone was party to.

It was a slight disappointment for us, though, because we had asked the FIA to do something 80% similar in 2008, and they had said no. More than anything else, that's what buoyed us into thinking that we had to fight it, as it didn't seem to make sense to give two rulings on this point.

Once we saw these things and quickly realised what those three teams (Brawn, Toyota and Williams) were doing, we had a head start over the other teams without double diffusers and were the first to put one on, in China.

DOUBLE DIFFUSER IS A BIG DISTRACTION
We thought, 'wow, this is going to be night and day stuff, no wonder they're so quick,' but when we got into the wind tunnel the gains didn't come in dollops and it took a lot of effort to get it to work. It was fraught with all sorts of practical implications. It was a big, big distraction in terms of the tunnel time we spent on it, the intellectual time, thinking up the arguments for the legal battles. And of course the guys that had it were just sailing along developing and reaping the benefits.

Once we got that behind us, there was a continuous development programme, especially around the front wings that, if we had an area of weakness, was it. We haven't developed those as much as some and, if you look at our early-season wings versus teams like Brawn, you can see that theirs were more highly developed.

We tried hard to put development on for pretty much every race except the last three, and focused on diffusers, front wings, a little bit on rear wings. We did some interesting suspension developments that brought benefits to low-speed mechanical grip.

KERS PROVES A WEAKNESS
The other big thing was KERS. That's been an enormous frustration. By the start of the season, we'd spent about £10m on the project and I think it was particularly frustrating as Flavio [Briatore], and I'm not being critical of

him, was certain that it wouldn't happen and everyone would decide not to do it. He was so strong in his conviction that we only did lip service to KERS in its early development.

It meant that we had to do KERS in a condensed period and, I've got to say, in all of the things that I've seen us do in recent years to be proud of, that project is one of them. Although we haven't exploited it very much, the effort that went into getting it to be as good as anyone else's – there's nothing to choose between the systems despite what people say – and to have a system that hasn't let us down and was completely reliable, was a heck of an achievement for the small team that did it. And it really was a very small team, just three or four people.

That was another huge distraction and influenced the car's architecture significantly. Flavio was absolutely right in as far as it was a complete waste of time for F1 in its guise, particularly from a commercial and cost point-of-view.

KERS BRINGS CENTRE-OF-GRAVITY ISSUES
We had to fit the actual motor generator unit and the batteries under the fuel cell, which meant all the fuel got pushed up and we had to make the tank bigger and worry a bit more about the centre of gravity height of the fuel and the baffling of the tanks and thermal insulation. That was an issue because KERS generates more heat, which goes into the fuel.

At Viry, they had to redo the engine to accept the drive and that in itself was a big task. You also ended up with virtually no moveable ballast and so, if you got your centre of gravity in the wrong place, you were stuffed. We were lucky that we weren't too far out of bed and the little bit of ballast we had allowed us to put it where we needed it.

We had a different tank for when we weren't using KERS, but it was a big scene to change between the two. Cutting a long story short, when we ran with KERS the drivers couldn't really feel the fundamental performance improvement but they all – Fernando [Alonso], Nelson [Piquet Jr] and Romain [Grosjean] – felt that it was affecting the balance under braking.

They weren't comfortable with it and they weren't comfortable that it was increasing the cockpit load on them or that the control system engineers had to spend more time setting it up

THE TEAM

PERSONNEL
PRESIDENT Bernard Rey
MANAGING DIRECTOR Jean-Francois Caubet
DEPUTY MANAGING DIRECTOR, ENGINE Rob White
DEPUTY MANAGING DIRECTOR, SUPPORT OPERATIONS Laurent Chedorge
TECHNICAL DIRECTOR Bob Bell (above)
DEPUTY TECHNICAL DIRECTOR James Allison
HEAD OF VEHICLE TECHNOLOGY Tad Czapski
OPERATIONS DIRECTOR John Mardle
HEAD OF AERO Dirk de Beer
CHIEF DESIGNER Tim Densham
RS27 ENGINE PROJECT MANAGER Malcolm Stewart
HEAD OF TRACKSIDE ENGINE OPERATIONS Remi Taffin
SPORTING MANAGER Steve Nielsen
CHIEF RACE ENGINEER Alan Permane
DRIVERS Fernando Alonso, Romain Grosjean, Nelson Piquet Jr
RACE ENGINEER (Alonso) Simon Rennie
RACE ENGINEER (Piquet Jr, Grosjean) Phil Charles
TEST TEAM MANAGER Carlos Nunes
TEST/THIRD DRIVERS Lucas di Grassi, Romain Grosjean
CHIEF MECHANIC Gavin Hudson
TOTAL NUMBER OF EMPLOYEES 600
NUMBER IN RACE TEAM Undisclosed
TEAM BASE Enstone, England
TELEPHONE +44 (0)1608 678000
WEBSITE www.renaultf1.com

TEAM STATS
IN F1 SINCE 1977–1985 then from 2002 **FIRST GRAND PRIX** Britain 1977, then Australia 2002 **STARTS** 263 **WINS** 35 **POLE POSITIONS** 50 **FASTEST LAPS** 29 **PODIUMS** 93 **POINTS** 1146 **CONSTRUCTORS' TITLES** 2 **DRIVERS' TITLES** 2

SPONSORS
ING, Elf, Total, Pepe Jeans, Bridgestone

7 FERNANDO ALONSO

8 NELSON PIQUET JR

8 ROMAIN GROSJEAN

TECHNICAL SPECIFICATIONS

ENGINE
MAKE/MODEL Renault RS27
CONFIGURATION 2400cc V8 (90 degree)
SPARK PLUGS Not disclosed
ECU FIA standard issue
KERS Magneti-Marelli
FUEL Total
OIL Elf
BATTERY Renault F1

TRANSMISSION
GEARBOX Renault F1
FORWARD GEARS Seven
CLUTCH AP Racing

CHASSIS
CHASSIS MODEL Renault R29
FRONT SUSPENSION LAYOUT
Carbon-fibre top and bottom wishbones operating an inboard rocker via a pushrod system connected to a torsion bar and inboard dampers

REAR SUSPENSION LAYOUT
Carbon-fibre top and bottom wishbones operating angled torsion bars and transverse-mounted dampers mounted on top of the gearbox casing
DAMPERS Not disclosed
TYRES Bridgestone
WHEELS OZ Racing
BRAKE DISCS Hitco
BRAKE PADS Hitco
BRAKE CALIPERS AP Racing
FUEL TANK ATL
INSTRUMENTS Renault F1

DIMENSIONS
LENGTH 4800mm
WIDTH 1800mm
HEIGHT 950mm
WHEELBASE 3110mm
TRACK front 1450mm
rear 1400mm
WEIGHT 605kg (including driver and camera)

RENAULT F1 Team

when they could have been setting up the diff mapping or basic things like that. Our feeling after the Bahrain GP was that it was net negative.

ONE LAST TRY WITH KERS AT MONZA
We were painfully slow at that part of the season and we thought, let's go back to basics, pull KERS off the car and get the centre of gravity back down again. When we got ourselves sorted on the fundamentals, we looked at it again and it went back on at Monza, where I think you get the most lap-time gain, and it was relatively competitive. But it was the same story again: the drivers didn't like it and we pulled it off for the rest of the season.

It was a great shame, as it was a huge effort that most of the outside world didn't see. For example, the effort we went to getting UN certification to fly the batteries around the world was a huge undertaking. I think that we're the only team with it, as the rest flew the batteries around under some sort of prototype status. Then there was all the work you have to do to educate everybody about the safety.

THE R29 LACKED AERO DEVELOPMENT
I don't think the R29 had any particular vices, it just lacked aero development compared to some teams. Brawn are probably the best example, as they had far longer developing the car in the wind tunnel than we had. We did a reasonable job catching up, as the development curve is so steep with these rules, but nonetheless we were always playing catch-up.

Fernando was his normal self and all credit to him. The car has been pretty poor this year, but he has given it his best and has got as much out of it as it's going to give.

Nelson does have talent, there's no doubt. But I think he gets really spooked by qualifying. He just doesn't seem to be able to deal with it in its current guise and ended up at the back of the grid in a car that was off the pace. It was a recipe for a lot of accidents.

Romain is different, but didn't have a lot of luck. He's quick. In Singapore he was 0.2–0.3s from Fernando most of the time and I think he does have the pace. He just needs to have more opportunity to show it in a race. This year it came home to me just how much confidence you need to get a lap time out of a car, particularly one that's handling badly. Fernando can do it and Romain showed that too. I think he has a lot of potential."

FORCE INDIA

CONCERTED EFFORT DRIVES TEAM FORWARD

**By James Key
(Technical Director)**

"We finalised the new deal with McLaren fairly late, November 10, and the agreement included a KERS and a gearbox. It was a much bigger task with many more ramifications than a simple engine change, which we'd been through a number of times of course.

The collaboration with McLaren and Simon Roberts worked out well, and they supplied an excellent engine. Mercedes-Benz High Performance Engines is only just up the road from us, at Brixworth, so that was another plus. The McLaren gearbox and hydraulics took away a considerable reliability concern and allowed us to concentrate on development.

There are always pros and cons when not everything is under your direct control, and you can't always do everything you'd like to, but the positives outweighed the negatives.

BODYWORK REDESIGN REQUIRED
Installation-wise, the engine/chassis interface was all we really needed to deal with, because although we'd already designed our gearbox for 2009, with it suddenly coming from McLaren we had no problems. All we needed to do was get the back of the tub right and the fuel and cooling systems correct, so the new engine itself wasn't as much of a compromise as the significant architectural changes that go with installing an engine and a gearbox so late in the day and making a space for the KERS.

Fundamentally, a lot of the car had to be either tweaked from where it was, or fundamentally redesigned. We just got on with the job and concentrated on hitting the track as soon as we could.

It was a packaging exercise that knocked out quite a bit of plans for the bodywork. Obviously, we would have developed around that from the outset, had we known earlier, but the bodywork was probably the biggest hit and, although we recovered from it, I think we lost about a month's wind-tunnel time adapting.

UPDATES MADE A REAL DIFFERENCE
It seemed to go well but, having said that, we didn't start off that strongly. It was probably a better start than previous years, but we didn't get out of Q1 until Monaco. The updates were what really made the difference. There was the double-diffuser situation to contend with

as well, and for Bahrain we had a twin diffuser on both cars. We'd actually clocked it the year before as a loophole, but not quite to the level of Brawn, Williams and Toyota, who obviously launched their cars with them.

We had some working knowledge of how the airflow-exit conditions worked, so it was just a case of getting the entry conditions right. As soon as we realised what they were doing and formed our own interpretation, we targeted the Chinese GP, but could only spend a couple of weeks in the wind tunnel and couldn't get it working until Bahrain. It did work, though, and it was a really good effort.

DROPPING KERS HELPED PACKAGING
To begin with, we had the packaging disadvantages of KERS and took a bit of a knock, but when we did the Valencia update, we assumed we wouldn't run KERS, and so knocked out the volume originally taken up with the installation that could now be utilised by aero surfaces.

We had four major updates throughout the year, but the Valencia one was the most significant. We expected it to be worth around 0.7s per lap, and that translated on the track. I don't think that we perhaps realised the full potential in Valencia, but at subsequent races we did. We'd actually made a big step at Silverstone that we couldn't take advantage of because Adrian had a big qualifying shunt that also affected Giancarlo's lap.

One of the design aims was always to keep tabs on the efficiency of the car, because before this year we'd not been especially competitive on lift/drag ratio numbers. However, it wasn't necessarily the driving force behind everything we did, and given a totally fresh set of regulations we didn't want to go into the season with a compromise.

HIGH-SPEED CORNERS SUITED THE CAR
We did, however, seem to have a car that coped well with high-speed corners at places like Suzuka and Silverstone, and it was also good in a straight line. So we thought we'd be pretty good at Spa-Francorchamps because of the efficiency and the fact that most of it is high-speed corners, but obviously it was still great to do as well as we did and it certainly created excitement.

We were thinking that we could get both cars through to Q3, but we weren't anticipating

THE TEAM

PERSONNEL
CHAIRMAN & TEAM PRINCIPAL Vijay Mallya
CO-OWNER Michiel Mol
TEAM DIRECTOR & DEPUTY TEAM PRINCIPAL Bob Fernley
CHIEF TECHNICAL OFFICER Simon Roberts then Otmar Szafnauer
DIRECTOR OF BUSINESS AFFAIRS Ian Phillips
TECHNICAL DIRECTOR James Key (above)
DESIGN DIRECTOR Mark Smith
PRODUCTION DIRECTOR Bob Halliwell
DESIGN PROJECT LEADER 2009 Ian Hall
DESIGN PROJECT LEADER 2010 Akio Haga
HEAD OF R&D Simon Gardner
HEAD OF AERO Simon Phillips
HEAD OF ELECTRONICS Mike Wroe
HEAD OF COMPOSITE DESIGN Bruce Eddington
HEAD OF MECHANICAL DESIGN Dan Carpenter
TEAM MANAGER Andy Stevenson
DRIVERS Giancarlo Fisichella, Vitantonio Liuzzi, Adrian Sutil
CHIEF ENGINEER Dominic Harlow
RACE ENGINEER (Fisichella, Liuzzi) Jody Eggington
RACE ENGINEER (Sutil) Bradley Joyce
TEST/THIRD DRIVER Vitantonio Liuzzi
CHIEF MECHANIC Andy Deeming
TOTAL NUMBER OF EMPLOYEES 280
NUMBER IN RACE TEAM 46
TEAM BASE Silverstone, England
TELEPHONE +44 (0)1327 850800
WEBSITE www.forceindiaf1.com

TEAM STATS
IN F1 SINCE 1991, as Jordan then Midland **FIRST GRAND PRIX** USA 1991 **STARTS** 320 **WINS** 4 **POLE POSITIONS** 3 **FASTEST LAPS** 3 **PODIUMS** 21 **POINTS** 301 **CONSTRUCTORS' TITLES** 0 **DRIVERS' TITLES** 0

SPONSORS
Kingfisher, Whyte & Mackay, Medion, Reliance, ICICI, Royal Challenge, Bridgestone

20 ADRIAN SUTIL   **21** GIANCARLO FISICHELLA   **21** VITANTONIO LIUZZI

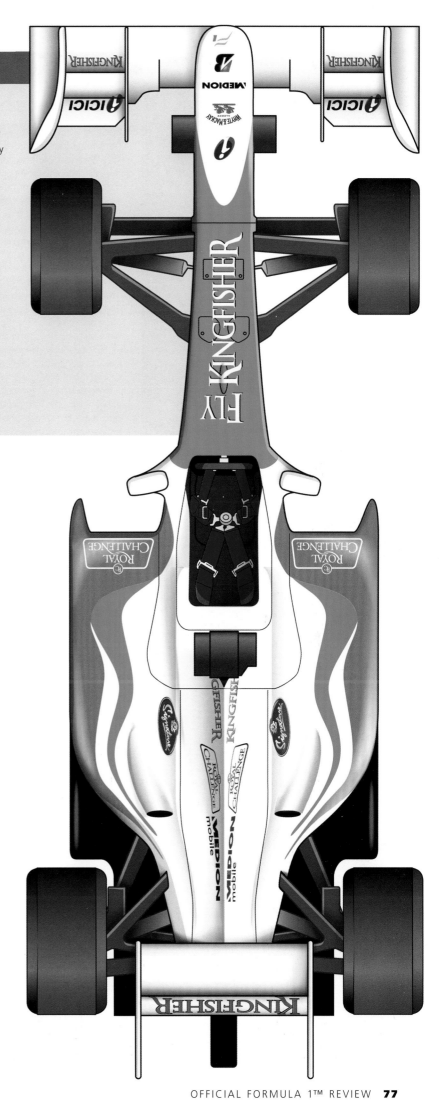

TECHNICAL SPECIFICATIONS

ENGINE
MAKE/MODEL Mercedes-Benz
FO 108W
CONFIGURATION 2400cc V8
(90 degree)
SPARK PLUGS NGK
ECU FIA standard issue
KERS n/a
FUEL Mobil 1
OIL Mobil 1
BATTERY Force India design

TRANSMISSION
GEARBOX McLaren
FORWARD GEARS Seven
CLUTCH AP Racing

CHASSIS
CHASSIS MODEL Force India VJM02
FRONT SUSPENSION LAYOUT
Aluminium MMC uprights with carbon-
fibre composite wishbones and pushrod.
Inboard chassis-mounted torsion springs,
dampers and and anti-roll bar assembly

REAR SUSPENSION LAYOUT
Aluminium MMC uprights
with carbon-fibre composite
wishbones, trackrod and pushrod.
Inboard-mounted torsion springs,
dampers and anti-roll bar assembly
DAMPERS Penske
TYRES Bridgestone
WHEELS BBS
BRAKE DISCS Carbon Industrie
BRAKE PADS Carbon Industrie
BRAKE CALIPERS
AP Racing
FUEL TANK Not disclosed
INSTRUMENTS Not disclosed

DIMENSIONS
LENGTH Approx 5000mm
WIDTH 1800mm
HEIGHT 950mm
WHEELBASE Not disclosed
TRACK front 1480mm
rear 1418mm
WEIGHT 605kg (including
driver and camera)

pole! It was real too, on a dry track, and down to the car
working well and a great effort from the driver. So it was
very satisfying, and I'm sure that without the safety car
and Giancarlo's vulnerability to Kimi's KERS-assisted Ferrari
at the restart, about which he could do little, we could
have won the race. Fisi did a fantastic job that weekend.
He believed that the car could do it and he went out and
almost made it happen.

THE DRIVERS RESPONDED TO COMPETITIVE CAR
I think both Adrian and Giancarlo certainly responded to
having a more competitive car. When the car has been
capable of getting to Q2 and Q3, they have done the job
more often than not. I think their psychology changed.
Early in the season, it was difficult to look beyond going
out in Q1 and a mentality builds up around that.

The only thing I'd say, and it's not the drivers' fault
necessarily, but in general we could have had more
championship points on the board. There were lots of
opportunities which, for one reason or another, weren't
capitalised on. Whether it was going off or somebody
hitting us, there were a number of occasions when we
missed out on scoring. However, certainly at Monza and
Spa, the drivers did make the most of the car.

Tonio Liuzzi came in at Monza completely fresh and did a
tremendous job. It was a great shame that he couldn't finish
there, because I think he was destined for fifth place. We
continued to perform strongly with Adrian third on the grid
at the Brazilian GP before the unfortunate altercation with
Jarno Trulli. Suzuka and the Nürburgring were the other
grands prix in which we would have scored points if we had
finished in the positions in which we had been racing.

I was a little bit surprised that Giancarlo seemed to
struggle when he moved to Ferrari, but all the cars are
different, there's a lot of aero development and he also
had to cope with KERS, as well as working with a new
team, so it was never going to be easy.

THE YEAR WAS A REALLY STRONG TEAM EFFORT
Overall, I want to emphasise how much of a team effort the
year was. The aero department worked very hard on all the
updates, which passed through the design and production
departments, both of which responded extremely well. The
way that the team pulled together was vital and there was
impressive reliability."

TORO ROSSO

THE TEAM

PERSONNEL

TEAM OWNER Dietrich Mateschitz
TEAM PRINCIPAL Franz Tost
TECHNICAL DIRECTOR Giorgio Ascanelli (above)
TEAM MANAGER Gianfranco Fantuzzi
CHIEF DESIGNER Alex Hitzinger (Red Bull Technology)
CHIEF ENGINEER Laurent Mekies
DRIVERS Jaime Alguersuari (from Hungarian GP),
Sebastien Bourdais (up to Hungarian GP), Sebastien Buemi
TECHNICAL CO-ORDINATOR Sandro Parrini
LOGISTICS MANAGER Domenico Sangiorgi
RACE ENGINEER (Bourdais, Alguersuari) Claudio Balestri,
then Andrea Landi
RACE ENGINEER (Buemi) Riccardo Adami
TEST/THIRD DRIVERS Jaime Alguersuari, Brendon Hartley
CHIEF MECHANIC Paolo Piancastelli
ASSISTANT CHIEF MECHANIC Marco Campoduni
NO 1 MECHANIC (Bourdais, Alguersuari) Alberto Gavarini
NO 1 MECHANIC (Buemi) Gabriele Vegnana
RELIABILITY MANAGER Gianvito Amico
SENIOR ENGINE ENGINEER Ernst Knoorst
RACE ENGINES MANAGER Mattia Binotto
TOTAL NUMBER OF EMPLOYEES 230
NUMBER IN RACE TEAM 52
TEAM BASE Faenza, Italy
TELEPHONE +39 (0)546 696111
WEBSITE www.tororosso.com

TEAM STATS

IN F1 SINCE 1985, as Minardi until 2005 **FIRST
GRAND PRIX** Brazil 1985 **STARTS** 411 **WINS** 1 **POLE
POSITIONS** 1 **FASTEST LAPS** 0 **PODIUMS** 1 **POINTS** 94
CONSTRUCTORS' TITLES 0 **DRIVERS' TITLES** 0

SPONSORS

Red Bull, Red Bull Cola, Hangar-7, Puma

11 SEBASTIEN
BOURDAIS
11 JAIME
ALGUERSUARI
12 SEBASTIEN
BUEMI

A YEAR OF BEING CONSISTENTLY SLOW...

By Giorgio Ascanelli
(Technical Director)

"We were vastly improved with our timing this year. In the 2008 World Championship, we did the first five grands prix with the previous year's car, whereas this time around we had the new car for the first race. We did a test at the beginning of the year, then went off to the Australian GP, reducing our time deficit to Red Bull Racing from two months to 22 days.

It was also a bit more difficult this time because the cars – Toro Rosso's and Red Bull's – had more differences between them. Some of that was down to the engine installation, but more so because of the KERS. The two cars were quite different and that conditioned our work. There was a lot more work to do on the chassis than in 2008, and I think that we made a good job of that.

We had the car in Red Bull launch specification and had the same wheelbase, but we couldn't match the same weight distribution, and so we had to work on a few tweaks. We did the first four grands prix in launch specification. Then at the Spanish GP at Barcelona, Red Bull introduced a higher-downforce wing package, which we then got for Monaco.

SLOW TO ADOPT DOUBLE-DECK DIFFUSERS
We then missed the boat with the first version of the double-deck diffuser. Red Bull generated two different packages and we couldn't afford to make the first one for resource reasons. It wasn't just the money, though, but also because the cars were so different that there would have been a major redesign involved. We got the second version, which was better, and took it to the Hungarian GP, which was a delay because we wanted it for the British GP, where Red Bull was so dominant.

There was of course a significant rules change for 2009, and the learning curve of development has been extremely productive, although it's been very important this season to do your development fast. That hasn't really suited us, and it's been tough to try to cope with the changes.

ALL TEAMS RESPONDED DIFFERENTLY
This year, there have been many changes in the relative performances of different cars. Part of it was intrinsically the cars, but another part of it was the way in which the teams work. The

Belgian and Italian GPs looked very different, for example, with Williams not so good in low-drag specification. It is a philosophy, and what works well at those circuits is very different to what works at Valencia or Monaco.

Our season was complicated by the decision of the FIA to allow the double-deck diffusers. I respect their position, but it opened up a different way of packaging the car. Making the evolution for Hungary meant redoing a large part of the hydraulics because there was something in the way because of the electronics for the KERS.

LACK OF FEEL A PROBLEM FOR DRIVERS
Some people had issues with the tyres, but I don't think there was a problem there for us. More of a problem was what you feel. I'm a big fan of John McEnroe who says you have to feel the ball over the net. Only when you have that feel can you spin it and attack it. However, it's very difficult to connect the feeling with what you actually get. It's clear that it's extremely difficult to drive the current tyres to the point that you want them. The drivers with experience can feel them and Jaime [Alguersuari] has been very good in saying he doesn't feel them yet.

Slalom skiing champion Alberto Tomba used to talk about the centrality of weight on the skis: you start going fast when you can feel it and learn how to control it, but it takes time. I don't think our car was particularly good or bad on the tyres. As the circuit changes – and it does over the course of a grand prix meeting – and the car changes around it, it's difficult for the driver to feel the effect, especially if he's not so experienced. At least we were consistent: consistently slow, but consistent!

A LACK OF TESTING HURT YOUNG DRIVERS
The drivers were the second side of our story really. In 2008, I never wanted the credit that was given to me for the performance because we had [Sebastian] Vettel, a great driver. Well, he wasn't with us anymore. That's no disrespect to the other drivers, and the situation with [Sebastien] Buemi has been positive. At the beginning of the year he drove a lot of miles in the old car, but now you can't test anymore and every time you've got a new tweak you've got to understand it. It's natural that people who are not used to this find it difficult, and it's difficult for an experienced driver, let alone

TECHNICAL SPECIFICATIONS

ENGINE
MAKE/MODEL Ferrari 056
CONFIGURATION 2398cc V8
(90 degree)
SPARK PLUGS Not disclosed
ECU FIA standard issue
KERS n/a
FUEL Not disclosed
OIL Not disclosed
BATTERY Not disclosed

TRANSMISSION
GEARBOX Not disclosed
FORWARD GEARS Seven
CLUTCH Sachs

CHASSIS
CHASSIS MODEL Toro Rosso STR4
FRONT SUSPENSION LAYOUT
Upper and lower carbon wishbones,
torsion-bar springs and anti-roll bars

REAR SUSPENSION LAYOUT
Upper and lower carbon wishbones,
torsion-bar springs and anti-roll bars
DAMPERS Sachs
TYRES Bridgestone
WHEELS Advant Racing
BRAKE DISCS Brembo
BRAKE PADS Brembo
BRAKE CALIPERS Brembo
FUEL TANK ATL
INSTRUMENTS
Scuderia Toro Rosso

DIMENSIONS
LENGTH Not disclosed
WIDTH Not disclosed
HEIGHT Not disclosed
WHEELBASE
Not disclosed
TRACK front Not disclosed
rear Not disclosed
WEIGHT 605kg (including
driver and camera)

SCUDERIA Toro Rosso

a new guy. You have to learn how to drive it and so this has has slowed us down.

The obvious question: [Sebastien] Bourdais. He didn't do for us what was reasonable to expect of him: he outqualified his rookie team-mate on just two occasions out of nine. That's acceptable because one can only do one's best. What is not acceptable is not to try to go to the limit, not try to improve yourself. It undermines the confidence of the team. Most people say it's impossible to have a difference. in lap time of more than two tenths between drivers. Really?

Our position in the championship was bad. We were helped in 2008 by the fact that the Honda and Force India cars were handfuls. This year we were faster than Force India at the beginning of the year, but again they became better and the big step they made at the European GP at Valencia took them very far clear until we improved at the end of the season. But, if you look at in-car Force India footage, the drivers are not properly on the edge, so I think their car was very good.

LOOKING TO EXPAND AND ADD A TUNNEL
We have targeted boosting our staff numbers for the beginning of next year. We're in the middle of hiring, but our constraints are time and the ability to attract people. When it comes to attracting the best engineers, we can't exactly pull like Brad Pitt!

Although we signed off on our new chassis, the wind tunnel wasn't ready in step because we didn't manage to put it together in time. I think it's a miracle that we are even at the stage of calibrating the Bicester wind tunnel, but it's going to be a long time between calibrating it and having confidence in it. It will probably be December before we are, and if we are successful next year it will be sheer luck, but I've been given a task and I'm doing the best that I can.

I'm thankful to the ownership that they've made a big investment in computing capacity in terms of computational fluid dynamics. The whole philosophy of the company has to be changed, though, as it has to be independent of Red Bull now. We couldn't use the tools that were familiar to us anymore and had to cope with this at the same time as trying to do a new car."

THE RACES

Brawn GP hit the ground running as F1 was shaken up by a new set of rules and Red Bull Racing joined them in usurping the established front-running teams

2009 FORMULA 1 ING AUSTRALIAN GRAND PRIX
MELBOURNE

BOLT FROM THE BLUE

Less than a month before the season's opening race, Jenson Button was out of a job yet, in an amazing turnaround, here he was a winner again for Ross Brawn's new team

The Australian GP signalled the start of a new world order in Formula One, as Jenson Button and Rubens Barrichello completed a clean sweep for the Brawn GP team. Just 23 days after the announcement that the former Honda Racing outfit had been saved, its Mercedes-powered cars were the dominant force as the sport began what promised to be a fascinating season.

Lurking in the background, however, was the controversy over the double diffusers used by Brawn GP as well as by the Williams and Toyota teams, and which were used pending an FIA Court of Appeal hearing. Depending on what side of the fence you sat, those teams had either cynically exploited an unintended loophole in the rules, or used brilliant ingenuity to pursue a route that the usual frontrunners had missed. Crucially, the FIA's opinion leaned towards the latter.

However, come Sunday evening, few outside the defeated teams were suggesting that the result was anything but a wonderful fillip for the sport, as it produced a superb start to the season that saw not just Brawn GP but several other teams leaving the established favourites trailing. A combination of low downforce, skittish cars and tricky tyre management spiced up the show, as did the debut of KERS. In the end, only Ferrari, McLaren, Renault and BMW Sauber (with Nick Heidfeld's car) came equipped with the much-vaunted energy storage and release technology.

In qualifying, Button and Barrichello claimed the front row, and had so much in hand that they still carried heavier fuel loads than most of those behind. Ross Brawn's new team was at or near the front from the start of practice, but nobody could match the pace of the white cars in qualifying. In the end, Button beat team-mate Barrichello to pole position by over 0.3s.

The fight for third on the grid was much closer, with just 0.2s covering the next five drivers, and the expected domination by the teams equipped with the double diffuser not quite materialising. Quickest of those five was Sebastian Vettel, the young German having a great first outing for Red Bull Racing. Robert Kubica qualified fourth for BMW Sauber, while Nico Rosberg was disappointed with fifth after being higher up for Williams in most of the practice sessions. Timo Glock underlined Toyota's potential with sixth, although along with team-mate Jarno Trulli, he was put to the back for a wing-flexing infringement.

McLaren was just not quick enough for this opening round but, to make matters worse, Lewis Hamilton suffered a gearbox failure after just scraping through to Q2 in 15th, and was not able to take part in that session. A penalty for a change of gearbox dropped him further back on the grid.

Button made his escape at the start, helped by a first-corner tangle in which his team-mate – who got away badly – was involved. Among the victims was Heikki Kovalainen, adding to McLaren's woes, while local hero Mark Webber was also delayed.

Button soon opened up a huge lead, only to lose most of it when a safety car came out after 19 laps due to Kazuki Nakajima crashing his Williams. Things could have gone badly wrong for Button, and he did lose his big advantage, but fortunately the safety car took a while to emerge, so he got in and out of the pits safely. At the restart, he was pursued hard by Vettel, with the German doing a brilliant job. Adrian Newey's Red Bull RB5 was clearly the second-fastest car, despite not using a double diffuser.

Things got more exciting in the closing laps as tyres played a part. Everyone knew that the supersoft option tyre, which had to be used for at least one

OPPOSITE Nelson Piquet Jr started his second campaign for Renault with a bang

BELOW Turn 1, lap 1, always produces fireworks. Mayhem ensues as Mark Webber is tipped around by Rubens Barrichello, who's been hit by Heikki Kovalainen

stint, tailed off badly after a few laps. Button and Vettel had to run on the option in the closing laps, and they were caught rapidly by Kubica, who had used them – and suffered – in the first stint. One of six drivers to start on them, he did a better job than all the others of converting that initial handicap into a viable strategy. The Pole was flying on the prime tyre at the end, and that's precisely what the team was banking on.

With three laps to go, Kubica even had a sniff of victory but, as he tried to pass the struggling Vettel for second place, the two made heavy contact and he crashed out. Another safety car came out and Vettel tried to drive his by now three-wheeled RB5 home, but inevitably he was told by race control to pull over and stop.

After the race, Kubica displayed remarkable candour when asked for his thoughts on the conduct of his former BMW Sauber team-mate, but when they actually met in the paddock there was a bit of a public scene as the Pole made his displeasure known. Vettel tried to put a consoling arm around him, but the offer was rejected in no uncertain terms. However, at least Vettel scored points of a

INSIDE LINE
ROSS BRAWN
**BRAWN GP
TEAM PRINCIPAL**

"I've had some great experiences, but that was moving. After the emotions of the past three months, to be here was great, to be quick was great and to win the race was just sensational! I feel so pleased and proud for the team. I've had some of those experiences, they haven't. It's a great group of people. I was very quiet at the end. I needed some time. You just sit there and think: this can't be true, it can't be happening…

I'd like to think we are going to have a season like the one I had with Benetton and Michael [Schumacher] in 1994, but you can never assume that. The rate of progress will be very rapid with the new regulations. Some people have forgotten what happens when new rules are introduced. At Benetton we sacrificed 1993, and in '94 we won the title. It was an anomaly in a way, as we were a small T-shirt manufacturer that won the World Championship. People didn't like it. We've got a long way to go and people will progress rapidly but, a bit like then, we started this car 15 months ago and we're the only team that did.

Since we introduced the BGP 001, I don't think either Jenson or Rubens has had a spin or major excursion. That tells you the car is predictable and responds well. People talk about downforce and that's important, but it's also key that you have a stable aerodynamic platform. With these new regulations, and a very low, wide front wing, there are difficulties because the wing can be pitch or ride-height sensitive.

On top of that, the vehicle dynamics group, headed by Craig Wilson, has done a superb job of analysing how the tyres should work and what geometry changes we should make. If you look at where the car is very quick, it's in the slow and medium-speed stuff. I watched on the circuit at the Barcelona test and there are some low and medium-speed corners before the final turns, and the car was exceptional through them.

I'd like to think we can develop the car well. In restructuring the company, we've been mindful of performance. We have an upgrade planned for Barcelona and everybody will be incredibly motivated. It's not easy to find performance, but it won't be for want of trying. We haven't downsized the company to a level from which we can't operate, but perhaps we no longer have some of the niceties we had under Honda. Genuinely, the management at Honda are pleased for us. Without them we wouldn't have got here."

TALKING POINT
THE BRAWN FAIRYTALE

Honda announced its withdrawal from F1 in December 2008, amid a global credit crunch, a haemorrhaging motor industry, and in the wake of two appalling F1 seasons. In Brackley, with an uncertain future, the 700-plus F1 staff worried about their futures. A management buy-out under Ross Brawn saved the day for around 450.

Less than four months later, Jenson Button and Rubens Barrichello finished 1–2 in Melbourne.

Brawn looked shell-shocked. "You don't often find Ross lost for words, but I think even the Big Bear was struggling a bit!" the victorious Button grinned.

The car's double diffuser, also used by Toyota and Williams, was the talk of the paddock. Naturally, it was protested. With the stewards finding it legal, appeals were lodged and a World Motor Sport Council hearing scheduled.

"Let's be clear," McLaren's Martin Whitmarsh said, "the concept circumvents the intentions of the Overtaking Working Group regulations and generates more downforce. It's undoubtedly a way of extending the diffuser and heightening it beyond the intention of the regulations.

"In first iterations, people are seeing 10–15 points of downforce from their double diffusers, and you can probably think of 20 points being around one second," Whitmarsh expounded. "But it's not just that: you create a virtuous circle. People struggled to switch the tyres on – Ferrari, ourselves, and others – and if the diffuser helps get the tyre to the right temperature, you've got performance beyond what would be mathematically available with the additional downforce."

Brawn was walking a tight-rope in Melbourne. The team was blowing off The Establishment, having got to the grid courtesy of the goodwill of one of its major players, namely McLaren-Mercedes, which supplied an engine at the 11th hour – and one reputed to be the best on the grid. Arguably, Brawn was a bit cheeky in acting as FOTA's technical representative at the same time as going very quickly with a floor that circumvented the intentions of the OWG's new rules, a point that Renault's Flavio Briatore wasn't slow to make.

Then there was billionaire Sir Richard Branson. He arrived on Saturday for a hastily arranged press conference for a Virgin/Brawn deal inked four hours before he got on his plane.

On Sunday night Branson said: "I'm completely hooked after today, so it's a good time for the team to sit down, twist my arm and ply me with champagne! We'll stay involved for a long time. The team needs and deserves funding. Many of my decisions are based on gut feelings. I knew about Ross Brawn and liked him. I knew he was capable of producing miracle cars and it seemed wrong that he was about to go out of business. Sometimes my intuition works, like today."

different kind when he held up his hands to his error on meeting the stewards. He was given a 10-place grid penalty for the following race in Malaysia.

The collision allowed Button to take a breather, and indeed the race finished under caution. Thanks to the chaos ahead, into second place came Barrichello, who pushed hard after requiring a new nose at his first pit stop. After being in the middle of the first corner mess, he'd also had contact with Kimi Räikkönen, but got away without a penalty.

"It's been a good day," said Button. "You'd think that it would be easy in front, but it's not, it's still a tough race. We came away with victory and I've got to say congratulations to everyone involved. We've had it tough, and I know I keep saying it, but it's the truth. We deserve this, so hopefully this is the first of many. This is an amazing moment for me, and I'm sure it was very emotional for my family and the rest of the team when I crossed that line first.

"It was good to see so many fans being supportive of us. I think that people understand what we've been through the past few months, and I think we've got a lot of support out there. I think we're the people's team, hopefully."

Team boss Brawn could barely believe the way the weekend unfolded: "It's a little surreal. It's my name, but it had to be called something. I still feel awkward about it, to be honest. It wasn't the masterplan, it evolved the way it did. Maybe it hasn't sunk in. Whenever anyone refers to it as a Brawn, I think what are they talking about? And then I suddenly realise. So it is a bit weird. It was very much a team effort to put this team together with the management group we had and the staff. I'm very proud that my name's on the car, but I don't think of it as my team, it's our team!"

Third place went initially to Trulli, who drove a great race after starting his Toyota from the pitlane. The Italian had been running a couple of seconds ahead of Hamilton when the Vettel/Kubica shunt triggered the safety car to be deployed as they approached the end of the lap. In truth, Hamilton was never really on the pace, but he charged hard and a good strategy moved him up the order.

At the penultimate corner, Trulli skated over the grass (team-mate Glock did exactly the same a few seconds later), and a surprised and grateful Hamilton dived through. The McLaren was thus in third place

OPPOSITE Nico Rosberg started his season with points for Williams

BELOW LEFT Rubens Barrichello's Brawn is given a new nose, but he was still able to finish second

BELOW RIGHT Lewis Hamilton pushes Jarno Trulli, but their battle carried on in front of the stewards

BOTTOM Robert Kubica was fastest in the closing stages, but crashed after clashing with Vettel

as the cars crossed the timing line at the end of lap 56, the first completed under the safety car.

In theory, Hamilton had passed Trulli under the safety car, but if someone has gone off the road you are not obliged to wait for them, and can legitimately claim the place. Further around lap 57, though, the pair swapped places, so Trulli was ahead when they came past the pits.

After the embarrassment of the qualifying penalty, Trulli's third place came as a tremendous boost, and the outwardly dry and colourless Toyota team celebrated the result in style in the paddock. And then came the news that Trulli had been given a 25s

penalty. Since the field finished the race behind the safety car, it had a disproportionately large effect, dropping him to 12th, last on the lead lap.

Race control had been astonished when the timing screens showed third place changing from Hamilton to Trulli on lap 57, the penultimate lap – while the safety car was out. It was clearly something that warranted investigation.

When Hamilton emerged from *parc fermé*, he explained what had happened: "I slowed down as much as I could. I was told to let him back past, but I mean... I don't know if that's the regulations, and if it isn't, then I should have really had third."

However, that was not the story that he and team manager Dave Ryan shared with the stewards when they were making their decision. When the FIA discovered the anomaly, the stewards were reconvened in Sepang. Ultimately, Hamilton was disqualified and Trulli got third place back (see Malaysian GP report).

None of that affected the rest of the results. The remaining points went to Trulli, Glock, Fernando Alonso (delayed by the first-lap shunt), Rosberg (who struggled badly on soft rubber in the final stint), Toro Rosso rookie Sebastien Buemi and Sebastien Bourdais. Webber had another bad home race, and was badly delayed after being hit by Barrichello at the start, struggling around to finish 13th, a lap down.

Ferrari had a disastrous weekend. The team had better pace than McLaren, but Felipe Massa was only seventh fastest in qualifying, even with a light fuel load. Both he and Räikkönen made good starts, but lost a lot of time on the softer tyre and had to make premature first stops. They then lucked in with the safety car, but neither was able to take advantage, as Massa suffered an upright failure and Räikkönen – who spun and clipped the wall – retired with diff problems. What a difference a year makes...

SNAPSHOT FROM
AUSTRALIA

CLOCKWISE FROM RIGHT Turn 1, seen from the air, with the lake in the top left of the photo; Scuderia Toro Rosso's new boy Sebastien Buemi; Buttons father and son celebrate after Jenon's fairytale victory; Lewis Hamilton tries cricket, rounders-style; Sir Richard Branson brought some Virgin pizzazz to Brawn GP; Fernando Alonso is dwarfed by a paddock beauty; bear-faced cheek; Mark Webber admires Sebastian Vettel's handiwork on the beach overlooking Melbourne Bay

WEEKEND NEWS

■ David Coulthard faced the prospect of an unexpected comeback when he was named as Red Bull Racing's third driver after Brendon Hartley was not granted a superlicence in time for the Australian GP. The 19-year-old Kiwi would eventually be awarded a licence several races into the season, allowing DC to focus on his BBC TV duties.

■ Jarno Trulli recorded his 200th grand prix start in Melbourne, and unusually the anniversary came at the same venue where the Toyota driver made his debut with Minardi back in 1997. His special weekend didn't work out too well when he was forced to start from the pitlane and was, initially at least, disqualified from third place...

■ Virgin boss Richard Branson caused a considerable stir when he arrived in the Albert Park paddock accompanied by some stewardesses from his airline. He held a press conference behind the Brawn GP garage and kept a conspicuously high profile all weekend. Although the Brawn BGP 001s carried Virgin logos, there was no firm word on what the deal entailed.

■ The celebrations didn't continue for long for some members of Brawn GP. Shortly after the race, CEO Nick Fry confirmed that the team would be trimming its staff from 700 to around 450. The general idea was to get back to the staffing levels of 2004, before the then BAR team was officially taken over by Honda.

■ During the winter, F1 drivers expressed their dissatisfaction at a hike in the price of their superlicences. However, a compromise was reached after a meeting between the leading lights of the GPDA and Max Mosley in the run-up to the Australian GP. Meanwhile, Lewis Hamilton confirmed that he was finally willing to sign up as a member of the Grand Prix Drivers' Association.

RACE RESULTS
AUSTRALIA MELBOURNE

Official Results © [2009]
Formula One Administration Limited,
6 Princes Gate, London, SW7 1QJ.
No reproduction without permission.
All copyright and database rights reserved.

RACE DATE March 29th
CIRCUIT LENGTH 3.295 miles
NO. OF LAPS 58
RACE DISTANCE 191.110 miles
WEATHER Sunny and dry, 22°C
TRACK TEMP 31°C
ATTENDANCE 286,900
LAP RECORD Michael Schumacher,
1m24.125s, 141.016mph, 2004

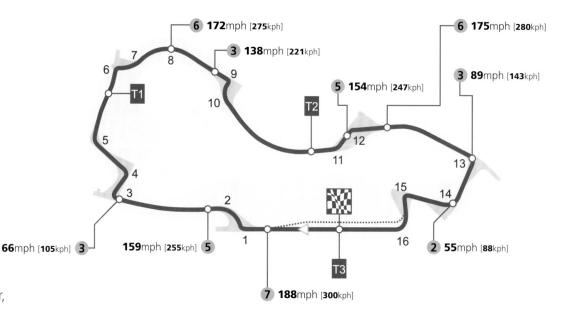

6 172mph [**275**kph]
3 138mph [**221**kph]
6 175mph [**280**kph]
3 89mph [**143**kph]
5 154mph [**247**kph]
66mph [**105**kph] **3**
159mph [**255**kph] **5**
2 55mph [**88**kph]
7 188mph [**300**kph]

PRACTICE 1				PRACTICE 2				PRACTICE 3				QUALIFYING 1			QUALIFYING 2	
	Driver	Time	Laps		Driver	Time	Laps		Driver	Time	Laps		Driver	Time		Driver	Time
1	N Rosberg	1m26.687s	19	1	N Rosberg	1m26.053s	36	1	N Rosberg	1m25.808s	21	1	R Barrichello	1m25.006s	1	R Barrichello	1m24.783s
2	K Nakajima	1m26.736s	21	2	R Barrichello	1m26.157s	38	2	J Trulli	1m25.811s	19	2	J Button	1m25.211s	2	J Button	1m24.855s
3	K Räikkönen	1m26.750s	24	3	J Trulli	1m26.350s	42	3	J Button	1m25.981s	20	3	M Webber	1m25.427s	3	S Vettel	1m25.121s
4	R Barrichello	1m27.226s	21	4	M Webber	1m26.370s	30	4	F Massa	1m26.020s	17	4	T Glock	1m25.499s	4	N Rosberg	1m25.123s
5	H Kovalainen	1m27.453s	15	5	J Button	1m26.374s	38	5	K Nakajima	1m26.078s	18	5	N Heidfeld	1m25.827s	5	R Kubica	1m15.152s
6	J Button	1m27.467s	12	6	T Glock	1m26.443s	42	6	R Barrichello	1m26.348s	19	6	F Massa	1m25.844s	6	M Webber	1m25.241s
7	F Massa	1m27.642s	24	7	K Nakajima	1m26.560s	33	7	M Webber	1m26.355s	16	7	N Rosberg	1m25.846s	7	J Trulli	1m25.265s
8	T Glock	1m27.710s	24	8	S Vettel	1m26.740s	19	8	T Glock	1m26.410s	25	8	K Räikkönen	1m25.899s	8	T Glock	1m25.281s
9	A Sutil	1m27.993s	20	9	A Sutil	1m27.040s	29	9	R Kubica	1m26.514s	18	9	R Kubica	1m25.922s	9	F Massa	1m25.319s
10	F Alonso	1m28.123s	16	10	F Massa	1m27.064s	35	10	N Heidfeld	1m26.555s	19	10	S Vettel	1m25.938s	10	K Räikkönen	1m25.380s
11	N Heidfeld	1m28.137s	20	11	K Räikkönen	1m27.204s	32	11	H Kovalainen	1m26.652s	13	11	F Alonso	1m26.026s	11	N Heidfeld	1m25.504s
12	J Trulli	1m28.142s	21	12	F Alonso	1m27.232s	28	12	L Hamilton	1m26.714s	18	12	K Nakajima	1m26.074s	12	F Alonso	1m25.605s
13	R Kubica	1m28.511s	22	13	G Fisichella	1m27.282s	32	13	S Vettel	1m27.009s	12	13	H Kovalainen	1m26.184s	13	K Nakajima	1m25.607s
14	G Fisichella	1m28.603s	16	14	N Heidfeld	1m27.317s	34	14	A Sutil	1m27.062s	12	14	J Trulli	1m26.194s	14	H Kovalainen	1m25.726s
15	S Buemi	1m28.785s	27	15	R Kubica	1m27.398s	36	15	S Bourdais	1m27.152s	16	15	L Hamilton	1m26.454s	15	L Hamilton	No time
16	L Hamilton	1m29.042s	18	16	S Bourdais	1m27.479s	36	16	S Buemi	1m27.192s	17	16	S Buemi	1m26.503s			
17	M Webber	1m29.081s	7	17	H Kovalainen	1m27.802s	35	17	F Alonso	1m27.357s	18	17	N Piquet Jr	1m26.598s			
18	N Piquet Jr	1m29.461s	25	18	L Hamilton	1m27.813s	31	18	G Fisichella	1m27.492s	20	18	G Fisichella	1m26.677s			
19	S Bourdais	1m29.499s	21	19	N Piquet Jr	1m27.828s	35	19	N Piquet Jr	1m27.739s	22	19	A Sutil	1m26.742s			
20	S Vettel	1m32.784s	4	20	S Buemi	1m28.076s	33	20	K Räikkönen	1m28.801s	5	20	S Bourdais	1m26.964s			

Best sectors – Practice			Speed trap – Practice			Best sectors – Qualifying			Speed trap – Qualifying		
Sec 1	J Trulli	28.535s	1	S Buemi	191.693mph	Sec 1	R Barrichello	28.115s	1	S Buemi	191.817mph
Sec 2	F Massa	23.090s	2	F Massa	191.568mph	Sec 2	R Barrichello	22.734s	2	N Heidfeld	191.631mph
Sec 3	N Rosberg	33.979s	3	L Hamilton	191.382mph	Sec 3	R Kubica	33.702s	3	F Massa	191.568mph

IN 2008

This was a race that put the smiles back on the faces of the McLaren crew, when Lewis Hamilton raced from pole to victory as both Ferraris failed. Nick Heidfeld was second for BMW Sauber, while Nico Rosberg claimed his first podium result by finishing third for Williams. Five cars were eliminated in a first-corner clash.

Lewis Hamilton
"I was trying to get one point, so to get six is great. Considering the package we've got, I wrung every last ounce of pace out of the car. I drove one of my best races ever."

Felipe Massa
"We ran into trouble with the soft tyres, pitted early and switched to an aggressive strategy, but it proved to be wrong, as soon after the stop, the safety car came out."

Robert Kubica
"I think Sebastian was a bit too optimistic. Had this been the last corner OK, but there were three laps to go and he had no realistic chance to defend his position."

Fernando Alonso
"I started in a poor position, was pushed wide at Turn 1 and fell back. After that, it was hard and so it's great to score. I was a bit disappointed at how the KERS worked."

Jarno Trulli
"When the safety car came out near the end of the race Lewis passed me when I was caught out by a shadow on the track, but soon after that he suddenly slowed."

Heikki Kovalainen
"Obviously, my race was very short. Webber had a moment at the first corner and his front wheel hit my left-front. It was a racing accident, these things happen."

Kimi Räikkönen
"When I ended up in the wall, it was my mistake and I reckon I could've come second. The KERS worked well at the start, but there wasn't room to go anywhere."

Nick Heidfeld
"I had a good start and made up places. Then under braking for Turn 1 there was no car next to me, but suddenly I got a bang. I had to pit for tyres and a new front wing."

Nelson Piquet Jr
"When the safety car came out I started to have brake problems. I overtook Rosberg at the restart, but when I touched the brakes again they were gone, and I spun."

Timo Glock
"To be fighting at the front like that after we started from the pits is proof that our car has pace. The race was exciting but I was stuck behind Alonso for quite a while."

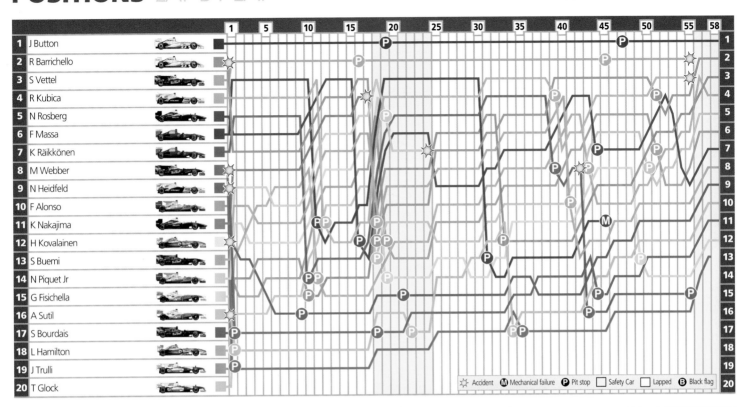

	Driver		
1	J Button		
2	R Barrichello		
3	S Vettel		
4	R Kubica		
5	N Rosberg		
6	F Massa		
7	K Räikkönen		
8	M Webber		
9	N Heidfeld		
10	F Alonso		
11	K Nakajima		
12	H Kovalainen		
13	S Buemi		
14	N Piquet Jr		
15	G Fisichella		
16	A Sutil		
17	S Bourdais		
18	L Hamilton		
19	J Trulli		
20	T Glock		

☆ Accident Ⓜ Mechanical failure Ⓟ Pit stop ☐ Safety Car ☐ Lapped Ⓑ Black flag

QUALIFYING 3

	Driver	Time
1	J Button	1m26.202s
2	R Barrichello	1m26.505s
3	S Vettel	1m26.830s
4	R Kubica	1m26.914s
5	N Rosberg	1m26.973s
6	T Glock	1m26.975s
7	F Massa	1m27.033s
8	J Trulli	1m27.127s
9	K Räikkönen	1m27.163s
10	M Webber	1m27.246s

GRID

	Driver	Time
1	J Button	1m26.202s
2	R Barrichello	1m26.505s
3	S Vettel	1m26.830s
4	R Kubica	1m26.914s
5	N Rosberg	1m26.973s
6	F Massa	1m27.033s
7	K Räikkönen	1m27.163s
8	M Webber	1m27.246s
9	N Heidfeld	1m25.504s
10	F Alonso	1m25.605s
11	K Nakajima	1m25.607s
12	H Kovalainen	1m25.726s
13	S Buemi	1m26.503s
14	N Piquet Jr	1m26.598s
15	G Fisichella	1m26.677s
16	A Sutil	1m26.742s
17	S Bourdais	1m26.964s
18*	L Hamilton	No time
19^	T Glock	-
20^	J Trulli	-

* Five-place grid penalty for gearbox change
^ Sent to back of grid for illegal rear wing

RACE

	Driver	Car	Laps	Time	Avg. mph	Fastest	Stops
1	J Button	Brawn-Mercedes BGP 001	58	1h34m15.784s	121.649	1m28.020s	2
2	R Barrichello	Brawn-Mercedes BGP 001	58	1h34m16.591s	121.631	1m29.066s	2
3	J Trulli	Toyota TF109	58	1h34m17.388s	121.610	1m28.916s	2
D^	L Hamilton	*McLaren-Mercedes MP4-24	58	1h34m18.698s	121.587	1m29.020s	2
4	T Glock	Toyota TF109	58	1h34m20.219s	121.554	1m28.416s	2
5	F Alonso	* Renault R29	58	1h34m20.663s	121.544	1m28.712s	2
6	N Rosberg	Williams-Toyota FW31	58	1h34m21.506s	121.526	1m27.706s	2
7	S Buemi	Toro Rosso-Ferrari STR4	58	1h34m21.788s	121.520	1m29.230s	2
8	S Bourdais	Toro Rosso-Ferrari STR4	58	1h34m22.082s	121.514	1m29.823s	2
9	A Sutil	Force India-Mercedes VJM02	58	1h34m22.119s	121.513	1m28.943s	3
10	N Heidfeld	*BMW Sauber F1.09	58	1h34m22.869s	121.496	1m28.283s	3
11	G Fisichella	Force India-Mercedes VJM02	58	1h34m23.158s	121.491	1m29.005s	2
12	M Webber	Red Bull-Renault RB5	57	1h34m16.197s	119.543	1m28.508s	2
13	S Vettel	Red Bull-Renault RB5	56	Accident	-	1m28.140s	2
14	R Kubica	BMW Sauber F1.09	55	Accident	-	1m27.988s	2
15	K Räikkönen	*Ferrari F60	55	Accident	-	1m28.488s	3
R	F Massa	*Ferrari F60	45	Chassis	-	1m29.141s	2
R	N Piquet Jr	*Renault R29	24	Spun off	-	1m30.502s	1
R	K Nakajima	Williams-Toyota FW31	17	Accident	-	1m29.923s	0
R	H Kovalainen	*McLaren-Mercedes MP4-24	0	Accident	-	-	0

* Denotes car fitted with KERS
^ Disqualified for providing misleading information about Trulli's passing move behind the safety car

CHAMPIONSHIP

	Driver	Pts
1	J Button	10
2	R Barrichello	8
3	J Trulli	6
4	T Glock	5
5	F Alonso	4
6	N Rosberg	3
7	S Buemi	2
8	S Bourdais	1

Fastest lap
N Rosberg 1m27.706s
(135.252mph) on lap 48

Fastest speed trap
A Sutil 191.693mph

Slowest speed trap
H Kovalainen 147.575mph

Fastest pit stop
1 N Heidfeld 19.325s
2 J Trulli 19.369s
3 T Glock 19.676s

	Constructor	Pts
1	Brawn-Mercedes	18
2	Toyota	11
3	Renault	4
4	Williams-Toyota	3
5	Toro Rosso-Ferrari	3

Sebastien Bourdais
"After three laps, the option tyres were graining. Several cars passed me, so the team called me in. When the safety car came out, it was clear we had to fuel to the finish."

Mark Webber
"I was trying to get through Turn 1 clean, but Rubens came into the side of me hard and I picked up a lot of damage and wasn't going to be a threat to anyone after that."

Nico Rosberg
"I left the door open at Turn 3 on lap 1, and then we had a problem on my first pit stop. The restart after the first safety car on cold tyres was very difficult, I had no grip."

Adrian Sutil
"I had a good start, but in the first corner Webber slowed and I damaged my wing and had to get the car back to the pits. I then lost some time behind Heidfeld."

Jenson Button
"This is just a fairytale ending to our first race together for Brawn GP. It may have looked like an easy win but it wasn't at all. This win is for me, my family and my team."

Sebastien Buemi
"First race, first point, so I am very happy. Maybe we had a bit of luck with the accidents, but even without that we weren't too bad and our strategy worked well."

Sebastian Vettel
"I was second, but a few laps from the end, I had a stupid accident with Robert. When I turned in I was ahead, but when we hit we was in front, but I had nowhere to go."

Kazuki Nakajima
"I had a quite big accident on lap 17 when I ran wide at Turn 4, hit the kerb and then I lost the rear. It was quite a fast impact, so I had a precautionary medical check up."

Giancarlo Fisichella
"I'm disappointed with the error I made in the pits. I was confused with last year when we had the last slot in the pitlane, so I overshot and had to be pulled back."

Rubens Barrichello
"The anti-stall kicked in at the start which cost me a few places off the line and then I was hit from behind going into Turn 1 and thought that was it. Luckily the car survived."

2009 FORMULA 1 PETRONAS MALAYSIAN GRAND PRIX
KUALA LUMPUR

IT'S TWO FROM TWO

Jenson Button and Brawn GP did it again, but the weather had the last laugh, bringing the grand prix to a premature halt, then stopping it for good as darkness approached

After his first nine seasons of Formula One had produced just one grand prix victory, a dramatic afternoon in Malaysia led to Jenson Button continuing his outstanding start to the 2009 World Championship by taking his second win in eight days.

In Australia he'd taken the chequered flag with the field lined up under caution behind him, but in Malaysia he didn't even manage that, learning that he'd won while sitting in his car on the grid and waiting for a restart that never came.

A storm of monsoon proportions caused the race to be suspended and, while the weather cleared, the impending gloom of nightfall made it impossible to run the remaining laps. The much-criticised decision to move the local start time from 3pm to 5pm, mainly for the benefit of European TV audiences, left no safety net. The premature conclusion meant that Button and the rest of the top-eight finishers scored only half points, but the man himself was certainly happy enough to log another victory.

"This was a difficult race in difficult circumstances," said the Brawn GP driver. "One day hopefully we'll have a race that has no safety cars, no accidents and no rain that stops play! It's been a couple of difficult races. People might say that our car is the best and it's easy from there, but it's definitely not..."

In fact, the eventful race finally allowed everyone to take their minds off the big story of the week. The reconvening of the Australian GP stewards and subsequent disqualification of Lewis Hamilton from his third place dominated the headlines, and the beleaguered driver and McLaren were under fire from all sides. It was an extraordinary few days that took the focus off what was happening on the track.

With rain threatening, an exciting qualifying session had Ferrari and McLaren both struggling as the 'new boys' continued to upset the established order. There was drama in Q1 when both Ferrari drivers stuck with their times from their first runs, assuming that they would be fast enough to get through. However, the field was so closely packed that as Felipe Massa sat helpless in the garage he was bumped down to 16th and so out of Q2. Team-mate Kimi Räikkönen scraped through by two places.

Then, in the second qualifying session it was McLaren's turn to suffer, as Hamilton ended up 13th and Heikki Kovalainen 14th, neither man thus progressing into the vital Q3 session.

Having struggled a little in practice on Friday, Button got it just right to take his second pole in two attempts this year, and it was starting to look as though Brawn GP was going to be hard to catch.

Button's closest challenger was Jarno Trulli, the Toyota driver coming within 0.106s of Button's time as he claimed the other front-row spot. Sebastian Vettel continued to show great form as he took third for Red Bull Racing, but he was carrying a 10-place grid penalty after his clash with Robert Kubica in Australia, and thus dropped to 13th. Rubens Barrichello was fourth in the other Brawn, but he moved back five places after having to take a new gearbox.

After the long wait until 5pm, the field finally got away in dry conditions but, with rain in the air. Button made it hard for himself from the start, as he was beaten away by Nico Rosberg (promoted to fourth on the grid by the Vettel/Barrichello penalties), Trulli and the KERS-boosted Fernando Alonso.

Crucially, Button soon got back past the fuel-heavy Renault, but he still had two cars ahead. The significance of the ongoing twin-diffuser controversy was made only too clear, as the Williams, Toyota and Brawn – three cars thus equipped – left everyone else trailing. Meanwhile, Kovalainen had another short race, sliding off on the opening lap.

Button had carried a few extra laps of fuel in qualifying and, having sat patiently in third place until his two rivals pitted – Rosberg on lap 15, Trulli two laps later – he took advantage of a clear track to put on an extraordinary spurt. The true potential of the Brawn BGP 001 was evident as he then recorded a best lap that was a full second quicker than those of the team's main challengers.

When Button pitted, he emerged in the lead, still on slicks despite the darkening skies and signs of a storm on the horizon. Ferrari, meanwhile, made an ill-advised decision to put Räikkönen onto rain tyres.

BELOW Nico Rosberg blasts past Jenson Button to take the lead

BOTTOM Robert Kubica's BMW Sauber lasted just one lap before his engine caught fire and he retired

OPPOSITE This was the only type of massed attention that Lewis Hamilton enjoyed all weekend

INSIDE LINE
LEWIS HAMILTON
McLAREN DRIVER

Friday, Sepang press conference room: "In Melbourne, I had a great race (he finished fourth from the back of the grid) and as soon as I got out of the car I had the TV interviews at the back of the garage. I gave an account of what happened (when he passed Trulli, who had run off the circuit during a safety-car period in the closing stages in the Australian GP five days earlier).

After being requested by the stewards and while waiting for them, I was instructed and misled by my team manager (Dave Ryan) to withhold information (that I had been instructed by radio to allow Trulli to re-pass). I sincerely apologise to the stewards for wasting their time and making them look silly.

I'm very sorry for the situation, for my team, for Dave, who has been a good member of the team for many years and is a good guy.

I went into the meeting and wanted to tell the story, but I was misled. I want to say a big sorry to all my fans. I have showed who I am for the past three years. That is who I am. I'm not a liar. I'm a team player and every time I've been told to do something, I've done it.

This time I realise that it was a huge mistake and I'm learning from it. It's taken a huge toll on me and I apologise to you guys for not speaking yesterday, but it was a lot to take in and deal with.

It's not an easy thing to do, to realise I'm in the wrong, but I owe it to my fans to let them know. But I was misled. I acted as a team member and didn't have time to think about what I was going to do. I felt awkward, very uncomfortable, and I guess the stewards could see that. I have never felt so bad. I've never gone through my life lying or being dishonest, and so for people to say that, and for the world to think that, hurts.

The decision to suspend Dave is nothing to do with me. He's a great guy who's worked for the team for many years, so he's feeling it just as much as the whole team.

The situation is the worst thing I've experienced. It's right for me to tell you all what went on, and to put my hands up. I can't tell you how sorry I am. I'm sorry to my team and my family for the embarrassment."

The Finn then tumbled down the race order as he waited in vain for the rain to come, and his rain tyres were soon destroyed.

When the first drizzle finally arrived, Button initially extended his advantage with some great driving on slicks on a gradually soaking track. When he finally pitted, he was one of many drivers to go straight to extreme-wet tyres, only to find that the track wasn't quite wet enough. Timo Glock, meanwhile, had gone to intermediates, and was really flying. Button soon changed to intermediates, but then the heavens opened and he had to make a fourth stop to go back to extreme wets.

Ordinarily, that sort of indecision, which brought back memories of Donington Park 1993, would have scuppered his chances. But just about everyone else was equally confused and also making multiple stops. With cars slithering around everywhere, and rivers running across the track, race control took the decision to send out the safety car. And that was followed almost immediately by a red flag, so the field stopped on the grid and the race went into suspended mode.

"After my first change to wet tyres, I was just skating around all over the place, I was just so slow," Button said later. "But nobody else on the extreme wet was really much quicker. I was trying to look after the rears, as I was getting oversteer, knowing that it was probably going to rain. The guys came on the radio and said Timo was very quick on inters, so I pitted for inters and came out behind him. Then, as soon as he went past me into Turn 1, I saw that his tyres were all but slick. After that, I struggled massively to try and get the tyres working, but then Timo was struggling more, and then it was about making the call for wets, which we did, and then it was just crawling round after the safety car."

It was clear that Button was in the lead, but there was still a little confusion as to the race order behind while officials sorted out who was where when the flag came out. As the minutes ticked by, the rain abated and drivers either sat in their cars or mooched nervously around the grid.

However, it wasn't getting any lighter, and it was eventually decided that there was not enough daylight left to justify restarting the race. Inevitably, this caused some questions to be asked about the wisdom of moving the start time so late, especially when the risk of bad weather meant that it was always going to be hard to squeeze in the full race distance.

BELOW LEFT Mark Webber and Nick Heidfeld were both heading for the podium, but only Heidfeld made it

BELOW RIGHT This is Kazuki Nakajima's Williams, but it's very hard to tell through the spray

BOTTOM Heavy rain came too late for Ferrari, who gambled too early on rain tyres. Felipe Massa was classified in ninth place

TALKING POINT
MOUNTAINS OUT OF MOLE HILLS…

Australia hadn't been great. From the back of the grid, Lewis Hamilton had salvaged fourth, which became third when the stewards awarded a 25s penalty to Jarno Trulli for re-passing the McLaren driver behind the safety car. When both parties gave evidence to the Melbourne stewards, Trulli claimed Hamilton had slowed to let him re-pass, which was true. Hamilton and McLaren's Dave Ryan denied it.

Ryan was angry at himself for not reacting more quickly and telling the calm, unflappable Richard Hopkirk (team tactician for Hamilton, who was heard clearly on the radio telling Hamilton to allow Trulli by) that it wasn't necessary. Hamilton was cross that they'd ceded a podium.

Interviews given by Hamilton as soon as he got out of the car after the race didn't square with what he said in the stewards' room, and once the FIA listened to the radio transmissions it was all too obvious.

By the time team principal Martin Whitmarsh arrived at Sepang not quite four days later (he'd been holidaying in Indonesia between races), all hell had broken loose. Hamilton had been disqualified, Trulli reinstated and headlines about lying were shooting around the world. Whitmarsh was descended upon by the media and, naturally enough, defended his troops. When he said they hadn't lied, it added to the confusion.

In reality, Trulli/Hamilton had been a nothing incident. Every time two drivers are called before stewards, they have a different version of events. Sometimes, one is telling the truth, sometimes both.

For the press, though, it was wilful lying involving the World Champion! The media moved into overdrive. Ryan was a senior member of McLaren and he'd made an error of judgement. But as McLaren's name was besmirched once more, it became an error with a consequence entirely disproportionate to its actuality.

Whitmarsh spoke to Ryan long into Thursday night before taking the decision to suspend him. It was, he admitted, the most difficult thing he'd ever had to do. Damned for scapegoating if he did and damned for failing to take the matter seriously if he didn't.

Ryan wasn't just a colleague but also a friend. He was the man on the front-left wheel when James Hunt won the World Championship in a McLaren at Fuji in 1976. Cut Dave Ryan and he bled McLaren. And yet there he was heading for the airport on Friday morning. Yes he'd been wrong, but it was as big an injustice as many could recall. Hamilton's apology to the media in which he repeatedly fingered Ryan, only left a worse taste.

All of that was of little consequence to Button who, on learning the news, alighted from his car and kicked off the celebrations.

"The boys couldn't tell me because the radios weren't working as it had all got too wet," he explained. "They came over to the car and said you've won the race. I was very happy obviously, winning the race. You only get half points, but for me it was the win that matters, it wasn't the points. And it was the right decision, to call the race off when they did. So I jumped out, gave everyone a hug. It was nice to have my engineer, Andrew Shovlin, on the podium with us. He's been through a lot, he's been with me as my engineer since I started with the team. He deserves a lot of credit."

Second place went to BMW Sauber's Nick Heidfeld, who had made a good call for extremes that coincided with his first scheduled stop. Indeed, by resolutely staying out on them, he jumped up the order to earn a position that was unrepresentative of the team's real form. In fact, he'd spun just before the red flag and been passed by Glock, but on a countback to the previous lap, he got the place back.

Glock's good decisions – initially for intermediates and then an early move to extremes – also paid dividends, and he still secured the final podium place, ahead of team-mate Trulli. Barrichello moved up to fifth, but both he and Trulli were lucky to get away with pit stops just as the flag came out, as the final order was taken from the previous lap.

Mark Webber was classified a frustrated sixth after getting himself into a prime spot to challenge for the podium. He was actually several places ahead of that when the race was suspended and, had the race run a lap or two longer, he would certainly have been on the podium. His team-mate Vettel meanwhile was one of the victims of the flooded track, spinning into retirement.

ABOVE Conditions became wetter and wetter, and darker and darker, and it was Jenson Button who was in front when the red flag was shown

ABOVE Jenson Button is pushed into position on the grid for a restart that didn't come due to insufficient light as evening fell

RIGHT There's the evidence: it's 18:45 and that's the race order, with Button top of the tree, but Glock and Heidfeld are the wrong way around in second and third

Webber finished ahead of Hamilton (who spun just before the stoppage) and Rosberg, the latter's early lead squandered by strategic fumbles.

One point for Hamilton was small consolation for the McLaren team after its nightmare weekend, but things were even worse at Ferrari, as Massa finished outside the points in ninth place, while Räikkönen retired to the pits just as the grand prix was suspended. Incredibly, the two Ferraris had scored no points at all in two outings, and were officially classified last, behind even Force India. This was going to be a strange season...

"In a sense, the rule changes have caused a fair amount of chaos," said McLaren team principal Martin Whitmarsh. "Because of two significantly different sets of interpretations, and also because it's meant that teams that committed to these regulations a long time before Ferrari and ourselves are down the road from us at the moment.

"As a team we don't like it, but the truth is for F1 it was a good and a healthy shake-up, and it's a kick up the backside for ourselves and Ferrari. We've got to make sure that we restore what we consider the natural order as quickly as we can. It's a lot of work..."

SNAPSHOT FROM
MALAYSIA

CLOCKWISE FROM RIGHT April in Malaysia means thunderstorms; Button is ready for action with a cool vest; fitting a wing back-to-front is surely going to lead to uplift not downforce; a local fan wearing Ferrari's colours with pride; the drummers enjoyed a rare period of sunshine on the grid; it says 'dry' on the tyre wraps behind them, but getting excess water off awnings made these guys anything but; presumably one was being prepared that said 'unbelievably wet race'...

WEEKEND NEWS

■ McLaren Sporting Director Dave Ryan was suspended from duty on Friday morning in Sepang for his part in the Melbourne safety-car affair. Just two days after the race, the team confirmed that he had officially parted company with the team. A popular figure in the F1 paddock, Ryan had been with McLaren since 1974.

■ At Sepang, BMW Sauber confirmed officially that it was joining the appeal against the decision by the Australian GP stewards on the legality of double diffusers. Ferrari, Renault and Red Bull Racing had all made protests in Australia – and had them rejected – but BMW Sauber didn't get its paperwork done on time at the first race. Later, it was revealed that McLaren would also be at the appeal hearing in Paris on 14 April.

■ Incredibly, the Malaysian GP was only the fifth time in F1 history that half points had been awarded for a race that had to be stopped prematurely. The previous examples were the Spanish and Austrian GPs in 1975, Monaco in 1984 and Australia in 1991. The last named still holds the record as the shortest grand prix ever, having been abandoned after just 14 laps, with McLaren's Ayrton Senna declared the winner.

■ The Grand Prix Drivers' Association further strengthened its numbers when Felipe Massa decided to rejoin, while Adrian Sutil and newcomer Sebastien Bourdais were also added to the membership after lobbying by Pedro de la Rosa and Mark Webber. The only leading driver to remain outside the group was Kimi Räikkönen.

■ After the Malaysian GP weekend, Renault made a considerable PR effort in Dubai with a series of demonstration runs featuring a pair of R28s, including a blast up a motorway. Alas, things went a little awry when rally star and occasional FIA F1 Steward Mohammed bin Sulayem had a massive accident when he lost control in a drag race against a Ford GT at the Dubai circuit.

RACE RESULTS
MALAYSIA
SEPANG

Official Results © [2009]
Formula One Administration Limited,
6 Princes Gate, London, SW7 1QJ.
No reproduction without permission.
All copyright and database rights reserved.

RACE DATE April 5th
CIRCUIT LENGTH 3.444 miles
NO. OF LAPS 31
RACE DISTANCE 106.777 miles
WEATHER Overcast then rain, 31°C
TRACK TEMP 37°C
ATTENDANCE 194,736
LAP RECORD Juan Pablo Montoya, 1m34.223s, 131.995mph, 2004

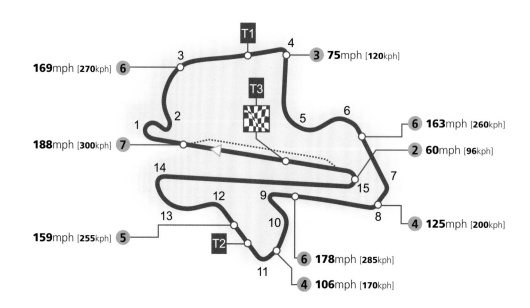

169mph [270kph] 6
3 75mph [120kph]
T1
T3
6 163mph [260kph]
188mph [300kph] 7
2 60mph [96kph]
7
15
4 125mph [200kph]
159mph [255kph] 5
8
T2
6 178mph [285kph]
4 106mph [170kph]

	PRACTICE 1				PRACTICE 2				PRACTICE 3				QUALIFYING 1			QUALIFYING 2	
	Driver	Time	Laps		Driver	Time	Laps		Driver	Time	Laps		Driver	Time		Driver	Time
1	N Rosberg	1m36.260s	27	1	K Räikkönen	1m35.707s	40	1	N Rosberg	1m35.940s	19	1	R Barrichello	1m34.681s	1	J Button	1m33.784s
2	K Nakajima	1m36.305s	25	2	F Massa	1m35.832s	38	2	M Webber	1m36.048s	13	2	J Trulli	1m34.745s	2	J Trulli	1m33.990s
3	J Button	1m36.430s	20	3	S Vettel	1m35.954s	40	3	F Massa	1m36.089s	13	3	T Glock	1m34.907s	3	M Webber	1m34.222s
4	R Barrichello	1m36.487s	22	4	N Rosberg	1m36.015s	39	4	J Trulli	1m36.132s	21	4	S Vettel	1m34.935s	4	T Glock	1m34.258s
5	F Massa	1m36.561s	21	5	M Webber	1m36.026s	36	5	T Glock	1m36.189s	22	5	H Kovalainen	1m35.023s	5	S Vettel	1m34.276s
6	K Räikkönen	1m36.646s	18	6	R Barrichello	1m36.161s	37	6	S Vettel	1m36.194s	14	6	M Webber	1m35.027s	6	R Barrichello	1m34.387s
7	L Hamilton	1m36.699s	16	7	J Button	1m36.254s	31	7	K Räikkönen	1m36.322s	14	7	J Button	1m35.058s	7	K Räikkönen	1m34.456s
8	M Webber	1m36.703s	23	8	K Nakajima	1m36.290s	35	8	K Nakajima	1m36.325s	18	8	N Rosberg	1m35.083s	8	N Rosberg	1m34.547s
9	S Vettel	1m36.747s	25	9	H Kovalainen	1m36.397s	40	9	R Barrichello	1m36.519s	19	9	N Heidfeld	1m35.110s	9	R Kubica	1m34.562s
10	T Glock	1m36.980s	27	10	N Piquet Jr	1m36.401s	35	10	J Button	1m36.541s	17	10	R Kubica	1m35.166s	10	F Alonso	1m34.706s
11	J Trulli	1m36.982s	26	11	L Hamilton	1m36.515s	30	11	R Kubica	1m36.563s	18	11	F Alonso	1m35.260s	11	N Heidfeld	1m34.769s
12	G Fisichella	1m37.025s	20	12	J Trulli	1m36.516s	34	12	L Hamilton	1m36.657s	15	12	L Hamilton	1m35.280s	12	K Nakajima	1m34.788s
13	R Kubica	1m37.039s	18	13	S Buemi	1m36.628s	32	13	H Kovalainen	1m36.742s	13	13	K Nakajima	1m35.341s	13	L Hamilton	1m34.905s
14	N Piquet Jr	1m37.199s	20	14	T Glock	1m36.639s	29	14	F Alonso	1m37.004s	16	14	K Räikkönen	1m35.476s	14	H Kovalainen	1m34.924s
15	A Sutil	1m37.241s	18	15	F Alonso	1m36.640s	20	15	N Heidfeld	1m37.026s	18	15	S Bourdais	1m35.507s	15	S Bourdais	1m35.431s
16	F Alonso	1m37.395s	12	16	A Sutil	1m36.875s	36	16	N Piquet Jr	1m37.032s	18	16	F Massa	1m35.642s			
17	S Buemi	1m37.634s	22	17	R Kubica	1m37.267s	38	17	A Sutil	1m37.118s	18	17	N Piquet Jr	1m35.708s			
18	N Heidfeld	1m37.640s	17	18	S Bourdais	1m37.278s	30	18	S Buemi	1m37.282s	17	18	G Fisichella	1m35.908s			
19	S Bourdais	1m38.022s	19	19	G Fisichella	1m37.432s	27	19	S Bourdais	1m37.322s	16	19	A Sutil	1m35.951s			
20	H Kovalainen	1m38.483s	7	20	N Heidfeld	1m37.930s	37	20	G Fisichella	1m37.398s	19	20	S Buemi	1m36.107s			

Best sectors – Practice			Speed trap – Practice			Best sectors – Qualifying			Speed trap – Qualifying		
Sec 1	L Hamilton	24.757s	1	N Piquet Jr	191.382mph	Sec 1	F Alonso	24.470s	1	N Heidfeld	189.456mph
Sec 2	N Rosberg	31.681s	2	S Vettel	188.834mph	Sec 2	J Trulli	31.079s	2	F Alonso	188.896mph
Sec 3	K Räikkönen	38.919s	3	A Sutil	188.524mph	Sec 3	J Button	38.108s	3	N Piquet Jr	188.772mph

IN 2008

Ferrari bounced back from its disappointing visit to Melbourne, as Kimi Räikkönen notched up a dominant win, although Felipe Massa made a mess of things as he tried to fight back after being forced wide at Turn 2. Robert Kubica gave BMW Sauber its second second place of the year, with Heikki Kovalainen third for McLaren.

Lewis Hamilton
"It was impossible to drive in the rain. These were the most dangerous conditions I've ever faced. It was correct to stop it: I love it when it rains, but this was too much."

Felipe Massa
"It was chaotic: we fitted rain tyres, then I came back for intermediates and immediately after that the downpour arrived. It's a shame, as I could have scored."

Robert Kubica
"My engine made strange noises on the formation lap and there was little power. I started the race and asked what to do, but before I got an answer the car caught fire."

Fernando Alonso
"I made a good start from P9 to P3, then had to defend as I was slow. It was hard to decide what tyre to take at our stop, as we didn't know how heavy the rain would be."

Jarno Trulli
"I was fighting with Rosberg for the lead. Then the rain came and we went for full wets. Being quickest car on full wets wasn't enough as they went off after two laps."

Heikki Kovalainen
"My start was alright. I was taking it quite carefully and was trying to slot in behind Lewis, then I just lost the rear [at Turn 5] and spun out. It was my mistake. Game over."

Kimi Räikkönen
"I was in a good position at the first stop. Then we made a mistake, fitting the rain tyres when the rain had yet to fall. And that was where my race was pretty much over."

Nick Heidfeld
"I pitted early and went for rain tyres. They wore quickly, but the team told me to stay out, but the tyres felt like slicks. Intermediates would have been much quicker."

Nelson Piquet Jr
"Just before the red flag, it was impossible to drive. We tried to call the right decision at the right time and there's nothing more we could have done in these conditions."

Timo Glock
"I struggled, then made the right call for intermediates. When the heavy rain came, I had to go to full wets and was running second when the red flags came out."

Pos	Driver
1	J Button
2	J Trulli
3	T Glock
4	N Rosberg
5	M Webber
6	R Kubica
7	K Räikkönen
8	R Barrichello
9	F Alonso
10	N Heidfeld
11	K Nakajima
12	L Hamilton
13	S Vettel
14	H Kovalainen
15	S Bourdais
16	F Massa
17	N Piquet Jr
18	G Fisichella
19	A Sutil
20	S Buemi

☆ Accident Ⓜ Mechanical failure Ⓟ Pit stop ☐ Safety Car ☐ Lapped ▢ Race Stopped Ⓑ Black flag

QUALIFYING 3

	Driver	Time
1	J Button	1m35.181s
2	J Trulli	1m35.273s
3	S Vettel	1m35.518s
4	R Barrichello	1m35.651s
5	T Glock	1m35.690s
6	N Rosberg	1m35.750s
7	M Webber	1m35.797s
8	R Kubica	1m36.106s
9	K Räikkönen	1m36.170s
10	F Alonso	1m37.659s

GRID

	Driver	Time
1	J Button	1m35.181s
2	J Trulli	1m35.273s
3	T Glock	1m35.690s
4	N Rosberg	1m35.750s
5	M Webber	1m35.797s
6	R Kubica	1m36.106s
7	K Räikkönen	1m36.170s
8*	R Barrichello	1m35.651s
9	F Alonso	1m37.659s
10	N Heidfeld	1m34.769s
11	K Nakajima	1m34.788s
12	L Hamilton	1m34.905s
13^	S Vettel	1m35.518s
14	H Kovalainen	1m34.924s
15	S Bourdais	1m35.431s
16	F Massa	1m35.642s
17	N Piquet Jr	1m35.708s
18	G Fisichella	1m35.908s
19	A Sutil	1m35.951s
20	S Buemi	1m36.107s

* Five-place grid penalty for gearbox change
^10-place grid penalty for causing an accident in Australian GP

RACE

	Driver	Car	Laps	Time	Avg. mph	Fastest	Stops
1	J Button	Brawn-Mercedes BGP 001	31	55m30.622s	115.407	1m36.461s	3
2	N Heidfeld	*BMW Sauber F1.09	31	55m53.344s	114.625	1m39.084s	1
3	T Glock	Toyota TF109	31	55m54.135s	114.598	1m39.406s	3
4	J Trulli	Toyota TF109	31	56m16.795s	113.829	1m37.591s	3
5	R Barrichello	Brawn-Mercedes BGP 001	31	56m17.982s	113.789	1m37.484s	3
6	M Webber	Red Bull-Renault RB5	31	56m22.955s	113.622	1m37.672s	4
7	L Hamilton	*McLaren-Mercedes MP4-24	31	56m31.355s	113.340	1m39.141s	3
8	N Rosberg	Williams-Toyota FW31	31	56m42.198s	112.979	1m37.598s	4
9	F Massa	*Ferrari F60	31	56m47.554s	112.802	1m39.250s	3
10	S Bourdais	Toro Rosso-Ferrari STR4	31	57m12.786s	111.973	1m39.242s	3
11	F Alonso	*Renault R29	31	57m20.044s	111.736	1m39.006s	3
12	K Nakajima	Williams-Toyota FW31	31	57m26.752s	111.519	1m39.387s	3
13	N Piquet Jr	*Renault R29	31	57m27.335s	111.500	1m39.268s	3
14	K Räikkönen	*Ferrari F60	31	57m53.463s	110.661	1m38.453s	3
15	S Vettel	Red Bull-Renault RB5	30	Spun off	-	1m38.427s	3
16	S Buemi	Toro Rosso-Ferrari STR4	30	Spun off	-	1m38.938s	2
17	A Sutil	Force India-Mercedes VJM02	30	55m58.426s	110.760	1m39.464s	2
18	G Fisichella	Force India-Mercedes VJM02	29	Spun off	-	1m39.407s	1
19	R Kubica	BMW Sauber F1.09	1	Engine	-	-	0
20	H Kovalainen	*McLaren-Mercedes MP4-24	0	Spun off	-	-	0

* Denotes car fitted with KERS

CHAMPIONSHIP

	Driver	Pts
1	J Button	15
2	R Barrichello	10
3	J Trulli	8.5
4	T Glock	8
5	N Heidfeld	4
6	F Alonso	4
7	N Rosberg	3.5
8	S Buemi	2
9	M Webber	1.5
10	L Hamilton	1
11	S Bourdais	1

Fastest lap
J Button 1m36.461s
(128.303mph) on lap 18

Fastest speed trap
A Sutil 190.636mph
Slowest speed trap
R Kubica 157.766mph

Fastest pit stop
1	J Trulli	24.458s
2	M Webber	24.550s
3	L Hamilton	25.236s

	Constructor	Pts
1	Brawn-Mercedes	25
2	Toyota	16.5
3	BMW Sauber	4
4	Renault	4
5	Williams-Toyota	3.5
6	Toro Rosso-Ferrari	3
7	Red Bull-Renault	1.5
8	McLaren-Mercedes	1

Sebastien Bourdais
"We were low on fuel so were hoping for rain. It didn't come, but we gambled on wets then changed to inters before it did arrive and I had to pit for wets."

Mark Webber
"The guys made the best call to stop the race. It would have been nice to have had some more laps to give us a crack at the podium, so I've got mixed emotions."

Nico Rosberg
"I took the lead and it's a while since Williams have been in front on pure performance. I opened out a gap, then the rain came and the situation just didn't go our way."

Adrian Sutil
"When the rain came it was nearly impossible to drive. We were in first gear at 20kph, sliding around. It was unbelievable, so it was a good decision to stop the race."

Jenson Button
"I went deep into Turn 1 and got snap oversteer which dropped me to fourth, but I passed Alonso at the end of the lap and then Trulli and Rosberg at the first pit stops."

Sebastien Buemi
"I was P8 and was due to pit the next lap, but I went off at Turn 5 as my extreme tyres were gone. I slowed, but not enough, so I spun, went into the gravel and stalled."

Sebastian Vettel
"I was on the inters and they were worn as it wasn't very wet before the downpour. I was going into Turn 7 and there was suddenly lots of water. I could do nothing."

Kazuki Nakajima
"I had wheelspin off the line and dropped a few places to the KERS cars, and ended up behind Piquet. This affected my plan as I dropped quite a lot of time behind him."

Giancarlo Fisichella
"I came in too early for wets and did four laps that destroyed the tyres. Then it was raining and the grip was getting better and better, but the tyres were almost slicks."

Rubens Barrichello
"After a good start, I felt that I had the pace to catch the front-runners. But, once the conditions deteriorated, I lost just a little too much time with my pit stops."

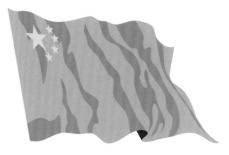

2009 FORMULA 1
CHINESE GRAND PRIX
SHANGHAI

RED BULL STRIKES

Just as he had for Scuderia Toro Rosso at Monza in 2008, Sebastian Vettel put on a masterclass of driving in the wet, this time giving Red Bull Racing its maiden victory

Just three races into his career with Red Bull Racing, Sebastian Vettel scored a brilliant victory in a rain-affected Chinese GP in Shanghai. It was the young German's second success in a wet race, after his win for Scuderia Toro Rosso in Italy some seven months earlier, but it was the first for RBR, at its 74th attempt.

Meanwhile, third place was enough to allow Jenson Button to consolidate his championship lead, on a day when Red Bull Racing's dark blue cars clearly had an advantage in the tricky conditions.

An exciting dry qualifying session saw the top five cars cross the line almost together in the closing seconds. For the first time in 2009, Brawn was edged out of the limelight as Mark Webber seemed to put his RB5 on pole, only for team-mate Vettel to steal it away again moments later. To everyone's surprise, the blue cars were split by Fernando Alonso, who slipped his Renault into second, helped by a very light fuel load.

The Red Bull RB5s had an Achilles' heel, however, as both drivers suffered driveshaft-related problems that restricted their running, and which gave the team some cause for concern for race day.

Alonso's performance came after a busy weekend for the Renault's mechanics. The Spaniard was not

ABOVE The race started behind the safety car because of standing water. This is the midfield group of Sebastien Buemi, Nick Heidfeld, Heikki Kovalainen and Felipe Massa

OPPOSITE TOP These fans are already saving up for a seat in a covered grandstand for 2010...

OPPOSITE BOTTOM Rubens Barrichello leads Jenson Button in the early laps, but the English driver was ahead by the finish, in third

running KERS, so the system had to be removed, and then on Friday night his car was fitted with the team's prototype double diffuser. He had problems on Saturday morning and did very few laps, but had clearly found some speed. The Brawns were restricted to fourth and fifth, with Rubens Barrichello just edging out Button. However, the white cars had been carrying a significantly heavier fuel load than those ahead.

Like Renault, Ferrari also temporarily abandoned KERS, mainly for reliability reasons. Kimi Räikkönen was eighth, while Felipe Massa made a mistake in Q2, and was down in 13th. Meanwhile, McLaren had a new diffuser and front wing on Lewis Hamilton's car, and there were some signs of progress as he qualified ninth.

After two dry days, rain began to fall at Sunday lunchtime, and the race thus started behind the safety car. That eradicated much of the advantage of anyone with an ultra-light fuel load and, as the laps behind the safety car began to mount, Renault and Alonso blinked first and came in for more fuel at just the wrong time.

It was a disastrous decision, although obviously the team wasn't to know that the FIA would call the safety car in within seconds of Alonso heading down the pitlane. Had he remained out for just a few

laps at the front before pitting, he would have been considerably better off.

There's an established theory that in the wet it's good to start with a heavy fuel load and give yourself maximum flexibility on strategy. However, as Vettel proved at Monza in 2008, there is no substitute for using a lighter load to help you start at the front, as long as you can clear off into the distance. Once again Vettel was handed an ideal situation, but he had to make the most of it. And, while there are advantages to being in front and not being in anyone's spray, you don't have anyone else's wheel tracks to drive in either, and you're the first one to have to judge conditions that can change with every lap.

When the race finally went green after eight laps, Vettel had just seven flying laps in which to make the most of his strategy before he needed fuel. He remained 3s clear of Webber, who pitted on lap 14 (despite running with slightly more fuel in qualifying). When Vettel came in a lap later, he'd extended his advantage on Button to 13s, and on a brake-troubled Barrichello to 23s. In just seven flying laps...

He dropped only to third, behind the Brawns. A few laps later, the safety car came out again after

INSIDE LINE
SEBASTIAN VETTEL
RED BULL RACING DRIVER

"To get pole and take the first win for Red Bull, having done it for Toro Rosso at Monza last year, feels special!

Pole position was really satisfying, as we had some driveshaft problems and I only had one run in Q1 on the hard tyre, then one run at the end of Q2 on the soft and also only one run in Q3. We were very concerned about reliability, but when you only have one lap, there's no second chance so it was really a bit unbelievable that we made pole.

I think it was the right decision to start the race under the safety car. It was OK at some points, but at certain corners you were aquaplaning. It was very, very difficult throughout the whole race.

Mark and I both were both on the short strategy, so when the safety car went in we had to push to get away from the pack, but it was tricky. Sometimes you were only just catching the car and keeping it on the circuit.

I had the best of the conditions, as I had no cars running in front of me for almost the whole race, but still it was really difficult with the aquaplaning, especially in the last corner. It goes a bit uphill on the way in and the water goes down and so there are some places where you have no control, so you just try not to downshift or brake too much there.

It was great that we were able to fix the reliability issues overnight. That speaks for the quality of the team. My worst moment was when Buemi hit me. I thought Rubens was in front of me, took care, moved to pass him and didn't see that Buemi was coming. I didn't want to run into the car in front of me. Obviously, it was impossible to see anything in the mirrors as there was so much spray, so I moved to the right, checked and then I realised it was a Toyota ahead and not Rubens. By then, Buemi had hit me. It was a shame for his race and I was very lucky to finish mine!

About 10 laps from the end, I tried to observe the gap to the car behind, Mark's, and was trying to adapt to his pace, trying to have everything in control. I realised I mustn't lose focus, so started to think corner by corner and not look too far ahead.

I'm delighted for the whole team and hope we can continue working in this direction."

Robert Kubica hit Jarno Trulli and scattered debris on the track. Button and Barrichello were able to dive into the pits and refuel without problem, while Vettel regained his lead. After that, Vettel drove a perfect race, regularly setting fastest laps.

Clearly, the RB5 package was working to perfection in the wet. Button gave an insight into just how good it looked from where he was sitting: "In the dry, I think we would have been a lot more competitive. But in the wet, we don't have Red Bull's pace. You can see it in high-speed corners. When I was behind them – not for long because they soon disappeared – they can keep a really tight line.

"We turn in and end up on the outside of the corner. It feels that we're not going through the water, but just floating across it. That's something that we need to look at. Maybe we're just running the cars too low at the front, but it's costing us quite a bit of time."

This was one of those rare races where the cars ran throughout on extreme wets (everyone except Nico Rosberg, who went for slicks near the end), and on every lap there were multiple chances for things to go wrong. The race ran for just under two hours, and as several drivers showed – and Vettel himself

demonstrated in Fuji in 2007 when he hit Webber – even those laps behind the safety car required utmost concentration. But fortune was smiling on him, not least when he survived an assault from Toro Rosso's Sebastien Buemi without incurring any harm.

"It was a very difficult race, a very long race," said Vettel. "We did 56 laps but, in terms of time, I don't know how long it took to complete these laps. It was extremely difficult, as there was some standing water, some rivers, even some lakes. Cars were going off, the team was telling me by radio 'be careful, be careful'. So I had all the time a warning.

"I had a lot of moments with aquaplaning where the car just started to slide. Fortunately with all these moments I got control of the car back.

"Ten laps to go I thought 'OK, I have a big gap, so it should be no problem,' but then I tried to forget and focus on every single corner, because there was so much water on the circuit. It was extremely difficult. I was continuing to push. I could see the gaps to the guys behind, and at the end I'm very, very happy to have won of course."

Vettel was asked if he could compare himself with that other regenmeister, Michael Schumacher, replying: "I think he was outstanding, no matter if it was wet or dry. Comparing anyone to Michael is a bit over the top. I think I keep my feet on the ground. I like driving in the wet. Both times now I've won the grand prix when it was wet, so let's see..."

It was a pretty good effort too from Webber. Not many people fully appreciated how competitive he was in Malaysia in the rain. Had the red flag arrived a couple of laps later, he could very well have finished second. And, had there been a restart, he would have had at least some chance of overhauling Button.

In China, Webber's chance of staying on terms with Vettel was spoiled when Button got ahead during the safety-car sequence, so the Australian was stuck

TALKING POINT
DID RON PAY THE PRICE?

Dominating paddock gossip in Shanghai was the question of whether Ron Dennis had fallen on his sword to ensure that McLaren did not face draconian penalties when the FIA World Motor Sport Council met to consider 'Liargate' on 29 April.

The subject of diffusers had even made CNN news in the aftermath of the World Motor Sport Council passing them legal before the paddock decamped to Shanghai, but it was Dennis 'stepping away' from F1 after 43 years that caught the attention.

Given its recent history with the governing body, and the 2007 'spygate' saga in particular, McLaren had serious concerns ahead of the hearing. Their sponsors and partners had not deserted them, but those who know about these things hinted that 'disrepute' get-out clauses would have been inserted into contracts since then. On top of that, we were now in the middle of a worldwide recession and the team was hardly covering itself in glory on the circuit. The fear was that if there was any kind of suspension, ban or disrepute charge, the implications for the team could be catastrophic.

Dennis, often engaging, but sometimes condescending and aloof, tends to polarise opinion, but there can be no doubting his passion for F1 nor his achievements, culminating in the team's Norman Foster-designed McLaren Technology Centre HQ. There are many who feel that Dennis, already a CBE, is thoroughly deserving of a knighthood, but that the chances of it happening may have been terminally damaged by the public besmirching of McLaren and the $100m fine in 2007.

Dennis's successor at the helm of McLaren Racing, Martin Whitmarsh, readily conceded in China: "It would be healthier for all of us at McLaren to have a more positive, constructive relationship with the FIA." Whitmarsh added that, like everyone, he has his own personal faults, but doesn't hold grudges quite as long as Dennis.

The fall-out from 'Liargate' had been considerable. The Hamiltons had been so upset by the headlines that they had allegedly spoken to Max Mosley and his aides about the possibility of quitting the sport. Nobody believed that likely, but emotions ran high. No matter how the picture was painted, it can't have been coincidence that Dennis was hosting a group of automotive journalists to tell them of his changing priorities within the group – even if he was indeed enthusiastic about that new direction.

There was no dispelling the facts. Dennis is the most successful team boss in the history of F1. During his tenure, McLaren has won 138 grands prix, stretching back to John Watson's popular success in the British GP at Silverstone in 1981. His demise in these circumstances left as bad a taste as had Dave Ryan's fate in Malaysia.

ABOVE Drenched but happy, the Red Bull Racing crew celebrate the team's first victory as Sebastian Vettel splashes across the line

BELOW Sebastian Vettel bathes in the glory on the podium, flanked by Mark Webber and Jenson Button

behind him at the restart. By the time he got through, Vettel was 10s up the road. At the flag 24 laps later, the gap was still 10s, although obviously the German had paced himself.

"They were challenging conditions," said Webber. "Sebastian had a nice clear run at it, but he drove a very good race. Second was the next best thing I could do. He drove a fantastic race, and we were pushing each other at times. It's never easy in the rain to try and close the gap, and after the safety car Jenson was ahead (of me). That was a great opportunity for Sebastian to escape.

"But for Red Bull today it's absolutely incredible.

We had driveshaft problems coming into the race, and yet Red Bull was unbeatable today and we scored a 1–2. Sebastian and I hit each other in these conditions a few years ago and got no results. Today there were also Red Bulls hitting each other a little bit. We've still got work to do in the dry. Jarno was very fast in qualifying yesterday, as were the Brawns, so we have work to do."

As the race progressed, Button couldn't match the pace of the Red Bulls, but was happy to keep his title lead by coming home third, ahead of Barrichello. A single-stop strategy helped the McLaren drivers, as Heikki Kovalainen came home fifth ahead of team-mate Hamilton who had several off-track excursions. Timo Glock (handicapped five grid places by a gearbox change) and Sebastien Buemi completed the points scorers. The Toyota driver survived contact with Nick Heidfeld while, as noted, the Scuderia Toro Rosso man hit Vettel under the safety car, fortunately without consequences for either.

Unluckiest driver of the day was Adrian Sutil, who was doing a great job in sixth place before he crashed out a few laps from home. We never found out whether he needed a splash-and-dash for fuel, but it was going to be close.

It was another bad day for Ferrari, as Massa retired from a strong early position with a throttle problem, having chosen a one-stop strategy that could have earned him decent points. Räikkönen failed to score after another difficult race, while both BMW Sauber and Renault also failed to score.

Looking at the points situation, Vettel was left to ponder what might have happened had he not got involved with Kubica in Australia. He would have been at least third there, and gone to Malaysia without a 10-place penalty – where he had a very good chance of being on the podium with or without the rain. The collision had proved even more expensive than it appeared at the time...

SNAPSHOT FROM
CHINA

Lewis Hamilton swings onto the start/finish straight, but clearly not in race conditions; second place in Malaysia clearly boosted Nick Heidfeld's popularity; a splash of colour; Kimi Räikkönen had his own fans too; Nelson Piquet Jr points out his lap time to Renault F1 boss Flavio Briatore; matching nail colour and waterproof, now that's attention to detail at an F1 level; "You get in there, and I'll tell you how to drive"

WEEKEND NEWS

■ Just over a week before the Chinese GP, an FIA Court of Appeal hearing in Paris upheld the decision of the stewards of the Australian GP regarding double diffusers, much to the frustration of the teams that had protested against them. Inevitably, the outcome kickstarted a rush by the seven teams that didn't have them to be ready with their own versions.

■ The Chinese GP was far from the first time in recent years that a team has scored its maiden win in the wet, and with both cars to the fore. It happened with Jordan at Spa in 1998 (a 1–2), with Red Bull Racing's forerunner, Stewart, at the Nürburgring in 1999 (1–3), with BAR at Hungary in 2006 (1–4), and of course with Toro Rosso at Monza last year, when Sebastien Bourdais would have been close to winner Vettel had he not been left behind on the formation lap.

■ Red Bull Racing's concerns over driveshaft boot failures were resolved by borrowing spares from Scuderia Toro Rosso. Under parc fermé rules, teams can only replace damaged or suspect parts with identical ones, but team boss Christian Horner insisted that was the case, and that they'd come out of the same mould. Not so long ago, the two teams used to tell us that everything was different in order to take the heat off the customer-car controversy...

■ While the F1 media regulars were away in China, Ron Dennis chose a press conference about the new McLaren Automotive division to announce that he would henceforth be cutting his formal ties with the race team. He had already outlined a gradual step back at the MP4-24 launch in January. Most observers surmised that his latest move was not unconnected with the post-Melbourne controversy.

■ Ferrari confirmed that Luca Baldiserri – the race engineering guru who doubled up as team manager – had been switched to a factory-based role. The news came in the light of a poor start to the season for the Italian team, and in particular some bad decisions over the weekend of the Malaysian GP. Baldiserri's new job was to co-ordinate track and factory activities.

RACE RESULTS
CHINA SHANGHAI

RACE DATE April 19th
CIRCUIT LENGTH 3.390 miles
NO. OF LAPS 56
RACE DISTANCE 189.680 miles
WEATHER Heavy rain, easing off, 20°C
TRACK TEMP 22°C
ATTENDANCE 120,000
LAP RECORD Michael Schumacher,
1m32.238s, 132.202mph, 2004

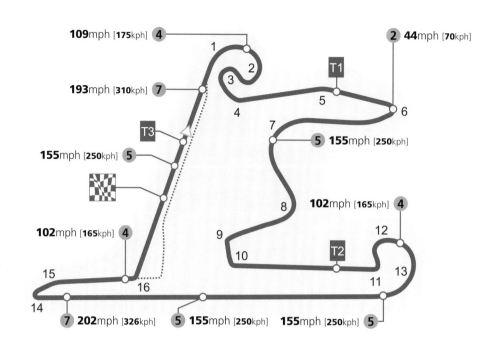

PRACTICE 1				PRACTICE 2				PRACTICE 3				QUALIFYING 1			QUALIFYING 2	
	Driver	Time	Laps		Driver	Time	Laps		Driver	Time	Laps		Driver	Time		Driver	Time
1	L Hamilton	1m37.334s	22	1	J Button	1m35.679s	35	1	N Rosberg	1m36.133s	17	1	J Button	1m35.533s	1	S Vettel	1m35.130s
2	J Button	1m37.450s	18	2	N Rosberg	1m35.704s	36	2	J Trulli	1m36.272s	22	2	R Barrichello	1m35.701s	2	M Webber	1m35.173s
3	R Barrichello	1m37.566s	19	3	R Barrichello	1m35.881s	35	3	L Hamilton	1m36.330s	17	3	M Webber	1m35.751s	3	R Barrichello	1m35.503s
4	H Kovalainen	1m37.672s	23	4	M Webber	1m36.105s	32	4	J Button	1m36.463s	16	4	L Hamilton	1m35.776s	4	J Button	1m35.556s
5	M Webber	1m37.752s	20	5	S Vettel	1m36.167s	22	5	N Piquet Jr	1m36.464s	16	5	N Rosberg	1m35.941s	5	J Trulli	1m35.645s
6	J Trulli	1m37.764s	19	6	J Trulli	1m36.217s	42	6	F Massa	1m36.528s	18	6	K Räikkönen	1m36.137s	6	L Hamilton	1m35.740s
7	N Rosberg	1m37.860s	24	7	K Nakajima	1m36.377s	32	7	H Kovalainen	1m36.547s	13	7	F Massa	1m36.178s	7	F Alonso	1m35.803s
8	T Glock	1m37.894s	21	8	T Glock	1m36.548s	40	8	K Nakajima	1m36.560s	17	8	S Buemi	1m36.284s	8	N Rosberg	1m35.809s
9	F Alonso	1m38.089s	19	9	H Kovalainen	1m36.674s	34	9	K Räikkönen	1m36.568s	17	9	J Trulli	1m36.308s	9	K Räikkönen	1m35.856s
10	S Bourdais	1m38.195s	24	10	S Bourdais	1m36.800s	34	10	R Barrichello	1m36.642s	17	10	T Glock	1m36.364s	10	S Buemi	1m35.965s
11	K Räikkönen	1m38.223s	23	11	A Sutil	1m36.829s	30	11	N Heidfeld	1m36.702s	14	11	F Alonso	1m36.443s	11	N Heidfeld	1m35.975s
12	S Vettel	1m38.274s	20	12	F Massa	1m36.847s	34	12	R Kubica	1m36.742s	14	12	N Heidfeld	1m36.525s	12	H Kovalainen	1m36.032s
13	S Buemi	1m38.307s	26	13	L Hamilton	1m36.941s	28	13	S Buemi	1m36.742s	16	13	S Vettel	1m36.565s	13	F Massa	1m36.033s
14	A Sutil	1m38.319s	18	14	K Räikkönen	1m37.054s	33	14	S Bourdais	1m36.834s	17	14	H Kovalainen	1m36.646s	14	T Glock	1m36.066s
15	F Massa	1m38.418s	20	15	S Buemi	1m37.219s	34	15	M Webber	1m37.330s	8	15	K Nakajima	1m36.673s	15	K Nakajima	1m36.193s
16	N Heidfeld	1m38.456s	21	16	N Piquet Jr	1m37.273s	36	16	S Vettel	1m37.349s	7	16	S Bourdais	1m36.906s			
17	G Fisichella	1m38.460s	19	17	R Kubica	1m37.491s	34	17	A Sutil	1m37.534s	17	17	N Piquet Jr	1m36.908s			
18	R Kubica	1m38.463s	18	18	N Heidfeld	1m37.544s	28	18	G Fisichella	1m37.732s	18	18	R Kubica	1m36.966s			
19	K Nakajima	1m38.730s	25	19	F Alonso	1m37.638s	28	19	F Alonso	1m38.003s	6	19	A Sutil	1m37.669s			
20	N Piquet Jr	1m38.825s	20	20	G Fisichella	1m37.750s	31	20	T Glock	1m39.110s	6	20	G Fisichella	1m37.672s			

Best sectors – Practice		Speed trap – Practice			Best sectors – Qualifying		Speed trap – Qualifying	
Sec 1 N Rosberg	25.156s	1	K Räikkönen	197.161mph	Sec 1 S Vettel	24.870s	1 S Buemi	191.506mph
Sec 2 J Trulli	28.300s	2	A Sutil	195.794mph	Sec 2 M Webber	28.123s	2 K Räikkönen	190.574mph
Sec 3 J Button	41.937s	3	F Massa	195.483mph	Sec 3 J Button	41.974s	3 G Fisichella	189.953mph

IN 2008					

IN 2008

Held as the last race but one in 2008, Shanghai's race was all about Lewis Hamilton as he homed in on his first world title by winning as he pleased. Kimi Räikkönen was next fastest, but let Ferrari team-mate Felipe Massa through to the second place he needed to keep his title hopes alive, leaving China seven points behind Hamilton.

 **Lewis Hamilton**

"It was almost too difficult to drive at the start, but I had some fun in the opening laps. Unfortunately I destroyed my tyres and made a few too many mistakes."

Felipe Massa

"I was third and lapping as fast as the leaders, even though I had enough fuel on board to go for a one-stop. Then, without warning, the accelerator wouldn't work."

Robert Kubica

"There were a lot of situations when I could see nothing, and this led to my accident with Trulli. When he braked I hit some standing water and then his rear tyre."

Fernando Alonso

"We thought the safety car would be out for 15 laps so we came in to get fuel, and at the same time the safety car came in, so we found ourselves starting the race last."

Jarno Trulli

"I made a solid start, but I started struggling for grip, and the longer it went on the more ground I lost. On lap 17, I felt a big hit from behind and lost my rear wing."

 Heikki Kovalainen

"The visibility was unbelievably poor, but our pace was good and, during the last laps of the race, I could get close to Rubens – just not enough to start an attack."

Kimi Räikkönen

"After my stop, I lost grip and was no longer able to push, as it meant the car slid a lot. A few times, the engine seemed to lose power, especially behind other cars."

Nick Heidfeld

"Glock hit me on lap 13, which damaged my car, but I still had the chance to score, but then I hit a wheel from Sutil's crash, with damage costing me four places."

Nelson Piquet Jr

"The conditions were so difficult. I had a few moments, but I managed to keep the car going, although I lost a lot of time and dropped to the back of the pack."

 Timo Glock

"I made up some ground, but damaged my front wing when I misjudged my braking point and hit Nick, forcing us to bring our stop forward by a few laps to fix it."

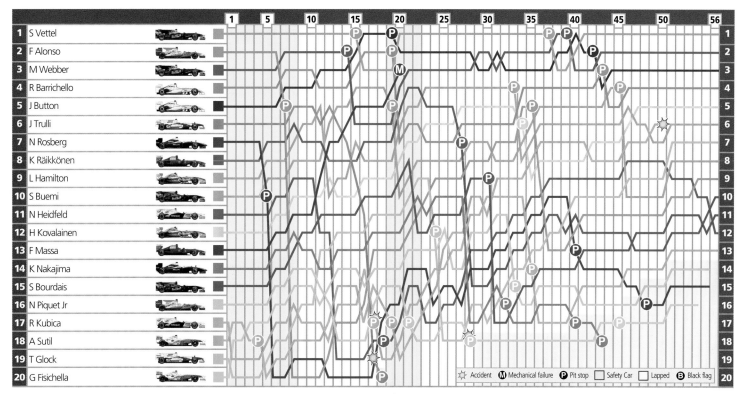

1	S Vettel	
2	F Alonso	
3	M Webber	
4	R Barrichello	
5	J Button	
6	J Trulli	
7	N Rosberg	
8	K Räikkönen	
9	L Hamilton	
10	S Buemi	
11	N Heidfeld	
12	H Kovalainen	
13	F Massa	
14	K Nakajima	
15	S Bourdais	
16	N Piquet Jr	
17	R Kubica	
18	A Sutil	
19	T Glock	
20	G Fisichella	

☆ Accident Ⓜ Mechanical failure Ⓟ Pit stop ☐ Safety Car ☐ Lapped Ⓑ Black flag

QUALIFYING 3

	Driver	Time
1	S Vettel	1m36.184s
2	F Alonso	1m36.381s
3	M Webber	1m36.466s
4	R Barrichello	1m36.493s
5	J Button	1m36.532s
6	J Trulli	1m36.835s
7	N Rosberg	1m37.397s
8	K Räikkönen	1m38.089s
9	L Hamilton	1m38.595s
10	S Buemi	1m39.321s

GRID

	Driver	Time
1	S Vettel	1m36.184s
2	F Alonso	1m36.381s
3	M Webber	1m36.466s
4	R Barrichello	1m36.493s
5	J Button	1m36.532s
6	J Trulli	1m36.835s
7	N Rosberg	1m37.397s
8	K Räikkönen	1m38.089s
9	L Hamilton	1m38.595s
10	S Buemi	1m39.321s
11	N Heidfeld	1m35.975s
12	H Kovalainen	1m36.032s
13	F Massa	1m36.033s
14*	T Glock	1m36.066s
15	K Nakajima	1m36.193s
16	S Bourdais	1m36.906s
17	N Piquet Jr	1m36.908s
18	R Kubica	1m36.966s
19	A Sutil	1m37.669s
20	G Fisichella	1m37.672s

* Started from pitlane after five-place grid penalty for gearbox change

RACE

	Driver	Car	Laps	Time	Avg. mph	Fastest	Stops
1	S Vettel	Red Bull-Renault RB5	56	1h57m43.485s	96.611	1m52.627s	2
2	M Webber	Red Bull-Renault RB5	56	1h57m54.455s	96.461	1m52.980s	2
3	J Button	Brawn-Mercedes BGP 001	56	1h58m28.460s	96.000	1m53.546s	2
4	R Barrichello	Brawn-Mercedes BGP 001	56	1h58m47.189s	95.748	1m52.592s	2
5	H Kovalainen	*McLaren-Mercedes MP4-24	56	1h58m48.587s	95.729	1m54.516s	1
6	L Hamilton	*McLaren-Mercedes MP4-24	56	1h58m55.351s	95.638	1m54.665s	1
7	T Glock	Toyota TF109	56	1h58m57.961s	95.603	1m52.703s	1
8	S Buemi	Toro Rosso-Ferrari STR4	56	1h58m59.924s	95.577	1m54.590s	2
9	F Alonso	Renault R29	56	1h59m07.794s	95.472	1m54.481s	2
10	K Räikkönen	Ferrari F60	56	1h59m15.235s	95.372	1m55.396s	1
11	S Bourdais	Toro Rosso-Ferrari STR4	56	1h59m17.641s	95.340	1m53.474s	1
12	N Heidfeld	*BMW Sauber F1.09	56	1h59m19.319s	95.318	1m54.158s	1
13	R Kubica	BMW Sauber F1.09	56	1h59m30.338s	95.171	1m55.350s	2
14	G Fisichella	Force India-Mercedes VJM02	55	1h58m08.816s	94.546	1m56.239s	1
15	N Rosberg	Williams-Toyota FW31	55	1h58m31.069s	94.249	1m54.243s	3
16	N Piquet Jr	Renault R29	54	1h58m16.406s	92.726	1m55.535s	3
17	A Sutil	Force India-Mercedes VJM02	50	Accident	-	1m54.777s	2
R	S Nakajima	Williams-Toyota FW31	43	Transmission	-	1m56.167s	2
R	F Massa	Ferrari F60	20	Electrics	-	1m56.484s	0
R	J Trulli	Toyota TF109	18	Collision damage	-	2m00.330s	0

* Denotes car fitted with KERS

CHAMPIONSHIP

	Driver	Pts
1	J Button	21
2	R Barrichello	15
3	S Vettel	10
4	T Glock	10
5	M Webber	9.5
6	J Trulli	8.5
7	N Heidfeld	4
8	F Alonso	4
9	H Kovalainen	4
10	L Hamilton	4
11	N Rosberg	3.5
12	S Buemi	3
13	S Bourdais	1

Fastest lap
R Barrichello 1m52.592s
(108.298mph) on lap 42

Fastest speed trap
F Alonso 183.491mph
Slowest speed trap
F Massa 174.046mph

Fastest pit stop
1 N Rosberg 25.038s
2 R Barrichello 25.105s
3 S Buemi 25.109s

	Constructor	Pts
1	Brawn-Mercedes	36
2	Red Bull-Renault	19.5
3	Toyota	18.5
4	McLaren-Mercedes	8
5	BMW Sauber	4
6	Renault	4
7	Toro Rosso-Ferrari	4
8	Williams-Toyota	3.5

Sebastien Bourdais
"I started 15th and finished 11th, even with two spins. I don't think we should have raced, as there was so much aquaplaning and I could have spun 15 or 20 times."

Mark Webber
"When Jenson repassed me, I was very keen to try to win, so I passed him around Turn 7, as I knew he wouldn't know I'd be there. It was one of the moves of my career."

Nico Rosberg
"Fifteen laps from the end, I switched to intermediates as I had to try something. For the first few laps, they were good, but more rain came and it was all over."

Adrian Sutil
"We took a risk with a very early stop and it was a long way to go with one set of tyres. It's hard to believe when you lose it and it's all over from such a great position."

Jenson Button
"The conditions were crazy with rivers of water all over the circuit that changed every lap. Webber and I had a good fight for a few laps but I couldn't stay with him."

Sebastien Buemi
"The incident with Vettel happened under safety-car conditions: I didn't see him and tried to swerve to the right, but it just wasn't enough to avoid him."

Sebastian Vettel
"Ten laps from the end, I tried to control the gap to the car behind, adapt my pace, but it was hard. Scoring my second win, my first for Red Bull, makes me so happy!"

Kazuki Nakajima
"I had a transmission problem so couldn't go on. There was a lot of standing water and it was hard to keep the car on the track, particularly on the exit of the last corner."

Giancarlo Fisichella
"My main problem was graining tyres. It was hard keeping the car on the ground and many times I had moments, but the strategy was good and we can be pleased."

Rubens Barrichello
"I had only three brake discs working for the first 19 laps which made it really difficult. Luckily the problem resolved itself when the brakes heated up at my first stop."

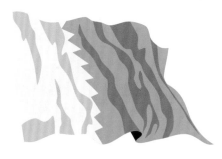

2009 FORMULA 1 GULF AIR BAHRAIN GRAND PRIX
SAKHIR

FOURTH TO FIRST

Jenson Button displayed a cool head as he fought his way past Hamilton, ran longer than the Toyotas and then controlled the race from the front. Sebastian Vettel was fast but frustrated

Jenson Button joked after winning at Sakhir: "It's the first time I've seen a chequered flag without a safety car or red lights in front of me. It was a great race and a very tough race, because we haven't had the pace that we expected. So, to get the win here is just amazing, and going back into Europe with 31 points on the board, a 12-point lead I think it is, I couldn't wish for any more."

Most observers were wishing for a straightforward, dry race in Bahrain to give us a better understanding of the true status quo among the teams, and we certainly got that. The battle at the front saw a game of chess between three teams, one that ultimately went Brawn and Button's way.

This was certainly a great drive from Button, not least because he won despite starting from fourth for the second race in succession – and that definitely wasn't where he was predicted to be. In the first couple of races, the Brawns were able to run significantly heavier than the opposition and still claim pole. This time life was much harder over one lap, possibly because the temperatures were costing the Mercedes engine a little power.

Meanwhile, Toyota's Jarno Trulli and Timo Glock

"Everyone was feeling the pressure a bit after such a difficult start to our season, with no points from the first three races. People were already starting to ask whether we were going to write off 2009 to concentrate on next year, but that's a luxury we don't have.

Scoring points here in Bahrain was the minimum step, but we should have done it with both of our cars. Kimi finishing sixth is a start, but when the race begins and you see your cars touch at the first corner, you do think 'Mamma Mia'! In terms of overall performance, though, the pace wasn't bad.

Luca di Montezemolo is solidly behind the team and I can only echo what he said, that you have difficult moments as well as success and that it's all part of competition. We have won eight World Championships in the past 10 years and there are three main reasons why we are in the middle of a black tunnel at the moment.

First, we have seen 'grey' rules. The second thing is KERS, introduced to have a link between F1 and advanced research for road cars. We did it immediately, even though it cost a lot and meant problems with safety and reliability. Finally, we started the new car late.

We will have a double-deck diffuser on the car in time for the Spanish GP, but I think it would be wrong to only focus under the car. Lewis Hamilton's pace in Bahrain was good even though he didn't have a double diffuser and the Red Bull is quick without one too.

Also, we have to give our drivers better performing, reliable cars and then I'm pretty sure we'll have all the elements to come back strongly. Before the start here, we had a telemetry problem with Felipe's car and were basically completely blind. Then the KERS wasn't running at the start for him. We need to understand that fully, but it was basically a temperature problem. On top of that, we had a flange issue that delayed Kimi's stop and prevented him possibly beating Barrichello to fifth place.

I'm sure we will have a better car and be more competitive in Spain, but the others will also have updates and we'll have to see what they do.

Nobody sleeps in F1 and so I don't want to say that Barcelona is our last chance saloon."

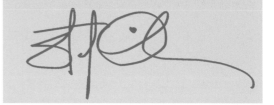

OPPOSITE TOP Timo Glock and Jarno Trulli congratulate each other after Toyota qualified first and second, but the race wasn't so kind

OPPOSITE BOTTOM Sebastien Bourdais had to work hard as he advanced from 20th to 13th

ABOVE Adrian Sutil's front wing goes flying after a clash with Kazuki Nakajima, as Mark Webber and Giancarlo Fisichella steer clear

ABOVE LEFT Jenson Button had to try several moves on Lewis Hamilton on lap 1 before getting past on lap 2

took a clean sweep of the front row. It was the Italian's first pole since the 'phantom' race at Indianapolis in 2005, when he qualified light knowing that all the Michelin runners were not going to take the start proper after problems earlier in the weekend.

Toyota had shown good form in the first three grands prix, but had not really been able to take full advantage of its position as one of the three pioneers of the double diffuser. Sebastian Vettel continued to show great form for Red Bull Racing, as he qualified third, just edging out Button, while Lewis Hamilton was the surprise package for McLaren, qualifying fifth with an aggressive fuel load. Rubens Barrichello would line up sixth in the other Brawn.

From fourth, Button knew he had to get away well. Not for the first time in 2009, he struggled. The Toyotas made their escape as Glock got ahead of Trulli, while Hamilton made a great start and ran third. However, he was passed by Button at the start of the second lap, which was a crucial move that would help secure victory for the Brawn driver.

However, Button didn't blame KERS for Hamilton's charge off the line: "The start was difficult as I had a lot of clutch slip and was lucky to get away as cleanly

as I did. In Turn 1, I knew I had to get past Vettel, and I had looked after my tyres on the way to the grid very well. Lewis was already past me before he hit the KERS button. And then really it was lining myself up for Turn 1. The outside was clear, so I headed there and braked late. I got around the outside of Sebastian. Then I was trying to fight my way past Lewis. I had a couple of goes at it, and eventually got him on the home straight into Turn 1."

There was good reason for the urgency. A fascinating aspect of KERS is that if you use it off the start line and for defence purposes later around the first lap, you will probably have nothing left for the regular blast out of the last corner. In other words, the end of the first lap is your most vulnerable time at that point on the circuit. You can't have another push until you cross the start/finish line, where you can use up some of your lap 2 boost. That's exactly what happened to Hamilton, and Button was savvy enough to be prepared to take advantage.

"In a way, I had to overtake him on the first lap," explained Button, "because on the first lap of the race the KERS cars use it off the startline. They have a little bit in reserve, about 3s, which he used on the back straight when I tried to pass him. Then I knew that he didn't have any more left. We got to the last corner, he ran wide, I got up the inside, was alongside him. But I knew as soon as I got to the startline he had a new KERS allowance, so he hit the button. He pulled past me, so I pulled in behind, and followed him down to Turn 1. Amazing speed that thing's got, when it's got KERS! The front of my car was lifting off the ground... Then I pulled to the inside and did him into Turn 1. A great move, and making that move stick was very important to me. That meant that I could chase down the Toyotas on a clear track. If I'd remained stuck behind Lewis, we would have struggled with temperatures."

It certainly was a great move, as not many people can get past Hamilton, even in a superior car. It's worth speculating that having used his boost at the start/finish line, Hamilton might have arrived at Turn 1 going a little faster than he had been used to all weekend and, in adjusting his braking to compensate, didn't quite get it right.

As Button noted, it was important that he didn't get stuck behind someone, so he could control the temperatures. Thus he wasn't too bothered about

sitting 3s back from Glock for the first 11 laps. The four extra laps of fuel he had over the German, and the three over leader Trulli, were crucial – as was Toyota's ultimately misguided decision to put both cars on the prime tyre, which cost them a lot of time over those critical laps. When Button came out after his lap-15 stop, he had comfortably jumped them.

"I thought they were going to do a three-stop race, because they were struggling, they said, with brake temperatures and brake wear on Friday and Saturday," said Button. "I thought maybe they were sticking [the prime] on to do a 12-lap run and then get back onto the option. That wasn't the case. That helped us enormously, as obviously Vettel was stuck behind Trulli. If Vettel had got past him, I don't know what the race outcome would have been, but I think our pace was very similar on both tyres.

"When I saw that Trulli was eight-tenths slower than me and Vettel was stuck behind, I just thought, 'Wow, this is what we need.' I pulled away 14–15s on Vettel, but even with that lead you're still wary, not sure exactly how the race is going to pan out."

Button made it look easy but, as he says, it certainly wasn't. Barrichello had a lighter fuel load

BELOW Fernando Alonso pressed hard all weekend and came away with a point for eighth for Renault

OPPOSITE Jarno Trulli holds off Sebastian Vettel and Lewis Hamilton for second on the opening lap

in qualifying and yet still could only convert that into a fifth place finish, having switched to a three-stop strategy and then got caught in the wrong place at the wrong time.

Button may have hogged the headlines, but Vettel showed that his first dry-weather victory couldn't be too far away, with another superb performance. Fuel-corrected, only Trulli was quicker in qualifying and, had Red Bull Racing been a little more aggressive, he could have started on the front row, in which case he could well have won. Even from third he was well placed to do so, as he was ahead of Button. But he blew it with a mediocre start.

"Going to Turn 1, Lewis was next to me and Jenson was on the outside," Vettel explained, "so I was caught in the middle and had to give way to both of them, which put me fifth. We lost quite a bit there. Unfortunately, I was not able to pass them immediately. Then you suffer a lot with your tyres and you get some degradation."

Thus, the German spent the first chunk of the race behind Hamilton. Matters weren't helped by Vettel's heavier fuel load, which eventually took him four laps further than the McLaren driver.

TALKING POINT
IS WEIGHT A SAFETY ISSUE?

At the end of the race in Sakhir, run in an ambient temperature approaching 40 degrees, Fernando Alonso attempted to do a TV interview and passed out.

Alonso's drinks pump had failed during the race and, told about it, Mark Webber nodded knowingly. For some time, Webber and Robert Kubica have lamented the difficulties faced by taller, heavier drivers under the current weighing system. The lighter you are, the more scope to play with ballast. The need for forward weight distribution with the current Bridgestone tyres has exacerbated the problem and KERS has multiplied it again.

Alonso is not quite jockey-sized, but does not carry an ounce of body fat and had managed to drop another couple of kilos to assist Renault with KERS.

The easiest way to lose weight is through body fluid, and fighters regularly drop 5% of body weight – the more extreme as much as 10% – to make a weigh-in. They then re-hydrate, and a 65kg fighter can be a full 7kg heavier when he steps into the ring. Rehydrating is vital because medical evidence says you are more likely to suffer brain injury in a dehydrated state.

One team's physical trainer said: "I'm not saying that's what's happening here, but asking someone to lose body fluid temporarily is very different from asking them to perform in a dehydrated state. The effect of that could be reduced endurance, loss of concentration and the more serious implications of a head blow. I would feel very uncomfortable with that combination if my client was a racing driver. Offering them an enticement to do it, is asking for it..."

And yet, F1's Technical Working Group rejected plans to neutralise weight disadvantages by subtracting the weight of the driver plus seat and helmet before minimum weight considerations. Predictably enough, Red Bull Racing and BMW had been keen on the change.

Williams Technical Director Sam Michael said: "I actually agree with them. It was rejected on the basis of a couple of teams saying that if a driver is heavier, he's stronger, so that's an advantage. I've heard Webber say that's bollocks and I've got to agree with him. The cars have power steering and you just can't say that the lightest driver on the grid isn't strong enough.

"We're not in that position at Williams right now, but we have been, as we've had both Mark [Webber] and Alex Wurz in our cars, and I do feel for what they're going through. It's not a level playing field."

"The more fuel you have, the more you ask of the tyres," said Vettel. "I had one good opportunity, but I ended up braking a little bit too late, locked up the rears in the last corner, and lost momentum to the main straight. So that was the closest I was. After that, the tyres started to go off, and I was unable to follow really closely. He did a good job, no mistakes."

In fact, Vettel dropped a couple of seconds back from Hamilton. He finally had a clear track ahead when Hamilton pitted on lap 15, but immediately after his own stop on lap 19, found himself behind Trulli. Since the Italian was struggling a little on the prime tyre, this time he stayed right with the Toyota, eventually getting past at the final round of stops.

Toyota had been leaning towards a three-stop strategy, which would have justified the low fuel loads at the start. However, last minute concerns over coming out in traffic caused the team to switch to a more common two-stop strategy, and as part of the change it was decided to use up the prime tyres in the second stint. It didn't work, and the team had to rue its choice afterwards.

Trulli was at least able to hold on to third place as Hamilton faded a little in the final stint when he had to use the harder tyre. Nevertheless, in fourth place Hamilton was only 22s behind the winner.

As noted earlier, Barrichello went for a three-stop strategy in an unsuccessful attempt to get out of traffic, and he lost time behind Nelson Piquet Jr's Renault. He was still able to secure fifth place as his strategy played out.

Watched by team boss Luca di Montezemolo, Kimi Räikkönen took sixth place for Ferrari's first points of the year, and even had the consolation of leading a few laps of the race by being the last frontrunner to make his first pit stop. He finished ahead of a frustrated Glock and Fernando Alonso, who were the final points scorers.

The Bahrain GP was another frustrating day for Felipe Massa, who damaged his Ferrari's nose in a first-lap squeeze between Barrichello and Räikkönen, and had to pit for a replacement.

Robert Kubica and Nick Heidfeld also had to pit for new noses for their BMW Saubers after early tangles, and they finished 18th and 19th after a terrible afternoon for BMW Sauber. A year earlier, Kubica had been on pole position here...

ABOVE LEFT Kimi Räikkönen gave Ferrari the first points of its campaign, albeit only for sixth place

LEFT Fernando Alonso checks the opposition's level of tyre degradation post-race in *parc fermé*

SNAPSHOT FROM
BAHRAIN

CLOCKWISE FROM RIGHT Robert Kubica, alone with the desert, and far from the pace; birthday celebrations for Felipe Massa, joined by his parents, Stefano Domenicali and Kimi Räikkönen; rock legend Robert Plant dropped in; these tyres are not nice to drive on, but almost a work of art; stewardesses from event sponsor Gulf Air; Nelson Piquet is reunited with his 1982-vintage Brabham-BMW BT50; Rubens Barrichello does his best to keep cool before the start of the grand prix

WEEKEND NEWS

■ The saga of a cost cap for 2010 and beyond rumbled on when, just after the Bahrain GP, the FIA announced an upwardly-revised figure of £40m, with engine costs taken out of the equation for the first season at least. Teams running to the cap would have adjustable front and rear wings, and could use an engine with no rev limit. The established FOTA teams continued to protest that a two-tier system was unacceptable.

■ Having made his feelings about the FIA clear to the media in Bahrain, Ferrari chairman Luca di Montezemolo subsequently wrote a letter to FIA President Max Mosley that insisted that a cost cap was unacceptable for Formula 1. Mosley responded by telling the press that the sport could live without Ferrari.

■ Speculation about the identity of potential new teams for Formula 1 for 2010 began to gather momentum, as it became clear that the FIA was serious about its cost-cap category. Among those making it clear that the idea had appeal was Prodrive boss David Richards. He had won an entry for the 2008 season, but had not used it after the goalposts moved on the use of customer cars.

■ Three days after the Bahrain GP, the World Motor Sport Council held a hearing into the Australian GP Hamilton affair. McLaren team principal Martin Whitmarsh attended on his own, and in essence admitted to mistakes by the team, while insisting that there had now been a change of culture. The team received a suspended three-race ban, and a warning that it would be applied should any more evidence of wrongdoing emerge.

■ Richard Branson continued his brilliant PR assault on the grand prix world by announcing in Bahrain that Niki Lauda wanted to be become a space pilot once the new Virgin Galactic service was up and running. He also revealed that Brawn GP driver Rubens Barrichello was one of the first recipients of a $200,000 ticket.

RACE RESULTS

BAHRAIN SAKHIR

Official Results © [2009]
Formula One Administration Limited,
6 Princes Gate, London, SW7 1QJ.
No reproduction without permission.
All copyright and database rights reserved.

RACE DATE April 26th
CIRCUIT LENGTH 3.363 miles
NO. OF LAPS 57
RACE DISTANCE 191.862 miles
WEATHER Sunny, dry, 36°C
TRACK TEMP 46°C
ATTENDANCE 93,682
LAP RECORD Michael Schumacher,
1m30.252s, 134.262mph, 2004

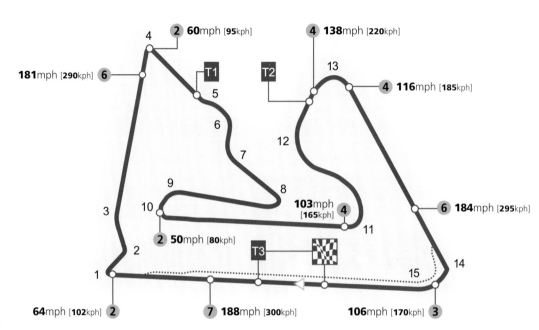

PRACTICE 1				PRACTICE 2				PRACTICE 3				QUALIFYING 1			QUALIFYING 2	
	Driver	Time	Laps		Driver	Time	Laps		Driver	Time	Laps		Driver	Time		Driver	Time
1	L Hamilton	1m33.647s	19	1	N Rosberg	1m33.339s	36	1	T Glock	1m32.605s	16	1	S Vettel	1m32.680s	1	S Vettel	1m32.474s
2	N Heidfeld	1m33.907s	17	2	F Alonso	1m33.530s	25	2	F Massa	1m32.728s	20	2	J Trulli	1m32.779s	2	T Glock	1m32.612s
3	R Kubica	1m33.938s	17	3	J Trulli	1m33.616s	37	3	N Rosberg	1m32.906s	18	3	L Hamilton	1m32.851s	3	J Trulli	1m32.671s
4	N Rosberg	1m34.227s	24	4	S Vettel	1m33.661s	29	4	L Hamilton	1m32.975s	16	4	J Button	1m32.978s	4	K Räikkönen	1m32.827s
5	J Button	1m34.434s	15	5	M Webber	1m33.676s	32	5	K Räikkönen	1m32.986s	18	5	R Barrichello	1m33.116s	5	R Barrichello	1m32.842s
6	H Kovalainen	1m34.502s	24	6	J Button	1m33.694s	35	6	N Piquet Jr	1m33.176s	19	6	K Räikkönen	1m33.117s	6	J Button	1m32.842s
7	R Barrichello	1m34.531s	18	7	A Sutil	1m33.763s	30	7	R Kubica	1m33.195s	13	7	T Glock	1m33.165s	7	F Alonso	1m32.860s
8	F Massa	1m34.589s	17	8	T Glock	1m33.764s	37	8	K Nakajima	1m33.302s	17	8	K Nakajima	1m33.221s	8	L Hamilton	1m32.877s
9	M Webber	1m34.827s	21	9	R Barrichello	1m33.885s	30	9	J Trulli	1m33.397s	19	9	F Massa	1m33.297s	9	F Massa	1m33.014s
10	K Räikkönen	1m34.827s	19	10	K Nakajima	1m33.899s	36	10	N Heidfeld	1m33.415s	14	10	N Heidfeld	1m33.377s	10	N Rosberg	1m33.166s
11	K Nakajima	1m34.880s	24	11	L Hamilton	1m33.994s	30	11	S Vettel	1m33.443s	16	11	H Kovalainen	1m33.479s	11	H Kovalainen	1m33.242s
12	S Vettel	1m34.938s	21	12	G Fisichella	1m34.025s	23	12	H Kovalainen	1m33.478s	12	12	R Kubica	1m33.495s	12	K Nakajima	1m33.348s
13	N Piquet Jr	1m34.974s	21	13	S Buemi	1m34.127s	37	13	F Alonso	1m33.482s	13	13	N Piquet Jr	1m33.608s	13	R Kubica	1m33.487s
14	A Sutil	1m35.021s	18	14	S Bourdais	1m34.366s	26	14	A Sutil	1m33.534s	17	14	F Alonso	1m33.627s	14	N Heidfeld	1m33.562s
15	J Trulli	1m35.036s	22	15	N Piquet Jr	1m34.411s	29	15	J Button	1m33.586s	17	15	N Rosberg	1m33.672s	15	N Piquet Jr	1m33.941s
16	G Fisichella	1m35.042s	16	16	F Massa	1m34.564s	34	16	R Barrichello	1m33.686s	17	16	A Sutil	1m33.722s			
17	T Glock	1m35.333s	20	17	R Kubica	1m34.605s	31	17	S Buemi	1m33.720s	15	17	S Buemi	1m33.753s			
18	F Alonso	1m35.348s	24	18	K Räikkönen	1m34.670s	28	18	M Webber	1m33.726s	14	18	G Fisichella	1m33.910s			
19	S Bourdais	1m35.353s	22	19	H Kovalainen	1m34.764s	35	19	G Fisichella	1m33.964s	15	19	M Webber	1m34.038s			
20	S Buemi	1m35.369s	15	20	N Heidfeld	1m34.790s	33	20	S Bourdais	1m34.990s	7	20	S Bourdais	1m34.159s			

Best sectors – Practice			Speed trap – Practice			Best sectors – Qualifying			Speed trap – Qualifying		
Sec 1	L Hamilton	29.720s	1	G Fisichella	196.601mph	Sec 1	L Hamilton	29.634s	1	G Fisichella	194.737mph
Sec 2	N Rosberg	39.913s	2	A Sutil	196.229mph	Sec 2	S Vettel	39.856s	2	A Sutil	194.427mph
Sec 3	T Glock	22.786s	3	L Hamilton	196.104mph	Sec 3	J Trulli	22.846s	3	S Bourdais	194.116mph

IN 2008

Felipe Massa displayed a clear affinity with this desert track as he won for a second year in a row, with team-mate Kimi Räikkönen following him home. Lewis Hamilton failed to score after making a poor start and hitting Fernando Alonso's Renault, leaving Robert Kubica clear to take another podium finish with Nick Heidfeld fourth.

Lewis Hamilton
"My start was quite good, but I wasn't able to keep third place – Jenson was just so fast. The Red Bulls, Toyotas and Brawns were so fast in the high-speed corners."

Felipe Massa
"I was sandwiched between Kimi and Rubens and my front wing got broken against Kimi's rear wheel. Then I found myself in traffic and my hopes evaporated."

Robert Kubica
"My race was destroyed at the first corner. I was between Nick and Heikki and broke my wing. I was only able to pit after lap 2. Then I was in a heavy car on prime tyres."

Fernando Alonso
"I lost a position at the start that dropped me to eighth. After that, nothing happened and there were no retirements so we were eighth fastest and we finished eighth."

Jarno Trulli
"Timo beat me into Turn 1, but we went for a long second stint on the hard tyres and Vettel got ahead of me after my last stop. After that, I was on the soft, but couldn't pass."

Heikki Kovalainen
"My start was a disaster. Clearly, to begin the race on the prime tyre was the wrong choice. The harder tyres didn't have the right grip and soon started to deteriorate."

Kimi Räikkönen
"I'm happy to have picked up a few points, but I can't be that pleased with our performance. I've been around long enough not to get excited about a sixth place."

Nick Heidfeld
"The result is a disaster, though we were unlucky with the collision in the first corner. I thought the suspension was broken, but I only had to have a new nose fitted."

Nelson Piquet Jr
"It would have been better if I could have made the first stint shorter and the second longer, but I'm happy with the day as we had a solid race, which we needed."

Timo Glock
"I was surprised to get ahead of Jarno from the dirty side. I was the first to pit, but when I went out on the primes I lost a lot of time on the first two laps as I struggled for grip."

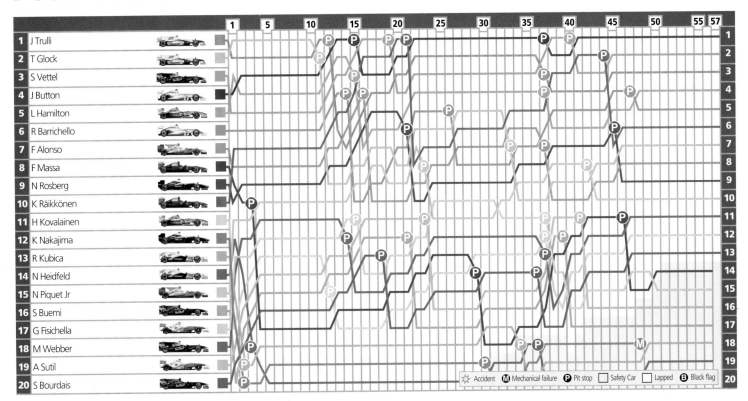

1	J Trulli	
2	T Glock	
3	S Vettel	
4	J Button	
5	L Hamilton	
6	R Barrichello	
7	F Alonso	
8	F Massa	
9	N Rosberg	
10	K Räikkönen	
11	H Kovalainen	
12	K Nakajima	
13	R Kubica	
14	N Heidfeld	
15	N Piquet Jr	
16	S Buemi	
17	G Fisichella	
18	M Webber	
19	A Sutil	
20	S Bourdais	

☆ Accident Ⓜ Mechanical failure Ⓟ Pit stop ☐ Safety Car ☐ Lapped Ⓑ Black flag

QUALIFYING 3

	Driver	Time
1	J Trulli	1m33.431s
2	T Glock	1m33.712s
3	S Vettel	1m34.015s
4	J Button	1m34.044s
5	L Hamilton	1m34.196s
6	R Barrichello	1m34.239s
7	F Alonso	1m34.578s
8	F Massa	1m34.818s
9	N Rosberg	1m35.134s
10	K Räikkönen	1m35.380s

GRID

	Driver	Time
1	J Trulli	1m33.431s
2	T Glock	1m33.712s
3	S Vettel	1m34.015s
4	J Button	1m34.044s
5	L Hamilton	1m34.196s
6	R Barrichello	1m34.239s
7	F Alonso	1m34.578s
8	F Massa	1m34.818s
9	N Rosberg	1m35.134s
10	K Räikkönen	1m35.380s
11	H Kovalainen	1m33.242s
12	K Nakajima	1m33.348s
13	R Kubica	1m33.487s
14	N Heidfeld	1m33.562s
15	N Piquet Jr	1m33.941s
16	S Buemi	1m33.753s
17	G Fisichella	1m33.910s
18	M Webber	1m34.038s
19*	A Sutil	1m33.722s
20	S Bourdais	1m34.159s

* 3-place grid penalty for obstructing Webber in Q1

RACE

	Driver	Car	Laps	Time	Avg. mph	Fastest	Stops
1	J Button	Brawn-Mercedes BGP 001	57	1h31m48.182s	125.179	1m34.588s	2
2	S Vettel	Red Bull-Renault RB5	57	1h31m55.369s	125.015	1m34.756s	2
3	J Trulli	Toyota TF109	57	1h31m57.352s	124.971	1m34.556s	2
4	L Hamilton	*McLaren-Mercedes MP4-24	57	1h32m10.278s	124.679	1m34.915s	2
5	R Barrichello	Brawn-Mercedes BGP 001	57	1h32m25.961s	124.326	1m34.901s	3
6	K Räikkönen	*Ferrari F60	57	1h32m30.239s	124.230	1m35.498s	2
7	T Glock	Toyota TF109	57	1h32m31.062s	124.211	1m34.574s	2
8	F Alonso	*Renault R29	57	1h32m40.945s	123.991	1m35.722s	2
9	N Rosberg	Williams-Toyota FW31	57	1h32m46.380s	123.869	1m35.816s	2
10	N Piquet Jr	*Renault R29	57	1h32m53.331s	123.715	1m35.441s	2
11	M Webber	Red Bull-Renault RB5	57	1h32m55.823s	123.660	1m35.165s	2
12	H Kovalainen	*McLaren-Mercedes MP4-24	57	1h33m06.006s	123.435	1m35.520s	2
13	S Bourdais	Toro Rosso-Ferrari STR4	57	1h33m06.987s	123.413	1m35.410s	2
14	F Massa	*Ferrari F60	56	1h31m55.017s	122.828	1m35.065s	3
15	G Fisichella	Force India-Mercedes VJM02	56	1h32m01.893s	122.675	1m36.376s	2
16	A Sutil	Force India-Mercedes VJM02	56	1h32m04.350s	122.621	1m36.219s	2
17	S Buemi	Toro Rosso-Ferrari STR4	56	1h32m05.906s	122.586	1m36.473s	2
18	R Kubica	*BMW Sauber F1.09	56	1h32m06.822s	122.566	1m35.706s	2
19	N Heidfeld	*BMW Sauber F1.09	56	1h32m12.682s	122.436	1m35.924s	2
20	K Nakajima	Williams-Toyota FW31	48	Oil pressure	-	1m36.153s	2

* Denotes car fitted with KERS

CHAMPIONSHIP

	Driver	Pts
1	J Button	31
2	R Barrichello	19
3	S Vettel	18
4	J Trulli	14.5
5	T Glock	12
6	M Webber	9.5
7	L Hamilton	9
8	F Alonso	5
9	N Heidfeld	4
10	H Kovalainen	4
11	N Rosberg	3.5
12	K Räikkönen	3
13	S Buemi	3
14	S Bourdais	1

Fastest lap
J Trulli 1m34.556s
(128.033mph) on lap 10

Fastest speed trap
G Fisichella 195.421mph
Slowest speed trap
J Trulli 189.145mph

Fastest pit stop
1	R Barrichello	25.197s
2	N Rosberg	25.525s
3	A Sutil	25.545s

	Constructor	Pts
1	Brawn-Mercedes	50
2	Red Bull-Renault	27.5
3	Toyota	26.5
4	McLaren-Mercedes	13
5	Renault	5
6	BMW Sauber	4
7	Toro Rosso-Ferrari	4
8	Williams-Toyota	3.5
9	Ferrari	3

Sebastien Bourdais
"I started so far back, which meant that I couldn't get into the points. The team adopted the right strategy starting me on prime tyres and after that I was quite quick."

Mark Webber
"I got stuck behind Piquet, as it's hard to pass a car with KERS on the straights. We converted to a two-stop strategy, but the grip was not so good on the prime tyres."

Nico Rosberg
"I lost so many places at the start as all the KERS cars came flying past, which was shocking as I had a very good start. We need to push hard to catch up with the others."

Adrian Sutil
"I lost three positions in the first lap as Nakajima drove into my car. It was a shame, but it was a good race, and the upgrades have put us right back into the midfield."

Jenson Button
"I got Sebastian round the outside on Turn 1, then knew that Lewis would pull away from me on the straight so dropped back and used the tow to overtake him at Turn 1."

Sebastien Buemi
"My start was bad with a lot of wheelspin, and then I was unable to attack and sliding a lot. I'm not sure why I struggled with the car, as its behaviour was strange."

Sebastian Vettel
"I got caught between Lewis and Jenson into the first corner and had to give way. Then in the second stint, I was behind Jarno, which was a shame as I was on the soft tyres."

Kazuki Nakajima
"It got very close going into the first corner on lap 2 and I damaged my front wing, so I had to pit early. Then my oil pressure was spiking so we decided to retire the car."

Giancarlo Fisichella
"The temperatures were the hottest so far and I was in pain as my seat was rubbing my right hip, bruising it. Late on, Massa got past and there was a little contact."

Rubens Barrichello
"I lost time behind Piquet after my first stop. We went for a three-stop strategy and decided to come in early for my second stop as I was being held up behind Hamilton."

2009 FORMULA 1 GRAN PREMIO
DE ESPANA TELEFONICA 2009
CATALUNYA

DOWN TO STRATEGY

Rubens Barrichello took the lead at the start and thought he'd done enough for his first win for Brawn, only to find that team-mate Jenson Button had changed strategy and beaten him

Jenson Button scored his fourth win of the 2009 season in Spain after another dominant performance by Brawn GP. However, his victory came at the expense of team-mate Rubens Barrichello, who looked set to beat him before the two drivers were put onto different race strategies.

The Brazilian's body language told the story in the backstage television shots of the drivers as they prepared for the podium ceremony.

"I don't know how the hell I lost that race," he said to Button. As honest as ever, the winner said that he was happy for himself, "but I feel for you."

Afterwards, Barrichello made it clear to the media that he was more than disappointed, although eventually the team persuaded him that there had been no conspiracy, and that a lack of speed on one set of tyres had counted against him.

Button had taken his third pole of the season after a dramatic dash to the line at the end of qualifying. He left the pits to start his last run later than scheduled and had to race around in order to commence his hot lap. He made it 1.6s before the clock ran out, then took full advantage of his good fortune by putting in a scorching lap that pipped Sebastian Vettel by 0.133s.

"I'm disappointed that I didn't win. I thought I had it in the bag. I had a great reflex and made a better start than Jenson, who was on pole. I used his slipstream and was able to carry that momentum into the first corner to lead.

I knew I was a lap or two longer on fuel than Jenson in the first stint. He caught me up a little bit on the strategy because of the safety car, but I was quite happy knowing that I was going longer and being in front. We were both running three-stop strategies and I had the race in my pocket, so I was actually quite surprised when they told me they had switched Jenson to two stops. From then on, I had to go flat-out.

It's a group that makes the decisions. Ross is involved. In the morning, we decided that three stops was the way to go and I will have some answers after our meeting later.

As far as having to move over for Michael at Austria in 2002 and things like that, well, I'm very experienced with that, and if it happens I won't follow team orders any more. I'm making that clear now, so everybody knows.

But it's also true that it's a much different position than it used to be at Ferrari. We have a much more friendly situation, so I'm not sitting down blaming this or that. The race only finished half an hour ago and that's the way it went. There's no way I'm going to sit here crying. It's in my best interests to learn what went wrong today because I had the ability to win the race but I didn't.

Jenson is on a flier and doing very well. I think this weekend was really good for me though. I worked hard on the car's set-up. We both learned and improved, and we're pushing each other very well. There's a bit more pressure on my side, obviously, because he's won four races and I've won nothing, but I'm there, I'm working and I won't stop working.

I'm definitely raising my hands to the sky and giving thanks because this is a great car. It was not long ago that people were putting flowers on my grave and saying 'Thank you very much for your job'. But I'm here, I'm very much alive and happy. And I'm going to make it work."

Running a little heavier than Button, Barrichello was quicker for most of the weekend, but had to settle for third. There was a big surprise as Felipe Massa put his Ferrari fourth on the grid, after updates – including a double diffuser – made a clear difference. Kimi Räikkönen, though, was stranded in 16th after failing to make it out of Q1, as once again Ferrari gambled on being able to make it through with a single run. Mark Webber qualified fifth in the second Red Bull.

Lewis Hamilton would start 14th as he struggled for speed on a track whose fast corners revealed a lack of downforce. He had the heaviest fuel load in the field for Sunday as the team took a strategic gamble.

One thing that Barrichello certainly got right was the start of the race. He was immediately behind Button on the clean side of the grid, which gave him a good run on Vettel, but to pass his team-mate as well was pretty impressive.

"I had a brilliant start, it was a great reflex on the light, and then I used the slipstream a lot," said Barrichello. "I think I surprised Jenson a bit. I presumed the focus was on Massa with the KERS, and although I knew he had everything to play with I was on the right side of the grid, and if I used Jenson's slipstream I could keep at least Massa at bay. That's what I was focused on, and it worked perfectly, as I went around the outside. I didn't even see Felipe coming, I just went around the outside, and had a great first lap."

In fact, both Brawn drivers were helped by the fact that Massa's KERS didn't work off the start.

However, the real action was behind, as Jarno Trulli went off, came back onto the track and was hit hard by Adrian Sutil. In the confusion, the Toro Rossos of Bourdais and Buemi made heavy contact. All four were out immediately, and a short safety-car interlude was called for while the mess was cleared up.

Barrichello knew he was going to pit later than his team-mate, and thus being in front of him was perfect. If the person you're racing pits before you, you can react by ensuring that you also pit later than him next time, and so on. However, matters can be complicated when your rival is in the same team.

The Brazilian had a short first stop compared to Button's, and it became apparent that he was going to stop three times, Button just once more. Later, the team explained that both drivers were scheduled to stop three times, and that Button was switched to two to prevent him from getting caught in traffic.

OPPOSITE Jarno Trulli comes back onto the track at Turn 3 and triggers mayhem behind as he collects Adrian Sutil and both Toro Rossos

ABOVE Fernando Alonso and Mark Webber go wheel-to-wheel on the run down to Turn 1 after the withdrawal of the safety car

"The agreement was before the race that both cars would be doing three stops," explained Barrichello. "So I wondered why they didn't change me, who was the longer one, to two stops. I had more fuel than Jenson, so I was quite safe."

That was a good point. The safety car didn't help anyone on a short first stint, as it obviously gave them less opportunity to get away and use a lighter fuel load to full advantage.

The team's explanation was a logical one, though. If Button had continued on a three-stop strategy, after his first pit visit he would have come out just behind Nico Rosberg, who was on a long first stint. Since he would have been stuck behind, Button wouldn't have been able to take advantage of his light fuel load.

In contrast, a slightly longer pit stop (thanks to the extra fuel required for a two-stop strategy) dropped him a little further behind the Williams. And, because he was now heavier, his potential speed was lower, and he was unlikely to catch Rosberg and thus be delayed by the Williams driver.

The numbers suggest that that was a good call. After stopping on lap 18, Button came out 6s behind Rosberg. He was now carrying fuel for 30 laps

(approximately 68kg), while Rosberg had just seven to go on his run (16kg). That was a huge difference, even if you're driving a Brawn, and by the time Rosberg pitted, the gap was still fluctuating at around 4–5s.

As noted, a shorter stop and lighter load (27kg if he'd matched Barrichello's 12-lap second stint) would have ensured that he'd soon have been right on the gearbox of the Williams, and unable to run at his true pace. The fear was that might be enough to make him vulnerable to the Massa/Vettel battle, even if that didn't appear to be the case.

"Rubens pulled a little bit of a gap on me and I was able to get the gap to Massa," said Button. "They realised I had enough of a gap to exit the pits in front of Massa even though he was stopping later, so they tried to cover both bases. We thought that the three-stopper would be quicker initially, but they put me on the two and it obviously worked.

"As soon as I came out of the pits in front of Massa, it was just a case of trying to put the laps in. It was difficult, as I had a lot of fuel on board on that second stint. I had to push so hard on a heavy load, and I damaged the tyres, but I could get the lap time out of the car by being aggressive with it."

Of course, none of this was known to Barrichello when he got out of the car after the race, and he was left to puzzle over it.

"For me, it came as a surprise when they said that Jenson was changing to two," he rued. "With the pace that I had, pulling away from him, I really thought that I had it in the bag. Then all of a sudden [before] my third stop I had a tyre that wasn't working particularly well, and then I saw he was in front of me, which was very disappointing."

That third stint was the key to it all. The team still insisted that Barrichello had the optimum strategy, and indeed in the second stint, things seemed to be going his way. But, he just didn't have the necessary

BELOW Three pit stops ought to have yielded victory to Rubens Barrichello, but it didn't...

BOTTOM Mark Webber made a long second stint work to his benefit and climbed from fifth to third place

OPPOSITE A double diffuser transformed Ferrari's form and Felipe Massa deserved better than sixth

CAMPDEVÀNOL CON ALONSO, NUNCA CAMINARAS SOLO

Torrecilla

TALKING POINT
RUBENS VS JENSON

When he climbed out of his car, Barrichello's face betrayed his disappointment. Brawn GP's simulations showed that a three-stop race was optimum, and from first (Button) and third (Barrichello) on the grid, they went for it. Barrichello had set fastest lap of all in Q2 and is often quicker than

Button at Barcelona. He was first into Turn 1. This one was his. However, to make three-stoppers work, you need to lap to your potential. A safety-car period for the first four laps spelled recalculations.

Button, due to pit a lap before Barrichello and now behind him, was compromised more, and when he was told they were swapping him to a two-stop, he assumed he hadn't gained enough time to eventually clear the Massa Ferrari and Vettel Red Bull, which both ran two laps longer to their first pit stops.

In fact, the problem was Rosberg. As they crossed the line on lap 17, one lap before Button was due in, Rosberg, helped by the safety car, was still just 18.5s

behind Button, despite being fuelled to run to lap 25. Button was going to come out behind him and, this being Barcelona, wouldn't be able to pass. So the three-stop strategy was abandoned.

For Barrichello, clearing Rosberg was going to be very close. He was 1.4s further ahead of Button and scheduled to run one lap further. He'd got the hammer down and cleared Rosberg by the smallest of margins. It should have won him the race.

Barrichello ran just a 12-lap second stint, part of the short stop needed to clear Rosberg, but the damage was done on his 19-lap third stint, where he had understeer. He fell behind Button, only just clearing Webber's two-stopping Red Bull at his final stop.

The distant look spoke volumes. It should have been 1–3 between he and Button but it was 0–4.

"I heard they had changed Jenson's strategy and that I had to keep on pushing," Rubens said. "I would like to understand why."

Had Barrichello been sacrificed in the interests of Button? Was this Ferrari all over again?

Button interjected: "I'm going to answer this as well because it affects me. Our strategy said a three-stop was quicker. Full stop. I don't even want to go down the avenue of talking about team orders because it's so far from the situation in our team," he said, half laughing.

It was a chortle that said "listen, you have no idea what I've just done and how chuffed I am to pull that one off".

have guaranteed pole position, and also down to bad getaways at the start.

In Bahrain, Vettel dropped behind Hamilton and Button, and this time it was Barrichello and Massa who got past. He ended up spending most of the race staring at the back of the Ferrari, even coming into the pits behind it at both stops, which meant that the status quo resumed when they returned to the track.

The clever bit by Webber's side of the garage was to give the Aussie a heavier load at his first stop and a much longer second stint. That meant he jumped both Massa and Vettel and suddenly popped up in third. There were reports afterwards of a little acrimony in the RBR camp, and specifically that Helmut Marko – the man behind all Red Bull's racing programmes, and the mentor of Vettel – wasn't exactly happy that his boy had been demoted by his own team-mate...

Massa should still have taken fourth place, but Ferrari had a refuelling problem, and at the last stop he didn't take on board all the fuel he was due to have. The team had no option but to ask him to cut his revs or he wouldn't make the flag. Vettel overtook him and then so did Fernando Alonso as the Ferrari crawled around in the closing laps.

In the end, Massa was lucky to scrape home in sixth before stopping on the slowing down lap. Nevertheless, the red car had shown a significantly improved performance, thanks largely to the team's adoption of a double diffuser. Nick Heidfeld took seventh place after a solid run for BMW Sauber, while Rosberg completed the scorers in eighth.

Hamilton ran an ultra-long first stint in an attempt to make up ground, and it appeared to be working, but the strategy didn't pay out as he struggled for grip, and in the end he could not better ninth. At least he did better than team-mate Heikki Kovalainen, who retired early with a gearbox failure, and Ferrari's Räikkönen, who stopped after a throttle problem.

ABOVE Jenson Button comforts his vanquished team-mate Rubens Barrichello on the podium, after changing tactics and winning by 13s

BELOW BMW Sauber's Nick Heidfeld abandoned KERS for Spain and climbed from 13th to seventh

pace in the third stint, complaining of understeer, and that tipped the race in Button's favour.

The Spanish GP wasn't a wheel-to-wheel thriller, but there was plenty more to keep us busy. Webber's stealthy drive into third place was pretty impressive, and showed that Red Bull Racing could pull off a great strategy – even if one of the two places gained involved passing a sister car.

In Bahrain and again in Spain, Vettel had spent much of his time stuck behind someone, and had thus not been able to demonstrate his true potential. That was down to running a little too much fuel in qualifying, when a more aggressive approach might

SNAPSHOT FROM
SPAIN

CLOCKWISE FROM RIGHT There was only one star in the eyes of the local fans: Fernando Alonso; Bernie Ecclestone joins Lewis Hamilton in the unveiling of his plaque in the circuit's Champions Avenue; Lewis Hamilton's girlfriend tries a McLaren for size; Michael Schumacher was still in demand; Ross Brawn comes face-to-face with a robot from *Terminator Salvation*; photographers play at *Easy Rider*; things didn't go well for Scuderia Toro Rosso, with both cars out on lap 1

WEEKEND NEWS

■ For the Spanish GP weekend, Brawn GP enjoyed a tie-up with upcoming Hollywood movie *Terminator Salvation*, following on from similar deals involving Jaguar (*Ocean's 12* and *Terminator 3*) and Red Bull Racing (*Superman* and *Star Wars*) in the past. A robot from the film was on prominent display in the team's garage.

■ The debate over the FIA's cost cap and the proposed changes for 2010 gathered momentum over the Spanish GP weekend. In the days after the race, Ferrari made it clear that it would not continue in a two-tier championship with different rules for the new teams, while Renault indicated that it shared a similar stance. A meeting in London on 15 May failed to produce a compromise.

■ Lewis Hamilton was honoured by the Barcelona authorities with a plaque in his name on the circuit's Champions Avenue, which already celebrated previous World Champions Ayrton Senna, Nigel Mansell, Nelson Piquet, Michael Schumacher and Fernando Alonso. The plaque bore the message "Thank you for your passion and support" in Hamilton's own handwriting.

■ Doubts continued to surface about the likelihood of Donington Park being ready for its first British GP in 2010, although promoter Simon Gillett insisted that all was well and work was on schedule. Bernie Ecclestone said he had no problem with waiting a year should there be a delay.

■ Potential entries for the 2010 Formula 1 World Championship continued to appear. Lola indicated that it had a serious project planned and that its R&D was well underway, while British Formula 3 team Litespeed was a surprise candidate. Run by ex-Lotus personnel, the team had joined forces with erstwhile Toyota and Force India technical boss Mike Gascoyne.

RACE RESULTS
SPAIN
CATALUNYA

Official Results © [2009]
Formula One Administration Limited,
6 Princes Gate, London, SW7 1QJ.
No reproduction without permission.
All copyright and database rights reserved.

RACE DATE May 10th
CIRCUIT LENGTH 2.892 miles
NO. OF LAPS 66
RACE DISTANCE 190.872 miles
WEATHER Dry and bright, 24°C
TRACK TEMP 42°C
ATTENDANCE 213,030
LAP RECORD Kimi Räikkönen,
1m21.670, 127.500mph, 2008

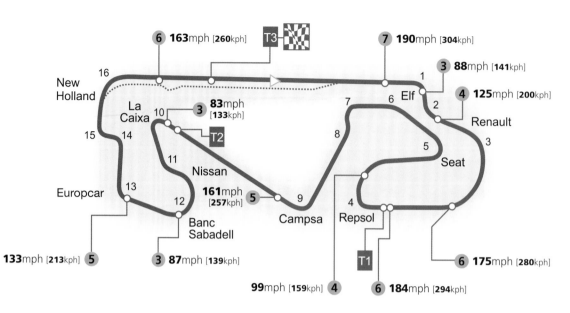

	PRACTICE 1				PRACTICE 2				PRACTICE 3				QUALIFYING 1			QUALIFYING 2	
	Driver	Time	Laps		Driver	Time	Laps		Driver	Time	Laps		Driver	Time		Driver	Time
1	J Button	1m21.799s	21	1	N Rosberg	1m21.588s	43	1	F Massa	1m20.553s	18	1	F Massa	1m20.484s	1	R Barrichello	1m19.954s
2	J Trulli	1m22.154s	30	2	K Nakajima	1m21.740s	40	2	K Räikkönen	1m20.635s	22	2	M Webber	1m20.689s	2	M Webber	1m20.007s
3	R Kubica	1m22.221s	24	3	F Alonso	1m21.781s	36	3	J Button	1m21.050s	19	3	J Button	1m20.707s	3	T Glock	1m20.107s
4	N Heidfeld	1m22.658s	14	4	R Barrichello	1m21.843s	39	4	R Barrichello	1m21.163s	17	4	S Vettel	1m20.715s	4	F Massa	1m20.149s
5	K Nakajima	1m22.659s	24	5	M Webber	1m22.027s	37	5	R Kubica	1m21.239s	21	5	N Rosberg	1m20.745s	5	J Button	1m20.192s
6	N Rosberg	1m22.667s	26	6	J Button	1m22.052s	35	6	J Trulli	1m21.256s	23	6	R Barrichello	1m20.808s	6	S Vettel	1m20.220s
7	N Piquet Jr	1m22.753s	24	7	S Vettel	1m22.082s	45	7	L Hamilton	1m21.346s	16	7	K Nakajima	1m20.818s	7	N Rosberg	1m20.256s
8	T Glock	1m22.828s	29	8	N Piquet Jr	1m22.349s	26	8	T Glock	1m21.377s	26	8	T Glock	1m20.877s	8	R Kubica	1m20.408s
9	F Massa	1m22.855s	15	9	S Buemi	1m22.571s	17	9	S Buemi	1m21.424s	19	9	R Kubica	1m20.931s	9	J Trulli	1m20.420s
10	R Barrichello	1m22.859s	24	10	K Räikkönen	1m22.599s	40	10	F Alonso	1m21.499s	17	10	L Hamilton	1m20.991s	10	F Alonso	1m20.509s
11	K Räikkönen	1m22.873s	20	11	S Bourdais	1m22.615s	30	11	H Kovalainen	1m21.519s	15	11	S Buemi	1m21.033s	11	K Nakajima	1m20.531s
12	M Webber	1m22.934s	25	12	G Fisichella	1m22.670s	32	12	N Rosberg	1m21.594s	20	12	N Heidfeld	1m21.095s	12	N Piquet Jr	1m20.604s
13	S Vettel	1m22.959s	24	13	L Hamilton	1m22.809s	31	13	M Webber	1m21.629s	19	13	N Piquet Jr	1m21.128s	13	N Heidfeld	1m20.676s
14	L Hamilton	1m23.077s	21	14	H Kovalainen	1m22.876s	29	14	S Bourdais	1m21.649s	19	14	F Alonso	1m21.186s	14	L Hamilton	1m20.805s
15	S Bourdais	1m23.088s	30	15	F Massa	1m22.878s	35	15	N Piquet Jr	1m21.685s	18	15	J Trulli	1m21.189s	15	S Buemi	1m21.067s
16	G Fisichella	1m23.089s	25	16	R Kubica	1m22.948s	40	16	S Vettel	1m21.689s	18	16	K Räikkönen	1m21.291s			
17	F Alonso	1m23.157s	18	17	N Heidfeld	1m23.173s	39	17	G Fisichella	1m21.909s	19	17	S Bourdais	1m21.300s			
18	S Buemi	1m23.185s	31	18	T Glock	1m23.360s	46	18	K Nakajima	1m22.043s	19	18	H Kovalainen	1m21.675s			
19	H Kovalainen	1m23.522s	17	19	J Trulli	1m23.623s	47	19	A Sutil	1m22.232s	19	19	A Sutil	1m21.742s			
20	A Sutil	1m23.536s	19	20	A Sutil	No time	-	20	N Heidfeld	1m23.457s	8	20	G Fisichella	1m22.204s			

Best sectors – Practice				Speed trap – Practice			Best sectors – Qualifying				Speed trap – Qualifying	
Sec 1	F Massa	22.509s	1	A Sutil	195.545mph	Sec 1	S Vettel	22.370s	1	G Fisichella	194.302mph
Sec 2	F Massa	30.319s	2	G Fisichella	194.551mph	Sec 2	R Barrichello	29.896s	2	A Sutil	193.867mph
Sec 3	F Massa	27.549s	3	M Webber	193.743mph	Sec 3	J Button	27.461s	3	S Buemi	193.308mph

IN 2008

Kimi Räikkönen was back in control, winning the battle to be the faster Ferrari driver as the red cars stretched clear of all but Lewis Hamilton. The British driver was right with them at the finish, in third, but it was a mixed day for McLaren, as Heikki Kovalainen suffered a hefty accident when a wheel failed. He was shaken, but OK.

 **Lewis Hamilton**

"It was a difficult race, as we lack downforce. I was worried about my tyres after hitting debris, but I came out of it OK, though ninth doesn't feel like a proper reward."

Felipe Massa

"It's a shame to have lost two places late on. We'd got ahead of the Red Bulls and, but for a fuel problem, I could have stayed ahead of both Vettel and Alonso."

Robert Kubica

"I lost a few places at the start due to a clutch problem. Then, after the safety-car period, my car had no grip. I don't understand what happened. Up to Q3, it had been going well."

Fernando Alonso

"Our simulations suggested I'd finish ninth or 10th, but I made a good start and was up to sixth after the first corner. Then I was able to pass Massa on the last lap."

Jarno Trulli

"I had a poor start and was behind Alonso and Rosberg into Turn 1. Rosberg went off, then came back next to me. I swerved, went onto the grass, so spun and was hit."

Heikki Kovalainen

"Luck doesn't seem to be going my way. It was gearbox failure this time. But we shouldn't forget that we've improved our car a lot since we tested here in the winter."

Kimi Räikkönen

"I'm very unhappy, as I could have finished in the points. Unluckily, my car had a hydraulic problem linked to the control of the accelerator which meant I had to retire."

Nick Heidfeld

"The start was decisive as I gained my position. It wasn't easy to defend my position against Kimi later on, and our fight slowed me, so I lost the contact with those ahead."

Nelson Piquet Jr

"I was lucky not to get caught in the first-lap accident, but I don't have a fully updated car yet so I hope that we can make some improvements for the next race."

Timo Glock

"My car didn't pull away well, but I got through Turn 1, then was behind Nico and couldn't get close enough to him in the slipstream. Every time I was close, my tyres went off."

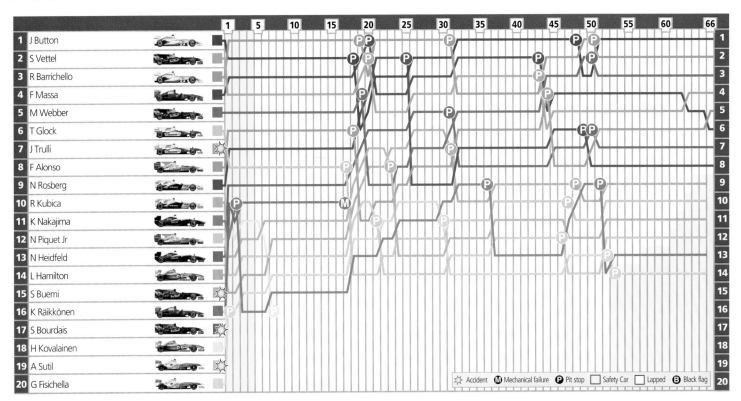

1 J Button
2 S Vettel
3 R Barrichello
4 F Massa
5 M Webber
6 T Glock
7 J Trulli
8 F Alonso
9 N Rosberg
10 R Kubica
11 K Nakajima
12 N Piquet Jr
13 N Heidfeld
14 L Hamilton
15 S Buemi
16 K Räikkönen
17 S Bourdais
18 H Kovalainen
19 A Sutil
20 G Fisichella

☆ Accident Ⓜ Mechanical failure Ⓟ Pit stop ☐ Safety Car ☐ Lapped Ⓑ Black flag

QUALIFYING 3

	Driver	Time
1	J Button	1m20.527s
2	S Vettel	1m20.660s
3	R Barrichello	1m20.762s
4	F Massa	1m20.934s
5	M Webber	1m21.049s
6	T Glock	1m21.247s
7	J Trulli	1m21.254s
8	F Alonso	1m21.392s
9	N Rosberg	1m22.558s
10	R Kubica	1m22.685s

GRID

	Driver	Time
1	J Button	1m20.527s
2	S Vettel	1m20.660s
3	R Barrichello	1m20.762s
4	F Massa	1m20.934s
5	M Webber	1m21.049s
6	T Glock	1m21.247s
7	J Trulli	1m21.254s
8	F Alonso	1m21.392s
9	N Rosberg	1m22.558s
10	R Kubica	1m22.685s
11	K Nakajima	1m20.531s
12	N Piquet Jr	1m20.604s
13	N Heidfeld	1m20.676s
14	L Hamilton	1m20.805s
15	S Buemi	1m21.067s
16	K Räikkönen	1m21.291s
17	S Bourdais	1m21.300s
18	H Kovalainen	1m21.675s
19	A Sutil	1m21.742s
20	G Fisichella	1m22.204s

RACE

	Driver	Car	Laps	Time	Avg. mph	Fastest	Stops
1	J Button	Brawn-Mercedes BGP 001	66	1h37m19.202s	117.648	1m22.899s	2
2	R Barrichello	Brawn-Mercedes BGP 001	66	1h37m32.258s	117.385	1m22.762s	3
3	M Webber	Red Bull-Renault RB5	66	1h37m33.126s	117.368	1m23.112s	2
4	S Vettel	Red Bull-Renault RB5	66	1h37m38.143s	117.267	1m23.090s	2
5	F Alonso	Renault R29	66	1h38m02.368s	116.785	1m23.420s	2
6	F Massa	*Ferrari F60	66	1h38m10.029s	116.632	1m23.089s	2
7	N Heidfeld	BMW Sauber F1.09	66	1h38m11.514s	116.603	1m23.878s	2
8	N Rosberg	Williams-Toyota FW31	66	1h38m24.413s	116.348	1m23.621s	2
9	L Hamilton	*McLaren-Mercedes MP4-24	65	1h37m20.216s	115.844	1m23.839s	2
10	T Glock	Toyota TF109	65	1h37m20.990s	115.829	1m24.134s	2
11	R Kubica	BMW Sauber F1.09	65	1h37m23.811s	115.773	1m24.078s	2
12	N Piquet Jr	Renault R29	65	1h37m26.107s	115.728	1m24.266s	2
13	K Nakajima	Williams-Toyota FW31	65	1h37m37.113s	115.510	1m24.155s	3
14	G Fisichella	Force India-Mercedes VJM02	65	1h37m50.740s	115.242	1m23.796s	4
R	K Räikkönen	*Ferrari F60	17	Hydraulics		1m24.490s	0
R	H Kovalainen	*McLaren-Mercedes MP4-24	7	Gearbox		1m28.719s	0
R	J Trulli	Toyota TF109	0	Accident	-	-	0
R	S Buemi	Toro Rosso-Ferrari STR4	0	Accident	-	-	0
R	S Bourdais	Toro Rosso-Ferrari STR4	0	Accident	-	-	0
R	A Sutil	Force India-Mercedes VJM02	0	Accident	-	-	0

* Denotes car fitted with KERS

CHAMPIONSHIP

	Driver	Pts
1	J Button	41
2	R Barrichello	27
3	S Vettel	23
4	M Webber	15.5
5	J Trulli	14.5
6	T Glock	12
7	L Hamilton	9
8	F Alonso	9
9	N Heidfeld	6
10	N Rosberg	4.5
11	H Kovalainen	4
12	F Massa	3
13	K Räikkönen	3
14	S Buemi	3
15	S Bourdais	1

Fastest lap
R Barrichello 1m22.762s
(125.817mph) on lap 28

Fastest speed trap
G Fisichella 195.359mph

Slowest speed trap
J Trulli 176.407mph

Fastest pit stop
1 G Fisichella 21.999s
2 N Heidfeld 22.232s
3 L Hamilton 22.265s

	Constructor	Pts
1	Brawn-Mercedes	68
2	Red Bull-Renault	38.5
3	Toyota	26.5
4	McLaren-Mercedes	13
5	Renault	9
6	BMW Sauber	6
7	Ferrari	6
8	Williams-Toyota	4.5
9	Toro Rosso-Ferrari	4

Sebastien Bourdais
"I became aware everything was slowing and didn't even have time to brake before I was flying over the back of my team-mate's car and I thought I was going to roll."

Mark Webber
"We planned a long second stint, as we knew Felipe would be a lap longer and he would be the key to my race. We had to get by him and that second stint was the key."

Nico Rosberg
"I believe we could have taken fifth. I had a good first few laps but, after 10 laps, I started to experience a problem at the rear that caused a lot of oversteer."

Adrian Sutil
"As I accelerated away from Turn 3, I saw a car flying into me. Jarno had spun on the inside and I could not do anything about it. My car was damaged and I had to stop."

Jenson Button
"I had a good start from pole, but Rubens had a flier. Having lost the lead, and with the prospect of being caught behind Rosberg, we switched to a two-stopper."

Sebastien Buemi
"Räikkönen and Kovalainen passed me before Turn 1. At the exit of Turn 2, Trulli spun. My team-mate didn't see that I was slowing and his car went over mine."

Sebastian Vettel
"My start wasn't the best: by Turn 1 Rubens was first and I was fourth, behind Massa. I was then stuck behind him. He was impossible to overtake, making no mistakes."

Kazuki Nakajima
"I damaged my front wing in the lap-one incident. Luckily, I didn't lose a massive amount of time as the safety car was deployed, but my race was really over from there."

Giancarlo Fisichella
"Trulli spun in front of me at Turn 1. We changed tyres under the safety car and so changed strategy, but I had a refuelling problem at the last pit stop so I had to pit again."

Rubens Barrichello
"I passed Sebastian and Jenson out of Turn 1. Getting out from my first stop ahead of Nico helped, but I suffered on my third set. I'm disappointed not to have won."

FORMULA 1 GRAND PRIX DE MONACO 2009
MONTE CARLO

FIVE WINS FROM SIX

Tyre management was key to his success, as Jenson Button led from the front, and team-mate Rubens Barrichello did him a service by riding shotgun in the early stages

Jenson Button made it five wins out of six after a faultless performance for Brawn GP in the most prestigious race of the year. In fact, his only mistake of the Monaco weekend came after the flag.

Five years after his previous Monaco podium appearance, Button had forgotten that the top three go to the grid, and no one in the team had reminded him. Having stopped in *parc fermé*, he finally got the message from an FIA official, and set off at a jog back to the last corner, then along the pit straight. It would have been a lot quicker to head down the pitlane but, by chance, Jenson created a little bit of sporting magic and provided a great bit of TV. You never know, it might even become something of a tradition, a bit like drinking the milk at Indianapolis.

"I parked in the wrong place," he grinned later, "so I ran round to the startline. Four hundred metres with your helmet on after a race in Monaco, normally you'd think 'crazy' but, when the adrenaline's pumping, you'll do anything. It was really an emotional moment. I'm sure that everyone who wins Monaco is going to want to do the same, because it's different, and you're running down the straight and everyone's high-fiving you."

INSIDE LINE
JENSON BUTTON
BRAWN GP DRIVER

"This victory is massive for us. I got off the pole clean, with Rubens behind, and then he had problems with his rear tyres, I got a gap and it really didn't change.

I was surprised when the covers came off and most people were on the harder tyres. We never thought twice about running the option, but I did start struggling with a bit of oversteer, although not as much as Rubens. That's why they called me in and I stuck the primes on.

Before the weekend, I said that Monaco doesn't mean anything different, but that was more to stop the pressure: we all know the truth. As I crossed the line, I shouted on the radio to my engineers, 'We've got Monaco, baby!'

Pole position was obviously important here and I did a great lap – I was a tenth quicker with fuel in Q3 than I had been in Q2 when I'd struggled with a bit of understeer. For sure I pushed harder in Q3, and the fuel effect wasn't anywhere near like I thought it was going to be. I could not have got anything more out of the car on that lap.

I had been nowhere near Rubens through the Swimming Pool, but I went as fast as I could through there and thought I was going to end up on Flavio's boat!

All through the weekend until then, I'd been fighting with Rubens and he had the upper hand. The McLarens have been up there, the Ferraris have been up there, the Red Bulls, the Williams. I was right on the edge on that lap and I was chuffed to bits to snatch pole. It was definitely one of the best laps I've ever done.

When the weekend started, I was really struggling, as I just had no front end on the car. We changed a few things and improved the car dramatically, especially on the prime tyre. At first, I couldn't get the prime to work at all and I was a second off Rubens on it. I was trying to be more aggressive in the first session on Thursday and it didn't really work. I sort of scraped a few barriers and it looked pretty cool, but the lap time wasn't there. To come from there to take pole, then look after the tyres and win the race, and for the team to get a 1–2, was just fantastic."

of the time sheets. However, the most distraught man in Monaco on Saturday was Lewis Hamilton, the World Champion crashing early in qualifying and ending up 16th. A penalty for a gearbox change then put him to the very back of the grid.

Tyres were the big questionmark for Sunday. Brawn really surprised the opposition when the covers came off on the grid and both cars were revealed to be on the supersoft tyre. For Vettel, back in fourth grid slot with his ultra-short opening stint, it seemed a logical choice. But would they last long enough on the two Brawns?

Button got over the first hurdle by getting a great start for once. Räikkönen's KERS was never going to be a huge help on the short run to Ste Devote and, crucially, he was jumped by Barrichello, who was helped by a little extra push from those supersofts. This gave Button a priceless advantage, as he knew exactly what he was dealing with, whereas a Ferrari in his mirrors would have created a lot more stress.

Button didn't pull away for the first few laps, but you had to be following the timing to really understand what was happening. In fact, Button pretty much drove those laps as slowly as he could, mindful of the need to keep the tyres in good shape.

"For the first three or four laps," he explained, "I didn't push the car too much, I didn't plant the throttle on corner exits, and it really worked for me. Rubens was dropping back and I wasn't really giving the car 100%. I then pushed a bit more and was able to pull out a big gap."

His first three flying laps went 1m19.3s, 1m18.5s, 1m18.3s. Then it was time to get a move on as he did 1m17.7s, 1m17.2s, 1m16.6s, and then a succession of laps in the 1m17.1s bracket. On lap 5, the gap to Barrichello was 1.5s, by lap 10 it was 4.2s. Then, as the Brazilian began to suffer severe graining on his tyres, it shot up to 12.5s by lap 15.

LEFT The narrowness of the start straight is emphasised by this shot, with Jenson Button on pole from Kimi Räikkönen and Rubens Barrichello

BELOW Nico Rosberg rounds La Rascasse on his way to sixth place

Button's wrong slot on the slowing-down lap was a rare mishap during what was a fabulous weekend for him. Taking pole and leading all the way is a great achievement at any race, even if you have a wonderful car. But at Monaco it's extra special, as there are so many hurdles that can catch you out.

He made it all look so easy, but obviously it wasn't. On Thursday, Button was eighth and fourth in the two free practice sessions, and in both he was slower than team-mate Rubens Barrichello, albeit by less than 0.2s in the afternoon. In Spain, he'd had to borrow Barrichello's set-up, and again this time he had to work to get the car to his liking for Saturday.

Button then did a brilliant job to grab pole position right at the end of the session, much to the frustration of Kimi Räikkönen. Ferrari was on form at this track, and the Finn enjoyed his best outing of the year as he secured second. Barrichello was disappointed to be third, having outpaced Button for much of the weekend. Sebastian Vettel had a very light fuel load, but traffic meant he was stuck in fourth, ahead of Felipe Massa and Nico Rosberg.

It was a disastrous qualifying session for BMW Sauber and Toyota, whose cars were at the bottom

La Rascasse

TALKING POINT
WHAT A FINE MESS

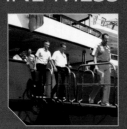

Monaco is a special venue and a special race, but in the paddock, politics was ramping up to levels not seen since the days of the FISA/FOCA wars of the late 1970s and early 1980s.

The sport appeared to be stuck between a rock and a hard place. The FIA had proposed two-tier regulations for 2010. The economic crisis, said the governing body, was the driving force behind a £40 million budget cap. Teams running to that would be allowed a raft of competitive advantages including four-wheel drive, stronger KERS systems, moveable front and rear wings, as well as engines that could be revved to 20,000rpm instead of 18,000rpm.

The budget cap, said the FIA, was necessary to make F1 sustainable and to open up entry to new teams. The FOTA (Formula One Teams Association) acknowledged the need for cost-cutting, but they certainly didn't want a budget cap and teams of FIA auditors trampling through their business. As for two-tier regulations, forget it…

With the entry deadline for the 2010 championship just five days in the future, and the list of potential new teams expanding seemingly by the second (Campos, Epsilon Euskadi, Formtech, iSport, Litespeed, Lola, Manor, March, Prodrive, RML, Lotus, USF1), it was time for some resolutions.

With the FOTA teams all pledging solidarity, allegedly on pain of a £50 million forfeit, all the team principals met, with delicious irony, on Flavio Briatore's yacht, reputedly chartered at a cost of around a quarter-of-a-million a week, to work out how they were going to go about saving money…

Meanwhile, for the prospective new entrants, the time to put up or shut up was fast approaching. The problem was that they didn't know what they were signing up to. A group of investors willing to back a company to take on a Ferrari team with a £40m budget was understandably less keen to commit if they were taking on a Ferrari team with a budget ten times that. It was an extremely complex mess.

The upshot of Monaco was that the FOTA teams had a Sunday-morning meeting with FIA President Max Mosley, at which they said they would commit to F1 until 2012 if the projected 2010 regulations were scrapped and replaced with less stringent budget cuts and more stable governance.

In the background was the threat that, if not, the FOTA teams would break away and organise their own championship.

That came as no surprise to Button: "Mark [Webber] had said to me 'those option tyres are going to be tough aren't they, they're graining after 13–14 laps.' 'Really?' I was stopping on lap 20–21! We knew that we'd have to look after them for the first few laps, and the engineers, if you heard on my radio, were saying 'Jenson look after the rear tyres'. I did.

"We actually thought the supersoft tyre would be the better tyre. We didn't think it would grain. The supersoft tyre always works in Monaco. The circuit grips up through the weekend and you lose the rear graining. To be fair, I was happy with my tyre, and I pulled a good lead. If Rubens wasn't there, I don't think Kimi would have caught me, he would still have been 15s behind. It was the right call."

"I guess that my problem was that I was running too close to Jenson in the early laps," Barrichello explained later. "I had a pace that was really good to begin with, I was even saving fuel, big time. I was amazed that I could keep up with him so well, still saving fuel. But as I ran too close I was probably losing downforce, and with that, I was forcing the tyres more. The rear graining came in too suddenly. In four laps, he was winning three-and-a-half seconds on me, and that really made his race."

Meanwhile, a huge queue of cars built up behind Vettel as he began to struggle for grip. Keen to find a way by, Massa jumped the chicane when he tried to overtake. He then had to slow to let the Red Bull Racing driver back through, and he was also passed by a cheeky Rosberg. Vettel then made a premature pit stop to go onto the soft tyre, but he crashed shortly afterwards at Ste Devote.

Barrichello had to call at the pits as early as lap 16, while Button, whose tyres had also begun to suffer, pitted a lap later.

"My first stop I had to anticipate quite a lot, and that was the cause of everything," said Barrichello.

"I was aiming for 23 laps, and I don't know which lap I stopped, but it was so early because of my tyres graining at the rear."

After the first stops, Button crucially came out just in front of Massa – the quickest driver not to have pitted – so he was able to continue at his own pace. Barrichello had fallen 16–17s back and was containing the threat from Räikkönen, so now it was a question of just bringing it home for Button.

"You've got a big enough lead, you run on the good tyre for the rest of the race, the deal's done," said Button. "It was the right choice for us, and we made the best out of it, we didn't destroy the tyres.

OPPOSITE Kimi Räikkönen was frustrated at being pushed back to third by Brawn's Rubens Barrichello

ABOVE Sebastien Buemi assaults Renault's Nelson Piquet Jr on lap 11

BELOW Heikki Kovalainen threw it all away at Piscine late in the race

"Having a 16s lead at the first pit stop meant a lot. I knew that I'd looked after the tyres more than Rubens had. We put the primes on, the car was working well. Rubens was catching me a bit. I don't want to sound like I had it under control, but I think I did. Then I pushed at the end of the stint and pulled out two to three seconds.

"Even when you're out in the lead with a big gap, you've got to concentrate like you wouldn't believe. I did slow down on the last two laps, taking it all in. It was a very enjoyable two laps. I had the biggest smile on my face, my jaw was hurting, but it was a great end to the weekend..."

Monaco was another frustrating race result for Barrichello, albeit not to the same degree as his second place in Spain had been, although everything was still going Button's way and, when it counted, Barrichello remained just that little step behind. A win in the principality would have been a great way to celebrate his 37th birthday.

"I'm knocking on the door, I won't stop fighting," insisted the Brazilian. "I lost the race yesterday in qualifying, that's how I see it. I had a perfect weekend in terms of set-up, I had a perfect weekend in terms of dominating everything, but not the final qualifying. You could see at the start of the race that I had a better pace than Jenson, and I just struggled with graining at the rear, and that set me back."

As the race progressed, Räikkönen and Massa (who had got by Rosberg) kept Barrichello on his toes, but they were not close enough at the second pit stops to be able to do anything about him, and the top four remained unchanged to the end. Ferrari's 3–4 finish was a clear sign that the team had made good progress since its shaky start to the season.

Webber worked his way up from eighth on the grid to take fifth place for Red Bull, while Rosberg earned sixth after a good effort. A long first stint for Fernando Alonso didn't make much difference to his overall race, although he moved up from ninth to seventh after Vettel and Heikki Kovalainen retired. The latter was heading for seventh place before he crashed heavily at Piscine. The final point went to Sebastien Bourdais, one of several drivers to start with a full fuel tank and run an ultra-long first stint.

An early first pit stop didn't seem to help Hamilton, who was also hampered by front wing damage on his way to 12th place. Among those who failed to see the chequered flag were Sebastien Buemi and Nelson Piquet Jr, after the Toro Rosso man misjudged his braking and hit the Renault driver.

ABOVE LEFT The FIA's Herbie Blash reminds Jenson Button that he left his car in the wrong place

LEFT Once he reached the podium, Jenson Button showed his delight, flanked by Rubens Barrichello and Ferrari's Kimi Räikkönen

SNAPSHOT FROM
MONACO

CLOCKWISE FROM RIGHT It could only be Monaco – the view down from the castle to Virage Antony Nogues; Lewis Hamilton appears to be heading for Piscine...; ... and so do these girls; Jacques Villeneuve was prominent in the paddock as he made it known that he wanted to make an F1 racing comeback; Kazuki Nakajima's Williams hits new heights after he crashed out on the last lap; Toyota's Timo Glock enjoys his Friday away from the circuit; FIA President Max Mosley was the centre of media attention again as a two-tier F1 was discussed for the 2010 season

WEEKEND NEWS

■ Discussions over the future of Formula 1, and specifically the cost cap, continued to dominate the Monaco GP meeting. The FOTA bosses met on Flavio Briatore's yacht before a crunch meeting with FIA President Max Mosley at the Automobile Club de Monaco office on Friday evening. However, very little progress appeared to have been made in their negotiations.

■ Ferrari lost its bid to launch an injunction against the FIA regarding the introduction of a cost cap for 2010. In the course of the legal procedure, details of Ferrari's veto over future rules – which had been in place for several years – were revealed for the first time.

■ The Dallara name was set for a return to F1, after it was confirmed that the Italian constructor was part of a bid by Adrian Campos for one of the three 2010 entry slots. A former Minardi driver himself, the Spaniard had sold his GP2 team but remained involved with an F3 operation.

■ Another Spanish project that appeared to promise much on paper was Epsilon Euskadi, run by former Benetton operations director Joan Villadelprat. Already active as a constructor in sportscars, the Bilbao-based team had good production facilities in place and seemed to have more going for it than some of the other potential contenders for 2010.

■ Former World Champion Jacques Villeneuve was in Monaco and keen to spread the word that he was interested in returning to F1 in 2010, since he liked the idea of racing on slick tyres once again. Alain Prost and Nigel Mansell were among the other former World Champions in town, the latter keeping an eye on his son Greg's exploits in the Renault 3.5 support race.

RACE RESULTS
MONACO MONTE CARLO

Official Results © [2009]
Formula One Administration Limited,
6 Princes Gate, London, SW7 1QJ.
No reproduction without permission.
All copyright and database rights reserved.

RACE DATE May 24th
CIRCUIT LENGTH 2.075 miles
NO. OF LAPS 78
RACE DISTANCE 161.850 miles
WEATHER Dry and bright, 26°C
TRACK TEMP 45°C
ATTENDANCE Not available
LAP RECORD Michael Schumacher, 1m14.439s, 100.373mph, 2004

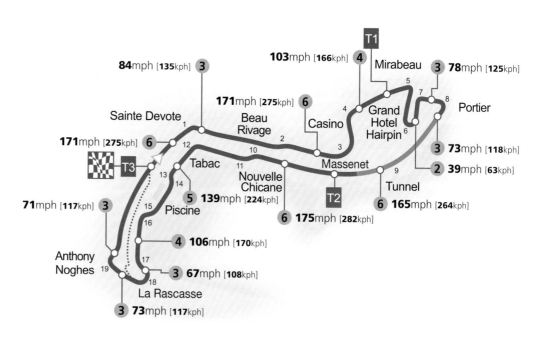

PRACTICE 1			
	Driver	Time	Laps
1	R Barrichello	1m17.189s	26
2	F Massa	1m17.499s	31
3	L Hamilton	1m17.578s	26
4	H Kovalainen	1m17.686s	30
5	K Räikkönen	1m17.839s	30
6	K Nakajima	1m18.000s	29
7	N Rosberg	1m18.024s	27
8	J Button	1m18.080s	28
9	F Alonso	1m18.283s	31
10	M Webber	1m18.348s	22
11	S Buemi	1m18.695s	37
12	N Piquet Jr	1m19.204s	36
13	S Vettel	1m19.233s	16
14	S Bourdais	1m19.255s	31
15	G Fisichella	1m19.534s	28
16	R Kubica	1m19.560s	20
17	N Heidfeld	1m19.579s	23
18	A Sutil	1m19.600s	24
19	T Glock	1m19.698s	24
20	J Trulli	1m19.831s	28

PRACTICE 2			
	Driver	Time	Laps
1	N Rosberg	1m15.243s	45
2	L Hamilton	1m15.445s	35
3	R Barrichello	1m15.590s	41
4	J Button	1m15.774s	36
5	F Massa	1m15.832s	42
6	S Vettel	1m15.847s	33
7	H Kovalainen	1m15.984s	45
8	K Räikkönen	1m15.985s	43
9	K Nakajima	1m16.260s	43
10	N Piquet Jr	1m16.286s	43
11	F Alonso	1m16.552s	39
12	M Webber	1m16.579s	27
13	A Sutil	1m16.675s	38
14	J Trulli	1m16.915s	43
15	S Buemi	1m16.983s	48
16	S Bourdais	1m17.052s	48
17	N Heidfeld	1m17.109s	40
18	T Glock	1m17.207s	45
19	G Fisichella	1m17.504s	45
20	R Kubica	No time	2

PRACTICE 3			
	Driver	Time	Laps
1	F Alonso	1m15.164s	24
2	J Button	1m15.233s	29
3	H Kovalainen	1m15.278s	24
4	R Barrichello	1m15.286s	26
5	F Massa	1m15.293s	23
6	K Räikkönen	1m15.382s	25
7	L Hamilton	1m15.389s	23
8	S Vettel	1m15.722s	23
9	N Rosberg	1m15.758s	23
10	M Webber	1m15.985s	24
11	K Nakajima	1m16.103s	22
12	A Sutil	1m16.228s	30
13	S Bourdais	1m16.301s	23
14	G Fisichella	1m16.317s	29
15	N Piquet Jr	1m16.382s	27
16	S Buemi	1m16.432s	22
17	T Glock	1m16.527s	29
18	R Kubica	1m16.599s	26
19	N Heidfeld	1m16.661s	22
20	J Trulli	1m16.810s	26

QUALIFYING 1		
	Driver	Time
1	N Rosberg	1m15.094s
2	J Button	1m15.210s
3	M Webber	1m15.260s
4	F Massa	1m15.340s
5	R Barrichello	1m15.425s
6	H Kovalainen	1m15.495s
7	K Räikkönen	1m15.746s
8	S Buemi	1m15.834s
9	F Alonso	1m15.898s
10	S Vettel	1m15.915s
11	K Nakajima	1m15.930s
12	N Piquet Jr	1m16.013s
13	G Fisichella	1m16.063s
14	S Bourdais	1m16.120s
15	A Sutil	1m16.248s
16	L Hamilton	1m16.264s
17	N Heidfeld	1m16.264s
18	R Kubica	1m16.405s
19	J Trulli	1m16.548s
20	T Glock	1m16.788s

QUALIFYING 2		
	Driver	Time
1	K Räikkönen	1m14.514s
2	H Kovalainen	1m14.809s
3	M Webber	1m14.825s
4	R Barrichello	1m14.829s
5	N Rosberg	1m14.846s
6	S Vettel	1m14.879s
7	F Massa	1m15.001s
8	J Button	1m15.016s
9	F Alonso	1m15.200s
10	K Nakajima	1m15.579s
11	S Buemi	1m15.833s
12	N Piquet Jr	1m15.837s
13	G Fisichella	1m16.146s
14	S Bourdais	1m16.281s
15	A Sutil	1m16.545s

Best sectors – Practice			Speed trap – Practice			Best sectors – Qualifying			Speed trap – Qualifying	
Sec 1	N Rosberg	19.708s	1	K Räikkönen	178.582mph	Sec 1	K Räikkönen	19.643s	1	G Fisichella	179.265mph
Sec 2	F Alonso	34.791s	2	L Hamilton	178.520mph	Sec 2	K Räikkönen	34.516s	2	A Sutil	178.582mph
Sec 3	F Alonso	20.365s	3	F Massa	178.209mph	Sec 3	K Räikkönen	20.244s	3	H Kovalainen	178.520mph

IN 2008

This race could have been a disaster for Lewis Hamilton, as there was blinding spray, a wet track and he suffered two punctures. But, somehow, the fates were with him and he raced to victory ahead of Kubica and Massa. The saddest sight was seeing Räikkönen crash into Adrian Sutil's Force India, taking it out of fourth.

Lewis Hamilton
"I raced my heart out, but bent a front-wing footplate when I hit Heidfeld going into Ste Devote, giving me understeer. Fitting a new wing made it a bit better."

Felipe Massa
"It's clear that we are on the way up. I lost a lot of time behind Vettel and then, as I made a mistake, I was passed by Rosberg. After that, I quickly got back up the order."

Robert Kubica
"I had a problem at the start and fell to the back. Then I had a puncture. After that pit stop, I was lapping well with a very heavy car, but retired with brake problems."

Fernando Alonso
"It was a hard race and very tight from the start, but in Monaco the starting position is essential and so starting ninth and gaining two places and two points is satisfying."

Jarno Trulli
"It was going to be difficult from where we were on the grid and my strategy didn't work, as I seemed to always be in the wrong place at the wrong time with the traffic."

Heikki Kovalainen
"I had trouble making my tyres work, but I passed Vettel. My second set was better, but I hit the kerb at the chicane and the rear stepped out and I hit the barriers."

Kimi Räikkönen
"This podium is very satisfying and if some details had worked out differently, like missing out on pole by a fraction of a second, the result could have been very different."

Nick Heidfeld
"I tried to make up places at the start, even being hit by Lewis at Ste Devote, but it didn't work and I was then stuck for ages behind Adrian who had tyre problems."

Nelson Piquet Jr
"I made a decent start and was in good shape, as I was running a long first stint. However, I then got hit on the straight by Buemi, which damaged the rear of my car."

Timo Glock
"Coming in the top 10 was more than I expected considering how the weekend had gone to then. When you start from the pits in Monaco you can't expect to score."

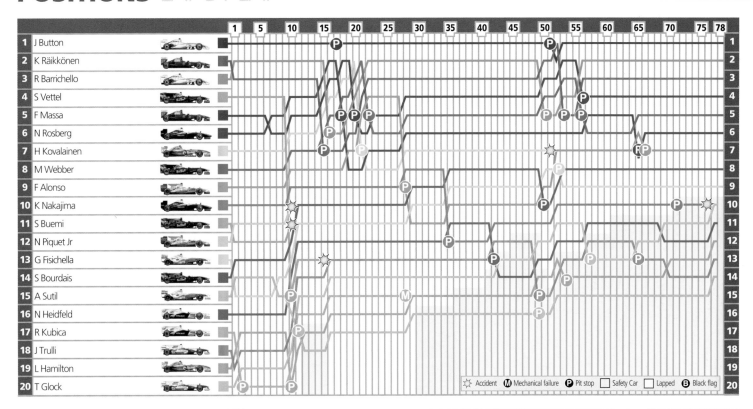

1	J Button
2	K Räikkönen
3	R Barrichello
4	S Vettel
5	F Massa
6	N Rosberg
7	H Kovalainen
8	M Webber
9	F Alonso
10	K Nakajima
11	S Buemi
12	N Piquet Jr
13	G Fisichella
14	S Bourdais
15	A Sutil
16	N Heidfeld
17	R Kubica
18	J Trulli
19	L Hamilton
20	T Glock

☆ Accident Ⓜ Mechanical failure Ⓟ Pit stop ▢ Safety Car ▢ Lapped Ⓑ Black flag

QUALIFYING 3

	Driver	Time
1	J Button	1m14.902s
2	K Räikkönen	1m14.927s
3	R Barrichello	1m15.077s
4	S Vettel	1m15.271s
5	F Massa	1m15.437s
6	N Rosberg	1m15.455s
7	H Kovalainen	1m15.516s
8	M Webber	1m15.653s
9	F Alonso	1m16.009s
10	K Nakajima	1m17.344s

GRID

	Driver	Time
1	J Button	1m14.902s
2	K Räikkönen	1m14.927s
3	R Barrichello	1m15.077s
4	S Vettel	1m15.271s
5	F Massa	1m15.437s
6	N Rosberg	1m15.455s
7	H Kovalainen	1m15.516s
8	M Webber	1m15.653s
9	F Alonso	1m16.009s
10	K Nakajima	1m17.344s
11	S Buemi	1m15.833s
12	N Piquet Jr	1m15.837s
13	G Fisichella	1m16.146s
14	S Bourdais	1m16.281s
15	A Sutil	1m16.545s
16	N Heidfeld	1m16.264s
17	R Kubica	1m16.405s
18	J Trulli	1m16.548s
19*	L Hamilton	1m16.264s
20^	T Glock	1m16.788s

* 5-place grid penalty for gearbox change
^ Started from pitlane

RACE

	Driver	Car	Laps	Time	Avg. mph	Fastest	Stops
1	J Button	Brawn-Mercedes BGP 001	78	1h40m44.282s	96.415	1m15.190s	2
2	R Barrichello	Brawn-Mercedes BGP 001	78	1h40m51.948s	96.294	1m15.685s	2
3	K Räikkönen	*Ferrari F60	78	1h40m57.724s	96.202	1m15.382s	2
4	F Massa	*Ferrari F60	78	1h40m59.392s	96.175	1m15.154s	2
5	M Webber	Red Bull-Renault RB5	78	1h41m00.012s	96.166	1m15.321s	2
6	N Rosberg	Williams-Toyota FW31	78	1h41m17.868s	95.883	1m15.772s	2
7	F Alonso	Renault R29	78	1h41m22.121s	95.816	1m15.371s	1
8	S Bourdais	Toro Rosso-Ferrari STR4	78	1h41m47.424s	95.419	1m16.178s	1
9	G Fisichella	Force India-Mercedes VJM02	78	1h41m49.322s	95.389	1m16.419s	1
10	T Glock	Toyota TF109	77	1h41m05.998s	94.839	1m16.066s	1
11	N Heidfeld	BMW Sauber F1.09	77	1h41m25.243s	94.539	1m16.268s	1
12	L Hamilton	*McLaren-Mercedes MP4-24	77	1h41m26.882s	94.513	1m15.706s	2
13	J Trulli	Toyota TF109	77	1h41m28.869s	94.482	1m16.011s	1
14	A Sutil	Force India-Mercedes VJM02	77	1h41m31.730s	94.438	1m16.245s	2
15	K Nakajima	Williams-Toyota FW31	76	Spun off	-	1m15.792s	2
R	H Kovalainen	*McLaren-Mercedes MP4-24	51	Spun off	-	1m15.672s	2
R	R Kubica	BMW Sauber F1.09	28	Brakes	-	1m17.558s	2
R	S Vettel	Red Bull-Renault RB5	15	Spun off	-	1m17.634s	1
R	N Piquet Jr	Renault R29	10	Accident	-	1m18.514s	1
R	S Buemi	Toro Rosso-Ferrari STR4	10	Accident	-	1m18.582s	0

* Denotes car fitted with KERS

CHAMPIONSHIP

	Driver	Pts
1	J Button	51
2	R Barrichello	35
3	S Vettel	23
4	M Webber	19.5
5	J Trulli	14.5
6	T Glock	12
7	F Alonso	11
8	K Räikkönen	9
9	L Hamilton	9
10	F Massa	8
11	N Rosberg	7.5
12	N Heidfeld	6
13	H Kovalainen	4
14	S Buemi	3
15	S Bourdais	2

	Constructor	Pts
1	Brawn-Mercedes	86
2	Red Bull-Renault	42.5
3	Toyota	26.5
4	Ferrari	17
5	McLaren-Mercedes	13
6	Renault	11
7	Williams-Toyota	7.5
8	BMW Sauber	6
9	Toro Rosso-Ferrari	5

Fastest lap
F Massa 1m15.154s
(99.414mph) on lap 50

Fastest speed trap
F Massa 180.197mph
Slowest speed trap
S Vettel 174.170mph

Fastest pit stop
1 J Trulli 22.284s
2 J Button 22.539s
3 G Fisichella 22.636s

Sebastien Bourdais
"I hadn't done a good job in qualifying, so I'm happy with eighth given the small number of incidents. It was fun, with the satisfaction of scoring from 14th."

Mark Webber
"We're pretty happy with fifth. There were a few more people in on the act, so for us to still come away with a few points is good for us in the championship."

Nico Rosberg
"I'm happy with sixth, as more wasn't possible. It was a great start with lots going on, but I managed to get through it all to set me up well. I always enjoy racing here."

Adrian Sutil
"I started on a one-stop strategy, that would have been OK, but we used the supersoft tyre from the start and they grained. I had to pit and lost a lot of time there."

Jenson Button
"To win in Monaco is a special feeling. The race felt as if it went on forever: you feel the barriers are getting ever closer. It was then all capped by my run to the podium."

Sebastien Buemi
"I lost a place to Piquet at the start, but then tried to pass him. I was in his slipstream and when I tried to make my move he hit the brakes and I couldn't avoid him."

Sebastian Vettel
"I was braking maybe a little bit too late, locked the rears, lost the car and hit the wall. It's disappointing, but in Monaco you make a small mistake and pay the price."

Kazuki Nakajima
"The start was good, but I always seemed to be picking up traffic out of the pitlane or responding to blue flags. I was pushing perhaps too hard when I had my accident."

Giancarlo Fisichella
"Ninth is great. I lost a place at the start and perhaps it was this that cost me the point. It was a step forward, to get two cars into Q2, then to get within 2s of a point."

Rubens Barrichello
"I was able to pass Kimi before the first corner, but following so closely behind Jenson affected my aero balance and I came in earlier than planned to keep second place."

2009 FORMULA 1 ING TURKISH GRAND PRIX
ISTANBUL

SEB SPINS, JB WINS

Sebastian Vettel mounted a serious attack on Jenson Button's supremacy, but it all came unstuck halfway around the opening lap, leaving the Brawn driver to win as he pleased

Jenson Button made it a remarkable six wins out of seven with yet another victory for Brawn GP in Istanbul. It wasn't quite as straightforward as some of his earlier successes, however, as he faced stiff competition from Red Bull Racing's Sebastian Vettel. The German driver just pipped him to pole position, only to make a silly first-lap mistake.

After a slightly dodgy start to the weekend – he was only 12th on the slippery, "green" track on Friday – Button emerged with the fastest package come qualifying and the race. And he made full use of it, putting in another faultless performance.

Vettel may have taken pole, but he had to run 6kg lighter than Button to do it. Fuel-corrected, Button was actually fastest, something that the man himself would not have expected after his form in practice on Friday. Yet, not for the first time, he worked away with the Brawn GP engineers until things were just so. Given that the track changed dramatically over the weekend as rubber went down, it was a good effort by all concerned.

Button wasn't entirely happy with his quick lap and hinted at a little gamesmanship from Mark Webber. It's not like Button to make excuses so, from where he

INSIDE LINE
NICK FRY
**BRAWN GP
CHIEF EXECUTIVE OFFICER**

"When you score the first win, you're pleased. But, when you get to where we are now, you've kind of run out of words. After the first one, there was the challenge of racing in the rain, for which we'd had no preparation. Then Barcelona went well, then a low-speed circuit like Monaco went well, then Turkey which, with some justification, was judged to be better for Red Bull. We were expecting a big fight and potentially to come out second, but the guys did a marvellous job identifying the cause of a high-speed weakness in the car and, as Jenson said, it was perfect.

It's working well, and there is a clear division of responsibility between Ross and myself. I run the commercial side, the factory, and the second part of the partnership is good communication. We speak numerous times a day. The third part is that we are in a position to make every decision in real time and so the speed of decision-making is incredibly quick and efficient. If we get something wrong, we only have to look at each other.

That really does help when we have to be so efficient in our use of resources. We can't develop three or four different routes in parallel and choose the best one. Today, we've only got the money for one course of action. But we have developed possibly the best F1 manufacturing facility in the world and we've got one of the best technical teams run by the best guy in the business.

After Melbourne, we had the extremely distressing situation of having just won the first race and at the same time having to downsize the company. I was fully occupied back at the factory with the restructuring. It wasn't a job I relished. The head count was 720 at the start of the year. Today it's 450.

The commercial and sponsorship side is obviously important to our future. We are winning and, while slapping some logos on in a tactical way would earn a little bit of money in the short-term, and indeed we've done some of that – the deal with Sony and the Terminator robot is one example – the amount of money you get does not make the difference between life and death in the future. What will is significant title sponsorship, and when you're asking for £30–40m, those deals aren't done overnight."

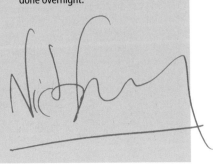

was sitting, it must have looked deliberate, even if that wasn't the Australian driver's intention.

"It wasn't the tidiest lap for sure, which was a pity," said Button. "On the first timed lap in qualifying I've struggled to get the tyres to work, and I've had to push really hard on the out-lap. I think Mark might have known that, and I think the Red Bulls can do a much slower out-lap. I was behind him and I kept slowing, but it wasn't enough. And I got to the last three corners of the out-lap and I didn't have the right tyre temperature up. Anyway, P2 is good, and I might not have beaten Vettel anyway."

Red Bull Racing had not hit headline pace in practice, but when it mattered in qualifying Vettel was to the fore. He was quickest in Q1 and Q2 before sealing pole in Q3. Rubens Barrichello followed the form book by qualifying his Brawn third, while Red Bull's pace was underlined by fourth place for Webber.

The chase was led by Jarno Trulli, who hadn't shown much speed until Q3. Ferrari seemed to have slipped a little since its Monaco upturn, as Kimi Räikkönen qualified sixth, and Felipe Massa – winner in Turkey for the past three years – only seventh.

Vettel seemed to have a good chance of stopping the Brawn steamroller and scoring the first dry win of his career, although his lighter fuel load meant that he would be pitting a lap or too earlier than Button. In fact, from the dirty side of the grid, Button was worried about losing out to Barrichello.

Vettel duly beat Button off the line, but later in the lap ran wide, saying after the race that the wind direction had changed and caught him out. He did a good job to regain control, but Button nipped through.

"Sebastian ran wide at Turn 10, and I knew there was an opportunity," said Button. "I actually thought he was going to spin completely, so I was quite cautious, I thought he was going to hit me in the side, but I was able to get in front and he kept it on the circuit."

Button must have had a huge smile on his face as he accelerated through the big space where the RB5 should have been. Far from being pitched down to third place as he'd feared before the start, he was now in front, and in control of his own destiny.

Barrichello had endured another bad start. Both Brawn drivers have had trouble this year, but this one was a disaster, dropping him to 12th.

"I couldn't imagine any different scenario than overtaking Jenson at the start, because I had the perfect line and everything," said Barrichello. "I had a good getaway on the formation lap, and then we had a faulty clutch. I can say this time that I didn't do

OPPOSITE Sebastian Vettel leads Jenson Button and Jarno Trulli into Turn 1, ahead of the pursuing pack

ABOVE Nico Rosberg made a great start from ninth on the grid, and kept the places he had gained to finish the race fifth

BELOW Button had to work hard to keep Vettel behind him after he passed the Red Bull driver when he ran wide on the opening lap

anything wrong, and it was just the clutch didn't bite. There was an overtorque situation because it was anti-stall and I had to come off it and then on again."

Button meanwhile pulled away from Vettel: "He was sitting behind me for a couple of laps, and I just took it easy on the tyres, because I didn't want to damage them. Then I started pushing and the car felt fantastic. Most races this year the car has felt pretty good, but it's not been completely to my liking. From then, I knew that I was stopping one or two laps later than him, just in case of safety cars. I was able to pull out a 5s lead, but the car just felt great in that stint."

Barrichello found himself stuck behind Heikki Kovalainen's McLaren, and was given a useful lesson in the benefits of KERS as a defensive tool.

"To make things horrible, I was eight seconds [per lap] on the limiter," said the Brazilian. "It was just a wrong gear ratio, and I was fighting with the fastest car on the straight, I was fighting with Kovalainen, and he's on top of the speed sheets. I had to be a go-karter and try silly things, try the inside line here and the outside there just to make it work..."

On lap 8, his frustration became apparent as he hit the Finn and spun, falling back even further. A few laps

later, Barrichello bumped into Adrian Sutil, crunching his front wing and necessitating a premature first stop. After that, all hope was lost and he eventually retired.

When Vettel pitted, RBR decided to keep him on the three-stop strategy that had been agreed before the race. That would have made more sense if he was still leading, but Vettel himself was surprised when told he was not switching to a more logical two stops.

In the second stint, things became more interesting. With a significantly lighter load – his second stop was to come on lap 29, Button's on lap 43 – Vettel was able to reel in the English racer. Had he been able to force his way by, there might have been more of a race but, as soon as he got into Button's wheel tracks, he lost any momentum he'd had. Again, Button made it all look so easy.

It wasn't, though, as Button explained: "It's difficult, you can either push that little bit extra – he's on lower fuel than me, so he's going to be quicker than me – or you can just back off that little bit and cover your lines, and that's what I did.

"Even when Seb was on low fuel, catching me from behind, I wasn't too worried, because my car was so nice to drive and I knew that we had the pace. I just had a lot more fuel on board. Even so, when you see a car in your mirrors it's a strange feeling knowing that he's catching you for your position. It doesn't matter whether he's on a three-stopper, you still don't like that feeling, and there's so much can go wrong in that situation. But it didn't, and we were the quicker team and had the faster car."

Indeed, the need to make an extra pit stop later on dropped Vettel back to third place behind team-mate Webber. With the Red Bull Racing cars out of contention for victory, Button had things under control as he cruised home in front.

After an equally faultless drive, Webber was delighted to take second place for his third podium

BELOW Kimi Räikkönen chases after Robert Kubica, but the Ferrari driver was to miss out on points

BOTTOM Rubens Barrichello's problems left him fighting for position with Heikki Kovalainen

OPPOSITE Jarno Trulli made up places at the start, but brake problems restricted him to fourth

TALKING POINT
IS PASSING ANY EASIER?

With the season a few races old there were suggestions that the work done by F1's Overtaking Working Group (OWG) was ineffective, that the show had not improved noticeably. However, as always, these matters are complex.

Adrian Newey, perhaps F1's most competent aerodynamicist, thinks that it's actually the circuits that are a bigger influence on overtaking than the cars. And, he asks, is there really a problem?

"People have this rose-tinted idea that overtaking used to be fantastic and now it isn't. I think that's selective memory. You still get some great overtaking moves, just as we always used to. I don't see the need to make it a lot easier. If it becomes too easy, the car that is quicker simply goes by and disappears and you don't even get the excitement of two cars battling each other for a number of laps.

"At some of the IRL-type races, where everyone is changing places all the time, I'm of the opinion that it's actually quite dull because it just becomes commonplace. I personally don't find NASCAR races very interesting because the whole art seems to be to be in about fourth place with three laps to go. I don't think that's modern F1 and it would be a very artificial set of rules that came up with that. I don't think it's as much of a problem as people are making out."

Interestingly, Timo Glock explained that in Melbourne he had found all the cars easier to follow, except the Renault, which was a nightmare. Behind it, his Toyota was all over the place. Now, he says, following any of the cars is a nightmare.

What's changed since the beginning of the year is that everyone has developed a double diffuser, although it's odd that the Renault didn't actually have one at the Australian GP.

McLaren gave considerable assistance to the OWG during its research, but Martin Whitmarsh was candid when commenting on the findings of his drivers.

"To be honest, I'm not sure about the relevance," he smiled, "because anything we've been behind has normally been pulling away… Seriously, the OWG set out to halve downforce, go to more mechanical grip and then optimise the airflow behind the car, but we haven't halved the downforce and by putting on double diffusers we're working that lower element much more strongly than the OWG intended. So, to anyone who says the OWG screwed up, I'd say that it happened because this diffuser loophole was allowed when I don't think it was there."

finish of the year. Although the Vettel three-stop strategy gave him a chance to jump his German team-mate, he still had to do some fast laps and take the opportunity that fell into his lap.

Vettel was frustrated to have to settle for third as, not for the first time in 2009, the team's strategy didn't work out in his favour. However, there was no escaping the fact that it was his own first-lap mistake that had allowed Button to get through and make his escape.

Towards the end of the race, we heard Vettel's engineer telling him that Webber was faster. In other words "back off, save the car, and don't race him." That didn't make much difference to his pace and, but

for a little moment on the very last corner, he would have grabbed the race's fastest lap.

"They didn't really say you're not allowed to race him," Vettel said sheepishly. "I got the message 'Mark is faster than you'. I wanted to reply, but I think I had better keep this one for myself! As a racing driver, I tried to catch him, which I did. Unfortunately, I didn't have any extra laps to pass him, so that was third then. For the team, it's the same result, second and third. Obviously my target was to win. If you can't win, then you try to finish second."

Toyota continued its rollercoaster season, as Trulli recovered from qualifying at the back in Monaco to take an excellent fourth place. Nico Rosberg finished an encouraging fifth for Williams, as the original double-diffuser gang demonstrated that their cars were more developed than those of the teams who had been forced to follow that route and change their original designs to accommodate them.

After showing so well in Monaco, Ferrari's performance was a disappointment. At a track where he won from pole in 2006, 2007 and 2008, Massa could finish only sixth, conceding that his car felt good, but simply wasn't fast enough. Räikkönen was ninth, having got away badly and damaged his front wing in an early skirmish with Fernando Alonso.

Robert Kubica finished in seventh place, as BMW Sauber at last showed some signs of progress, while the final point went to Timo Glock, despite the German starting only 13th. Alonso completed the top 10 after a gamble on a low qualifying fuel load failed to pay off for the Renault driver.

It was another terrible day for McLaren, as the cars struggled to find performance. Lewis Hamilton failed to make it out of Q1, ending up stranded in 16th on the grid and, after opting for a tricky one-stop strategy, only advanced to 13th. He did at least get ahead of team-mate Kovalainen, who was 14th.

SNAPSHOT FROM
TURKEY

CLOCKWISE FROM RIGHT This wonderful aerial shot shows the section of the track from Turn 7 (on right) to Turn 10; glamorous and cool; Jarno Trulli looks reflective before hitting the track; Lewis Hamilton spots the cameras; the Turkish fans have soon identified their favourites; dry ice was used to keep the engines cool on the grid; all the drivers were summoned to a meeting by FOTA on race morning; the Brawn GP crew celebrates points leader Jenson Button's sixth win of 2009

WEEKEND NEWS

■ On Sunday morning, the FOTA bosses called all the drivers of their respective teams together for a chat about the latest political situation. The meeting took place very publically in the Toyota hospitality area, and led some observers to believe that a boycott of the race was being planned. That did not prove to be the case...

■ The list of potential new teams for 2010 became ever more intriguing, as Litespeed confirmed that it wished to be known as Team Lotus, while the March and Brabham names were also connected with rival bids. The latter attempt, by the German Formtech organisation that had bought some of the Super Aguri team's assets, was immediately challenged by the Brabham family.

■ Yet another new F1 project was launched by Alexander Wurz, who had teamed up with former Minardi sponsor Superfund. The former Benetton, McLaren and Williams driver insisted that he was well down the road with the planning of the scheme, and intended to pursue a connection with an existing team.

■ The FOTA ranks were shrunk when first Williams and later Force India were suspended after they submitted unconditional entries for the 2010 World Championship. The teams claimed that they had commercial and legal obligations that committed them to entering the championship rather than standing firm with the manufacturer-led FOTA group.

■ Toyota indicated that it might not be willing to host the Japanese GP at Fuji Speedway in 2010, the year it was due to return after the event being run at Suzuka in 2009. The news was confirmed some weeks later, ensuring that the race would be back at Suzuka indefinitely. The expensively rebuilt Fuji had hosted the race twice, in 2007 and 2008.

RACE RESULTS

TURKEY
ISTANBUL

RACE DATE June 7th
CIRCUIT LENGTH 3.317 miles
NO. OF LAPS 58
RACE DISTANCE 192.386 miles
WEATHER Sunny and dry, 32°C
TRACK TEMP 49°C
ATTENDANCE Not available
LAP RECORD Juan Pablo Montoya,
1m24.770s, 138.056mph, 2005

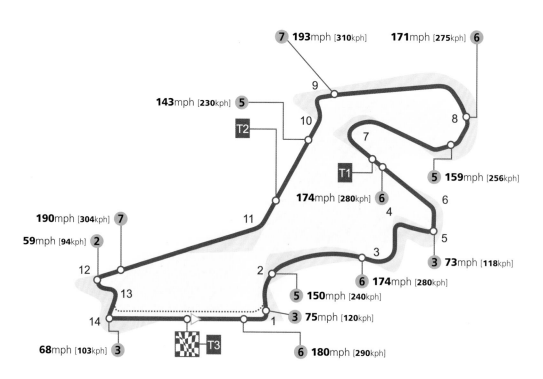

PRACTICE 1				PRACTICE 2				PRACTICE 3				QUALIFYING 1			QUALIFYING 2	
	Driver	Time	Laps		Driver	Time	Laps		Driver	Time	Laps		Driver	Time		Driver	Time
1	N Rosberg	1m28.952s	24	1	H Kovalainen	1m28.841s	37	1	F Massa	1m27.983s	26	1	S Vettel	1m27.330s	1	S Vettel	1m27.016s
2	L Hamilton	1m29.263s	23	2	F Alonso	1m28.847s	35	2	J Trulli	1m28.022s	21	2	J Button	1m27.355s	2	J Trulli	1m27.195s
3	J Trulli	1m29.271s	26	3	R Kubica	1m29.056s	35	3	T Glock	1m28.094s	23	3	R Barrichello	1m27.371s	3	J Button	1m27.230s
4	S Vettel	1m29.337s	17	4	K Nakajima	1m29.091s	37	4	K Nakajima	1m28.122s	19	4	M Webber	1m27.466s	4	F Massa	1m27.349s
5	F Massa	1m29.342s	22	5	S Vettel	1m29.202s	4	5	R Kubica	1m28.320s	20	5	F Massa	1m27.508s	5	K Räikkönen	1m27.387s
6	K Nakajima	1m29.371s	21	6	J Trulli	1m29.207s	41	6	R Barrichello	1m28.332s	21	6	N Rosberg	1m27.517s	6	M Webber	1m27.416s
7	K Räikkönen	1m29.398s	24	7	N Rosberg	1m29.257s	40	7	J Button	1m28.360s	19	7	J Trulli	1m27.529s	7	R Barrichello	1m27.418s
8	F Alonso	1m29.422s	24	8	R Barrichello	1m29.305s	35	8	N Rosberg	1m28.364s	19	8	K Räikkönen	1m27.556s	8	N Rosberg	1m27.418s
9	R Barrichello	1m29.525s	24	9	M Webber	1m29.383s	39	9	K Räikkönen	1m28.415s	16	9	K Nakajima	1m27.691s	9	R Kubica	1m27.455s
10	H Kovalainen	1m29.590s	19	10	N Piquet Jr	1m29.401s	38	10	S Vettel	1m28.451s	18	10	R Kubica	1m27.788s	10	F Alonso	1m27.473s
11	J Button	1m29.747s	20	11	F Massa	1m29.416s	38	11	N Piquet Jr	1m28.503s	15	11	N Heidfeld	1m27.795s	11	N Heidfeld	1m27.521s
12	A Sutil	1m29.864s	21	12	J Button	1m29.430s	33	12	L Hamilton	1m28.563s	19	12	F Alonso	1m27.988s	12	K Nakajima	1m27.629s
13	T Glock	1m29.934s	25	13	L Hamilton	1m29.435s	31	13	M Webber	1m28.678s	18	13	T Glock	1m28.160s	13	T Glock	1m27.795s
14	N Piquet Jr	1m30.132s	18	14	T Glock	1m29.518s	40	14	N Heidfeld	1m28.715s	19	14	H Kovalainen	1m28.199s	14	H Kovalainen	1m28.207s
15	M Webber	1m30.176s	21	15	K Räikkönen	1m29.520s	33	15	H Kovalainen	1m28.738s	19	15	A Sutil	1m28.278s	15	A Sutil	1m28.391s
16	R Kubica	1m30.645s	22	16	N Heidfeld	1m29.550s	40	16	A Sutil	1m29.050s	18	16	L Hamilton	1m28.318s			
17	N Heidfeld	1m30.689s	19	17	A Sutil	1m30.081s	33	17	S Bourdais	1m29.076s	19	17	N Piquet Jr	1m28.582s			
18	G Fisichella	1m30.729s	22	18	G Fisichella	1m30.091s	38	18	S Buemi	1m29.167s	21	18	S Buemi	1m28.708s			
19	S Bourdais	1m30.838s	24	19	S Bourdais	1m30.295s	39	19	F Alonso	1m29.261s	15	19	G Fisichella	1m28.717s			
20	S Buemi	1m30.944s	25	20	S Buemi	1m30.629s	37	20	G Fisichella	1m29.421s	17	20	S Bourdais	1m28.918s			

Best sectors – Practice			Speed trap – Practice			Best sectors – Qualifying			Speed trap – Qualifying		
Sec 1	N Rosberg	32.941s	1	K Räikkönen	192.625mph	Sec 1	R Kubica	32.568s	1	F Massa	192.563mph
Sec 2	F Massa	30.747s	2	A Sutil	192.376mph	Sec 2	S Vettel	30.378s	2	G Fisichella	192.500mph
Sec 3	F Massa	24.034s	3	F Massa	191.693mph	Sec 3	K Räikkönen	23.855s	3	K Räikkönen	192.376mph

IN 2008

Felipe Massa made it three wins in the past three visits to the Istanbul circuit to close the points gap to team-mate Kimi Räikkönen, but they were split by Lewis Hamilton who had an inspired run to handle a three-stop strategy to claim second place. The BMW Saubers, as ever, were best of the rest, finishing fourth and fifth.

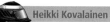

Lewis Hamilton
"It was an uneventful race, but I really enjoyed myself. I was very heavy at the start, but I pushed and pushed. That's why I can smile – as I think I drove to my full potential."

Felipe Massa
"We have to accept the fact sixth was the best we could do, as we weren't fast enough to fight those ahead. We must continue to push on the car development front."

Robert Kubica
"It's good to finally score. I think I raced well. The race was hard, as I nearly always had someone close behind, and the smallest mistake would have cost a position."

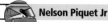

Fernando Alonso
"I started eighth, and having the lightest car on the grid penalised us because after the first pit stop we just couldn't keep up with the pace of the top contenders."

Jarno Trulli
"I made up two places into Turn 1, but struggled with locking brakes so fell to fourth. I fought Rosberg. He got ahead at the first stops, but I overtook him at the second."

Heikki Kovalainen
"At the start, I got 100% out of the car. I had a good fight with Rubens and it was satisfying to keep a faster car at bay with some good old-fashioned racing tactics."

Kimi Räikkönen
"Lap 1 was decisive: I lost places and it wasn't possible to get them back as we weren't quick enough. We aren't yet at the level of the best, especially at tracks like this."

Nick Heidfeld
"My car pulled to one side on the formation lap and the front left had no grip. The start was OK, but I more or less went straight on in the first turns due to my problems."

Nelson Piquet Jr
"My fate had been decided by the problems I had in qualifying. I had some fun battles, including the one with Lewis when I passed him, but my result is disappointing."

Timo Glock
"It was hard to score from 13th. I got caught out of Turn 1 and was pushed wide, losing places, so maybe the result could have been better. But I am happy to score."

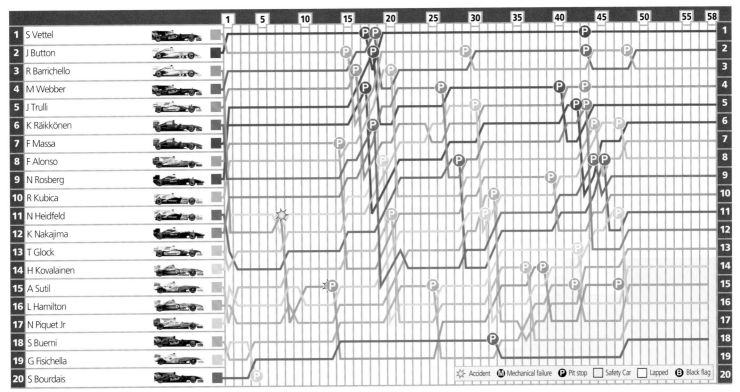

	Driver	Time
QUALIFYING 3		
	Driver	Time
1	S Vettel	1m28.316s
2	J Button	1m28.421s
3	R Barrichello	1m28.579s
4	M Webber	1m28.613s
5	J Trulli	1m28.666s
6	K Räikkönen	1m28.815s
7	F Massa	1m28.858s
8	F Alonso	1m29.075s
9	N Rosberg	1m29.191s
10	R Kubica	1m29.357s

	GRID	
	Driver	Time
1	S Vettel	1m28.316s
2	J Button	1m28.421s
3	R Barrichello	1m28.579s
4	M Webber	1m28.613s
5	J Trulli	1m28.666s
6	K Räikkönen	1m28.815s
7	F Massa	1m28.858s
8	F Alonso	1m29.075s
9	N Rosberg	1m29.191s
10	R Kubica	1m29.357s
11	N Heidfeld	1m27.521s
12	K Nakajima	1m27.629s
13	T Glock	1m27.795s
14	H Kovalainen	1m28.207s
15	A Sutil	1m28.391s
16	L Hamilton	1m28.318s
17	N Piquet Jr	1m28.582s
18	S Buemi	1m28.708s
19	G Fisichella	1m28.717s
20	S Bourdais	1m28.918s

	RACE						
	Driver	Car	Laps	Time	Avg. mph	Fastest	Stops
1	J Button	Brawn-Mercedes BGP 001	58	1h26m24.848s	133.485	1m27.579s	2
2	M Webber	Red Bull-Renault RB5	58	1h26m31.562s	133.312	1m27.809s	2
3	S Vettel	Red Bull-Renault RB5	58	1h26m32.309s	133.293	1m27.622s	3
4	J Trulli	Toyota TF109	58	1h26m52.691s	132.771	1m27.868s	2
5	N Rosberg	Williams-Toyota FW31	58	1h26m56.387s	132.677	1m28.222s	2
6	F Massa	*Ferrari F60	58	1h27m04.844s	132.462	1m28.176s	2
7	R Kubica	BMW Sauber F1.09	58	1h27m11.095s	132.304	1m28.008s	2
8	T Glock	Toyota TF109	58	1h27m11.807s	132.288	1m27.883s	2
9	K Räikkönen	*Ferrari F60	58	1h27m15.094s	132.203	1m28.061s	2
10	F Alonso	Renault R29	58	1h27m27.268s	131.896	1m28.389s	2
11	N Heidfeld	BMW Sauber F1.09	58	1h27m29.175s	131.849	1m28.214s	2
12	K Nakajima	Williams-Toyota FW31	58	1h27m31.224s	131.797	1m27.988s	2
13	L Hamilton	*McLaren-Mercedes MP4-24	58	1h27m45.302s	131.445	1m28.562s	1
14	H Kovalainen	*McLaren-Mercedes MP4-24	57	1h26m33.885s	130.953	1m29.174s	2
15	S Buemi	Toro Rosso-Ferrari STR4	57	1h26m36.808s	130.879	1m28.624s	2
16	N Piquet Jr	Renault R29	57	1h26m40.349s	130.790	1m28.340s	2
17	A Sutil	Force India-Mercedes VJM02	57	1h26m46.214s	130.643	1m29.192s	2
18	S Bourdais	Toro Rosso-Ferrari STR4	57	1h26m48.471s	130.586	1m29.022s	1
19	R Barrichello	Brawn-Mercedes BGP 001	47	Gearbox	-	1m28.526s	2
20	G Fisichella	Force India-Mercedes VJM02	4	Brakes	-	1m34.070s	0

* Denotes car fitted with KERS

	CHAMPIONSHIP	
	Driver	Pts
1	J Button	61
2	R Barrichello	35
3	S Vettel	29
4	M Webber	27.5
5	J Trulli	19.5
6	T Glock	13
7	N Rosberg	11.5
8	F Massa	11
9	F Alonso	11
10	K Räikkönen	9
11	L Hamilton	9
12	N Heidfeld	6
13	H Kovalainen	4
14	S Buemi	3
15	R Kubica	2
16	S Bourdais	2

Fastest lap
J Button 1m27.579s
(136.342mph) on lap 40

Fastest speed trap	
H Kovalainen	194.365mph
Slowest speed trap	
G Fisichella	178.271mph

	Fastest pit stop	
1	S Vettel	24.271s
2	T Glock	24.399s
3	N Rosberg	24.485s

	Constructor	Pts
1	Brawn-Mercedes	96
2	Red Bull-Renault	56.5
3	Toyota	32.5
4	Ferrari	20
5	McLaren-Mercedes	13
6	Williams-Toyota	11.5
7	Renault	11
8	BMW Sauber	8
9	Toro Rosso-Ferrari	5

Sebastien Bourdais
"After the start, Fisichella was all over the place, so I couldn't take risks trying to get past and I lost between 3–4s on lap 1. I also had to deal with a heavy fuel load."

Mark Webber
"I had to hang on in the first stint, and managed to go a lap longer, saving fuel. It was about who would finish behind Jenson and I did enough in the middle stint."

Nico Rosberg
"I'm happy with fifth. I had a great start, and by the end of lap 1 I'd made up four positions. From there, I pushed hard to get past Trulli, but he had a quicker car."

Adrian Sutil
"I'd hoped for more. I lost two places at the start, but was able to get them back. It wasn't a problem with Barrichello: he touched me, but I was just defending position."

Jenson Button
"We showed what this car can do. I had a good start from the dirty side and took my chance on lap 1 when Sebastian went wide, and from there controlled the race."

Sebastien Buemi
"It was a tough but good race, as I attacked as hard as I could. We have to stay positive and, today, we looked a bit more competitive than over the rest of the weekend."

Sebastian Vettel
"The start was OK, but I nearly lost the car at Turn 9/10. And I nearly did the same on lap 2. After that, I thought the strategy might swap to a two-stop plan, but it didn't."

Kazuki Nakajima
"I had a good start and a strong first lap. It all went well until the second stop. What happened was a shame, as I think that was probably the best race of my career."

Giancarlo Fisichella
"We changed the brake systems, but it was actually worse. I was quite competitive, but then the brake pedal was getting longer and we decided to retire the car."

Rubens Barrichello
"A clutch problem put my car into anti-stall. I was hitting the limiter on the straights, so I had to take risks to pass. With the gearbox getting worse, I had to retire."

2009 FORMULA 1 SANTANDER BRITISH GRAND PRIX
SILVERSTONE

A DRIVE OF PERFECTION

Red Bull Racing's Sebastian Vettel controlled proceedings at Silverstone from start to finish for his first win in the dry, while team-mate Mark Webber was left frustrated in second

The best way to bounce back from a costly mistake is to follow up with a faultless drive, and that's exactly what Sebastian Vettel did at Silverstone. After hitting the wall in Monaco and going off the road on the first lap in Turkey, the rising German star didn't put a foot wrong for the duration of the British GP weekend. He turned in a performance that was so dominant that the race was still fascinating to watch, despite any lack of excitement over what the eventual outcome would be.

It was just the sort of result that Vettel and his team needed. On top in the rain in China, they might easily have won a couple of other races this season had luck gone their way, or strategy played out differently. With World Championship leader Jenson Button finishing only sixth at Silverstone, and Red Bull Racing looking ever stronger, suddenly the battle for the world title didn't seem as clear-cut as it had looked previously.

We knew going to Silverstone that RBR would be strong, and could well have the edge on Brawn, but their advantage was exacerbated by circumstances. In the cool conditions, Button in particular had trouble getting the tyres to work properly, as his anxious descriptions over the team radio on Friday made clear. This time there was no gradual progression to

"It's been a strange weekend with all the politics in the background, but it's a great feeling to come away with a 1–2, our second of the year. The factory is just a few miles away and there is always special interest in Silverstone. The credit goes to everyone who has worked so hard to get the updated car ready.

Perhaps the circuit didn't suit Brawn, and it looks as if the cooler conditions gave them problems with tyre temperature, but we were obviously very competitive and the changes to the car have certainly helped. I don't see why we shouldn't be competitive at the remaining races.

Both of our drivers were right with the programme straight away, but Mark made an error on his final run in Q3, when Räikkönen was ahead going into Stowe. He was expecting to be on the front row and so third on the grid was a disappointment, but Sebastian did a good job getting pole, and qualifying turned out to be the difference when Rubens managed to split them, which obviously compromised Mark's first stint in the race.

They are pushing each other hard. Obviously Sebastian has had two wins now and Mark is still looking for his first, which I'm sure he hoped was going to be here. It's still very impressive when you consider that lying in a hospital bed in Tasmania in November, he could hardly have been dreaming about grands prix wins. Certainly, we had some concerns because he forgot to tell us that he'd broken his shoulder as well as his leg...

The comeback has been remarkable and it's testimony to his determination and commitment that he has got himself back, got himself fit and is driving better than ever. I don't think Mark's at full fitness still, though.

As far as the World Championship is concerned, we will keep fighting to the end. Our car is working very well in a multitude of conditions, but we've still got a big hurdle to get over to catch Brawn, even if we have made some inroads this weekend.

We are pushing them very hard on development. We still have performance to come to the car and it will be a really exciting second half of the season. The pendulum may have swung, but I am sure it will swing back and forth over the next few events. We are just going to take each weekend, focus race by race, and the championship will take care of itself."

perfection over the course of the weekend, and it was left to the Red Bulls to fight over pole. In the end, it didn't quite go to plan for Mark Webber, and Vettel – with the heaviest car in the top six – got it just right.

Featuring a new aerodynamic package, the Red Bull RB5s looked quick all meeting, and Vettel signalled his intentions by topping Q2 before being fastest in the final qualifying session.

"I was surprised when I crossed the line and saw the lap time," admitted the German. "The lap was close to perfect, I was able to use the tyres when I needed to, therefore I am very pleased with the result."

Webber had been a good bet for pole position, and was faster than Vettel in Q1. However, when it mattered in the final session, he couldn't match his team-mate due to Kimi Räikkönen distracting him, and he had to settle for third. Rubens Barrichello came closest to pipping Vettel, as he outshone Brawn team-mate Button who would line up in sixth place.

Q1 was red flagged with 24s to go, after Adrian Sutil crashed heavily due to an apparent brake problem that curtailed the final laps of several drivers, including Lewis Hamilton. McLaren's hero of the 2008 race was thus a lowly 19th after yet another disastrous session.

Vettel had clearly learned from his first-lap mistake in Turkey and, as the race got underway, this time he didn't put a foot wrong. He not only headed off into the lead, but pulled away from Barrichello at an astonishing 1s per lap. Webber, undoubtedly his main rival for the win, was stuck behind the Brawn.

"The start was perfect, and the first stint was the most crucial one," Vettel noted afterwards. "The more of a gap I could build up, the more important it would be for the rest of the race, and probably I would have an easier life. Which was the case, so I was very pleased and was always in control."

After just a few laps, Vettel had no one in his mirrors, making it hard to judge his own performance: "It's true, it's not easy, as you're looking at the board, talking to the team, asking 'how is the pace?' Because you can't see anyone, you can't see if you're making progress. You have to trust some numbers... and it's quite strange. In the end, it's like qualifying and you try to nail every single lap, every single corner. I have to say it was a pleasure, because this circuit is fantastic."

However, even Vettel didn't quite achieve perfection, explaining: "I was sometimes slightly too late on the brakes in the first stint and missing the apex by a sniff,

OPPOSITE ABOVE The rather crowded calm before the storm, with a packed starting grid

OPPOSITE BELOW Jenson Button sported a special helmet for his home race, but could finish no higher than sixth, 46 seconds down on winner Vettel

ABOVE Sebastian Vettel led away from pole and controlled every facet of the race for his second 2009 win

TALKING POINT
BREAKAWAY THREAT

For the media, the British GP meeting traditionally kicks off with a Renault dinner on Thursday. This time, just down the road at Renault's Enstone HQ, a simultaneous Formula One Teams Association (FOTA) meeting was in full swing. Would they reach solutions to a stand-off with the FIA and submit unconditional entries to the 2010 championship by the next day, or would they announce a breakaway championship?

It was almost midnight when the statement came through. No deal. They were going it alone. The war was on. The teams were unhappy that recent changes to the F1 rule structure effectively rendered them powerless to influence regulatory change, and they did not like the fact that such a large portion of the sport's revenue disappears to commercial rights holders CVC Capital Partners.

The following day, the FIA responded: "The actions of FOTA as a whole, and Ferrari in particular, amount to serious violations of law, including wilful interference with contractual relations, direct breaches of Ferrari's legal obligations and a grave violation of competition law. The FIA will be issuing legal proceedings without delay."

Ferrari in particular because Ferrari had already committed to the FIA World Championship until 2012, in return for certain 'privileges' which, it had emerged, included rights of rule veto. Ferrari, however, pointed out that "on the 15th June last, it already instigated arbitration against the FIA to protect its contractual rights in its dealings with this Federation, including those relative to the respecting of procedures as regards the adoption of rules and the right to veto."

What Ferrari was effectively saying was, because you've not allowed us to veto your rules, then we are not obliged to play. With Ferrari on-side, Max and Bernie always had a strong hand in the past. But now?

The FOTA teams denied publicly that they wanted to be rid of Mosley, but there was little doubt that was part of the agenda. Everyone agreed that two separate championships was in nobody's interest but, if it was still to be an FIA series, then concessions would need to be made. The issue dominated the British GP.

By Sunday night, Mosley was talking not of litigation but consultation. Without it, CVC faced owning 75% of nothing. When you considered what Max had been through in the past year – the humiliating exposure of his private life, the fight for survival as FIA President and then, just a few weeks before the British GP, the death of his son, it was truly remarkable that he had the stomach for a fight.

but it wasn't costing me an awful lot, possibly half-a-tenth or a tenth some laps. In the end, I think I was gaining more by pushing so hard."

That was a characteristic understatement. When Barrichello pitted on lap 18, he was more than 18s behind, a clear demonstration of Vettel's metronomic progress. The next two stints were about bringing it home, and only a mistake could cost Vettel victory.

"I had quite a lot of traffic in the second stint due to lapped cars," said Vettel, "so it wasn't always easy, I had to be patient. I was counting the laps down. Ten laps from the end, I had a moment because I had a big rain drop on my visor all of a sudden in Stowe, and I thought if it starts to rain now it will be quite exciting!

"Fortunately it didn't. Obviously, when you are in the lead, having quite a margin to the guys behind, the last thing you want is something special to happen, whereas when you are maybe sitting behind and you can't really get the gap close that's just what you're waiting for."

Meanwhile, Webber had to settle for a distant second. He did get closer to Vettel over the second and third stints, but the German driver was only going as fast as he needed to. Those laps stuck behind Barrichello in the first part of the race had proved very costly for the

Australian and, had Räikkönen not spoiled his qualifying lap, things might have been different.

"We were going to try and do it off the line, but it didn't work so we took it to the first stint," said Webber of his tussle with Barrichello. "I saved fuel sitting behind him and jumped him at the first stop. After that, it was pretty straightforward with the fight with Rubens. Sebastian's gap was just too big, as the damage that Rubens cost me in the first stint was massive.

"Rubens drove as hard as he could, but that wasn't enough for us to stay in touch with Sebastian. It also would have been nice to maybe have landed the qualy position that we probably deserved, but I think I got the most I could out of today. Second is the first loser of course, but also it's still not a bad result."

A first dry-weather 1–2, just a few miles from the Milton Keynes factory, was a great result for RBR.

"We always highlighted this track as a circuit that would suit the characteristics of our car," said RBR boss Christian Horner. "We also brought a couple of modifications here that seem to be working well. What's been surprising is that we expected to be strong in the first two sectors, the high-speed stuff, and actually sector three has been very strong."

OPPOSITE Rubens Barrichello holds down second place in the first stint, holding up Mark Webber

BELOW Felipe Massa and Nico Rosberg tussle over the minor points-paying positions

BOTTOM Heikki Kovalainen clashed with Sebastien Bourdais, at Vale, and it certainly didn't improve his McLaren's handling

ABOVE Sporting conduct from Mark Webber as he congratulates team-mate Sebastian Vettel on the win that he himself would have liked to have gained

ABOVE Sporting conduct from Mark Webber as he congratulates team-mate Sebastian Vettel on the win that he himself would have liked to have gained

BELOW Giancarlo Fisichella finished 10th after showing increasingly strong form for the improving Force India team

Barrichello dropped away in third place after the first stops, and by the flag he almost fell into the clutches of Felipe Massa. The latter had a charging race and, having started only 11th, gained ground with a late first stop. Ferrari was the only team using KERS, and both drivers benefited at the start. Massa got up to eighth and then, by running until lap 22, jumped to fifth, before taking fourth place from Nico Rosberg at the second stops.

Rosberg nevertheless had a good run to fifth for Williams on the 30th anniversary of the team's first win. Button meanwhile started sixth and then dropped to ninth after getting boxed in at the start. He soon passed Massa and then spent a long time trying to get by Jarno

Trulli. He eventually finished where he had started, in sixth, having pushed Rosberg hard in the closing laps, albeit without finding a way past.

The final points went to Trulli and a low-key Räikkönen, who had been fifth in the first stint, but got blocked by the Toyota mid-race. Timo Glock finished a disappointed ninth, while Giancarlo Fisichella had a great race for Force India, finishing 10th on merit. Indeed, after charging past several cars in the first two laps, he benefited when the back half of the field got trapped behind Nick Heidfeld's BMW Sauber.

Once again, some of the big names struggled badly. Robert Kubica and Heidfeld finished 13th and 15th, split by Fernando Alonso's Renault. Hamilton came home 16th after struggling for grip and losing a bit of time with a quick spin. Nevertheless, he got a big cheer when he brought the car home.

The only incident of note in a relatively unexciting race was a collision between Sebastien Bourdais and Heikki Kovalainen that eliminated both drivers.

After such a flat performance, the Brawn GP guys were left scratching their heads, and in essence blaming the cool temperatures for the tyre problems. RBR looked strong, but could the team really start building title-winning momentum?

"I will answer this question in a couple of grands prix time!" said Vettel. "You never know what happens at the next one. That's sport, that's racing. For sure we are going the right way. We are here to fight and here to win, and today it was a good day for us. Every single venue counts, and in the end we will add up all the points we have collected and see if it is enough.

"I would say that we have made a step forward, I would say that the pace of the car is already very good, but we had a competitive car before as well. Obviously it worked perfectly here, so we can be very pleased with the results and hope to continue. We have a very strong package, and it's up to us to use it."

SNAPSHOT FROM
BRITAIN

CLOCKWISE FROM RIGHT It's go, go, go, as Sebastian Vettel leads away from pole position in front of a full house; cycling stars Victoria Pendleton and Chris Hoy were among the celebrities in attendance...; ...as was England football manager Fabio Capello; Stirling Moss offers Jenson Button some last-minute advice; Nelson Piquet Jr has a quiet moment; 'Button' was everywhere for his home race; home support was appreciated by both British drivers; Bernie Eccelstone meets 'The Stig'

WEEKEND NEWS

■ After a lengthy meeting of team bosses at Renault's Enstone factory, FOTA announced late on the Thursday evening ahead of the British GP that plans for a breakaway series were going ahead. The FIA responded on Friday morning, and for the rest of the weekend the subject dominated every conversation.

■ Shortly before the British GP, the FIA had confirmed that the three 2010 entry slots had been filled by the US F1, Campos Meta and Manor Motorsport teams. The last of these – with promised technical support provided by former Simtek boss Nick Wirth – had kept a low profile throughout the bidding process.

■ Silverstone did little to acknowledge that this was supposedly the last British GP to be held at the track, and indeed during the weekend there were increasingly strong signals that Donington Park might not be ready to replace it for 2010. Both Bernie Ecclestone and Max Mosley hinted that we could be returning to Northamptonshire in 2010, at least temporarily.

■ Jackie Stewart celebrated the anniversary of his 1969 British GP win by getting back behind the wheel of a Matra MS80 on Sunday morning. The race has forged a place in the history books thanks to his spectacular battle with the Lotus of his old pal Jochen Rindt.

■ As usual, Silverstone rivalled Monaco for its roll call of VIPs, although it was definitely more sporting excellence than Hollywood glitz. Among those on view were footballers Michael Ballack, Eric Cantona and England football manager Fabio Capello, plus Olympic cycling heroes Chris Hoy and Victoria Pendleton. Meanwhile, darts legend Bobby George demonstrated his skills in the Force India motorhome!

RACE RESULTS
GREAT BRITAIN SILVERSTONE

Official Results © [2009]
Formula One Administration Limited,
6 Princes Gate, London, SW7 1QJ.
No reproduction without permission.
All copyright and database rights reserved.

RACE DATE June 21st
CIRCUIT LENGTH 3.194 miles
NO. OF LAPS 60
RACE DISTANCE 191.640 miles
WEATHER Bright and dry, 17°C
TRACK TEMP 25°C
ATTENDANCE 310,000
LAP RECORD Michael Schumacher, 1m18.739s, 146.059mph, 2004

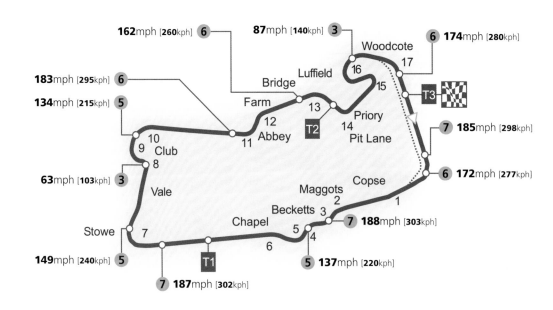

PRACTICE 1			
	Driver	Time	Laps
1	S Vettel	1m19.400s	20
2	M Webber	1m19.682s	19
3	J Button	1m20.227s	20
4	R Barrichello	1m20.242s	29
5	F Alonso	1m20.458s	26
6	F Massa	1m20.471s	23
7	J Trulli	1m20.585s	32
8	L Hamilton	1m20.650s	26
9	N Rosberg	1m20.815s	32
10	G Fisichella	1m20.838s	25
11	A Sutil	1m20.913s	22
12	H Kovalainen	1m21.029s	22
13	N Heidfeld	1m21.103s	24
14	K Räikkönen	1m21.179s	27
15	S Bourdais	1m21.384s	23
16	T Glock	1m21.386s	32
17	K Nakajima	1m21.489s	26
18	N Piquet Jr	1m21.525s	30
19	S Buemi	1m21.590s	37
20	R Kubica	1m21.801s	16

PRACTICE 2			
	Driver	Time	Laps
1	S Vettel	1m19.456s	39
2	M Webber	1m19.597s	35
3	A Sutil	1m20.141s	41
4	K Nakajima	1m20.209s	36
5	F Alonso	1m20.237s	36
6	R Barrichello	1m20.244s	26
7	L Hamilton	1m20.417s	35
8	J Trulli	1m20.458s	40
9	N Rosberg	1m20.468s	42
10	N Piquet Jr	1m20.608s	37
11	R Kubica	1m20.622s	23
12	H Kovalainen	1m20.733s	37
13	T Glock	1m20.762s	37
14	J Button	1m20.767s	28
15	N Heidfeld	1m20.932s	35
16	S Bourdais	1m20.945s	36
17	F Massa	1m21.005s	37
18	K Räikkönen	1m21.132s	38
19	G Fisichella	1m21.413s	40
20	S Buemi	1m21.668s	37

PRACTICE 3			
	Driver	Time	Laps
1	N Rosberg	1m18.899s	20
2	K Nakajima	1m19.102s	19
3	J Trulli	1m19.125s	15
4	S Vettel	1m19.371s	15
5	F Massa	1m19.596s	19
6	K Räikkönen	1m19.855s	13
7	T Glock	1m19.868s	19
8	F Alonso	1m19.917s	14
9	M Webber	1m19.946s	15
10	R Barrichello	1m20.028s	14
11	L Hamilton	1m20.048s	16
12	J Button	1m20.157s	17
13	N Piquet Jr	1m20.232s	18
14	S Bourdais	1m20.459s	17
15	A Sutil	1m20.548s	15
16	G Fisichella	1m20.572s	17
17	H Kovalainen	1m20.638s	18
18	N Heidfeld	1m20.696s	20
19	S Buemi	1m21.024s	11
20	R Kubica	1m21.039s	13

QUALIFYING 1		
	Driver	Time
1	K Nakajima	1m18.530s
2	M Webber	1m18.674s
3	S Vettel	1m18.685s
4	J Trulli	1m18.886s
5	J Button	1m18.957s
6	K Räikkönen	1m19.010s
7	F Massa	1m19.148s
8	F Alonso	1m19.167s
9	T Glock	1m19.198s
10	N Rosberg	1m19.228s
11	R Barrichello	1m19.325s
12	N Piquet Jr	1m19.555s
13	N Heidfeld	1m19.559s
14	R Kubica	1m19.730s
15	H Kovalainen	1m19.732s
16	G Fisichella	1m19.802s
17	S Bourdais	1m19.898s
18	A Sutil	1m19.909s
19	L Hamilton	1m19.917s
20	S Buemi	1m20.236s

QUALIFYING 2		
	Driver	Time
1	S Vettel	1m18.119s
2	M Webber	1m18.209s
3	J Trulli	1m18.240s
4	R Barrichello	1m18.335s
5	K Räikkönen	1m18.566s
6	K Nakajima	1m18.575s
7	N Rosberg	1m18.591s
8	J Button	1m18.663s
9	F Alonso	1m18.761s
10	T Glock	1m18.791s
11	F Massa	1m18.927s
12	R Kubica	1m19.308s
13	H Kovalainen	1m19.353s
14	N Piquet Jr	1m19.392s
15	N Heidfeld	1m19.448s

Best sectors – Practice			Speed trap – Practice			Best sectors – Qualifying			Speed trap – Qualifying		
Sec 1	J Trulli	25.218s	1	A Sutil	184.547mph	Sec 1	K Räikkönen	24.949s	1	A Sutil	184.920mph
Sec 2	S Vettel	33.918s	2	G Fisichella	183.863mph	Sec 2	R Barrichello	33.575s	2	J Trulli	184.485mph
Sec 3	N Rosberg	19.632s	3	N Heidfeld	183.366mph	Sec 3	M Webber	19.355s	3	K Räikkönen	184.050mph

IN 2008

Rain was the key feature of a dramatic race, with Lewis Hamilton mastering the changing conditions as Felipe Massa struggled, spinning five times. Kimi Räikkönen pushed, but a decision to keep him on inters took him out of contention, leaving the way clear for Nick Heidfeld to finish second and Rubens Barrichello third.

Lewis Hamilton
"We knew it would be hard, and I enjoyed my battle with Fernando, but we didn't have the pace to score points. The best thing about the weekend has been the fans."

Felipe Massa
"I feel as though I won! To start 11th and finish fourth is great. I had a good strategy and I pushed at the key moments. The KERS was a help, especially at the start."

Robert Kubica
"This was a difficult race. Starting 12th, we couldn't achieve much, so we decided to start the race with a high fuel load and on the prime tyres. But it didn't pay off."

Fernando Alonso
"We lost two places at the start and I was stuck behind Heidfeld who was heavy on fuel. Although I had some good fights, I'm really frustrated with the result."

Jarno Trulli
"I had a difficult start, as the car didn't pull away as normal, so I lost a couple of positions. I was trying to fight back all race, but it wasn't easy and the car was sliding a lot."

Heikki Kovalainen
"Until my retirement, I was on target. Then Bourdais ran into the back of me and damaged the left-rear corner. I then had to stop, as it made the car undriveable."

Kimi Räikkönen
"I got a good start, but couldn't push as much as I wanted as I was always in traffic. After the first stops, I was behind Trulli and from then on my race was really over."

Nick Heidfeld
"Given our poor qualifying, the result was as expected. At the start, I risked a lot going for a small gap. I damaged my front wing but was glad it wasn't worse than that."

Nelson Piquet Jr
"The result is disappointing. We must introduce upgrades, as I can be competitive if the car is good, but it's down to me to improve my performance in qualifying."

Timo Glock
"It's a pity to miss out on points, as I was quick out of traffic and was able to catch Kimi. The problem was at the first corner when I lost places and that left me in traffic."

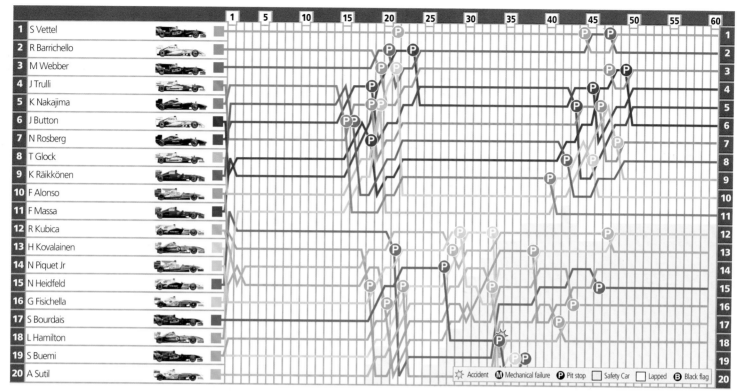

1	S Vettel				
2	R Barrichello				
3	M Webber				
4	J Trulli				
5	K Nakajima				
6	J Button				
7	N Rosberg				
8	T Glock				
9	K Räikkönen				
10	F Alonso				
11	F Massa				
12	R Kubica				
13	H Kovalainen				
14	N Piquet Jr				
15	N Heidfeld				
16	G Fisichella				
17	S Bourdais				
18	L Hamilton				
19	S Buemi				
20	A Sutil				

☆ Accident   Ⓜ Mechanical failure   Ⓟ Pit stop   ☐ Safety Car   ☐ Lapped   Ⓑ Black flag

QUALIFYING 3

	Driver	Time
1	S Vettel	1m19.509s
2	R Barrichello	1m19.856s
3	M Webber	1m19.868s
4	J Trulli	1m20.091s
5	K Nakajima	1m20.216s
6	J Button	1m20.289s
7	N Rosberg	1m20.361s
8	T Glock	1m20.490s
9	K Räikkönen	1m20.715s
10	F Alonso	1m20.741s

GRID

	Driver	Time
1	S Vettel	1m19.509s
2	R Barrichello	1m19.856s
3	M Webber	1m19.868s
4	J Trulli	1m20.091s
5	K Nakajima	1m20.216s
6	J Button	1m20.289s
7	N Rosberg	1m20.361s
8	T Glock	1m20.490s
9	K Räikkönen	1m20.715s
10	F Alonso	1m20.741s
11	F Massa	1m18.927s
12	R Kubica	1m19.308s
13	H Kovalainen	1m19.353s
14	N Piquet Jr	1m19.392s
15	N Heidfeld	1m19.448s
16	G Fisichella	1m19.802s
17	S Bourdais	1m19.898s
18	L Hamilton	1m19.917s
19	S Buemi	1m20.236s
20*	A Sutil	1m19.909s

* Started with spare chassis

RACE

	Driver	Car	Laps	Time	Avg. mph	Fastest	Stops
1	S Vettel	Red Bull-Renault RB5	60	1h22m49.328s	138.805	1m20.735s	2
2	M Webber	Red Bull-Renault RB5	60	1h23m04.516s	138.382	1m20.915s	2
3	R Barrichello	Brawn-Mercedes BGP 001	60	1h23m30.503s	137.665	1m21.429s	2
4	F Massa	*Ferrari F60	60	1h23m34.371s	137.558	1m21.509s	2
5	N Rosberg	Williams-Toyota FW31	60	1h23m35.243s	137.534	1m21.054s	2
6	J Button	Brawn-Mercedes BGP 001	60	1h23m35.613s	137.524	1m21.189s	2
7	J Trulli	Toyota TF109	60	1h23m57.635s	136.923	1m21.806s	2
8	K Räikkönen	*Ferrari F60	60	1h23m58.950s	136.887	1m21.656s	2
9	T Glock	Toyota TF109	60	1h23m59.151s	136.882	1m21.671s	2
10	G Fisichella	Force India-Mercedes VJM02	60	1h24m00.850s	136.836	1m21.810s	2
11	K Nakajima	Williams-Toyota FW31	60	1h24m03.351s	136.768	1m21.845s	2
12	N Piquet Jr	Renault R29	59	1h23m00.929s	136.173	1m22.505s	1
13	R Kubica	BMW Sauber F1.09	59	1h23m01.760s	136.150	1m22.182s	2
14	F Alonso	Renault R29	59	1h23m02.225s	136.137	1m21.852s	2
15	N Heidfeld	BMW Sauber F1.09	59	1h23m25.425s	135.507	1m21.956s	2
16	L Hamilton	McLaren-Mercedes MP4-24	59	1h23m52.322s	134.782	1m22.576s	2
17	A Sutil	Force India-Mercedes VJM02	59	1h23m53.434s	134.752	1m23.475s	1
18	S Buemi	Toro Rosso-Ferrari STR4	59	1h23m56.002s	134.684	1m22.711s	2
R	S Bourdais	Toro Rosso-Ferrari STR4	37	Water pressure	-	1m22.466s	2
R	H Kovalainen	McLaren-Mercedes MP4-24	36	Crash damage	-	1m22.418s	2

* Denotes car fitted with KERS

CHAMPIONSHIP

	Driver	Pts
1	J Button	64
2	R Barrichello	41
3	S Vettel	39
4	M Webber	35.5
5	J Trulli	21.5
6	F Massa	16
7	N Rosberg	15.5
8	T Glock	13
9	F Alonso	11
10	K Räikkönen	10
11	L Hamilton	9
12	N Heidfeld	6
13	H Kovalainen	4
14	S Buemi	3
15	R Kubica	2
16	S Bourdais	2

Fastest lap
S Vettel 1m20.735s
(142.442mph) on lap 16

Fastest speed trap
K Räikkönen 183.739mph
Slowest speed trap
H Kovalainen 179.203mph

Fastest pit stop
1 K Räikkönen 22.545s
2 S Buemi 22.952s
3 K Nakajima 22.977s

	Constructor	Pts
1	Brawn-Mercedes	105
2	Red Bull-Renault	74.5
3	Toyota	34.5
4	Ferrari	26
5	Williams-Toyota	15.5
6	McLaren-Mercedes	13
7	Renault	11
8	BMW Sauber	8
9	Toro Rosso-Ferrari	5

Sebastien Bourdais
"Heikki braked early, as he'd just left the pits on full tanks. I was trying to outbrake him, but he should not have changed line twice. Then at the end I lost water pressure."

Mark Webber
"I lost my chance for victory during qualifying. I saved fuel in the first stint, which meant I could jump Rubens at the first stop. I don't think I could have done more."

Nico Rosberg
"That was another good race. We still didn't get the result we're due, but Rubens was slow in the middle stint and I was stuck behind him, costing me the place to Massa."

Adrian Sutil
"We rebuilt the spare car after my crash damaged my race car, but then had a fuel pressure problem on the formation lap. We were able to start, but it was disappointing."

Jenson Button
"I had a bad start, as Trulli was slow away ahead of me. I struggled on the harder tyres in cool conditions, but on softer rubber was able to catch Rosberg and Massa."

Sebastien Buemi
"We struggled and must work out why, as we had been quicker than this earlier in the weekend. On worn tyres especially, the car was very difficult to drive."

Sebastian Vettel
"The car was fantastic, but the second stint wasn't so easy; there were a lot of lapped cars fighting. From the last stop, I was in clean air and counting down each lap."

Kazuki Nakajima
"That result was not ideal. I was pleased with my start, but was held up by the car in front before my first stop and then it was hard to keep up with those ahead of me."

Giancarlo Fisichella
"A top-10 finish was our target. I overtook many drivers on lap 1. I passed Kubica and the Renaults on lap 2. Perhaps we could have scored if we'd started higher."

Rubens Barrichello
"We knew if track temperatures didn't increase, it would be hard to beat the Red Bulls. I had a good start, but Sebastian ran away and so I knew I was racing for third."

FORMULA 1 GROSSER PREIS SANTANDER VON DEUTSCHLAND 2009
NÜRBURGRING

WEBBER AT LAST

The speed has always been there and, in mid-2009, Mark Webber had the car to do the job too. Finally, at the 130th time of asking, the popular Australian became a grand prix winner

It had been 28 years since the anthem *Advance Australia Fair* last rang out over a grand prix circuit. However, in the eighth year of his Formula 1 career, Mark Webber won the German GP for Red Bull Racing, and so became the first Australian driver to triumph in F1 since Alan Jones was victorious for Williams at Las Vegas back in 1981.

Finally, the monkey was off Webber's back. Prior to this grand prix, the popular Aussie had been cast as the new Chris Amon, a man who so often deserved to win a race but, for whatever reason (usually bad luck) it wasn't to be. Even here at the Nürburgring, it wasn't all plain sailing…

Seven months before this race, Webber was lying in the road with a broken leg and a broken shoulder. It was a gut-wrenching, possible career-threatening moment but, as he admitted after winning, the winter testing pace of the RB5 kept his motivation up.

In the subsequent months, Webber worked tirelessly on his rehabilitation with his physiotherapist Roger Cleary. And, while he's admitted his confidence was knocked early on in his convalescence, coming to Germany the plucky Australian was determined to reverse the outcome of the British Grand Prix

ABOVE Hamilton had got his nose ahead of Rubens Barrichello's going into the first corner, but contact with Mark Webber (behind) would hurt...

BELOW ...and his high hopes for the race went pop, along with his right-rear tyre. It was a long and doubly costly limp back to the pits

OPPOSITE Red Bull Racing's Sebastian Vettel leaves Felipe Massa's blurred Ferrari in his wake

and stop Sebastian Vettel's march in the title race. Webber's return to fitness (indeed, he had a couple of pins taken out of his leg prior to the race at the Nürburgring) proved that when he's down, he'll come back fighting…

"It is an incredible day for me and I wanted to win so badly after the British GP, as I thought I had a good chance at Silverstone," enthused Webber. "However, after yesterday's pole position I knew that I was in a good position to win. I've had great people around me to recover from the injuries that I suffered, and Sebastian showed in winter testing what the car could do, so that kept my motivation

very high when I was hurting a lot with all my rehab. It's just an incredible day for all the people who have helped me to get to where I am."

This was supposed to be Vettel's weekend, though, just as it should have been Webber's at Silverstone. Whether it was the pressure of competing in his home race or some other factor, though, Vettel admitted that he wasn't as quick as his team-mate, and so it transpired in qualifying when Webber took the first pole position of his career. With Vettel qualifying fourth and the Brawns struggling to get heat into their tyres, many people in the paddock were predicting that Webber would break his duck come Sunday afternoon.

However, they had their own idea down at McLaren about who might win. A new rear diffuser, new engine cover and a significant update to the front wing and sidepods for Lewis Hamilton gave the Woking team cause for optimism. The reigning World Champion had been fastest of all on Friday afternoon and again on Saturday morning, and was duly the first non-Brawn or Red Bull car on the grid, qualifying fifth. The top two teams were concerned too, particularly as Hamilton would be able to take advantage of the extra 80 or so horsepower from his KERS boost at the start.

Sure enough, when the five red lights flicked off to signal the start of the race, the McLarens made a blistering getaway from the third row. Hamilton blasted into an instant lead, while Heikki Kovalainen slotted into third, a significant third, as it transpired.

On the run down to the first corner, Hamilton was helped by front-row starters Webber and Rubens Barrichello coming together. With his lighter fuel load, the Brazilian driver managed to pull alongside Webber on the run to Turn 1. Knowing that leading the first lap would be crucial if he wanted to win, Webber tried to fend off Barrichello, but he did it

INSIDE LINE
LEWIS HAMILTON
McLAREN DRIVER

"To finish 18th definitely wasn't the result we were hoping for before this race. We'd had such an encouraging practice and qualifying, so I thought I could get a good result for myself and the team, but it just wasn't to be.

It was just unfortunate that I got a puncture at the first corner of the race and, as we now know, that it subsequently damaged the upper floor and brake duct. That was my race over, because I had a handling imbalance for the rest of the afternoon. There was no safety concern, but we did lose downforce and it made the car difficult to control.

But I feel optimistic going to Hungary that we've made good improvement with the car. If we had turned up at the Nürburgring and discovered that the upgrades we'd brought were a disappointment, then it would have been a huge blow to everyone. However, as far as we know, the upgrades made a considerable difference to our performance in Germany.

For the first time this year, I actually felt that I had a car under me that I could control instead of it controlling me.

Unfortunately the team were able to complete only one set of upgrades, so Heikki had to run with some of the older parts, but he had a great race and result considering, and I'm hopeful that we can carry that performance and more through to Hungary.

The team has more improvements planned, and it would be great if we could further close the gap to the leaders, as Red Bull Racing and Brawn have both got fantastic cars and it will be incredibly hard to just turn up and be able to compete with them.

At least we are now on the right track with our upgrades and the development process continues for both this year and next. While it's nice to think about race results and running at the front, as I've said before I now look at this year as a development year for all of us and one that will only make us stronger in the future.

I'm confident that we'll have some good showings in the next few grands prix, and then we should have a clearer idea of just how well we'll go at the end of the season."

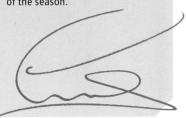

with a forceful bash that left a battle-scarred rubbery mark on the Brawn's left sidepod. As Webber straightened himself up, he just clipped Hamilton's right-rear tyre as the KERS-boosted McLaren was flying past. That touch was enough to puncture Hamilton's right rear tyre and his chance for a victory or podium was instantly over.

Barrichello did make it past Webber but, because Kovalainen had made it up to third place, the Finn neatly held up the other Brawn of Button, the other Red Bull of Vettel and the two Ferraris.

That allowed Barrichello and Webber to make their escape, and it was significant for Webber that they were able to, as after nine laps the stewards announced they were going to look more closely at the 'incident' between he and Barrichello just after the start. Two laps later, the inevitable came. Car 14 was issued with a drive-through-penalty for causing a collision. Had Webber been jinxed again?

Fortunately for Webber, thanks to Kovalainen holding up a train of cars, the top two had a 16s lead over the Finn and his group of followers, namely Button, Felipe Massa, Vettel, Kimi Räikkönen and Force India's Adrian Sutil. Yes, Sutil.

The Force India team has been working miracles this year thanks to the technical assistance from McLaren, and Sutil was actually set for a points finish at the Nürburgring. He'd made his way up to second place before his late first pit stop, but the dream ended when he clashed with Räikkönen (why is it always Kimi?) exiting the pits, necessitating a stop again for a new front wing.

Back at the front of the race, Barrichello and Webber pitted from the lead on the same lap. However, while Webber was serving his drivethrough penalty and continued back out of the pits with a clear track in front of him, Barrichello emerged in the middle of Kovalainen's train, right behind Massa.

Webber had five laps to put the hammer down, while it was another 11 laps before Massa was due to stop. And, from there, Barrichello's race was finished. Webber duly disappeared down the road, while Barrichello was seeing any chance of a successful three-stop strategy fall apart thanks to Massa.

KERS was introduced this year and one of the advantages that it was intended to bring was an 'overtaking boost' – however, it's also done a not insubstantial job of holding people at bay and keeping

BELOW Just as at Monaco in 2008, Kimi Räikkönen ruins Adrian Sutil's hopes of coming away with points

OPPOSITE Rubens Barrichello is guided in for a pit stop, but he was later truly livid with the way that the team handled his race strategy

the race order static, the reverse of what it had been intended to achieve…

With the temperatures much hotter on Sunday than they had been for the earlier part of the meeting, Brawn's hopes had been further compromised. They wanted to spend as little time as possible on the medium compound tyre, hence the three-stop strategy, but the increase in temperatures meant the medium tyre was working better than the teams had experienced, and the super-softs were graining more quickly than usual.

When Barrichello came in for his second stop, the intention was to switch him to a two-stop strategy, but when he asked the team if he was now able to run to the flag, the response was "negative".

A faulty fuel rig, meant the team had to swap hoses and not enough fuel went into the Brawn's tank, so Barrichello would have to stop again before the finish. If that wasn't bad enough, his Brawn team-mate Button was on his tail in the final stint of the race. Then, when the team pitted Barrichello first, it gave Button the chance to do a quicker in-lap and out-lap and emerge ahead of the Brazilian…

Barrichello (with Webber) had held a 16s lead in

TALKING POINT
REVOLVING DOORS

There was an interesting contrast of television pictures during the broadcast of the German Grand Prix. Just as Sebastien Bourdais was seen hugging Scuderia Toro Rosso's tech boss Giorgio Ascanelli on the pit wall – an image that said Formula 1 was saying goodbye to the Frenchman – so the television cameras cut to a man to whom the grand prix world was now saying hello.

As he strode confidently down the paddock in his dark tie and jacket, this was the first glimpse we'd seen of former World Rally Champion Ari Vatanen, who could become one of the most powerful men in motorsport, after he announced that he would stand for the role of FIA President in the October elections.

Max Mosley had conceded that he would not stand for re-election, following the on-going political storm surrounding FOTA and their plans for a breakaway F1

series, but had given his public support to the other candidate for the job, former Ferrari boss Jean Todt.

So it was Vatanen v Todt in the race for the premiership of the FIA, but Vatanen was the first to appear at a grand prix and spent a lot of time with reporters at the Nürburgring, talking about the need for greater transparency in the governing body.

"The President is the public face of the FIA – the role is to defend the one billion motorists in the world, but this must be in consultation," said Vatanen. "The President's role is not to get involved on a daily basis in the technical details. It is about simple, professional, transparent management."

Vatanen won the World Rally Championship in 1981 for Ford with former Benetton then British American Racing boss David Richards as his co-driver, and then also went on to drive for Peugeot, which at the time was run by one Mr Todt…

Bizarrely, Vatanen wasn't the only rallying connection with F1 at the German GP. That's because Kimi Räikkönen was talking about his upcoming debut on the Finnish Rally (which could one day lead to a full-time switch), while multiple World Rally Champion Sebastien Loeb was being touted for an F1 drive later in the year, in the place of guess who…? Outgoing F1 driver Sebastien Bourdais…

the opening stages and yet managed to finish the race back in sixth… How had he done that?

"I'm terribly upset with the way things have gone today, because it was a very good show of how to lose a race," said Barrichello in an extraordinary, emotional attack on his team immediately after the race. "I did everything I had to do. I had to go first into the first corner, and that's what I did. Then they [Brawn] made me lose the race basically. If we keep going on like this, then we'll end up losing both championships.

"To be honest, I wish I could just get on a plane and go home now. I don't want to talk to anyone in the team, because it would be a lot of blah, blah, blah, blah... And I don't want to hear it."

Barrichello had at his disposal a superior machine with the Brawn in 2009, but to see his team-mate take six wins and to have not won himself, indeed not having been victorious since the 2004 Chinese GP, you can imagine the frustration starting to build. Thankfully, Ross Brawn is a forgiving man…

The frustration was evident in Button too during the weekend and particularly the race. In the closing stages, he was weaving down the straight simply to do what he could to try to generate heat in his tyres. Also, when he spoke on the radio to his team, it sounded like an exasperated cry, rather than the controlled dialogue that other drivers offer. The wheels were ever so slightly starting to come off Brawn's championship campaign, and Webber's victory was a clear indication that this championship wasn't going to be about just Button and Vettel.

Webber was relaxed too, this weekend. Prior to his outstanding qualifying lap, he was asked whether he engaged in any sort of intense mental preparation? "Nah mate, I was watching my school mate Brad Haddin score some runs against England… It's good to see him doing so well!" Good to see Webber do well too, after the tribulations that he's suffered over the course of the past 12 months.

First of all a British driver – Button – won in Australia. Then a German – Vettel – won in Britain and now an Australian – Webber – won in Germany. What chance Barrichello winning in Brazil…?

ABOVE LEFT Nico Rosberg leads Robert Kubica and Giancarlo Fisichella in the early stages, when they circulated outside the top 10 after qualifying badly

LEFT Mark Webber punches the air with delight, having finally secured the win that many felt he deserved years earlier in his career

SNAPSHOT FROM
GERMANY

CLOCKWISE FROM RIGHT Nelson Piquet Jr dives into Turn 1 in what would be his last but one grand prix; a win for Vettel would have been appreciated; Timo Glock raced with a helmet livery designed by this eight-year-old; five photographers take the same photo of Kimi Räikkönen's Ferrari; one doubts that it said M. Webber on the back of one of the trouser legs...; the Nürburgring's off-track facilities provided a thrill too; Mark Webber just couldn't stop celebrating his first win

WEEKEND NEWS

■ Fuji International Speedway pulled the plug on hosting the Japanese Grand Prix. The volcanoside circuit had hosted the race for the past two seasons, and was planning to alternate hosting the Japanese GP with Suzuka from 2010. However, the global economic downturn forced Fuji's owners, Toyota, to abandon those plans.

■ Red Bull Racing confirmed at the German GP that Technical Director Geoff Willis had left the team. He had joined the outfit in 2007, having worked previously at Williams then Honda Racing.

■ German police tried to impound Force India's motorhome prior to the opening practice session at the German GP, due to a payment dispute relating to work conducted on the team's hospitality unit, but the matter was swiftly resolved.

■ Sebastien Bourdais was dropped from Scuderia Toro Rosso following his retirement in the German GP, and he issued a statement planning legal action against the team. "I am even more frustrated that the decision has come before a new, competitive package was due to be introduced by the team for the next race," said the disappointed Frenchman.

■ Following on from his victory in the German GP, Red Bull Racing confirmed that Mark Webber would remain at the team for a fourth year to race alongside Sebastian Vettel for 2010. "His recent results show that Mark is on the form of his life and he has the motivation to deliver at the highest level. It was therefore a straightforward decision to extend the relationship," said team principal Christian Horner.

■ Renault announced at the Nürburgring that Fernando Alonso would drive a Renault F1 car in his home town of Oviedo in Spain in September. The street demonstration was expected to attract more than 100,000 fans. Alonso was extremely excited, saying: "To drive an F1 car in my home town will be really special."

RACE RESULTS
GERMANY
NÜRBURGRING

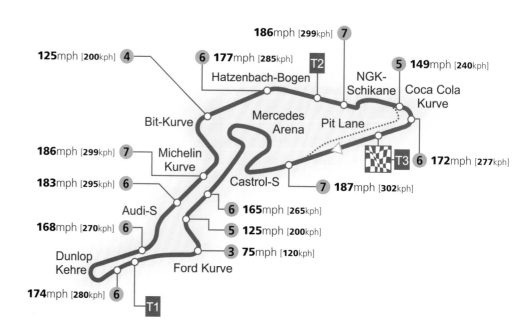

Official Results © [2009]
Formula One Administration Limited,
6 Princes Gate, London, SW7 1QJ.
No reproduction without permission.
All copyright and database rights reserved.

RACE DATE July 12th
CIRCUIT LENGTH 3.199 miles
NO. OF LAPS 60
RACE DISTANCE 191.940 miles
WEATHER Cloudy and dry, 19°C
TRACK TEMP 23°C
ATTENDANCE 250,000
LAP RECORD Michael Schumacher,
1m29.468s, 128.721mph, 2004

Track map labels:
125mph [200kph] 4 — Bit-Kurve
186mph [299kph] 7 — Hatzenbach-Bogen
6 177mph [285kph] T2
186mph [299kph] 7 — NGK-Schikane
5 149mph [240kph] — Coca Cola Kurve
186mph [299kph] 7 — Michelin Kurve
183mph [295kph] 6 — Mercedes Arena — Pit Lane
6 172mph [277kph] T3
7 187mph [302kph] — Castrol-S
168mph [270kph] 6 — Audi-S
6 165mph [265kph]
5 125mph [200kph]
3 75mph [120kph]
174mph [280kph] 6 — Dunlop Kehre — Ford Kurve — T1

PRACTICE 1			
	Driver	Time	Laps
1	M Webber	1m33.082s	19
2	J Button	1m33.463s	18
3	F Massa	1m33.745s	21
4	J Trulli	1m33.795s	23
5	G Fisichella	1m33.839s	26
6	K Räikkönen	1m33.840s	23
7	N Rosberg	1m33.902s	26
8	S Vettel	1m33.909s	13
9	K Nakajima	1m33.952s	25
10	F Alonso	1m34.148s	16
11	N Heidfeld	1m34.221s	25
12	R Barrichello	1m34.227s	17
13	L Hamilton	1m34.483s	14
14	R Kubica	1m34.694s	23
15	N Piquet Jr	1m34.738s	24
16	S Bourdais	1m34.827s	27
17	S Buemi	1m34.878s	28
18	H Kovalainen	1m34.893s	26
19	T Glock	1m34.911s	23
20	A Sutil	1m35.092s	6

PRACTICE 2			
	Driver	Time	Laps
1	L Hamilton	1m32.149s	23
2	S Vettel	1m32.331s	31
3	J Button	1m32.369s	32
4	M Webber	1m32.480s	28
5	J Trulli	1m32.511s	32
6	A Sutil	1m32.585s	32
7	R Barrichello	1m32.664s	26
8	F Alonso	1m32.774s	24
9	K Nakajima	1m32.872s	32
10	N Piquet Jr	1m32.992s	29
11	N Heidfeld	1m33.012s	36
12	F Massa	1m33.052s	34
13	N Rosberg	1m33.128s	34
14	R Kubica	1m33.161s	28
15	T Glock	1m33.172s	34
16	K Räikkönen	1m33.182s	29
17	H Kovalainen	1m33.724s	27
18	S Buemi	1m33.903s	30
19	S Bourdais	1m34.025s	30
20	G Fisichella	1m38.877s	3

PRACTICE 3			
	Driver	Time	Laps
1	L Hamilton	1m31.121s	16
2	F Alonso	1m31.340s	18
3	F Massa	1m31.351s	20
4	S Vettel	1m31.542s	17
5	M Webber	1m31.610s	16
6	K Räikkönen	1m31.615s	19
7	J Trulli	1m31.620s	23
8	N Rosberg	1m31.690s	20
9	K Nakajima	1m31.731s	20
10	N Heidfeld	1m31.928s	21
11	J Button	1m32.009s	22
12	T Glock	1m32.022s	20
13	A Sutil	1m32.104s	20
14	R Barrichello	1m32.124s	13
15	G Fisichella	1m32.135s	21
16	N Piquet Jr	1m32.223s	15
17	S Buemi	1m32.239s	23
18	R Kubica	1m32.269s	20
19	H Kovalainen	1m32.742s	18
20	S Bourdais	1m32.883s	21

QUALIFYING 1		
	Driver	Time
1	M Webber	1m31.257s
2	F Alonso	1m31.302s
3	S Vettel	1m31.430s
4	L Hamilton	1m31.473s
5	R Barrichello	1m31.482s
6	J Button	1m31.568s
7	N Rosberg	1m31.598s
8	F Massa	1m31.600s
9	J Trulli	1m31.760s
10	N Heidfeld	1m31.771s
11	K Räikkönen	1m31.869s
12	H Kovalainen	1m31.881s
13	K Nakajima	1m31.884s
14	A Sutil	1m32.015s
15	N Piquet Jr	1m32.128s
16	R Kubica	1m32.190s
17	S Buemi	1m32.251s
18	G Fisichella	1m32.402s
19	T Glock	1m32.423s
20	S Bourdais	1m33.559s

QUALIFYING 2		
	Driver	Time
1	R Barrichello	1m34.455s
2	N Piquet Jr	1m35.737s
3	A Sutil	1m35.740s
4	M Webber	1m36.038s
5	J Button	1m39.032s
6	L Hamilton	1m39.149s
7	S Vettel	1m39.504s
8	H Kovalainen	1m40.826s
9	F Massa	1m41.708s
10	K Räikkönen	1m41.730s
11	N Heidfeld	1m42.310s
12	F Alonso	1m42.318s
13	K Nakajima	1m42.500s
14	J Trulli	1m42.771s
15	N Rosberg	1m42.859s

Best sectors – Practice		
Sec 1	L Hamilton	30.040s
Sec 2	L Hamilton	37.487s
Sec 3	F Alonso	23.474s

Speed trap – Practice		
1	N Heidfeld	187.529mph
2	F Alonso	187.467mph
3	L Hamilton	187.343mph

Best sectors – Qualifying		
Sec 1	J Button	30.035s
Sec 2	M Webber	37.373s
Sec 3	L Hamilton	23.494s

Speed trap – Qualifying		
1	S Bourdais	187.902mph
2	K Räikkönen	187.219mph
3	F Massa	187.157mph

IN 2008

The 2008 German GP was at Hockenheim due to its alternation with the Nürburgring, and Lewis Hamilton fought his way back to the front after McLaren elected not to bring him into the pits after the safety car came out. He hunted down Felipe Massa, then Renault's Nelson Piquet who had pitted just as the safety car came out.

Lewis Hamilton
"I had a good launch and was braking when I felt a tap and went straight on. I think the flat tyre had damaged the floor and it felt like I was out there driving on ice."

Felipe Massa
"A great start and strategy were the keys to this result. In the first 15 laps I was struggling to keep Vettel behind me, but I think he was also struggling with his tyres."

Robert Kubica
"I gained a lot of places on lap 1. Rosberg was on primes ahead of me and was really quick. I changed to primes, but the pressures were not right and I had 20 laps to go."

Fernando Alonso
"My start was very poor and I lost quite a few places before the first corner. After that, I was stuck in traffic, but the car has clearly improved, as I set the fastest lap."

Jarno Trulli
"My race was over at the first corner when another car hit my front wing. The team changed it, but as soon as I caught up with the field I was always stuck in traffic."

Heikki Kovalainen
"Qualifying went well and our KERS hybrid helped me move from sixth to third at the start. From then on, it was all about defending and a hard way to earn points."

Kimi Räikkönen
"Germany really doesn't seem to bring me luck. I don't know how many times a problem beyond my control has forced me to retire, and this time it was down to debris."

Nick Heidfeld
"The start was good, but Sutil's defending was very tough. I made up ground in the middle stint, but had bad luck at the pit stop, as a Renault came in and I had to wait."

Nelson Piquet Jr
"I lost ground at the start, as I had some problems warming the tyres. After that, I got held up in traffic, which made it hard to progress in the second half of the race."

Timo Glock
"I am quite satisfied, as I started from the pits and came ninth on a track where overtaking is hard. If it wasn't for the traffic, I would have had a better chance of scoring."

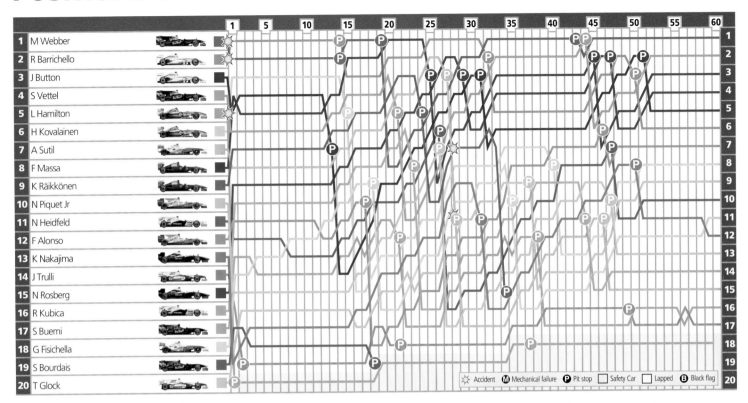

	Driver			1	5	10	15	20	25	30	35	40	45	50	55	60	
1	M Webber																1
2	R Barrichello																2
3	J Button																3
4	S Vettel																4
5	L Hamilton																5
6	H Kovalainen																6
7	A Sutil																7
8	F Massa																8
9	K Räikkönen																9
10	N Piquet Jr																10
11	N Heidfeld																11
12	F Alonso																12
13	K Nakajima																13
14	J Trulli																14
15	N Rosberg																15
16	R Kubica																16
17	S Buemi																17
18	G Fisichella																18
19	S Bourdais																19
20	T Glock																20

☆ Accident Ⓜ Mechanical failure Ⓟ Pit stop ☐ Safety Car ☐ Lapped Ⓑ Black flag

QUALIFYING 3

	Driver	Time
1	M Webber	1m32.230s
2	R Barrichello	1m32.357s
3	J Button	1m32.473s
4	S Vettel	1m32.480s
5	L Hamilton	1m32.616s
6	H Kovalainen	1m33.859s
7	A Sutil	1m34.316s
8	F Massa	1m34.574s
9	K Räikkönen	1m34.710s
10	N Piquet Jr	1m34.803s

GRID

	Driver	Time
1	M Webber	1m32.230s
2	R Barrichello	1m32.357s
3	J Button	1m32.473s
4	S Vettel	1m32.480s
5	L Hamilton	1m32.616s
6	H Kovalainen	1m33.859s
7	A Sutil	1m34.316s
8	F Massa	1m34.574s
9	K Räikkönen	1m34.710s
10	N Piquet Jr	1m34.803s
11	N Heidfeld	1m42.310s
12	F Alonso	1m42.318s
13	K Nakajima	1m42.500s
14	J Trulli	1m42.771s
15	N Rosberg	1m42.859s
16	R Kubica	1m32.190s
17	S Buemi	1m32.251s
18	G Fisichella	1m32.402s
19	S Bourdais	1m33.559s
20*	T Glock	1m32.423s

*Three-place grid penalty for obstructing Alonso in Q1

RACE

	Driver	Car	Laps	Time	Avg. mph	Fastest	Stops
1	M Webber	Red Bull-Renault RB5	60	1h36m43.310s	119.053	1m34.003s	3
2	S Vettel	Red Bull-Renault RB5	60	1h36m52.562s	118.864	1m34.089s	2
3	F Massa	*Ferrari F60	60	1h36m59.216s	118.728	1m34.458s	2
4	N Rosberg	Williams-Toyota FW31	60	1h37m04.409s	118.622	1m34.403s	2
5	J Button	Brawn-Mercedes BGP 001	60	1h37m06.919s	118.571	1m34.252s	3
6	R Barrichello	Brawn-Mercedes BGP 001	60	1h37m07.778s	118.554	1m34.676s	2
7	F Alonso	Renault R29	60	1h37m08.198s	118.545	1m33.365s	2
8	H Kovalainen	*McLaren-Mercedes MP4-24	60	1h37m42.002s	117.861	1m35.524s	2
9	T Glock	Toyota TF109	60	1h37m44.767s	117.806	1m35.369s	1
10	N Heidfeld	BMW Sauber F1.09	60	1h37m45.235s	117.796	1m34.559s	2
11	G Fisichella	Force India-Mercedes VJM02	60	1h37m46.186s	117.778	1m34.238s	2
12	K Nakajima	Williams-Toyota FW31	60	1h37m51.638s	117.668	1m34.876s	2
13	N Piquet Jr	Renault R29	60	1h37m52.865s	117.643	1m34.537s	2
14	R Kubica	BMW Sauber F1.09	60	1h37m55.251s	117.596	1m35.366s	2
15	A Sutil	Force India-Mercedes VJM02	60	1h37m55.251s	117.596	1m35.366s	3
16	S Buemi	Toro Rosso-Ferrari STR4	60	1h38m13.535s	117.231	1m36.279s	2
17	J Trulli	Toyota TF109	60	1h38m14.280s	117.216	1m33.654s	3
18	L Hamilton	*McLaren-Mercedes MP4-24	59	1h38m07.232s	115.400	1m35.367s	2
R	K Räikkönen	*Ferrari F60	34	Engine	-	1m36.080s	1
R	S Bourdais	Toro Rosso-Ferrari STR4	18	Hydraulics	-	1m37.498s	0

* Denotes car fitted with KERS

CHAMPIONSHIP

	Driver	Pts
1	J Button	68
2	S Vettel	47
3	M Webber	45.5
4	R Barrichello	44
5	F Massa	22
6	J Trulli	21.5
7	N Rosberg	20.5
8	T Glock	13
9	F Alonso	13
10	K Räikkönen	10
11	L Hamilton	9
12	N Heidfeld	6
13	H Kovalainen	5
14	S Buemi	3
15	R Kubica	2
16	S Bourdais	2

	Constructor	Pts
1	Brawn-Mercedes	112
2	Red Bull-Renault	92.5
3	Toyota	34.5
4	Ferrari	32
5	Williams-Toyota	20.5
6	McLaren-Mercedes	14
7	Renault	13
8	BMW Sauber	8
9	Toro Rosso-Ferrari	5

Fastest lap
F Alonso 1m33.365s
(123.341mph) on lap 49

Fastest speed trap
G Fisichella   188.586mph

Slowest speed trap
J Trulli   181.005mph

Fastest pit stop
1	J Button	23.210s
2	R Barrichello	23.614s
3	A Sutil	23.866s

Sebastien Bourdais
"We decided to start on the prime, which was a good call. But I began to lose hydraulic pressure and so lost the power steering, clutch and eventually everything else."

Mark Webber
"I thought Rubens was a bit to the left, so I went to the right and banged into him. I got a drive-through for that, but my engineer kept me calm, so it's a great day."

Nico Rosberg
"I started 15th and wasn't expecting much, but took a few chances on the first lap and ended it ninth! Although I had more fuel than anyone else, I kept pushing hard."

Adrian Sutil
"It was going well, as I was up to second by my first stop. When I left the pits I saw Kimi on the outside line and I tried to hold my line but we touched, damaging my nose."

Jenson Button
"I had a poor start to drop to fifth after Turn 1, but was able to pass Massa on lap 2, though just couldn't get past Kovalainen as I struggled with tyre degradation."

Sebastien Buemi
"It was a difficult race, although I made a good start. When we put on the soft tyres, I suffered with a loss of grip as I struggled to bring them up to temperature."

Sebastian Vettel
"I fell to eighth into Turn 1, then couldn't pass Felipe, as he used the KERS button when I got close. So I was lucky to have the strategy that got me back to second."

Kazuki Nakajima
"My race was defined by my first lap: I was hit by Jarno and almost went off, and dropped to the back of the field. It was a shame as my race was ruined from there."

Giancarlo Fisichella
"I thought it would be a difficult race, but I enjoyed it and again got close to the points. I had a good start and overtook a lot of cars. I could catch and pass people."

Rubens Barrichello
"I got ahead of Mark into Turn 1, despite our collision. After leading on lap 1, it's hugely disappointing to have finished sixth. It was a combination of things really."

FORMULA 1 ING
MAGYAR NAGYDIJ 2009
BUDAPEST

LEWIS RETURNS

Lewis Hamilton made the comeback of the season, taking a commanding victory, but McLaren's return to form was overshadowed by Felipe Massa's frightening head injury

Just two races before the Hungarian GP, Lewis Hamilton had struggled even to get through the first of the three stages of qualifying. And yet, at the Hungaroring, he scored a commanding victory, leaving usual 2009 pacesetters Red Bull Racing and Brawn GP trailing in his wake. A new aero package introduced at the previous race at the Nürburgring – where Hamilton was in effect eliminated by a first-lap collision – had clearly paid dividends. And, as it almost did for Damon Hill with Arrows in 1997, everything else just fell into place for Lewis in Hungary.

The weekend was dominated, however, by the accident that befell Felipe Massa in the second part of qualifying. The Brazilian was hospitalised after being struck on the helmet by a suspension spring that fell off Rubens Barrichello's Brawn.

Massa had been doing 160mph on an in-lap back to the pits after his qualifying run. There were reports from a marshal that the 800g spring – ejected from the back of the BGP 001 after leaking fluid had led to a damper failure – appeared to be heading off the track before it bounced back into the Ferrari driver's path.

Since he was on an in-lap, Massa had been obliged to look in his mirrors as he headed down the straight.

INSIDE LINE
LEWIS HAMILTON
McLAREN DRIVER

"It's an incredible feeling to win again after what feels such a long time away from the top step of the podium, and after such a struggle both for me and the team. They have never given up. We didn't expect to win here in Hungary, but the car felt fantastic.

We have made some serious improvements to the MP4-24, mainly aerodynamic, and now it is much better balanced.

Everything just fell into place here. The KERS was obviously important today, but I didn't really get a fantastic start initially, being on the dirty side of the grid. Kimi seemed to get an incredible one and was up alongside me, then I was level with him once I was on the KERS. Actually, we were both on KERS, I think!

I don't think Kimi saw me, but he was behind Mark Webber and when he moved to the right to go past him, we nearly touched. I went to the right and fortunately Vettel gave me enough space. I went a little bit wide at Turn 1, but got back onto the KERS and didn't lose out.

We knew that Fernando in front was running light, and the team told me to look after the tyres. I was really surprised to see that I was able to stay with Mark, then take second place from him and pull away while doing that.

When I passed him, I'd used my KERS down the straight because I thought that I'd be able to get him in Turn 1, but he blocked me, so I went to the outside in Turn 2. I used a little bit of KERS at the beginning of the move, but then I ran out.

Mark was in my blind spot eventually, so I gave him plenty of room. It was quite a straightforward move, but Mark was very smart, as he knows he's got to score points and there was no point in taking risks.

After that, it was all quite straightforward and so a big thank-you to the McLaren guys and all the fans who never gave up on me!

We need to take as much as we can from this weekend and continue to push. We have got some more improvements to bring to the car and for sure we still have more work to do to be able to beat these guys on a more regular basis. But this is one huge leap for us and hopefully we are now on the right track."

At the time of impact, he had his head turned slightly to the right, just enough to ensure that the spring hit the side of the helmet, in the area of the visor fixing, rather than head-on. The consequences could have been so very much worse.

Nevertheless, having been knocked out, he speared off into a tyre wall. His progress was thankfully slowed by the fact that his feet pressed both pedals, and eventually the software shut the engine down.

When qualifying resumed, Fernando Alonso took a surprise pole for Renault after the team opted to go for a light fuel load and a three-stop strategy. Sebastian Vettel qualified second for Red Bull, ahead of his team-mate Mark Webber. Hamilton would line up fourth, but knew that he had the benefit of KERS for the start.

Alonso got away safely in front, but Hamilton made it past Vettel to claim third place. With the other KERS-equipped cars also moving forward, it got rather crowded at Turn 1, and Vettel was bumped by Kimi Räikkönen's Ferrari. That cost the German driver several places and led to a costly retirement from the race with suspension damage a few laps later.

Meanwhile, Hamilton had passed Webber too, and began to chase after Alonso. The Spaniard's progress was slowed by a glitch that forced him to focus on playing with fuel-pump settings, which was a distraction that didn't help his lap times.

The Renault driver then had a problem at his first pit stop with the mechanism that secured his right-front wheel and, when he returned to the track, it was clear that he was in trouble. Part way around the lap, the wheel came off. He pitted for a replacement, and rejoined the race, but was soon forced to retire.

Later, the stewards imposed a ban on the Renault team from the following race for releasing the car with a potentially loose wheelnut, a decision prompted by the unfortunate Massa and Henry Surtees accidents (see 'Weekend News'). The team immediately appealed.

Alonso's problems left Hamilton alone in front, and thereafter the World Champion drove a faultless race, staying comfortably clear of Räikkönen. It was an astonishing turnaround in the fortunes of a team that had really been on the ropes.

"We clearly have got a good car," said Hamilton. "Well, we have made some serious improvements to it and now it's much better balanced. Even though we had fantastic pace today, it could have gone either way. The wind direction maybe could have changed and perhaps it would have suited Ferrari or Red Bull rather better than us.

"But everything just sort of fell in to place. I had quite a good start and a good little dice with Mark. He is very fair and fortunately I didn't get a puncture this time, unlike in Germany. We hope that we can compete for more podiums, but still have work to do. We have just got to keep pushing."

"No, I wasn't expecting it!" said team boss Martin Whitmarsh of the win. "We were aiming for it, of course. A month ago, no one would have predicted that one. We've had a tremendous effort from everybody, in Woking, Brixworth and Stuttgart, and at the track too. It's a massive team effort. Lewis did a

OPPOSITE Fernando Alonso was fuelled light, took pole and led the race, but ended up on the sidelines

BELOW Ferrari's crew shows support for Felipe Massa after he was badly injured in qualifying

BOTTOM Red Bull Racing's Sebastian Vettel chases after Heikki Kovalainen in the opening laps

achieve what we've achieved as a turnaround in the past four to six weeks."

Räikkönen's second place gave Ferrari some reason to cheer after Massa's accident, as he gave the team its best result to this point of the year. A glitch at his second stop cost him time, but didn't affect the result.

"It's nice to be second, for the team and for all the people who have put in a lot of effort," he said. "It hasn't been an easy year or an easy weekend with Felipe's accident yesterday, but we need to be happy. We knew that our car was probably not the fastest, but we still got a good result, good points. It was good, but not exactly what we wanted. You are never going to be happy unless you're first. Hopefully we can keep up this kind of speed and try to get good podium finishes and maybe at least one win this year."

However, there was a feeling in the camp that Massa would have had the speed with which to win. Meanwhile, having lost out to Räikkönen in the pits, Webber finished third and edged a little closer to championship leader Jenson Button.

"If we win and make it very, very boring, it's great for us but, in the end, to be honest, I think it was a good day for the sport," said the Australian. "Lewis is back and Ferrari are back and that's what Red Bull likes. We love racing these guys and fighting hard against them. We knew they would come back.

"KERS is going to play a bit of a role in the closing part of the championship, but thankfully we capitalised in the early part of the championship when these guys were struggling, so that was a big benefit to us. We're going to continue to be in the hunt. Our guys have got a lot of positive things to look forward to. Both drivers are trying to get the most out of the car and it was a good day for us."

Williams again showed signs of solid progress, as Nico Rosberg took fourth place for the second successive race, although this time he started fifth

great job again, but of course he can't do that unless we give him the car with which to do it.

"We knew when Fernando was stopping, we knew we were going to have him. We knew it was going to be tough with the Red Bulls, but I have to say from early on in that race Lewis was controlling the pace. Once he was in that zone, he could have driven quicker, but he just protected his lead and drove a mature, sensible race.

"I never gave up on the year and I don't think the team did. When you are as far back as we were, you struggle – particularly as McLaren – with the pressure. The fact is we didn't give up. You don't give up and

TALKING POINT
SAFETY FIRST

The fact that Felipe Massa survived a 160mph head impact with a spring from Rubens Barrichello's Brawn weighing almost a kilo, says an awful lot for the FIA's work on improving helmet standards.

Massa's Schuberth helmet was taken by the FIA for further analysis into the accident, but Arai's Peter

Buerger claimed that as recently as 15 years ago the outcome could have been very different.

"You could make a helmet and visor strong enough to survive every accident, but it wouldn't be wearable," he said. "Even 10 years ago, the spring would probably have destroyed much more than it did and gone through Felipe's head. The three manufacturers in F1 (Arai, Bell and Schuberth) work with a super-hard FIA standard and, even if the helmet was destroyed, it did its job and prevented him having even more serious head injuries."

The helmet work is a legacy of Ayrton Senna's fatal accident in 1994, after which Max Mosley commissioned an Advisory Expert Group under Professor Sid Watkins to improve all aspects of F1 safety.

The FIA worked with the Transport

Research Laboratory (TRL) in Bracknell, Bell and Snell, as well as with plastics experts, to look into ways of improving helmets, taking into account rotational forces, compressions, frontal impacts and testing methods.

The key to the problem was improving impact resistance at the same time as reducing weight, which had been identified as likely to worsen head and particularly whiplash neck injuries sustained in accidents. The reduced weight in collaboration with the HANS device was a considerable step forward.

Mosley presented the prototype helmet at Monaco in 2001 and claimed that it could absorb 70% more energy, as well as being 30% more resistant to penetration by sharp objects and up to 30% more effective at preventing rotational injuries. It was also 15%

lighter than the lightest helmet in use at the time – Mika Häkkinen's 1.43kg Bell.

The FIA made the final specifications available to any helmet manufacturer that wanted them, but Mosley added that sometimes manufacturers don't want to do too much development because it means expensive changes to their production methods. The new helmet, for instance, required an autoclave to cure the carbon outer shell. In this case, though, the governing body released all its funded developmental research.

Happily, there was take-up, and a new standard (FIA 8860 – 2004) was drafted. Arai, Bell and Schuberth all homologated new helmets and the World Motor Sport Council laid down compulsory use of them for F1 in July 2004.

BELOW Race winner Lewis Hamilton celebrates victory with the McLaren team, flanked by Heikki Kovalainen and Martin Whitmarsh

rather than 15th! He lost out to Räikkönen at the start, but then overtook Vettel and so retained fifth, before earning a place when Alonso retired. A delay at his last pit stop cost him a shot at overhauling Webber for third place.

Heikki Kovalainen took fifth in the second McLaren. From sixth on the grid, he was passed by a fast-starting Räikkönen, but gained places when Alonso and Vettel retired, and even led briefly thanks to a late pit stop. The Finn finished just ahead of Timo Glock. Both Toyota drivers struggled to find a good lap in qualifying, with Jarno Trulli starting the race 12th and Glock 14th. The team rolled the dice

by giving both men heavy fuel loads and so long first stints. Glock had the longer run, and it worked well as he made it to sixth by the flag, and was pushing Kovalainen hard in the closing laps. Trulli ran as high as second before his first pit stop, which was four laps earlier than Glock's. Ultimately, the drivers swapped places and the Italian finished eighth.

The Toyotas were split by Jenson Button. His title hopes took another knock as, for the third race in succession, the team was off the pace as it struggled to get the car and tyres to work together. He qualified only eighth and was overtaken by Kazuki Nakajima at the start, although he soon re-passed the Williams driver. Button duly gained two places from retirements, but finished behind Glock and could not better seventh. Barrichello's qualifying session was ruined by the suspension failure that led to Massa's injury, and he started the race only 13th. After a long first stint in the race, he finished 10th, following Trulli and Nakajima across the line.

BMW Sauber's painful season continued, as once again the cars were far from the points. In qualifying, neither driver made it out of Q1, with Nick Heidfeld taking 16th and Robert Kubica 19th. Both drivers made progress at the start, but Heidfeld lost a lot of time stuck behind other cars. He ran a short first stint, and pitted early, but it didn't make much difference and he finished 11th. Kubica was two places behind, after struggling throughout with tyre wear and heavy understeer. They were split by Nelson Piquet Jr, the Brazilian making what turned out to be his final appearance in a Renault.

Meanwhile, rookie Jaime Alguersuari became the youngest ever grand prix starter, at 19 years and 125 days, and managed to finish, beating his Toro Rosso team-mate Sebastien Buemi – who had a spin – to 15th place. It was a pretty good effort for a man who'd had so little preparation for his new role.

SNAPSHOT FROM
HUNGARY

CLOCKWISE FROM RIGHT BMW announced its withdrawal but Nick Heidfeld raced on; too hot to handle; Nelson Piquet Jr seeks the counsel of a three-time World Champion, his father; a young hopeful dreams of emulating F1's new youngest driver, Jaime Alguersuari; Lewis Hamilton congratulates Fernando Alonso (left) after the Spaniard took pole for Renault; there was considerable support for Ferrari after Felipe Massa's accident; the future's bright, the future's orange

WEEKEND NEWS

■ The racing world was shocked the weekend before the Hungarian GP by the tragic death of Henry Surtees, after an accident in an F2 race at Brands Hatch. The 18-year-old, son of 1964 World Champion John, was struck by a wheel that flew off a crashing car. The obvious parallels with the subsequent Massa accident in Hungary led to an FIA investigation.

■ By Sunday morning in Hungary, speculation was rife as to who would deputise for Felipe Massa at Ferrari in future grands prix. Three days later came the headline-grabbing news that seven-time World Champion Michael Schumacher would be making a comeback. With testing banned, he got a first taste by trying an obsolete Ferrari F2007 at Mugello, on GP2 slick tyres. Later, Schumacher's return was put on hold due to the slow healing of a neck injury sustained in a racing motorcycle test accident. Ferrari test driver Luca Badoer would stand in for Massa instead.

■ Just a few days after the Hungarian GP, BMW stunned the motorsport world by announcing that it was to withdraw from F1 at the end of the season. The decision was made by the company's board in the light of the bigger economic picture, although it was clear that the BMW Sauber team's poor on-track form had played a part.

■ Nelson Piquet Jr's future with Renault had been in doubt for some time and, a week after the Hungarian GP, the Brazilian driver announced on his own website that he had been dropped by the team. In an astonishing statement, he gave the reasons for his struggles and called team boss Flavio Briatore his 'executioner'.

■ Another key development during Formula 1's summer break in August was the confirmation that the Concorde Agreement had been signed, the FIA having first approved a 'resource restriction' deal that had been agreed by the teams. Only the BMW Sauber team (see above) was absent from the new Concorde arrangements, as Peter Sauber urgently sought new investment to continue in F1 in his own right.

RACE
RESULTS
HUNGARY
HUNGARORING

Official Results © [2009]
Formula One Administration Limited,
6 Princes Gate, London, SW7 1QJ.
No reproduction without permission.
All copyright and database rights reserved.

RACE DATE July 26th
CIRCUIT LENGTH 2.722 miles
NO. OF LAPS 70
RACE DISTANCE 190.540 miles
WEATHER Sunny and dry, 23°C
TRACK TEMP 36°C
ATTENDANCE 184,000
LAP RECORD Michael Schumacher,
1m19.071s, 123.828mph, 2004

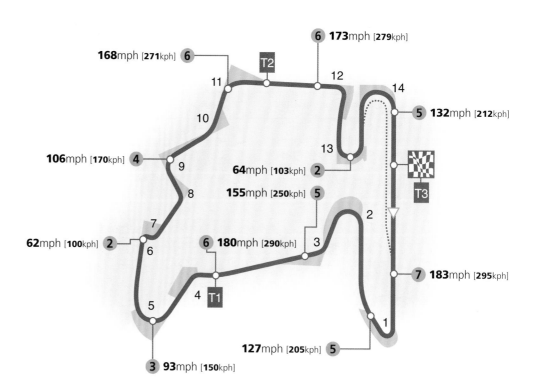

PRACTICE 1		
Driver	Time	Laps
1 H Kovalainen	1m22.278s	21
2 N Rosberg	1m22.337s	27
3 L Hamilton	1m22.554s	20
4 M Webber	1m22.615s	21
5 K Nakajima	1m22.619s	25
6 J Trulli	1m22.705s	17
7 K Räikkönen	1m22.796s	23
8 F Massa	1m22.855s	25
9 F Alonso	1m23.001s	28
10 J Button	1m23.130s	25
11 R Kubica	1m23.146s	24
12 N Heidfeld	1m23.154s	23
13 R Barrichello	1m23.209s	24
14 T Glock	1m23.234s	30
15 S Vettel	1m23.283s	25
16 G Fisichella	1m23.484s	20
17 N Piquet Jr	1m23.678s	22
18 A Sutil	1m23.845s	18
19 S Buemi	1m23.998s	37
20 J Alguersuari	1m24.228s	42

PRACTICE 2		
Driver	Time	Laps
1 L Hamilton	1m22.079s	36
2 H Kovalainen	1m22.126s	36
3 N Rosberg	1m22.154s	47
4 M Webber	1m22.369s	29
5 K Nakajima	1m22.426s	40
6 S Vettel	1m22.550s	30
7 R Barrichello	1m22.641s	38
8 J Trulli	1m22.663s	28
9 N Heidfeld	1m22.690s	43
10 T Glock	1m22.751s	45
11 K Räikkönen	1m22.763s	38
12 F Alonso	1m22.793s	37
13 J Button	1m22.806s	42
14 R Kubica	1m22.870s	36
15 N Piquet Jr	1m22.927s	36
16 A Sutil	1m22.978s	28
17 G Fisichella	1m23.029s	39
18 F Massa	1m23.156s	32
19 S Buemi	1m23.176s	45
20 J Alguersuari	1m23.942s	40

PRACTICE 3		
Driver	Time	Laps
1 L Hamilton	1m21.009s	19
2 N Heidfeld	1m21.408s	23
3 N Rosberg	1m21.509s	21
4 H Kovalainen	1m21.655s	20
5 S Buemi	1m21.800s	23
6 T Glock	1m21.849s	12
7 F Massa	1m21.911s	19
8 K Nakajima	1m21.935s	19
9 M Webber	1m21.936s	16
10 S Vettel	1m21.971s	21
11 R Kubica	1m22.076s	20
12 J Trulli	1m22.097s	25
13 R Barrichello	1m22.101s	22
14 N Piquet Jr	1m22.210s	17
15 K Räikkönen	1m22.270s	20
16 F Alonso	1m22.274s	19
17 J Button	1m22.312s	22
18 J Alguersuari	1m22.391s	20
19 G Fisichella	1m22.684s	23
20 A Sutil	1m23.231s	16

QUALIFYING 1	
Driver	Time
1 N Rosberg	1m20.793s
2 L Hamilton	1m20.842s
3 M Webber	1m20.964s
4 S Vettel	1m21.178s
5 N Piquet Jr	1m21.278s
6 F Alonso	1m21.313s
7 K Nakajima	1m21.407s
8 J Trulli	1m21.416s
9 F Massa	1m21.420s
10 J Button	1m21.471s
11 K Räikkönen	1m21.500s
12 R Barrichello	1m21.558s
13 S Buemi	1m21.571s
14 T Glock	1m21.584s
15 H Kovalainen	1m21.659s
16 N Heidfeld	1m21.738s
17 G Fisichella	1m21.807s
18 A Sutil	1m21.868s
19 R Kubica	1m21.901s
20 J Alguersuari	1m22.359s

QUALIFYING 2	
Driver	Time
1 M Webber	1m20.358s
2 L Hamilton	1m20.465s
3 K Nakajima	1m20.570s
4 S Vettel	1m20.604s
5 K Räikkönen	1m20.647s
6 J Button	1m20.707s
7 H Kovalainen	1m20.807s
8 F Massa	1m20.823s
9 F Alonso	1m20.826s
10 N Rosberg	1m20.862s
11 S Buemi	1m21.002s
12 J Trulli	1m21.082s
13 R Barrichello	1m21.222s
14 T Glock	1m21.242s
15 N Piquet Jr	1m21.389s

Best sectors – Practice	
Sec 1 H Kovalainen	29.016s
Sec 2 L Hamilton	29.073s
Sec 3 T Glock	22.635s

Speed trap – Practice	
1 L Hamilton	181.875mph
2 H Kovalainen	180.757mph
3 G Fisichella	178.520mph

Best sectors – Qualifying	
Sec 1 L Hamilton	28.784s
Sec 2 M Webber	28.744s
Sec 3 J Button	22.436s

Speed trap – Qualifying	
1 L Hamilton	180.570mph
2 H Kovalainen	179.949mph
3 S Vettel	179.079mph

IN 2008

This was a race in which Felipe Massa really showed his mettle, braving it around the outside of poleman Lewis Hamilton at the first corner and leading from there. Hamilton lost ground with a puncture. Then, with three laps to go, Massa's engine failed, leaving McLaren's Heikki Kovalainen to take his first grand prix victory.

Lewis Hamilton

"It's an incredible feeling to be back on the top spot. This was one of my best races. I never gave up and, crucially, neither did anyone in this team. The car was perfect."

Felipe Massa

Did not start due to head injury sustained in qualifying.

Robert Kubica

"I managed to make up a lot of places on lap 1. Unluckily, I had huge understeer and a lot of front tyre wear. About 10 laps into each stint, my fronts degraded a lot."

Fernando Alonso

"We missed a podium after a problem at my first stop fitting the right front. When I left the pits there was vibration, then a few corners later the wheel flew off."

Jarno Trulli

"I never give up and my result shows that, as I made up several places and finished up in the points. The car felt strong, but I got stuck in traffic. Later, I lost grip."

Heikki Kovalainen

"This was a great race for the team. Hopefully, next time it will be me! This victory proves just how much the team has improved our car in the past few months."

Kimi Räikkönen

"Today's result is important for the team in such a difficult weekend, due to what happened to Felipe. I got a good start, ending up fourth after the first few corners."

Nick Heidfeld

"From 15th, finishing 11th was the best I could do. I made up places at the start, but later on the lap somebody hit me from behind and later I went wide in Turn 11."

Nelson Piquet Jr

"I passed a few cars on lap 1, but then was stuck behind somebody. I was also unlucky with strategy and my race would have worked out better if I'd been in clean air."

Timo Glock

"To finish sixth after starting 13th is great. The car felt spot on, so it was a nice race for me. In the first stint, on a heavy load, I struggled but then found a good rhythm."

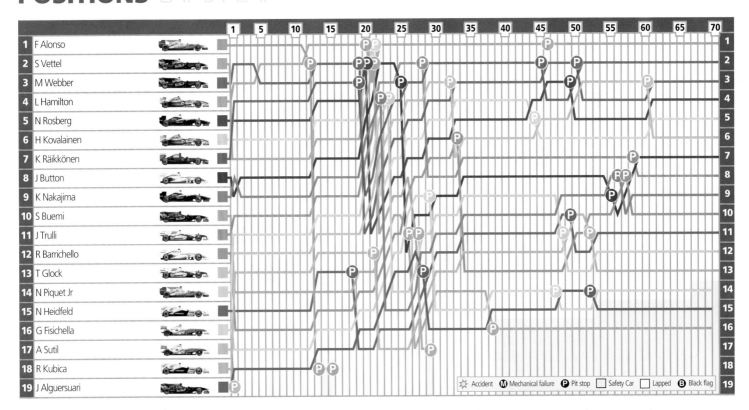

		1	5	10	15	20	25	30	35	40	45	50	55	60	65	70	
1	F Alonso																1
2	S Vettel																2
3	M Webber																3
4	L Hamilton																4
5	N Rosberg																5
6	H Kovalainen																6
7	K Räikkönen																7
8	J Button																8
9	K Nakajima																9
10	S Buemi																10
11	J Trulli																11
12	R Barrichello																12
13	T Glock																13
14	N Piquet Jr																14
15	N Heidfeld																15
16	G Fisichella																16
17	A Sutil																17
18	R Kubica																18
19	J Alguersuari																19

☆ Accident   Ⓜ Mechanical failure   Ⓟ Pit stop   □ Safety Car   □ Lapped   Ⓑ Black flag

QUALIFYING 3

	Driver	Time
1	F Alonso	1m21.569s
2	S Vettel	1m21.607s
3	M Webber	1m21.741s
4	L Hamilton	1m21.839s
5	N Rosberg	1m21.890s
6	H Kovalainen	1m22.095s
7	K Räikkönen	1m22.468s
8	J Button	1m22.511s
9	K Nakajima	1m22.835s
10	F Massa	No time

GRID

	Driver	Time
1	F Alonso	1m21.569s
2	S Vettel	1m21.607s
3	M Webber	1m21.741s
4	L Hamilton	1m21.839s
5	N Rosberg	1m21.890s
6	H Kovalainen	1m22.095s
7	K Räikkönen	1m22.468s
8	J Button	1m22.511s
9	K Nakajima	1m22.835s
10	S Buemi	1m21.002s
11	J Trulli	1m21.082s
12	R Barrichello	1m21.222s
13	T Glock	1m21.242s
14	N Piquet Jr	1m21.389s
15	N Heidfeld	1m21.738s
16	G Fisichella	1m21.807s
17	A Sutil	1m21.868s
18	R Kubica	1m21.901s
19	J Alguersuari	1m22.359s

RACE

	Driver	Car	Laps	Time	Avg. mph	Fastest	Stops
1	L Hamilton	*McLaren-Mercedes MP4-24	70	1h38m23.876s	116.179	1m22.479s	2
2	K Räikkönen	*Ferrari F60	70	1h38m35.405s	115.953	1m22.434s	2
3	M Webber	Red Bull-Renault RB5	70	1h38m40.762s	115.848	1m21.931s	2
4	N Rosberg	Williams-Toyota FW31	70	1h38m50.843s	115.651	1m22.468s	2
5	H Kovalainen	*McLaren-Mercedes MP4-24	70	1h38m58.268s	115.506	1m22.958s	2
6	T Glock	Toyota TF109	70	1h38m59.113s	115.490	1m22.506s	2
7	J Button	Brawn-Mercedes BGP 001	70	1h39m18.964s	115.105	1m22.706s	2
8	J Trulli	Toyota TF109	70	1h39m32.048s	114.853	1m23.261s	2
9	K Nakajima	Williams-Toyota FW31	70	1h39m32.650s	114.842	1m23.180s	2
10	R Barrichello	Brawn-Mercedes BGP 001	70	1h39m33.132s	114.832	1m23.024s	2
11	N Heidfeld	BMW Sauber F1.09	70	1h39m34.488s	114.806	1m23.282s	2
12	N Piquet Jr	Renault R29	70	1h39m35.388s	114.789	1m23.418s	2
13	R Kubica	BMW Sauber F1.09	70	1h39m37.922s	114.740	1m23.224s	2
14	G Fisichella	Force India-Mercedes VJM02	69	1h38m26.239s	114.474	1m23.174s	2
15	J Alguersuari	Toro Rosso-Ferrari STR4	69	1h38m44.598s	114.119	1m23.444s	2
16	S Buemi	Toro Rosso-Ferrari STR4	69	1h39m11.399s	113.605	1m22.955s	2
R	S Vettel	Red Bull-Renault RB5	29	Suspension	-	1m23.457s	2
R	F Alonso	Renault R29	15	Fuel pump	-	1m23.529s	2
R	A Sutil	Force India-Mercedes VJM02	1	Water temperature	-	-	0
NS	F Massa	*Ferrari F60	-	-	-	-	-

* Denotes car fitted with KERS

CHAMPIONSHIP

	Driver	Pts
1	J Button	70
2	M Webber	51.5
3	S Vettel	47
4	R Barrichello	44
5	N Rosberg	25.5
6	J Trulli	22.5
7	F Massa	22
8	L Hamilton	19
9	K Räikkönen	18
10	T Glock	16
11	F Alonso	13
12	H Kovalainen	9
13	N Heidfeld	6
14	S Buemi	3
15	R Kubica	2
	S Bourdais	2

Fastest lap
M Webber 1m21.931s
(119.612mph) on lap 65

Fastest speed trap
L Hamilton	186.100mph

Slowest speed trap
A Sutil	168.391mph

Fastest pit stop
1	T Glock	21.367s
2	R Barrichello	21.878s
3	J Button	22.203s

	Constructor	Pts
1	Brawn-Mercedes	114
2	Red Bull-Renault	98.5
3	Ferrari	40
4	Toyota	38.5
5	McLaren-Mercedes	28
6	Williams-Toyota	25.5
7	Renault	13
8	BMW Sauber	8
9	Toro Rosso-Ferrari	5

Jaime Alguersuari
"I am very happy to have finished, but the last five laps were difficult physically. 15th place is not so bad, but the main aim was to complete the 70 laps, with no mistakes."

Mark Webber
We knew it would be harder for us here so I'm happy. We would have had a better chance to fight Kimi if we'd chosen a different tyre for the middle stint, but that was my call."

Nico Rosberg
"I am quite pleased, as I had no chance off the line, but the first corner was a mess and I profited to climb back to fifth. As the race settled, I had to manage my tyres."

Adrian Sutil
"We had a water temperature problem: after a lap it had climbed to the max so the engine was very hot. We had suspicions going to the grid and so I had to retire."

Jenson Button
"I was heavily fuelled and our plan was to get a good start, stay with those in front and go longer to the first stop. But my rear tyres grained, taking away any chance I had."

Sebastien Buemi
"Starting on the harder tyres was not the right decision. I lost several places at the start and got stuck in traffic. The car was good, but I was the one who made the mistakes."

Sebastian Vettel
"I was on the inside at Turn 1, then Kimi hit my car. This was why my first pit stop was bad and, at some point, the front-left suspension gave up and so I had to retire."

Kazuki Nakajima
"After lap 1, when I passed Jenson, I couldn't hold the position and it dictated my race. It was a big moment for me and made it very hard to improve after that."

Giancarlo Fisichella
"I struggled for grip early on. On the second and third stints, the balance was good and I was faster than Barrichello and Kubica, but you just can't find a way past."

Rubens Barrichello
"My race was compromised from the start which is a shame as I could have scored, but I was hit when I turned into Turn 2, dropping me to the tail of the field."

2009 FORMULA 1 TELEFONICA GRAND PRIX OF EUROPE
VALENCIA

RUBENS HITS BACK

Frustrated by failing to win for Brawn GP in the opening 10 grands prix, Rubens Barrichello rediscovered his winning touch to take his first victory for five years, the first since Ferrari

It was what happened in Valencia that mattered, not how. The 'how' was just as devoid of interest as the inaugural race around the Spanish city's port district had been one year earlier. However, what happened; now that was significant. The headline was that Rubens Barrichello took his first F1 victory in five years, since China 2004 when he was still a Ferrari driver and a fellow called Schumacher was the talk of the paddock. After the engines had fallen silent in Spain, there was nothing but delight for the affable, engaging Brazilian. Even his team-mate Jenson Button managed a grudging smile.

There were more firsts, too, each of which left the distinct impression of a shift in momentum in this turbulent season. It was the first time Barrichello had beaten Button in a Brawn that was performing at its peak, free of its tyre-temperature woes, and in doing so he put himself firmly in the hunt for the drivers' title. It was the first time, too, that Brawn GP had outscored Red Bull Racing since the Turkish Grand Prix in early June. And, of course, it was the first time Ferrari's hapless Luca Badoer had driven in a grand prix for nearly 10 years, as he stood in for the injured Michael Schumacher, who had in turn hoped to stand in for the injured Felipe Massa. But we'll come to that later.

This European GP unfolded with the tense drama – and near-total absence of overtaking – of Max Mosley's beloved, strategy-dominated 'chess match'. At the front, it was a straight fight between the resurgent, KERS-enhanced McLarens and Barrichello's Brawn. Qualifying was tight, with Hamilton, Kovalainen and Barrichello covered by less than a tenth of a second. But Barrichello had fuel to run to lap 20, four laps longer than Hamilton's first stint and three laps advantage over Kovalainen. On pure pace, the Brawn was the quicker car, and Barrichello's comparatively heavy load had been a deliberate tactic: with KERS, the McLarens were likely to lead at the first corner if they qualified anywhere on the first two rows, so it was better for Barrichello to play the waiting game and let the race come to him.

Barrichello did that to perfection, driving with fluid precision and drawing everything from the nimble chassis. Hamilton made a perfect getaway, followed by Kovalainen, with Barrichello slotting into third place. Behind them, Räikkönen put his own KERS advantage to perfect use, jumping from sixth to

fourth and setting up a relentless, lonely race to the final podium spot. Button, though, paid the price for a tentative start – chopped by Sebastian Vettel, then swamped by Alonso, Rosberg and Webber. Running wheel-to-wheel with the Australian, he cut a chicane on lap 1 to nip ahead, which his rival immediately reported to his team and race control. The place had to be ceded four laps later. That left Button down in ninth place, behind every one of his title rivals. It promised to be a long afternoon.

Up front, Hamilton was driving beautifully. The stop-start layout played to the strengths of the greatly enhanced MP4-24 and masked its deficiencies in quicker, longer corners. By the time of his first pit stop, he had built an advantage of nearly nine seconds over Barrichello, who had been bottled up behind Kovalainen, who was driving for his seat with the team, if the paddock grapevine was to be believed.

The McLarens pitted in sync, Hamilton on lap 16 and Kovalainen one lap later. This was Barrichello's first opportunity. He didn't disappoint, turning on the pace to leapfrog Kovalainen and gaining five seconds on Hamilton, to emerge just over three seconds behind once the stops had shaken out. He shadowed

BELOW With the McLarens ahead, Rubens Barrichello holds off Kimi Räikkönen on the opening lap

OPPOSITE Fernando Alonso was relieved to be permitted to compete, and raced his Renault to sixth place

INSIDE LINE
LUCA BADOER
FERRARI DRIVER

"These have been very hard days, and it was a very hard weekend. However, this was the expectation from me and from the team as I said when I arrived in Valencia that this grand prix would be a time for me to dust the rust off my back, and get confident in the role of race driver again.

My life changed completely when the team told me I was going to be driving. It is a special time, because my dream ever since I was a small child was to drive for Ferrari in F1. So this is the best period in my life: it will not be long, but for me it will be enough.

The team did everything they could to make me feel comfortable, without putting me under any pressure. And Michael [Schumacher] was a great support throughout the weekend, too. It is important for me to count on his support, especially from the human point of view.

It was a tough race, because F1 is very different compared to 10 years ago when I last competed. After the race, I was fine from the physical point of view, so that was another cause for satisfaction. The priority for the team was for me to finish the race, so that I could have many more laps and have much more confidence with the car. At the end, we did the programme, and that is all.

I got a good start, making up a few places, but then I was hit by [Romain] Grosjean and that dropped me back down again. I tried to run my own race but it was not easy to maintain a consistent pace, especially when I had to let the leaders by.

At the first pit stop, I made a mistake which cost me one place to Grosjean – it was a misunderstanding with me, the team and the rules of the FIA. Then I was just a whisker over the white line, and so I picked up a drive-through penalty as well.

I think I improved a lot during the race – by about a second a lap. It is a reasonable step on a track like this. But I'm not a robot or Superman – I'm human and I needed time to get quick.

When I get to Spa, which is a track I know, I will be at a better level. I will have a better feeling with the car, with the team, with the track and with everything."

TOP **Kazuki Nakajima limps his Williams back to the pits after this complete failure of his left-rear tyre**

ABOVE **Heikki Kovalainen used his KERS well at the start to leap to second, and finished in fourth place**

OPPOSITE TOP **Luca Badoer keeps well out of the way as Jenson Button comes up to lap him**

OPPOSITE BOTTOM **Giancarlo Fisichella was the best of the one-stoppers, holding off Trulli for 12th**

the McLaren from there, a nagging presence in Hamilton's mirrors as tyre choice began to come into play. McLaren had run the softer compound for the first two stints, while Brawn had done the reverse. As Hamilton peeled into the pits on lap 37, Barrichello still had life in the tyres – and six laps worth of fuel with which to move past Hamilton. In retrospect, the race was already in the Brazilian's pocket.

However, he was then given a sizeable helping hand. As Hamilton dived into the pitlane, the team told him to stay out on track for another lap. He'd been saving fuel and the engineers had just established that he had enough to make it around again. This meant that Kovalainen would have to pit one lap early, to give his team-mate the strategic advantage, and his tyres were ready and waiting. The call, though, came too late. Suddenly, Hamilton was crawling down the pitlane while the mechanics waited for Kovalainen. Confusion ensued as tyres were swapped and Hamilton lost approximately five seconds before returning to the fray. Suddenly, Barrichello's job had become a whole lot easier.

It had become straightforward enough, in fact, that the Brazilian could pit safely three laps early in

order to avoid being caught out by a potential safety-car deployment, after Kazuki Nakajima's left-rear tyre disintegrated and he made his way slowly back to the pits, shedding rubber as he went. Barrichello had already done enough, though, setting the two fastest laps of the race up to that point on laps 38 and 39. He pitted on lap 40, re-emerging six seconds ahead. Even without McLaren's error, he would probably have emerged just in front.

In the same pit-stop shuffle, Räikkönen jumped Kovalainen. The Ferrari pitted on the same lap as Barrichello, nailing quick laps in similar fashion to the Brazilian, while the second McLaren struggled with the warm-up of its newly fitted hard tyres. During those crucial laps, Kovalainen's lap times were up to two seconds slower than Hamilton's. So Räikkönen claimed third place with a couple of seconds to spare, and secured Ferrari's third podium in three races, further confirming the resurgence of the traditional top teams. Fourth place was Kovalainen's best result of the year – but still not convincing enough, as his team-mate took a strong second.

And behind those four? The drives were solid, committed and unspectacular. Rosberg came home fifth, reinforcing the impression that, for the first season in a long time, Williams had kept pace in the development race. Alonso was sixth, reprieved by the Court of Appeal to compete in Spain, but unable to lift the fans to the heady heights of years past. Button finished a relieved seventh, taking solace from a day of damage limitation when two of his main championship rivals failed to score.

Vettel was accounted for by his second engine failure of the weekend, but he'd already dropped out of contention: at his first stop, a fuel-rig malfunction forced him to complete another lap before pitting again. As for Webber, he was never comfortable with the car or circuit – and Australia were busy losing the

TALKING POINT
RENAULT FIGHTS TO GO RACING

As Renault entered the summer break, the prospect of not competing at the European Grand Prix loomed large over the team. Following a mistake during Fernando Alonso's first pit stop at the Hungarian Grand Prix, his car was sent back out with a loose right-front wheel, which subsequently detached itself from the car and flew off during the next lap as Alonso tried to make his way slowly back to the pits.

The errant wheel was the third high-profile incident involving airborne debris in seven days: the day before, Felipe Massa had been struck on the head by a spring during qualifying, while F2 driver Henry Surtees was tragically killed at Brands Hatch a week earlier when he was struck on the head by a flying wheel assembly during a race.

The stewards came down hard on Renault, stating that the team "knowingly released" the car in an unsafe condition and subsequently failed to take any kind of corrective action.

The team was then suspended from the following grand prix, in Valencia. The decision left the race promoters aghast, as it raised the prospect of racing without the country's hero Fernando Alonso in the field, and left many onlookers questioning the consistency of the stewards' decision-making, given that comparable incidents had never before been punished in this way.

Renault's appeal was heard in Paris on the Monday before the European Grand Prix – by which time the team's trucks were already on their way to Valencia. The team accepted that it had been in "technical breach" of Articles 23.1.i and 3.2 of the Sporting Regulations, but strongly contested the assertion that it had deliberately or knowingly released the car back into the race in an unsafe condition. Renault argued instead that the car had been released as a result of mistakes and a flawed pit stop procedure.

Interestingly, and in a sign of the new-found unity between the teams, Renault's case was bolstered by letters of support from Red Bull, McLaren, Ferrari and Toyota, who admitted to using a similar pit stop procedure to that which had caught Renault out.

The court ultimately ruled in Renault's favour, accepting that the team had acted in good faith, quashing the one-race ban, and imposing instead a $50,000 fine plus a reprimand. This cleared the way for Frenchman Romain Grosjean to be confirmed as Alonso's team-mate following Nelson Piquet Jr's acrimonious departure from the team.

Furthermore, the court also took pains to highlight that "the penalty imposed in the present case appears to be significantly inconsistent with any penalty previously imposed (or not imposed) in other broadly comparable cases."

Romain Grosjean and Luca Badoer spent much of their race together on this harbourside circuit

Lewis Hamilton congratulates Rubens Barrichello after his first win for five years

Ashes, just to rub it all in. Matters were compounded when, in the laps before his second stop, he found himself bottled up behind Kovalainen. The stop itself was painfully slow – it took a full two-and-a-half seconds longer than Button's – and he dropped from seventh to ninth. The man who benefited was Kubica, excelling as usual on a circuit demanding plenty of heavy braking, to score his third point of the year.

Behind the points places, Buemi retired with brake problems, while Nakajima parked his Williams in the pits with three laps to go, citing damage from the earlier puncture. Down at the back, debutant Romain Grosjean and returnee Luca Badoer provided an amusing diversion. Grosjean ran into Badoer on lap 1, then mistook flying debris for parts of his own front wing, which he thought was disintegrating, and pitted. Badoer, meanwhile, toiled on in his Ferrari, whittling down his fastest lap until he was within 1.3 seconds of his team-mate. He and Grosjean pitted together on lap 28 and provided the only overtaking manoeuvre of the race: Badoer left the pits ahead then was told "traffic, traffic" on the radio. Thinking his engineer meant Grosjean, the hapless Italian pulled over to let his rival by in the pitlane exit – then realised the message referred to cars passing on the straight. In his frustration, he put a wheel over the white line as he rejoined the circuit – and was handed a drive-through penalty for doing so. It was an embarrassing return to the sport for Badoer, who many felt had been placed in an impossible position by the team. Grosjean showed better pace – setting a faster race lap than team-mate Alonso – but nevertheless trailed home 15th, as the last unlapped runner.

In a strange quirk of fate, the fastest lap went to Timo Glock, two tenths quicker than next best, Jenson Button. The pace came from nowhere after Glock had qualified 13th, while racing to 14th, the Toyota once more struggling on a low-grip street circuit. However, it made him the ninth different driver to set a fastest lap in 11 races – a small indication of the infinitely fine margin between success and failure in 2009.

Up front, though, none of that mattered. Barrichello savoured the moment; thought of Massa at home in Brazil; thought of Emerson, Nelson and Ayrton, too, as he took Brazil's 100th grand prix win. No doubt he remembered those days last winter when he changed his ring tone to a police siren, to make sure that he would couldn't miss it when the call came from Ross Brawn with news of the team's future. As he left Valencia, he'd finally proven what he believed and said all along: that he was a contender.

SNAPSHOT FROM
EUROPE

CLOCKWISE FROM RIGHT There were more yachts in the harbour this time around; TV pundit David Coulthard proves that it's not only drivers who can attract the girls; Michael Schumacher watches from Ferrari's pit balcony; taking on the paparazzi at their own game; Brawn GP's crew show their love for Rubens Barrichello, a winner again; engineer Rob Smedley talks, Luca Badoer focuses; Rubens Barrichello showed support for his friend Felipe Massa with a new helmet design

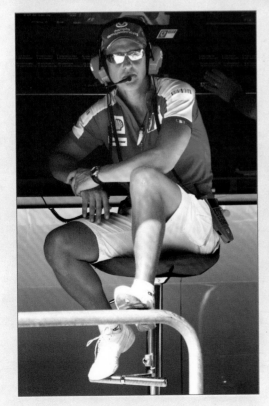

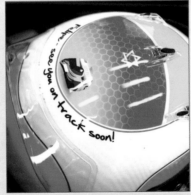

WEEKEND NEWS

■ The FIA published the 2010 Sporting and Technical regulations in the week before the European Grand Prix. As expected, refuelling will be banned and the minimum weight limit raised to 620kg. Qualifying will retain the successful knockout format, but the final session (Q3) will henceforth be conducted on low fuel, giving a truer picture of the teams' relative performance.

■ USF1 became the first new team to announce major commercial backing in the week before Valencia, when Chad Hurley – co-founder of YouTube – was unveiled as the team's main financial backer. "We're honoured to be a part of all this," said Hurley. "In years to come, I believe we can be quite competitive on the track."

■ Williams announced plans to establish the first Williams Foundation in Angola. It will be a non-profit organisation to help improve education, energy efficiency and road safety in Angola, which is not yet a member of the FIA. The project has been set up in co-operation with the team's partner Ridge Solutions.

■ Bernie Ecclestone issued an ultimatum to the owners of Donington Park, the planned venue for the 2010 British GP. Following myriad delays and funding problems at the Midlands circuit, Ecclestone said that he had demanded a bank guarantee from the organisers by the end of September. He also confirmed that the race would return to Silverstone should this not materialise.

■ In spite of speculation that the second grand prix at the harbourside Valencia circuit might prove to be the last, organisers confirmed after the race that the regional government had become a sponsor of the event for the next five years, at a cost of 18m euros per year. It will run under the banner of the European or Mediterranean GP.

RACE RESULTS
EUROPE
VALENCIA

RACE DATE August 23rd
CIRCUIT LENGTH 3.367 miles
NO. OF LAPS 57
RACE DISTANCE 191.919 miles
WEATHER Sunny and dry, 31°C
TRACK TEMP 48°C
ATTENDANCE 160,000
LAP RECORD Timo Glock,
1m38.683s, 122.837mph, 2009

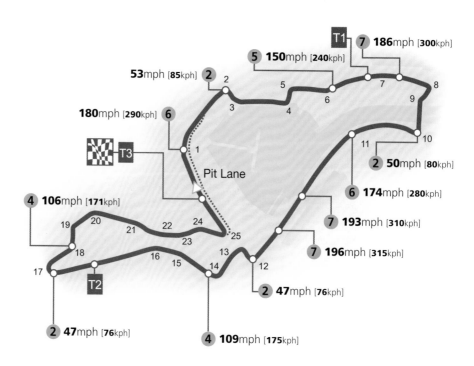

PRACTICE 1				PRACTICE 2				PRACTICE 3				QUALIFYING 1			QUALIFYING 2	
	Driver	Time	Laps		Driver	Time	Laps		Driver	Time	Laps		Driver	Time		Driver	Time
1	R Barrichello	1m42.460s	19	1	F Alonso	1m39.404s	33	1	A Sutil	1m39.143s	12	1	J Button	1m38.531s	1	R Barrichello	1m38.076s
2	H Kovalainen	1m42.636s	16	2	J Button	1m40.178s	33	2	K Nakajima	1m39.247s	12	2	L Hamilton	1m38.649s	2	L Hamilton	1m38.182s
3	L Hamilton	1m42.654s	18	3	R Barrichello	1m40.209s	34	3	R Kubica	1m39.513s	12	3	R Kubica	1m38.806s	3	H Kovalainen	1m38.230s
4	J Button	1m43.074s	19	4	N Rosberg	1m40.385s	39	4	H Kovalainen	1m39.553s	8	4	H Kovalainen	1m38.816s	4	S Vettel	1m38.273s
5	S Vettel	1m43.088s	17	5	K Nakajima	1m40.503s	35	5	N Rosberg	1m39.732s	11	5	K Räikkönen	1m38.843s	5	N Rosberg	1m38.346s
6	A Sutil	1m43.209s	13	6	A Sutil	1m40.596s	23	6	G Fisichella	1m39.764s	12	6	S Buemi	1m38.912s	6	J Button	1m38.601s
7	K Nakajima	1m43.225s	25	7	R Kubica	1m40.643s	34	7	J Button	1m39.883s	10	7	M Webber	1m38.983s	7	M Webber	1m38.625s
8	M Webber	1m43.243s	19	8	G Fisichella	1m40.681s	31	8	L Hamilton	1m39.950s	12	8	R Barrichello	1m39.019s	8	F Alonso	1m38.717s
9	F Alonso	1m43.345s	18	9	S Vettel	1m40.723s	33	9	J Trulli	1m40.017s	11	9	N Heidfeld	1m39.032s	9	R Kubica	1m38.747s
10	K Räikkönen	1m43.384s	23	10	H Kovalainen	1m40.738s	31	10	R Grosjean	1m40.088s	11	10	N Rosberg	1m39.039s	10	K Räikkönen	1m38.782s
11	S Buemi	1m43.389s	30	11	K Räikkönen	1m40.739s	39	11	S Buemi	1m40.118s	12	11	A Sutil	1m39.145s	11	N Heidfeld	1m38.826s
12	R Kubica	1m43.419s	20	12	J Trulli	1m40.770s	32	12	R Barrichello	1m40.192s	10	12	F Alonso	1m39.155s	12	A Sutil	1m38.846s
13	J Alguersuari	1m43.637s	30	13	R Grosjean	1m40.787s	35	13	N Heidfeld	1m40.230s	12	13	S Vettel	1m39.295s	13	T Glock	1m38.991s
14	N Rosberg	1m43.746s	22	14	M Webber	1m40.956s	37	14	K Räikkönen	1m40.260s	12	14	R Grosjean	1m39.322s	14	R Grosjean	1m39.040s
15	N Heidfeld	1m44.040s	23	15	T Glock	1m40.985s	30	15	F Alonso	1m40.402s	9	15	T Glock	1m39.459s	15	S Buemi	1m39.514s
16	G Fisichella	1m44.126s	17	16	S Buemi	1m41.156s	34	16	T Glock	1m40.443s	10	16	G Fisichella	1m39.531s			
17	R Grosjean	1m44.356s	23	17	N Heidfeld	1m41.350s	29	17	M Webber	1m40.879s	10	17	K Nakajima	1m39.795s			
18	J Trulli	1m44.638s	26	18	L Badoer	1m42.017s	37	18	S Vettel	1m40.916s	6	18	J Trulli	1m39.807s			
19	T Glock	1m44.732s	28	19	J Alguersuari	1m42.089s	34	19	J Alguersuari	1m41.125s	12	19	J Alguersuari	1m39.925s			
20	L Badoer	1m45.840s	25	20	L Hamilton	1m43.214s	3	20	L Badoer	1m42.198s	14	20	L Badoer	1m41.413s			

Best sectors – Practice			Speed trap – Practice			Best sectors – Qualifying			Speed trap – Qualifying	
Sec 1	F Alonso	26.342s	1	G Fisichella	193.930mph	Sec 1	H Kovalainen	26.121s	1 A Sutil	194.799mph
Sec 2	L Hamilton	44.775s	2	A Sutil	193.805mph	Sec 2	S Vettel	44.615s	2 G Fisichella	194.489mph
Sec 3	F Alonso	27.622s	3	R Barrichello	193.308mph	Sec 3	R Barrichello	27.233s	3 R Barrichello	194.427mph

IN 2008

Valencia's first scalp was claimed by Felipe Massa with a peerless performance, leading from pole to flagfall, save for when he pitted. Lewis Hamilton was the best of the rest, with Robert Kubica a distant third. Home fans were disappointed when Fernando Alonso was out after a first-lap clash with Kazuki Nakajima.

Lewis Hamilton
"Am I disappointed? Yes, we all are, but the call was marginal. What happened was a result of the team trying everything to turn a safe second place into a win."

Luca Badoer
"I made up a few places at the start, but was hit by Grosjean. At the first stop, I made a mistake that lost me a place and then I was just over the white line and got a penalty."

Robert Kubica
"I wasn't able to make up places at the start, and even lost a place to Nick. Although my stints were shorter, I was able to overtake Webber during his final stop."

Fernando Alonso
"Sixth is the best I could do, and the three points are a good result considering we started eighth. I'm confident we can keep this pace and deliver a better result at Spa."

Jarno Trulli
"I had the same problems as in qualifying, and the grip was not even close to how it had been in practice. I did my best, but there was nothing I could do to advance."

Heikki Kovalainen
"To start second and finish fourth isn't ideal, but we showed good performance. We don't have the pace of the frontrunners, but the team has done an incredible job."

Kimi Räikkönen
"My aim was to open a gap over Rosberg, who would stop after me. I realised that I could close on Kovalainen and try and make the most of the pit stops to get past."

Nick Heidfeld
"I had to defend my position against Sutil and lost contact with the front group. This turned out to be crucial, because after his pit stop Kovalainen came out ahead."

Romain Grosjean
"The opening lap didn't go well for me, but during the race there were a lot of positives and I gained some valuable experience. I'll aim to put this to good use at Spa."

Timo Glock
"I had to dive down the inside at the first corner, as the cars in front were braking heavily so I had to avoid them. Then I was hit from behind, ending all my hopes."

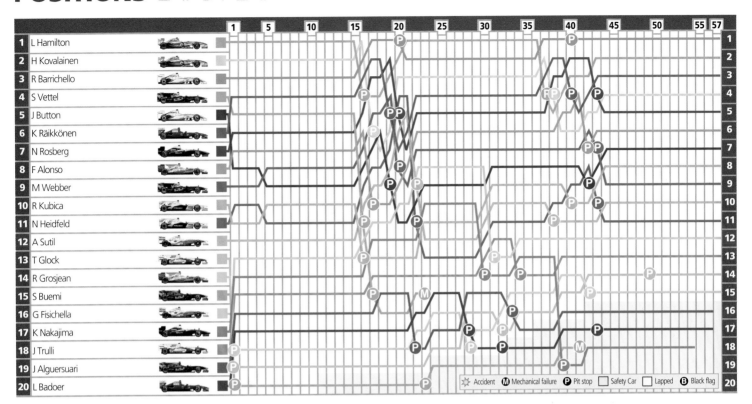

			1	5	10	15	20	25	30	35	40	45	50	55 57	
1	L Hamilton														1
2	H Kovalainen														2
3	R Barrichello														3
4	S Vettel														4
5	J Button														5
6	K Räikkönen														6
7	N Rosberg														7
8	F Alonso														8
9	M Webber														9
10	R Kubica														10
11	N Heidfeld														11
12	A Sutil														12
13	T Glock														13
14	R Grosjean														14
15	S Buemi														15
16	G Fisichella														16
17	K Nakajima														17
18	J Trulli														18
19	J Alguersuari														19
20	L Badoer														20

☆ Accident   Ⓜ Mechanical failure   Ⓟ Pit stop   ☐ Safety Car   ☐ Lapped   Ⓑ Black flag

QUALIFYING 3

	Driver	Time
1	L Hamilton	1m39.498s
2	H Kovalainen	1m39.532s
3	R Barrichello	1m39.563s
4	S Vettel	1m39.789s
5	J Button	1m39.821s
6	K Räikkönen	1m40.144s
7	N Rosberg	1m40.185s
8	F Alonso	1m40.236s
9	M Webber	1m40.239s
10	R Kubica	1m40.512s

GRID

	Driver	Time
1	L Hamilton	1m39.498s
2	H Kovalainen	1m39.532s
3	R Barrichello	1m39.563s
4	S Vettel	1m39.789s
5	J Button	1m39.821s
6	K Räikkönen	1m40.144s
7	N Rosberg	1m40.185s
8	F Alonso	1m40.236s
9	M Webber	1m40.239s
10	R Kubica	1m40.512s
11	N Heidfeld	1m38.826s
12	A Sutil	1m38.846s
13	T Glock	1m38.991s
14	R Grosjean	1m39.040s
15	S Buemi	1m39.514s
16	G Fisichella	1m39.531s
17	K Nakajima	1m39.795s
18	J Trulli	1m39.807s
19	J Alguersuari	1m39.925s
20	L Badoer	1m41.413s

RACE

	Driver	Car	Laps	Time	Avg. mph	Fastest	Stops
1	R Barrichello	Brawn-Mercedes BGP 001	57	1h35m51.289s	120.138	1m38.990s	2
2	L Hamilton	*McLaren-Mercedes MP4-24	57	1h35m53.647s	120.089	1m39.056s	2
3	K Räikkönen	*Ferrari F60	57	1h36m07.283s	119.805	1m39.207s	2
4	H Kovalainen	*McLaren-Mercedes MP4-24	57	1h36m11.321s	119.721	1m39.341s	2
5	N Rosberg	Williams-Toyota FW31	57	1h36m12.159s	119.704	1m39.329s	2
6	F Alonso	Renault R29	57	1h36m19.033s	119.562	1m39.494s	2
7	J Button	Brawn-Mercedes BGP 001	57	1h36m26.202s	119.413	1m38.874s	2
8	R Kubica	BMW Sauber F1.09	57	1h36m27.956s	119.377	1m39.374s	2
9	M Webber	Red Bull-Renault RB5	57	1h36m36.199s	119.207	1m39.528s	2
10	A Sutil	Force India-Mercedes VJM02	57	1h36m39.224s	119.145	1m39.622s	2
11	N Heidfeld	BMW Sauber F1.09	57	1h36m40.111s	119.127	1m39.704s	2
12	G Fisichella	Force India-Mercedes VJM02	57	1h36m54.903s	118.824	1m40.111s	1
13	J Trulli	Toyota TF109	57	1h36m55.816s	118.805	1m39.941s	1
14	T Glock	Toyota TF109	57	1h37m17.808s	118.357	1m38.683s	3
15	R Grosjean	Renault R29	57	1h37m23.063s	118.251	1m39.428s	3
16	J Alguersuari	Toro Rosso-Ferrari STR4	56	1h36m38.330s	117.073	1m40.935s	2
17	L Badoer	*Ferrari F60	56	1h37m13.273s	116.371	1m40.590s	3
18	K Nakajima	Williams-Toyota FW31	54	Car damage	-	1m39.747s	2
19	S Buemi	Toro Rosso-Ferrari STR4	41	Brake disc	-	1m41.042s	2
20	S Vettel	Red Bull-Renault RB5	23	Engine	-	1m39.992s	2

* Denotes car fitted with KERS

CHAMPIONSHIP

	Driver	Pts
1	J Button	72
2	R Barrichello	54
3	M Webber	51.5
4	S Vettel	47
5	N Rosberg	29.5
6	L Hamilton	27
7	K Räikkönen	24
8	J Trulli	22.5
9	F Massa	22
10	T Glock	16
11	F Alonso	16
12	H Kovalainen	14
13	N Heidfeld	6
14	R Kubica	3
15	S Buemi	3
16	S Bourdais	2

Fastest lap
T Glock 1m38.683s
(122.837mph) on lap 55

Fastest speed trap	
A Sutil	194.799mph
Slowest speed trap	
S Vettel	188.710mph

Fastest pit stop		
1	T Glock	16.941s
2	J Button	17.838s
3	N Heidfeld	18.505s

	Constructor	Pts
1	Brawn-Mercedes	126
2	Red Bull-Renault	98.5
3	Ferrari	46
4	McLaren-Mercedes	41
5	Toyota	38.5
6	Williams-Toyota	29.5
7	Renault	16
8	BMW Sauber	9
9	Toro Rosso-Ferrari	5

Jaime Alguersuari

"This was much tougher for me than Hungary, because of the heat and humidity. With 10 laps to go, I had a problem with my drinks system. It was really tough."

Mark Webber

"I've been struggling all weekend and I got the result I deserved, which was no points. We were a bit unlucky around the pit stops with Lewis coming out in front."

Nico Rosberg

"I enjoyed the race, but the heat took most of the fun out of it. Fifth again, after starting seventh, is not bad, and gives us more points. I was hoping to beat Räikkönen."

Adrian Sutil

"I was behind the two BMWs for my first stint and couldn't get past on the track, but the team did a really good stop and I was able to pass Heidfeld in the pitlane."

Jenson Button

"The small mistake in qualifying and a difficult start caught behind Vettel cost me, as I got caught in traffic and it's really tough to overtake around this circuit."

Sebastien Buemi

"I moved to the inside to avoid the bottleneck after the start and, as Glock accelerated, he drove over my wing. Later, I had braking problems and the disc broke."

Sebastian Vettel

"We weren't able to get fuel in the car at the first stop, so I had to come in again. The race was lost but, a few laps on, I had an engine problem and had to retire."

Kazuki Nakajima

"It was all over in qualifying really. I was 13th when I had the flat tyre, and that finished my race. Just a few laps before the end, I had some kind of problem so stopped early."

Giancarlo Fisichella

"It was a difficult race, as the grid position wasn't as good as we'd hoped, so we used a one-stop strategy. I made a very good start and 12th is a good result for us."

Rubens Barrichello

"Even after five years, you don't forget how to win! Although we were fuelled heavier than the McLarens, I knew that I would have to push really hard."

2009 FORMULA 1 ING BELGIAN GRAND PRIX
SPA-FRANCORCHAMPS

KIMI, BY A SECOND

Kimi Räikkönen helped Ferrari back to winning ways, but the formbook was turned on its head as the leading teams struggled and Force India's Giancarlo Fisichella chased him home

In the Spa-Francorchamps paddock on Saturday afternoon, a good number of people were scratching their heads. Seasoned campaigners with years of experience were hard pressed to explain exactly what had just happened in qualifying. Formula 1 is difficult to understand at the best of times, but then when one of the most bizarre dry qualifying sessions for years turned the formbook on its head it was even harder to comprehend.

On pole position was the Force India, yes the Force India, of Giancarlo Fisichella, who qualified ahead of Jarno Trulli's Toyota and Nick Heidfeld's BMW Sauber. That's the same BMW Sauber that had scored only nine points in the 11 rounds before the Belgian GP…

The championship protagonists struggled, as Jenson Button qualified 14th, while the Red Bull drivers were eighth and ninth. So, what exactly had happened to turn the grid upside down? There were mutterings of special tyres and, with Fisichella being linked to a move to Ferrari, someone suggested that he was getting special treatment. But, don't believe any of it, as the truth was that since Force India had moved into a technical partnership with McLaren-Mercedes in 2009, so a steady stream of

ABOVE Giancarlo Fisichella leads through Eau Rouge on lap 1, with Kimi Räikkönen already up to third behind Robert Kubica's BMW Sauber

OPPOSITE "Taxi for three to pick up at Les Combes!" With three wrecked cars, Jenson Button, Romain Grosjean and Lewis Hamilton had time on their hands

aerodynamic updates, and good ones at that, filtered onto the VJM02. At the previous race in Valencia, the little Silverstone-based outfit introduced a new aero package that was believed to be worth 0.7s a lap. Yet the high-downforce nature of the Spanish street track didn't show off its performance, whereas Spa was the first true low-downforce track of the year, so teams like Force India, BMW Sauber and Toyota could display the merits of their straight-line aero efficiency.

In addition, rapidly increasing track temperatures during qualifying made the call for soft or harder-compound tyres critical. Fisichella's team-mate Adrian Sutil preferred the harder tyre, and when he swapped to the soft, to be on the same rubber as Fisichella, found that he couldn't achieve the same speed, so temperamental was the effective use of the tyres.

Sitting alongside Fisichella on the front row of the grid was Trulli, and the Toyota was slightly slower because of its heavier fuel load, but that meant that it should have the advantage come the race. They were nervous at Toyota on race morning, but quietly confident that, if Trulli could stay ahead at the end of the first lap, then they were in a strong position to take their first World Championship victory.

The same was true of Force India and, indeed, Fisichella did stay at the head of the field at the end of the first lap. What scuppered him though was the arrival of the safety car. For Trulli, it was the first-corner melêe…

When the red lights were extinguished, Fisichella led into the La Source hairpin from BMW Sauber's Robert Kubica, who got ahead of his team-mate. In fact, Heidfeld backed off and in so doing caught Trulli by surprise. The Toyota tagged the back of Heidfeld's car, damaging his front wing and effectively ending any chance the Italian driver had to win the race. What was it the team had said about the opening lap?

Further back in the field, there was more trouble as Sutil's Force India was nudged around into a half-spin and clattered into Fernando Alonso's front-left wheel, which would lead to major problems for the Renault driver later in the race.

Meanwhile, as the field was rounding the tight hairpin for the first time, Räikkönen decided to stay clear of trouble and ran around the outside – going very wide over the run-off area. When he slotted back onto the track, half-way down to Eau Rouge, he was third (up from sixth on the grid) and challenging Kubica – who he out-powered, thanks to the use of his KERS

INSIDE LINE
VIJAY MALLYA
FORCE INDIA CHAIRMAN

"What a result – this will go down in the history books as India's first ever World Championship points. Qualifying was fantastic and then to get our first podium and points is just unbelievable. Giancarlo [Fisichella] drove an outstanding race: we can all be very proud of the entire effort.

We've worked very hard to get to this position, with a solid plan of upgrades coming through the factory – which has been different to before because last year we competed with an old Spyker car that we couldn't develop. This is the first true year for Force India where we have developed and designed our own car, and we always said we hoped to be a good midfield contender this year. So, from Australia, we have gradually improved and we put on a big update for Valencia, which was successful. We put on another for Spa and from the free practice sessions Giancarlo and Adrian [Sutil] have done well. Of course I was a little surprised, but it was fantastic to be on pole position, and to be on the podium is a big bonus and we feel very happy.

Obviously, KERS has played a part in the race for Ferrari, otherwise Giancarlo was very quick and right on his tail, less than one second behind. But I am happy, I don't want to get too greedy and I think we should all be very proud of our performance today.

KERS was part of the package offered to us and we elected not to take it, but nevertheless we are very pleased with the result. Luck hasn't been on our side until this race, as we have been in definite point-scoring positions at least three times this season and for one reason or another we were knocked out. But we've vindicated ourselves: we not only got points, but we finally got a podium, so I am feeling pretty good about that.

At the end of the day, when a driver sees a car that he now has confidence in, that he sees the team is giving him a machine that is constantly improving, he feels motivated. Giancarlo has been feeling very motivated since Bahrain when we first put the interim diffuser on. All of last year, I could understand if the drivers were somewhat frustrated, because the engineering we had in those days was promising improvement, but it wasn't coming through. Now it is there for them to see and to feel.

I'm very proud for the whole team."

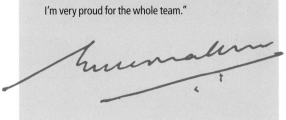

Button knew that, starting so far down the grid, it was always going to be hard to stay clear of trouble on the opening lap. "I had actually made up four places," he said ruefully, "and was about to overtake Kovalainen when Grosjean outbraked himself and hit my wheel. It's frustrating to be taken out when I'd made up so many places at the start. It's my first DNF of the year, but that's what happens when you start 14th on the grid."

It was an unusual sight to see Hamilton's wrecked McLaren in the wall too. Apart from a few mishaps in the pitlane, this was the McLaren driver's first on-track racing crash of his F1 career…

The arrival of the safety car was bad news for Fisichella, because now the KERS-equipped Räikkönen was sitting right behind him, ready to pounce when the green flag was shown again. Without that intervention, the raw speed of the Force India would probably have been good enough to keep Fisichella at the head of the field. However, it wasn't to be.

After a few laps under caution, Räikkönen set himself up to pass Fisichella with an almighty run through Eau Rouge, deployed his extra KERS boost and was already into the lead half way up the Kemmel straight. Fisichella had no answer to the Ferrari, but kept the pressure on throughout the race.

"I was actually quicker than Kimi," said Fisichella afterwards. "He could overtake me at the beginning of the race because of KERS and I am a little bit sad because of that, because I was quicker than him. We did exactly the same strategy in the race, so it's great because I finished second just one second behind the leader which is a great result for us, but actually we could have won the race."

Räikkönen and Fisichella traded quickest laps throughout the race, a tenth of a second here, two tenths there, but they were locked together and it was a rather surreal sight to see the Force India genuinely keeping up with the Ferrari. They pitted together on

ABOVE Red Bull Racing's Sebastian Vettel resisted Nico Rosberg in the early stages, then rose to third place

BELOW BMW Sauber's Robert Kubica ran third for much of the race, but Vettel demoted him to fourth at the second round of stops

OPPOSITE Luca Badoer had said that he would find his feet at Spa, but apparently he didn't find his throttle foot

boost and passed the Pole at the top of the hill. But only just… as Räikkönen then out-braked himself and had a wild moment running over the kerbs at Les Combes. Kubica came around the corner and tapped him, the field concertinaed and all of a sudden cars were flying everywhere.

Renault's Romain Grosjean went down the inside of Button and tapped the Brawn driver into a spin. Behind him, Lewis Hamilton tried to take avoiding action and was clipped by Jaime Alguersuari's Toro Rosso. In an instant, the rookies had taken the two British drivers out of the race. So the safety car was deployed while the four stricken cars and resulting mess was cleared up.

TALKING POINT
ALL WRONG FOR BADOER

The European and Belgian Grands Prix were a truly miserable couple of races for 38-year-old Luca Badoer – who'd achieved one of his lifetime ambitions of racing in a grand prix for Ferrari.

In his time, he'd been quick – remember he'd won the FIA Formula 3000 championship back in 1992, beating Rubens Barrichello, David Coulthard and Olivier Panis. Not only that, but in the past 10 years he's done more Formula 1 testing miles than any other driver – a good 80,000 miles. However, his races at Valencia and at Spa were characterised by errors, spins, penalties and a lack of speed…

He had the misfortune of twice qualifying last on the grid for Ferrari and extended his run of being the most 'pointless' driver in F1 history – it's now 50 grands prix without score.

Despite his considerable previous testing experience for Ferrari, Luca Badoer (dubbed "Look-how Bad-you-are") was always going to struggle to get to grips with the 2009-specification cars, with their low downforce and slick tyres, because of rules that prevent in-season testing.

One former driver said that endless amounts of testing was no substitute for actually racing, because of that extra level of competition that comes over a grand prix weekend. It's that final bit of performance that Badoer had lacked, given that it had been a full decade since he last competed in a race.

"In testing, it's more relaxed and there is less pressure," he admitted at Spa. "During a race weekend, I don't have a lot of track running and I don't have a lot of time. That is the biggest problem."

Badoer was fastest through the speed trap in qualifying at Spa – but that was because he forgot to brake and went straight on into the Les Combes barriers… He went on to finish the race 1m 42s behind his race-winning team-mate Kimi Räikkönen. Given the close battle between Ferrari and McLaren for third place in the constructors' championship, the Scuderia had little choice but to replace him for Monza, with Giancarlo Fisichella drafted in, replaced in turn at Force India by Vitantonio Liuzzi.

Yet, given the straightline-aero efficiency of the Force India, the betting started immediately after the news broke that Liuzzi would out-qualify Fisichella at Monza…

Badoer's future with Ferrari remained to be seen. He blamed the media following the announcement that he was being dropped. The media blamed the stopwatch…

lap 14 and even fuelled-up for identical 17-lap middle stints. However, Räikkönen is supreme on this classic track snaking through the Ardennes forest and, having won three of the previous four races here, he wasn't going to give Fisichella a sniff of victory. Indeed, the Finnish driver didn't put a foot wrong as he drove to his and Ferrari's first victory of the year.

"I think many drivers like it here, it's a proper circuit and it is good fun to drive," said Räikkönen. "Usually I have been pretty good here…"

So, while Button was suffering his fifth consecutive poor result, his nearest championship rivals were again, to his relief, making a meal of things. His team-mate Rubens Barrichello very nearly stalled on the grid, and the Brazilian was swamped in the opening laps and fell through the field like a stone dropped in water. He did manage to make up some positions through the race, but in the closing laps there was an ominous plume of blue smoke emanating from the rear of his Brawn. He nursed his sick machine home to cling on to seventh place for two points, although the car finally caught fire as he was in the pitlane heading to *parc fermé*.

For engine woes, though, you only had to look at Red Bull Racing. Sebastian Vettel again did very little running on Friday, and Mark Webber stayed in the pits on Saturday morning to conserve engine mileage. The pair of them were engaged in a titanic struggle on the opening lap, as the lighter Webber muscled his way past his team-mate climbing up to Les Combes. Unfortunately, the Australian's race was ruined when he fell foul of the stewards. He pitted on lap 14, the same lap as Heidfeld's BMW and, although Webber entered his pit first, he took on slightly more fuel and his lollipop man released him just as Heidfeld was coming down the pitlane. The German driver braked heavily to avoid the Red Bull as it pulled out, and the inevitable drive-through penalty came quickly for the Australian for the "unsafe release from the pit stop".

Another driver to suffer in the pits was Alonso. The Renault man was circulating in third place, on a one-stop strategy and eyeing up a podium finish when he pitted. The Renault team struggled to fit the front-left wheel properly, due to a problem with the wheel fairing, and TV replays showed that Sutil had damaged it during that opening-corner incident. The team, not wanting to risk any more problems with loose wheels, called him in to retire. Once again that pesky first lap put paid to Alonso's race ambitions, as it did for Trulli, Button, Hamilton and, ultimately, Fisichella.

That's the secret to Spa: it doesn't matter who starts where on the topsy-turvy upside-down grid. You need to stay away from everyone else on the opening lap, just as Räikkönen did on the outside of La Source. One wonders if everyone will try that move next year…

LEFT Kimi Räikkönen keeps his emotions in check on the podium while Giancarlo Fisichella acknowledges his Force India team

SNAPSHOT FROM
BELGIUM

CLOCKWISE FROM RIGHT Spa-Francorchamps looks great from any angle: this is looking down from La Source; 'Lewis Hamilton' and 'Robert Kubica' looked unusually cheerful; not everybody appreciated stand-in Luca Badoer's efforts for Ferrari; Rubens Barrichello finished, and then his Brawn caught fire; taking a look at Toyota's inner workings; Bernie Ecclestone and Giancarlo Fisichella appear bemused by this photo opportunity; Fisichella is greeted by his crew after finishing second

WEEKEND NEWS

■ The FIA announced that it was launching an investigation into the events surrounding the 2008 Singapore Grand Prix. Motor sport's governing body said that new evidence had come to light which suggested that Nelson Piquet Jr's crash on lap 14 of the race was deliberate and had been timed to bring out a safety car to help Renault team-mate Fernando Alonso's race strategy that resulted in victory for the Spaniard.

■ After considerable speculation, Ferrari confirmed after the Belgian Grand Prix that Force India's Giancarlo Fisichella would step in to replace Luca Badoer for the remainder of the season. "I'm in seventh heaven and I can't believe it – the dream of my life becomes true," said the 36-year-old Italian.

■ The organisers of the Abu Dhabi Grand Prix confirmed that they will hold the world's first day–night race, as they intended to start the 2009 season finale at five o'clock local time, with sunset due at 5.43pm.

■ The Formula 1 teams admitted at Spa-Francorchamps that they were to formally discuss the idea of running third cars in the 2010 season. Ferrari has been one of the key movers behind the idea in a bid to tempt Michael Schumacher to return to selected races in 2010.

■ Felipe Massa was told that he would not return to Formula 1 until 2010 after he underwent surgery to repair part of his skull following his Hungarian GP accident. The 28-year-old Brazilian was happy with progress and said he was looking forward to getting back behind the wheel of a kart again soon.

■ Donington Park insisted that it was still on schedule to hold a grand prix in 2010, despite it being listed with Silverstone as an alternative venue on a draft calendar that was circulated to the teams at Spa.

RACE
RESULTS
BELGIUM
SPA-FRANCORCHAMPS

Official Results © [2009]
Formula One Administration Limited,
6 Princes Gate, London, SW7 1QJ.
No reproduction without permission.
All copyright and database rights reserved.

RACE DATE August 30th
CIRCUIT LENGTH 4.352 miles
NO. OF LAPS 44
RACE DISTANCE 191.491 miles
WEATHER Sunny and dry, 19°C
TRACK TEMP 25°C
ATTENDANCE 100,000
LAP RECORD Sebastian Vettel,
1m47.263s, 146.065mph, 2009

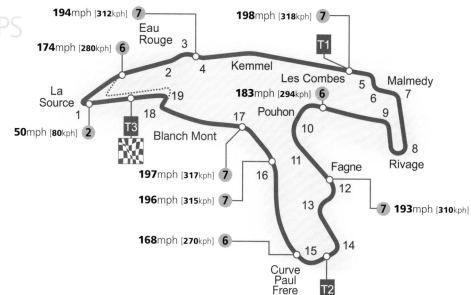

PRACTICE 1

	Driver	Time	Laps
1	J Trulli	1m49.675s	13
2	J Button	1m50.283s	18
3	F Alonso	1m50.368s	13
4	S Buemi	1m51.045s	20
5	J Alguersuari	1m51.529s	24
6	R Barrichello	1m52.321s	18
7	K Räikkönen	1m52.930s	16
8	H Kovalainen	1m53.383s	11
9	R Kubica	1m53.650s	12
10	L Badoer	1m55.068s	20
11	G Fisichella	2m03.972s	11
12	N Rosberg	2m04.505s	13
13	R Grosjean	2m05.513s	13
14	N Heidfeld	2m05.614s	14
15	K Nakajima	2m05.705s	15
16	A Sutil	2m05.839s	10
17	M Webber	2m06.181s	6
18	T Glock	2m06.331s	15
19	S Vettel	No time	1
20	L Hamilton	No time	4

PRACTICE 2

	Driver	Time	Laps
1	L Hamilton	1m47.201s	29
2	T Glock	1m47.217s	29
3	K Räikkönen	1m47.285s	26
4	M Webber	1m47.329s	31
5	R Grosjean	1m47.333s	34
6	G Fisichella	1m47.506s	27
7	J Trulli	1m47.559s	33
8	R Kubica	1m47.578s	33
9	J Alguersuari	1m47.579s	36
10	S Vettel	1m47.602s	25
11	S Buemi	1m47.702s	38
12	H Kovalainen	1m47.743s	33
13	A Sutil	1m47.790s	29
14	F Alonso	1m47.862s	30
15	K Nakajima	1m47.961s	32
16	N Heidfeld	1m48.017s	30
17	J Button	1m48.125s	34
18	R Barrichello	1m48.130s	37
19	N Rosberg	1m48.360s	29
20	L Badoer	1m49.211s	30

PRACTICE 3

	Driver	Time	Laps
1	N Heidfeld	1m45.388s	17
2	J Trulli	1m45.462s	18
3	A Sutil	1m45.677s	20
4	R Grosjean	1m45.878s	18
5	T Glock	1m45.908s	18
6	R Kubica	1m45.987s	18
7	N Rosberg	1m46.040s	19
8	G Fisichella	1m46.114s	21
9	L Hamilton	1m46.301s	17
10	J Button	1m46.406s	20
11	K Räikkönen	1m46.409s	19
12	S Buemi	1m46.417s	19
13	H Kovalainen	1m46.462s	17
14	S Vettel	1m46.747s	14
15	J Alguersuari	1m46.814s	22
16	R Barrichello	1m46.815s	19
17	F Alonso	1m46.926s	14
18	L Badoer	1m47.055s	20
19	K Nakajima	1m47.078s	19
20	M Webber	No time	3

QUALIFYING 1

	Driver	Time
1	G Fisichella	1m45.102s
2	J Trulli	1m45.140s
3	R Barrichello	1m45.237s
4	A Sutil	1m45.239s
5	M Webber	1m45.350s
6	S Vettel	1m45.372s
7	T Glock	1m45.450s
8	N Rosberg	1m45.486s
9	N Heidfeld	1m45.566s
10	K Räikkönen	1m45.579s
11	R Kubica	1m45.655s
12	H Kovalainen	1m45.705s
13	F Alonso	1m45.707s
14	J Button	1m45.761s
15	L Hamilton	1m45.767s
16	S Buemi	1m45.951s
17	J Alguersuari	1m46.032s
18	K Nakajima	1m46.307s
19	R Grosjean	1m46.359s
20	L Badoer	1m46.957s

QUALIFYING 2

	Driver	Time
1	J Trulli	1m44.503s
2	R Kubica	1m44.557s
3	S Vettel	1m44.592s
4	G Fisichella	1m44.667s
5	N Heidfeld	1m44.709s
6	R Barrichello	1m44.834s
7	T Glock	1m44.877s
8	M Webber	1m44.924s
9	K Räikkönen	1m44.953s
10	N Rosberg	1m45.047s
11	A Sutil	1m45.119s
12	L Hamilton	1m45.122s
13	F Alonso	1m45.136s
14	J Button	1m45.251s
15	H Kovalainen	1m45.259s

Best sectors – Practice

Sec 1	L Hamilton	30.810s
Sec 2	J Alguersuari	45.744s
Sec 3	L Hamilton	28.391s

Speed trap – Practice

1	J Button	194.986mph
2	R Barrichello	194.675mph
3	T Glock	193.992mph

Best sectors – Qualifying

Sec 1	L Hamilton	30.601s
Sec 2	N Rosberg	45.139s
Sec 3	R Kubica	28.304s

Speed trap – Qualifying

1	L Badoer	201.510mph
2	A Sutil	196.104mph
3	K Räikkönen	195.421mph

IN 2008

Rain late in the race turned this into a belter, with Lewis Hamilton winning a battle with Kimi Räikkönen before the Ferrari ace spun. But the stewards reckoned Hamilton hadn't ceded enough ground after crossing a chicane and added 25s to his finishing time, just enough to demote him to third behind Massa and Heidfeld.

Lewis Hamilton
"I got a poor start, the anti-stall kicked in and I got sandwiched at Turn 1. When Romain spun Jenson at Turn 5, I slowed to try and avoid the damage and got taken out."

Luca Badoer
"I flat-spotted my tyres at the first corner, so had vibrations. The situation improved when they were changed, but the harder compound was not as good."

Robert Kubica
"I was second after Turn 1. I was surprised to see Kimi next to me through Eau Rouge. We lacked a bit of pace, but it's good to be fighting for podiums again."

Fernando Alonso
"I missed a chance to be on the podium. I was third when I pitted, but it was seen that something was wrong on my left-front tyre and the team asked me to retire."

Jarno Trulli
"I can't say how disappointed I am. I was right behind Heidfeld at the first corner and just touched him at the exit and broke the front wing and had to make a pit stop."

Heikki Kovalainen
"A good race, even though our pace wasn't as good as in the past two races, our strategy worked perfectly and I was able to pass a lot of the guys stopping before me."

Kimi Räikkönen
"Behind the safety car I thought about keeping the tyres and brakes hot to be able to attack Fisichella, and that's how I was able to pass him easily at the restart."

Nick Heidfeld
"From third, I had higher expectations, but I lost the race on lap 1. I tried to outbrake Jarno into La Source, but lost ground as the tyres weren't warm enough."

Romain Grosjean
"I made a very good start, moving up to 13th, but then Button took me out at Turn 5 and it was the end for me. It's frustrating, as I would have loved to finish the race."

Timo Glock
"I was fourth when the safety car came out, but at my first stop we had trouble with the fuel rig. The crew did well to quickly change to the back-up rig but we lost time."

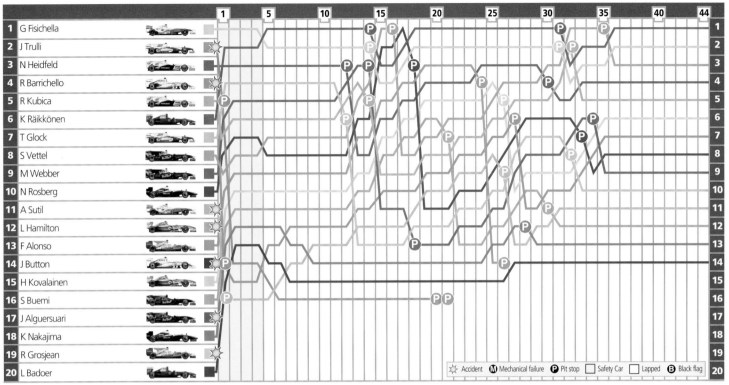

	Driver		1	5	10	15	20	25	30	35	40	44	
1	G Fisichella												1
2	J Trulli												2
3	N Heidfeld												3
4	R Barrichello												4
5	R Kubica												5
6	K Räikkönen												6
7	T Glock												7
8	S Vettel												8
9	M Webber												9
10	N Rosberg												10
11	A Sutil												11
12	L Hamilton												12
13	F Alonso												13
14	J Button												14
15	H Kovalainen												15
16	S Buemi												16
17	J Alguersuari												17
18	K Nakajima												18
19	R Grosjean												19
20	L Badoer												20

☆ Accident Ⓜ Mechanical failure Ⓟ Pit stop ☐ Safety Car ☐ Lapped Ⓑ Black flag

QUALIFYING 3

	Driver	Time
1	G Fisichella	1m46.308s
2	J Trulli	1m46.395s
3	N Heidfeld	1m46.500s
4	R Barrichello	1m46.513s
5	R Kubica	1m46.586s
6	K Räikkönen	1m46.633s
7	T Glock	1m46.677s
8	S Vettel	1m46.761s
9	M Webber	1m46.788s
10	N Rosberg	1m47.362s

GRID

	Driver	Time
1	G Fisichella	1m46.308s
2	J Trulli	1m46.395s
3	N Heidfeld	1m46.500s
4	R Barrichello	1m46.513s
5	R Kubica	1m46.586s
6	K Räikkönen	1m46.633s
7	T Glock	1m46.677s
8	S Vettel	1m46.761s
9	M Webber	1m46.788s
10	N Rosberg	1m47.362s
11	A Sutil	1m45.119s
12	L Hamilton	1m45.122s
13	F Alonso	1m45.136s
14	J Button	1m45.251s
15	H Kovalainen	1m45.259s
16	S Buemi	1m45.951s
17	J Alguersuari	1m46.032s
18	K Nakajima	1m46.307s
19	R Grosjean	1m46.359s
20	L Badoer	1m46.957s

RACE

	Driver	Car	Laps	Time	Avg. mph	Fastest	Stops
1	K Räikkönen	*Ferrari F60	44	1h23m50.995s	136.969	1m47.674s	2
2	G Fisichella	Force India-Mercedes VJM02	44	1h23m51.934s	136.943	1m47.737s	2
3	S Vettel	Red Bull-Renault RB5	44	1h23m54.879s	136.864	1m47.263s	2
4	R Kubica	BMW Sauber F1.09	44	1h24m00.961s	136.698	1m47.371s	2
5	N Heidfeld	BMW Sauber F1.09	44	1h24m02.271s	136.663	1m47.664s	2
6	H Kovalainen	*McLaren-Mercedes MP4-24	44	1h24m23.758s	136.083	1m48.348s	1
7	R Barrichello	Brawn-Mercedes BGP 001	44	1h24m26.456s	136.010	1m48.257s	2
8	N Rosberg	Williams-Toyota FW31	44	1h24m27.203s	135.990	1m47.766s	2
9	M Webber	Red Bull-Renault RB5	44	1h24m27.954s	135.970	1m47.783s	3
10	T Glock	Toyota TF109	44	1h24m32.485s	135.848	1m47.736s	2
11	A Sutil	Force India-Mercedes VJM02	44	1h24m33.631s	135.818	1m47.859s	2
12	S Buemi	Toro Rosso-Ferrari STR4	44	1h24m37.101s	135.725	1m47.763s	2
13	K Nakajima	Williams-Toyota FW31	44	1h24m45.236s	135.508	1m48.205s	1
14	L Badoer	*Ferrari F60	44	1h25m33.172s	134.243	1m49.803s	1
R	F Alonso	Renault R29	26	Crash damage	-	1m48.634s	1
R	J Trulli	Toyota TF109	21	Brakes	-	1m50.029s	2
R	L Hamilton	*McLaren-Mercedes MP4-24	0	Accident	-	-	0
R	J Button	Brawn-Mercedes BGP 001	0	Accident	-	-	0
R	J Alguersuari	Toro Rosso-Ferrari STR4	0	Accident	-	-	0
R	R Grosjean	Renault R29	0	Accident	-	-	0

* Denotes car fitted with KERS

CHAMPIONSHIP

	Driver	Pts
1	J Button	72
2	R Barrichello	56
3	S Vettel	53
4	M Webber	51.5
5	K Räikkönen	34
6	N Rosberg	30.5
7	L Hamilton	27
8	J Trulli	22.5
9	F Massa	22
10	H Kovalainen	17
11	T Glock	16
12	F Alonso	16
13	N Heidfeld	10
14	G Fisichella	8
15	R Kubica	8
16	S Buemi	3
17	S Bourdais	2

Fastest lap		
S Vettel 1m47.263s		
(146.065mph) on lap 38		

Fastest speed trap		**Fastest pit stop**	
R Barrichello	196.353mph	1 S Buemi	23.126s
Slowest speed trap		2 S Vettel	23.333s
L Hamilton	161.432mph	3 N Rosberg	23.380s

	Constructor	Pts
1	Brawn-Mercedes	128
2	Red Bull-Renault	104.5
3	Ferrari	56
4	McLaren-Mercedes	44
5	Toyota	38.5
6	Williams-Toyota	30.5
7	BMW Sauber	18
8	Renault	16
9	Force India-Mercedes	8
10	Toro Rosso-Ferrari	5

Jaime Alguersuari

"Jenson and Lewis had to move to the left to avoid Rubens, moving onto the part of the track that I was on. We collided and my car was too damaged for me to continue."

Mark Webber

"I had a good first lap but, at my first stop, I was released in front of Nick, and was given a drive-through penalty. After that, it was a case of damage limitation."

Nico Rosberg

"The car was difficult to drive today and it had a lot to do with the tyres. When the sun came out, the tyres worked well, especially the soft tyres in the final stint."

Adrian Sutil

"Someone crashed into me at the first corner. I think it was Alonso, who went straight into my rear and turned me around and destroyed my front wing."

Jenson Button

"I had a good run going down the straight to Turn 5. I was outside Heikki and turned in, but Romain outbraked himself and hit my back wheel. That was it for me today."

Sebastien Buemi

"It's a shame I couldn't overtake Heikki, even though I was faster than him, but at least I tried. Maybe a one-stop strategy would have worked better for me."

Sebastian Vettel

"I was too conservative when I saw Nick go off, as cars can come back on the track, so I lost a place to Nico. I lost too much ground to the leading cars in the first stint."

Kazuki Nakajima

"We struggled with our pace and qualifying was really tough, which of course affected our potential in the race. On balance, the race was slightly better than Saturday."

Giancarlo Fisichella

"It was an amazing day, but I could have won. I was unlucky with the safety car when Kimi passed me with KERS. But we can't take away from what was a fantastic result."

Rubens Barrichello

"The problem with the clutch at the start took away any chance of a podium, so we changed my strategy at the end of the first lap to fuel longer for the first stint."

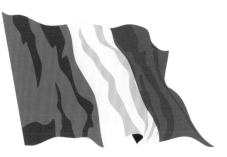

FORMULA 1 GRAN PREMIO
SANTANDER D'ITALIA 2009
MONZA

BRAWN WINNERS

The rot had set in, and this was Brawn GP's race of redemption as Rubens Barrichello led Jenson Button home for a 1–2 finish that pulled the team further clear of Red Bull

Two-stop, or not to two-stop? That was what it boiled down to at Monza. It was almost an old-fashioned fable, the race of the Brawn tortoises (on one-stop strategies) against Lewis Hamilton's hare (going for two). In the end, the tortoises had it – Barrichello ahead of Button, the order practically pre-ordained by the 0.015s gap between the pair in qualifying. That gave the Brazilian better track position and the optimum pit strategy. As a team, Brawn GP was flawless at Monza, and picked up a maximum score on a day when rivals Red Bull Racing scored a solitary point. It struck a decisive blow in Brawn GP's quest for the all-important (to the team and its balance sheet) constructors' championship.

As for Hamilton, he harried, hustled and cajoled his McLaren all afternoon, driving on the limit to chase down Button's second place during the final laps. Then he kissed a kerb too far, dropped his left-rear wheel in the dirt exiting the first Lesmo and ended his race against the barriers. He simply shrugged his shoulders as he clambered out, accepting an error that, in any other season, could have been the turning point in a championship campaign. "'tis better to have loved and lost," he might have said, "than never to have loved at

Ferrari made it onto the podium, but only thanks to Hamilton's late-race mishap – and he was hounded all the way by the Force India of Adrian Sutil, galloping along with Mercedes horsepower.

Events on track were overshadowed by the maelstrom of intrigue swirling through the paddock, as leaks from the FIA's case against Renault in 'Crashgate' became public. It was flamboyant stuff, each move on the political chessboard delivered with a flourish worthy of the greatest *comedia dell'arte* melodrama.

On track, Brawn clearly had the upper hand on raw pace. The question was how to make it count when faced with rivals running KERS – not just McLaren and Ferrari at this race, but Renault too. A light fuel load might secure the front row, but would carry the risk of being overtaken by KERS-enhanced cars on lap 1 – thereby nullifying the strategic gain of locking out the front row by running light. The only sensible option was to go for a one-stopper, and plan to out-run particularly Hamilton, and perhaps Räikkönen too, over the duration. It set up the first genuine contest between two different strategies since the intra-team duel between Button and Barrichello at Barcelona.

The plan was executed to perfection. The Brawn drivers were fuelled within 1.5kg of each other, with Barrichello slightly heavier. The Brazilian continued his run of midsummer form to outqualify Button; a solid race start took care of the rest, and he ran an accomplished race ahead of his team-mate.

The Brawns stopped on laps 28 (Button) and 29 (Barrichello) respectively, just past half distance, while Hamilton had made his first visit to the pits on lap 15, and then again on lap 34. He re-emerged 3.5s behind Button, who himself trailed Barrichello by 5s as he consolidated his championship lead. To all intents and purposes, the race was decided there and then, although Hamilton tried to harry a composed Button

all." At least Hamilton was going for it. The crumpled McLaren was ample proof that the British driver is a racer to the last.

To have any hope of victory in the Italian GP, you needed one thing above all else: a Mercedes engine. This is an era of notional engine parity, in which engine development is frozen to ensure that the 2.4-litre V8 is no longer a 'performance differentiator'. However, the engine from Stuttgart, via Brixworth, is most definitely first among equals. No circuit is a better indicator of engine performance than Monza; and six Mercedes engines in the top seven places in qualifying told a very clear story. Kimi Räikkönen's

ABOVE Robert Kubica gets onto the grass as Lewis Hamilton leads Kimi Räikkönen and Adrian Sutil down to the first chicane

LEFT Mark Webber clashed with Robert Kubica at the Roggia chicane on the opening lap and crashed out

INSIDE LINE
GIANCARLO FISICHELLA
FERRARI DRIVER

"Overall, I am happy with how things went in my first race weekend with Ferrari. To be honest, I was actually quite nervous going to the car on Friday, but totally focused. It was great to be working with Rob Smedley as my race engineer again, after our time together at Jordan. I had a good feeling straight away, as he knows how I work, and I know how he works.

I was pleased with my first day on Friday: I had a lot of fuel on board and we didn't go looking for performance. Compared to the Force India VJM02, you have to work a lot more with the steering wheel and the switches on the Ferrari. I was just concentrating on the driving before, but in this car I am quite busy.

The other major difficulty was gaining confidence with the KERS. I was concentrating so much on my first lap this morning that I wasn't even watching the Italian fans around the circuit. I only felt their presence when I was walking around the track afterwards, and they were very, very friendly.

My performance in qualifying was not up to the Ferrari standard. I lost valuable time to prepare when I crashed into the barriers at Parabolica, after I made a mistake at the beginning of third practice and couldn't run again.

The mechanics did a fantastic job to rebuild the car, but I knew I didn't have enough confidence in the car as I went into qualifying. I then didn't manage to put together a perfect lap in Q2, so I didn't make it through to the final part of qualifying, even though the potential was there.

In the race, I managed to make up a few positions at the start, but then I had a difficult moment with Sebastian Vettel: he closed the door on me going into Ascari, and let's say he was very decisive. I felt comfortable using the softer tyre in the first part of the race, but I struggled more on the harder one, especially after my pit stop.

I only just missed out on a points finish, in ninth place, but I did the best I could. I was mainly upset that I crashed in third practice, which prevented me from being as well prepared as possible for qualifying. If I had started a bit further forward, I might have been able to finish in the top eight."

TALKING POINT
CRASHGATE SCANDAL

Renault's litigious summer continued as the team arrived at Monza with the prospect of another trip to the World Motor Sport Council hanging over its head. One week before the Italian GP, the team was summoned to a hearing in Paris (on 21 September) to answer the charge that it had "conspired with its driver, Nelson Piquet Jr, to cause a deliberate crash at the 2008 Singapore Grand Prix."

At the time of Piquet's accident, many in the paddock aired their suspicions that its timing had been rather fortuitous, to put it politely. The accusation faded as the 2009 season began, but the storm was reignited following Piquet's dismissal from Renault after the Hungarian GP

In exchange for immunity, the Brazilian provided the FIA with a sworn statement that he had been asked by Renault boss Flavio Briatore and engineering director Pat Symonds to deliberately bring out the safety car on lap 14. The FIA's subsequent investigations, including interviews with the people involved, suggested that there was a case to be answered before the World Council.

During the Italian GP weekend, the affair acquired a new momentum when the FIA's dossier against the Renault team began to be leaked to the media. The leaks included telemetry data from Piquet's car, showing him maintaining throttle pressure after the car had begun spinning, when he would have been expected to have lifted off. Similarly, edited excerpts from conversations between the FIA investigators and Briatore and Symonds were made public. Testimony from Symonds in particular, in which he refused to answer potentially incriminating questions, appeared damning.

Briatore responded to the leaks by going on the offensive in an attempt to brazen it out. He told the media that the accusations were "outrageous lies". He also announced that he and the team had begun legal action against the Piquets for blackmail. Events had escalated sufficiently for Max Mosley to step in. He told the media "fixing is one degree worse than cheating" and urged caution because Renault had not yet submitted its defence case.

Three days after the race, Renault announced that Briatore and Symonds had left the team and that it would not be contesting the FIA's charges, following the testimony of an internal whistleblower who confirmed that the idea of causing a deliberate accident had been discussed.

The World Council subsequently sanctioned Renault with permanent exclusion from the championship, suspended for two years. Briatore was banned from all FIA-sanctioned championships for life, while Symonds was handed a five-year ban. Piquet Jr, having negotiated immunity in return for coming forward, remains free to compete.

to the flag – and paid the price on the final lap. It was just the second time in his F1 career that Hamilton had crashed out on circuit (rather than in the pitlane). And, by curious coincidence, the two incidents had occurred on consecutive weekends.

Behind the leading trio came an entertaining battle and, for once, it didn't end in tears. This was between Sutil and Räikkönen – the 'greatest rivalry in F1' suggested one paddock wag. There had been mutterings from the direction of Maranello that the surprise form of Force India at Spa and Monza was bad for the sport, because such lowly teams shouldn't be battling it out with the grandees. The former Jordan team took such tetchiness on the chin and delivered another great weekend. With former team leader Fisichella struggling to get his head around the second Ferrari, it was left to Sutil to lead the charge. And he did so ably, tracing Räikkönen's wheeltracks over the 53 laps. They were rarely more than 2s apart, and followed the same two-stop strategy. As fate would have it, they fuelled to exactly the same lap for their second pit stop, which thwarted any chance Sutil had of leapfrogging Räikkönen. Then the Ferrari faltered exiting the pits. providing an opportunity, but Sutil, over-eager to gain time, had overshot his pit – locking up his wheels, scattering startled mechanics. By the time they had sent their man on his way, he was once again staring at the 'Etihad' branding on the rear wing of the Ferrari.

Sutil, of course, had been dumped out of the points on several occasions by Räikkönen, and plenty were willing him on to return the favour by at least trying something. It would have been poetic justice, if nothing else. However, with his first F1 points at stake, the young German decided discretion was the better part of valour, on this occasion at least. For Räikkönen, it was his fourth, and Ferrari's fifth, consecutive podium, something of a resurgence in what has been an off-colour season.

Their respective team-mates provided contrasting studies in how to conduct one's debut weekend with a new team. Vitantonio Liuzzi, racing in a grand prix for the first time since Brazil in 2007, qualified his Force India an impressive seventh. He raced strongly, too, running as high as fourth until his retirement on lap 22 with a broken driveshaft. In the second Ferrari, the story was less happy. Fellow Italian Fisichella strutted through the paddock like a proud peacock, resplendent in Ferrari red. He was solid on Friday and then, on Saturday morning, crashed early in practice. That loss of track time meant he qualified 14th, then raced to a disappointing ninth place. This from a man who, a week earlier, had finished second in a Force India. There were mutterings about a lack of testing hampering his pace, and needing time to learn the car, but they sounded hollow when comparing his performance to Liuzzi, who had done nothing more than straightline running. Fisichella's ninth helped Ferrari's championship position as little as Badoer's 19th; how the unfortunate tester must have wished he'd been given another shot at a circuit he knew.

Behind Sutil and Räikkönen came Fernando Alonso, capable as ever of compartmentalising the

OPPOSITE Brawns to the fore, as Rubens Barrichello leads Jenson Button to a famous 1–2

ABOVE Kimi Räikkönen and Adrian Sutil fought hard over third

LEFT Kazuki Nakajima and Jarno Trulli get up close and personal as they enjoy a scrap late in the race

BELOW Vitantonio Liuzzi made an impressive return with Force India

ABOVE Lewis Hamilton was the only driver able to keep up with the Brawns, but a last-lap bid for second resulted in this tattered McLaren

BELOW Jenson Button congratulates Rubens Barrichello after they finished second and first

off-track drama and delivering a flawless performance on Sunday afternoon. The Renault was never the quickest car, but he gained a position on the opening lap, then ran consistently on a one-stop strategy to score more valuable points for his troubled team.

Next came another study in team-mate disappointment: Heikki Kovalainen in the second McLaren. He had been the pre-race favourite of many, after qualifying fourth as the first of the one-stoppers (he went to lap 27). A solid start would have put him in prime position for victory, but he suffered a disastrous opening lap, out-muscled by those around him. He was seventh as they crossed

the line for the first time, then eighth by lap 4. It put paid to any chances of even a podium, and he toiled to a disappointing sixth place. For many people, this was the opportunity the Finn needed to seize in order to prove he deserved another year with McLaren. His failure to do so, plus a fastest lap 0.3s off his team-mate's, told their own story.

Kovalainen was trailed home by Heidfeld, showing signs of BMW Sauber's continued late-season improvement, but still nearly a minute behind the winner prior to the last-lap safety car.

The final point went to Sebastian Vettel at the wheel of the out-of-sorts Red Bull. The team made noises about a deficit in engine performance, but that didn't explain why Alonso's demonstrably inferior works chassis finished ahead; as at Spa, it was simply a case of an opportunity missed. Vettel inherited eighth on lap 53, but that was 52 laps more than Mark Webber managed, after tangling with Robert Kubica at the second chicane and nerfing the barrier, which consigned him to an innocuous retirement – and practically ended his title chances. His momentum from the middle of the year had simply evaporated over three disappointing races.

The man who picked up the initiative, of course, was Barrichello: flawless throughout the weekend, controlled and composed on his way to his second win of the year – matching Vettel's total. If the Brazilian's win at Valencia was just reward for a season of nearly but not quite delivering, this Monza triumph felt altogether different; it was a commanding victory that laid down another marker for his team-mate.

The title fight was no longer about Brawn against Red Bull; it was now an in-house affair: Jenson against Rubens, with no team orders in sight. The big question was now not whether Button was cracking under the pressure, but how, and if, he could turn the tide of his team-mate's title charge…

SNAPSHOT FROM
ITALY

CLOCKWISE FROM RIGHT If the smell got bad for Renault's Pat Symonds at Monza, it was to get far worse later on; a ceremonial guard for the red trucks; there was only one team as far as the fans were concerned; the cars weren't the only things hugging the curves at Monza; the barriers on the old banking continue to rust; former F3 team-mates Adrian Sutil and Lewis Hamilton congratulate each other after claiming the front row

WEEKEND NEWS

■ To try and curb drivers' excesses, Monza officials installed higher 'combination kerbs' at the first and second chicanes, Rettifilo and Roggia, for the 2009 race. The design was approved by the FIA and had already been employed at Barcelona and the Nürburgring. It was judged a success by teams and drivers.

■ Ferrari announced a five-year deal with Spanish bank Grupo Santander at Monza. The move, widely held as a sign that Fernando Alonso would also be heading to Maranello, was confirmed by Luca di Montezemelo in a press conference on Thursday. Santander would also continue to sponsor McLaren in 2010.

■ Monza is traditionally where Ferrari confirms its driver line-up for the following year, and Ferrari President Luca di Montezemelo set tongues wagging when he told journalists that Fernando Alonso would join Ferrari "sooner or later." "I'll make it happen," said the Italian. "I've always liked Alonso, because he is a great driver. He won titles, and I've always thought that sooner or later, all great drivers come to Ferrari."

■ Williams co-owner Patrick Head spoke out strongly on the issue of race fixing and how the FIA should deal with offenders in the Renault case. "If that proved to be happening in a consistent way, nobody would have any interest in Formula 1 racing because you couldn't believe what you were looking at," said Head. "I hope that whatever punishments are handed out can be looked at and stand up to scrutiny."

■ During a media breakfast at the Italian GP, Sir Jackie Stewart revealed that a senior F1 figure had encouraged him to stand for the post of FIA President. Stewart declined and made it clear that his choice for the role was Ari Vatanen. "I think there's an enormous desire for change," said the Scot. "I don't think that the FIA will change much if Jean Todt gets in, because I think that regime will stay the same."

RACE
RESULTS
ITALY
MONZA

Official Results © [2009]
Formula One Administration Limited,
6 Princes Gate, London, SW7 1QJ.
No reproduction without permission.
All copyright and database rights reserved.

RACE DATE September 13th
CIRCUIT LENGTH 3.600 miles
NO. OF LAPS 53
RACE DISTANCE 190.800 miles
WEATHER Dry and bright, 27°C
TRACK TEMP 36°C
ATTENDANCE 110,000
LAP RECORD Rubens Barrichello,
1m21.046s, 159.909mph, 2004

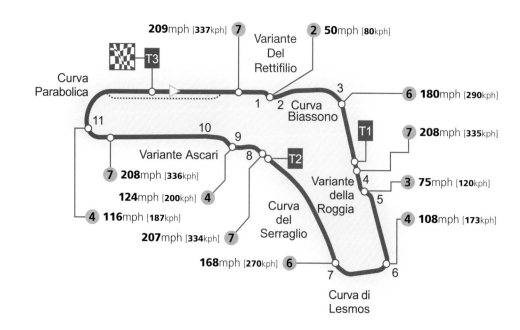

209mph [337kph] **7**   **2** 50mph [80kph]

Variante Del Rettifilio

Curva Parabolica

T3

3   **6** 180mph [290kph]

1 2 Curva Biassono

T1   **7** 208mph [335kph]

11

10

9

Variante Ascari

8   T2

7 208mph [336kph]

124mph [200kph] **4**

3 75mph [120kph]

4
5

Variante della Roggia

4 108mph [173kph]

4 116mph [187kph]

Curva del Serraglio

207mph [334kph] **7**

168mph [270kph] **6**

7   6

Curva di Lesmos

PRACTICE 1

	Driver	Time	Laps
1	L Hamilton	1m23.936s	26
2	H Kovalainen	1m24.332s	27
3	A Sutil	1m24.471s	24
4	F Alonso	1m24.477s	21
5	N Heidfeld	1m24.683s	25
6	S Buemi	1m24.703s	35
7	J Button	1m24.706s	21
8	G Fisichella	1m24.732s	24
9	M Webber	1m24.759s	19
10	K Räikkönen	1m24.761s	26
11	R Kubica	1m24.813s	20
12	R Barrichello	1m24.826s	24
13	N Rosberg	1m24.927s	29
14	K Nakajima	1m25.150s	28
15	R Grosjean	1m25.612s	18
16	V Liuzzi	1m25.689s	29
17	J Alguersuari	1m25.742s	30
18	S Vettel	1m25.951s	8
19	J Trulli	1m26.020s	23
20	T Glock	1m26.325s	17

PRACTICE 2

	Driver	Time	Laps
1	A Sutil	1m23.924s	28
2	R Grosjean	1m24.163s	31
3	F Alonso	1m24.297s	35
4	H Kovalainen	1m24.482s	41
5	R Kubica	1m24.622s	40
6	T Glock	1m24.634s	36
7	N Heidfeld	1m24.693s	34
8	K Räikkönen	1m24.796s	39
9	K Nakajima	1m24.799s	36
10	S Buemi	1m24.884s	44
11	L Hamilton	1m24.902s	32
12	V Liuzzi	1m24.921s	39
13	J Trulli	1m24.967s	40
14	M Webber	1m24.979s	25
15	J Alguersuari	1m25.003s	34
16	R Barrichello	1m25.140s	35
17	N Rosberg	1m25.215s	38
18	S Vettel	1m25.386s	27
19	J Button	1m25.424s	32
20	G Fisichella	1m25.543s	36

PRACTICE 3

	Driver	Time	Laps
1	A Sutil	1m23.336s	21
2	J Button	1m23.404s	21
3	N Heidfeld	1m23.490s	18
4	R Barrichello	1m23.575s	20
5	L Hamilton	1m23.633s	18
6	H Kovalainen	1m23.803s	20
7	V Liuzzi	1m23.849s	21
8	F Alonso	1m23.915s	17
9	T Glock	1m23.959s	21
10	R Kubica	1m23.996s	18
11	R Grosjean	1m24.197s	15
12	K Räikkönen	1m24.302s	20
13	J Trulli	1m24.326s	17
14	K Nakajima	1m24.392s	20
15	S Buemi	1m24.572s	23
16	N Rosberg	1m24.621s	21
17	M Webber	1m25.154s	13
18	S Vettel	1m25.244s	16
19	J Alguersuari	1m25.791s	10
20	G Fisichella	1m25.951s	10

QUALIFYING 1

	Driver	Time
1	K Räikkönen	1m23.349s
2	L Hamilton	1m23.375s
3	J Button	1m23.403s
4	R Barrichello	1m23.483s
5	H Kovalainen	1m23.515s
6	S Vettel	1m23.558s
7	A Sutil	1m23.576s
8	V Liuzzi	1m23.578s
9	N Heidfeld	1m23.584s
10	F Alonso	1m23.708s
11	M Webber	1m23.755s
12	G Fisichella	1m23.828s
13	R Grosjean	1m23.975s
14	R Kubica	1m24.001s
15	J Trulli	1m24.014s
16	T Glock	1m24.036s
17	K Nakajima	1m24.074s
18	N Rosberg	1m24.121s
19	S Buemi	1m24.220s
20	J Alguersuari	1m24.951s

QUALIFYING 2

	Driver	Time
1	J Button	1m22.955s
2	L Hamilton	1m22.973s
3	R Barrichello	1m22.976s
4	A Sutil	1m23.070s
5	V Liuzzi	1m23.207s
6	M Webber	1m23.273s
7	K Räikkönen	1m23.426s
8	F Alonso	1m23.497s
9	H Kovalainen	1m23.528s
10	S Vettel	1m23.545s
11	J Trulli	1m23.611s
12	R Grosjean	1m23.728s
13	R Kubica	1m23.866s
14	G Fisichella	1m23.901s
15	N Heidfeld	1m24.275s

Best sectors – Practice
Sec 1	H Kovalainen	27.299s
Sec 2	J Button	28.129s
Sec 3	A Sutil	27.632s

Speed trap – Practice
1	J Alguersuari	213.813mph
2	M Webber	213.068mph
3	V Liuzzi	212.943mph

Best sectors – Qualifying
Sec 1	L Hamilton	27.038s
Sec 2	R Barrichello	27.884s
Sec 3	M Webber	27.613s

Speed trap – Qualifying
1	M Webber	213.627mph
2	A Sutil	212.757mph
3	L Hamilton	212.695mph

IN 2008

Three days of rain at Monza didn't dampen Sebastian Vettel's enthusiasm, and he followed up becoming the youngest ever pole-sitter by being the youngest ever grand prix winner, at only just 21. Only Heikki Kovalainen could get close to his Toro Rosso, but not close enough to challenge, with Robert Kubica next up.

Lewis Hamilton

"I wasn't on the optimal strategy, so I really had to push to make my two-stopper work and I didn't make any mistakes – until the last lap. I can only say sorry to the team."

Giancarlo Fisichella

"I managed to make up a few places, then I had a difficult moment with Vettel, who closed the door on me going into Ascari in a way that was very decisive."

Robert Kubica

"Webber pushed me on the grass while I was on the brakes into the chicane. Then at Roggia, I wasn't able to avoid him and I ended up with a damaged front wing."

Fernando Alonso

"I'm very happy with the result, although the KERS didn't meet my expectations at the start, but the car behaved perfectly and our strategy worked well."

Jarno Trulli

"We expected a difficult race and that's what we got. I was behind Nakajima for much of the race and was getting a bit bored, so as soon as I saw a little space, I dived in."

Heikki Kovalainen

"My race began with a difficult start that cost me several places. Then I couldn't really push in the first stint as my prime tyres didn't have the grip to let me attack."

Kimi Räikkönen

"The strategy we chose prior to the race was the best one for us. In my battle with Sutil, I was never really in difficulty: I knew I only had to avoid making any mistakes."

Nick Heidfeld

"I'm totally happy, as for me it was a great race. Finishing seventh may not sound fantastic, but from 15th place on the grid that really was the best I could do today."

Romain Grosjean

"I'm very disappointed. My start was very poor and I need to understand why. I had some contact in the first chicane and so the car was damaged for the rest of my race."

Timo Glock

"It wasn't the result we wanted, but at least it was good entertainment. Towards the end, Jarno and I had a nice battle and made sure that we kept it clean."

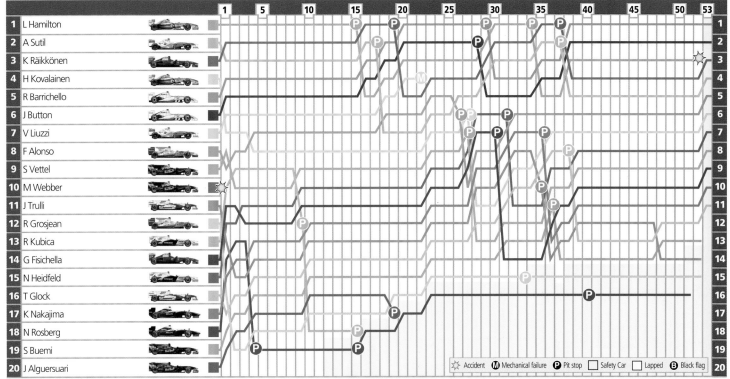

Key: ☆ Accident Ⓜ Mechanical failure Ⓟ Pit stop ☐ Safety Car ☐ Lapped Ⓑ Black flag

QUALIFYING 3

	Driver	Time
1	L Hamilton	1m24.066s
2	A Sutil	1m24.261s
3	K Räikkönen	1m24.523s
4	H Kovalainen	1m24.845s
5	R Barrichello	1m25.015s
6	J Button	1m25.030s
7	V Liuzzi	1m25.043s
8	F Alonso	1m25.072s
9	S Vettel	1m25.180s
10	M Webber	1m25.314s

GRID

	Driver	Time
1	L Hamilton	1m24.066s
2	A Sutil	1m24.261s
3	K Räikkönen	1m24.523s
4	H Kovalainen	1m24.845s
5	R Barrichello	1m25.015s
6	J Button	1m25.030s
7	V Liuzzi	1m25.043s
8	F Alonso	1m25.072s
9	S Vettel	1m25.180s
10	M Webber	1m25.314s
11	J Trulli	1m23.611s
12	R Grosjean	1m23.728s
13	R Kubica	1m23.866s
14	G Fisichella	1m23.901s
15	N Heidfeld	1m24.275s
16	T Glock	1m24.036s
17	K Nakajima	1m24.074s
18	N Rosberg	1m24.121s
19	S Buemi	1m24.220s
20*	J Alguersuari	1m24.951s

* Started from the pitlane

RACE

	Driver	Car	Laps	Time	Avg. mph	Fastest	Stops
1	R Barrichello	Brawn-Mercedes BGP 001	53	1h16m21.706s	149.750	1m24.967s	1
2	J Button	Brawn-Mercedes BGP 001	53	1h16m24.572s	149.656	1m24.935s	1
3	K Räikkönen	*Ferrari F60	53	1h16m52.370s	148.754	1m24.761s	2
4	A Sutil	Force India-Mercedes VJM02	53	1h16m52.837s	148.739	1m24.739s	2
5	F Alonso	Renault R29*	53	1h17m20.888s	147.840	1m25.199s	1
6	H Kovalainen	*McLaren-Mercedes MP4-24	53	1h17m22.399s	147.792	1m25.109s	1
7	N Heidfeld	BMW Sauber F1.09	53	1h17m44.118s	147.104	1m25.488s	1
8	S Vettel	Red Bull-Renault RB5	53	1h17m47.113s	147.009	1m25.194s	1
9	G Fisichella	*Ferrari F60	53	1h17m48.562s	146.964	1m25.498s	1
10	K Nakajima	Williams-Toyota FW31	53	1h19m03.869s	144.631	1m25.976s	1
11	T Glock	Toyota TF109	53	1h19m05.631s	144.577	1m25.751s	1
12	L Hamilton	*McLaren-Mercedes MP4-24	52	Accident	-	1m24.802s	2
13	S Buemi	Toro Rosso-Ferrari STR4	52	Followed safety car	-	1m25.564s	1
14	J Trulli	Toyota TF109	52	1h16m27.945s	146.722	1m25.700s	1
15	R Grosjean	Renault R29*	52	1h16m59.720s	145.713	1m25.609s	1
16	N Rosberg	Williams-Toyota FW31	51	1h17m07.169s	142.678	1m25.901s	3
R	V Liuzzi	Force India-Mercedes VJM02	22	Gearbox	-	1m26.041s	0
R	J Alguersuari	Toro Rosso-Ferrari STR4	19	Gearbox	-	1m27.819s	0
R	R Kubica	BMW Sauber F1.09	15	Oil leak	-	1m27.846s	1
R	M Webber	Red Bull-Renault RB5	0	Accident	-	-	0

* Denotes car fitted with KERS

CHAMPIONSHIP

	Driver	Pts
1	J Button	80
2	R Barrichello	66
3	S Vettel	54
4	M Webber	51.5
5	K Räikkönen	40
6	N Rosberg	30.5
7	L Hamilton	27
8	J Trulli	22.5
9	F Massa	22
10	H Kovalainen	20
11	F Alonso	20
12	T Glock	16
13	N Heidfeld	12
14	G Fisichella	8
15	R Kubica	8
16	A Sutil	5
17	S Buemi	3
18	S Bourdais	2

Fastest lap
A Sutil 1m24.739s
(152.923mph) on lap 36

Fastest speed trap
A Sutil   214.248mph
Slowest speed trap
M Webber   152.608mph

Fastest pit stop
1 A Sutil   25.396s
2 T Glock   25.400s
3 K Nakajima   25.562s

	Constructor	Pts
1	Brawn-Mercedes	146
2	Red Bull-Renault	105.5
3	Ferrari	62
4	McLaren-Mercedes	47
5	Toyota	38.5
6	Williams-Toyota	30.5
7	BMW Sauber	20
8	Renault	20
9	Force India-Mercedes	13
10	Toro Rosso-Ferrari	5

Jaime Alguersuari
"I started from the pits, so at least I kept out of the trouble on lap 1. After that my race was going OK and I was up behind Buemi. But then I had a gearbox problem."

Mark Webber
"I had a racing incident with Kubica. It seems his front wheel was inside my rear left at the second chicane. We had contact that flicked the car into the air."

Nico Rosberg
"I had a good first lap and I made up four places, overtaking on the left and the right. Then I was hit on the front left by some debris and the car felt suddenly very different."

Adrian Sutil
"I knew it would be really difficult to defend our position against Kimi and his KERS button at the start, and then I was stuck behind him for the whole race."

Jenson Button
"It's a fantastic feeling to be up on the podium again. The car worked well and I was able to get ahead of Heikki on the first lap and that was absolutely crucial for my race."

Sebastien Buemi
"Starting from the back of the grid, the race is never easy, but my lap times were good and consistent, especially in the second stint, so I am reasonably happy."

Sebastian Vettel
"We had a good start and a good first lap, but then I was struggling to stay with the cars in front. The biggest issue was the first five to 10 laps when I struggled for grip."

Kazuki Nakajima
"I managed to gain a couple of places in the first few corners. The pace wasn't enough, but it was positive to keep Glock behind me, even though he was going longer."

Vitantonio Liuzzi
"Finally, I am racing again and I gave it 100%. Everything was perfect until the transmission began making a strange noise and I lost drive and couldn't push."

Rubens Barrichello
"We had to think strategically in qualifying because of the KERS cars, and our one-stop strategy really paid off. Two wins in three races is pretty good going."

2009 FORMULA 1 SINGTEL SINGAPORE GRAND PRIX
SINGAPORE

STARRY NIGHT

Twelve months before, Lewis Hamilton had to be cautious as he aimed for his first title. This time around, with nothing to lose, he showed clear superiority to win with ease

Also twelve months before, a rather innocuous spin into the Turn 17 barriers brought out the safety car... We queried what happened at the time in a sidebar alongside the report in the *Season Review*, considering the incident suspicious, but who would have thought that Nelson Piquet Jr's crash would lead to so much controversy and turmoil? Yet, on the Monday before this year's Singapore GP, Renault were hauled up in front of the FIA World Motor Sport Council to answer charges of bringing the sport into disrepute. The team was given a suspended sentence, but bans were handed down to team boss Flavio Briatore and engineering chief Pat Symonds.

Renault flew to the Marina Bay street circuit, for the second ever F1 night race, hoping to draw a line under the events of the previous year. How gutting it then must have been, that title sponsor ING announced on the eve of practice that they were bringing to an end their deal with immediate effect. Then, to cap it all, during the first on-track running of the weekend, Piquet Jr's replacement, Romain Grosjean, re-enacted an almost carbon copy of the controversial 2008 shunt, losing control and crashing at, yes, Turn 17.

Sitting on the pit wall, new team principal Bob Bell

ABOVE Jenson Button had a steady run in Singapore's second night race, finishing in fifth place

OPPOSITE ABOVE Lewis Hamilton leads Nico Rosberg, Fernando Alonso, Sebastian Vettel *et al* before heading off to score his second win of 2009

could hardly believe it: "Oh, God, not there," he told reporters when he was asked how he felt when he saw the Renault spearing into the turn now dubbed 'Piquet's corner'. It was a baptism of fire for Bell. However, the reward at the end of the weekend was a podium finish for Fernando Alonso, although he then went and dedicated it to Flavio Briatore…

Ahead of the two-time World Champion on the floodlit podium were Toyota's Timo Glock and eventual winner Lewis Hamilton, with the latter significantly making up for his last-lap indiscretion at the Italian GP two weeks earlier. "I came here hoping to have a good result, hoping to redeem myself after the last race, and we did it, and I'm very, very happy," said the McLaren driver.

Hamilton, who excels on street circuits, was the star of the weekend. Quickest on Saturday morning and again in qualifying, he was untroubled from pole position. In fact, his biggest concern during the race was his KERS unit. After a wiring-loom problem during practice, the team found it easier to remove the engine, gearbox and suspension and fit it to a spare tub. Then, during the early stages of the race, Hamilton was given a radio order from the pit wall

that said: "Lewis, possible KERS defect: default X-three-zero." It was essentially an order to press a sequence of buttons and dials on his steering wheel to reset his KERS, at which point it began to work again. Not that he'd lost much time in the event.

From pole, Hamilton had eked out a small, but significant lead from Nico Rosberg – whose Williams he led by 2.5 seconds by the eighth lap. On the bumpy, twisty ribbon of tarmac that snakes around the imposing Far Eastern metropolis, Hamilton was as serene as ever, while behind him there was some driving that was a little less precise.

On the opening lap, Rosberg had made a better start on the cleaner, less dusty side of the grid and passed Sebastian Vettel into the first corner. Behind them, Mark Webber was eyeing up Alonso and, on the run down to Turn 7, the Renault slid wide, the Australian took to the outside of the corner to avoid him and, in so doing, overtook Alonso with all four wheels over the white line that defines the limits of the track. That's the same offence that caught out Button in Valencia, but with which Räikkönen seemed to get away at Spa-Francorchamps…

While Alonso was trying to gather up his slide out

of the left-hander, Glock also pounced and nipped past into the next turn, effectively sealing their order in the final race result.

For Webber, the command came via his team from race control a few laps later: "Let Alonso and Glock past," to which the Aussie quite rightly responded: "Why Glock?" It was the first of Red Bull Racing's problems, but worse was to come.

Further down the field, the race action was equally as frenetic in the hot, humid cauldron around the Marina Bay street circuit. The man doing most of the work was Force India's Adrian Sutil. He was cooped up behind Jaime Alguersuari's Toro Rosso, and his frustration was starting to show. He was then advised to gently drop away from the young rookie as the Mercedes engineers noted that his engine temperatures were rising. Behind him, Giancarlo Fisichella was given a radio order from his Ferrari engineer Rob Smedley, who advised the Italian driver to "Catch up and pass Sutil." These three were the closest battlers in the early stages of the race.

Then a seemingly quiet Singapore GP was interrupted when a yellow flag appeared just after Turn 7. A piece of debris had been thrown up from

INSIDE LINE
FERNANDO ALONSO
RENAULT DRIVER

"It's been absolutely fantastic to get this result, which is our first podium of the season. We didn't really have the fastest pace all weekend, so to achieve third place here was much better than we had expected to achieve when we arrived in Singapore.

The first lap was a little bit stressful, arriving in Turn 7 side-by-side with Mark Webber's Red Bull. We both ran wide and out over the kerb, and then Timo Glock benefited from this and overtook me into Turn 8. So, really, because of that battle with Webber, I think I lost the position to Timo and so that's why we finished the race behind his Toyota. But I have no real complaints about that. To be honest, it's a fantastic result for us.

Singapore is one of those circuits which you either like or don't, and there's no halfway about it. The people who don't like the circuit never find the right way around here because they don't have the confidence to attack the corners.

I think this weekend everything came to us and we took the benefit of some circumstances, such as qualifying when we took fifth position, which was certainly better than we had expected. Then, with the drive-through penalties for both Nico Rosberg and Sebastian Vettel, we made up these two positions and made it through to third.

We made no mistakes, I kept my concentration to 100% throughout the race, and we knew that we were not super fast here in Singapore this weekend but, if we didn't make any mistakes, we could be on the podium, and we did it.

The team have been fantastic, all season – from the mechanics, engineers, everybody in the factory, they all did their maximum. Sometimes we have got some good results, sometimes we have been a little bit unlucky. But finally this podium, after what has been a difficult time for the team, is very important.

Now we must put the difficulties behind us, because it's been hard for everybody. Now everything is clear, it's all behind us, and after this podium in Singapore we can concentrate on the remaining three races.

That said, I must dedicate this podium to Flavio Briatore, who is at home, as he is part of the success we had today."

Glock's Toyota and settled on the track. A number of laps passed while it was neatly avoided but, given the problems with debris on the circuit earlier in the season, notably with Felipe Massa's accident in Hungary, the race organisers didn't want to take any chances, and considered deploying the safety car. Fortunately, a brave marshal found a clear gap in the traffic and ran to collect the offending debris.

Then, a few laps later, the safety car was deployed anyway…

The safety car fed in at the head of the pack because, back in 15th place, Sutil had finally lunged towards Alguersuari. He backed off under braking, then lost control of his car and spun. In his eagerness to atone for his mistake, he floored the throttle, spin-turned, and collected the right-rear of Nick Heidfeld's BMW Sauber – which ripped the nose off the Force India, spewed debris all over the track and ended Heidfeld's race in an instant.

A year before, Rosberg benefited thanks to the emergence of the safety car. This time around, another good showing by Williams in this race was completely scuppered. Rosberg had pitted on lap 18, but it was while leaving the revised pitlane exit that

he was a little too quick, got caught out on the dust and ran over the kerb and the all-important white line. Despite changing his line to cut back into the pit exit, the deed was done and the inevitable drive-through penalty was given. The rules allow three laps before you must commit to taking the penalty. If he'd taken it straight away, then his race wouldn't have been so badly compromised. As it was, the emergence of the safety car meant Rosberg had to wait until the safety car came in before serving his penalty, the field was closed up, and when he stopped he effectively sunk to the back of the pack.

"It's hugely disappointing," shrugged the German. "I made a mistake by braking too late and running over the white line on the pitlane exit. Then the safety car came out at the worst possible moment. It left me with a horrible feeling, knowing that I wouldn't be in second place when I'd served my drive-through penalty and I would have to spend the rest of the race at the back of the field."

Following the rush of first pit stops under the safety car, the order at the front as the racing resumed was still Hamilton leading, now from Vettel, Glock, Alonso, Barrichello, Kovalainen, Button and Webber.

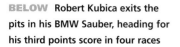

BELOW Robert Kubica exits the pits in his BMW Sauber, heading for his third points score in four races

ABOVE LEFT Fernando Alonso gave the Renault team a much-needed fillip by finishing third

ABOVE Nico Rosberg ought to have finished second, but crossing the pit exit line left him nowhere

LEFT Mark Webber also came away with nothing after his Red Bull RB5's brakes failed and put him out

TALKING POINT
BRIGHT SPARKS

There are some unique challenges to racing on Singapore's impressive Marina Bay street circuit that you simply do not get at any other grand prix on the Formula 1 calendar.

The most talked about of these challenges is the strange time-shifting that the F1 paddock experiences in order to have both their bodies and minds operating at peak efficiency at race time, after nightfall.

Living a nocturnal lifestyle for a week is actually a bizarre and sometimes rather unpleasant experience. Ordering dinner at 3.30am and then convincing your brain that going to sleep at daybreak is normal, er, isn't.

However, it's not only the teams' personnel that suffer on the streets of Singapore, as the cars do too…

For F1's second visit, every team fitted a metal plate to the underside of its gearboxes before sending the cars out onto the circuit. One of the side-effects of that was to create an incredible blur of sparks showering out behind the car, reminding more mature grand prix fans of the classic days of titanium skid-blocks on turbo-powered cars smacking the bumps on full tanks and producing a similar lightshow. The intention of this modification wasn't to improve the spectacle, even though the spectacle of the sparks attracted the photographers, rather to prevent electrical interference from any passing underground trains…

The reason for this modification was that Mark Webber suffered a mechanical problem on his Red Bull RB4 in 2008 when its gearbox selected two gears at once. This was put down to an electrical surge that was believed to have been caused by a passing underground train. On a section of the track, just two metres away, the sister Scuderia Toro Rosso team had suffered a similar problem earlier in the weekend.

"We had a failure on Mark's car last year that was very peculiar," explained Red Bull Racing team principal Christian Horner. "Basically, two valves were triggered that selected a couple of gears at once.

"There were a lot of theories last year as to why Mark had his problem, but we never found the real reason," he continued. "However, there were suspicions of static electricity, so we've taken some precautions to prevent a repeat of that, including a code change for the software and some protection that we've added to the bottom of the car. And, from what I understand, we're not the only team to add that protection."

Webber had his problem at Turn 13, close to the railway line near Raffles Place underground station, not far from one of the few restaurants that still serves food at four o'clock in the morning…

This was another weekend in which things were working less than perfectly for Brawn GP. On occasion the championship leaders were quick, notably in Friday practice as the low-speed downforce set-up and good mechanical grip led to them being more suited to the tight twists of Singapore, but there wasn't enough consistency throughout the weekend. Rubens Barrichello, in particular, suffered following his Turn 5 crash in the final stages of qualifying, which led to a gearbox change and a five-place grid penalty. His team-mate Jenson Button was also struggling as he played with the stiffness of his Brawn, encountering changing levels of grip – and he managed only the 12th quickest time, thus failing to make it to the final qualifying session. A measured drive in the race meant that Button was able to leapfrog his team-mate when the Brazilian stalled at his second pit stop. And so the Brawns picked up more minor points scores for finishing in fifth and sixth places.

As a result, Brawn GP had effectively presented Red Bull Racing with another open goal at which they had a free shot, but, once again, the Milton Keynes team shot wide… Vettel was all set for second place, when he was penalised for speeding in the pitlane during his second stop. Even more gutting for the team was the fact that his car's telemetry showed that he had never exceeded the mandatory 100kph but, given that the pitlane entrance is on a corner, and Vettel straightlined that corner, the official measuring equipment produced a skewed reading.

"So we have a speed limit and you are allowed to choose your own line, and the way the speed is measured is that it is divided into sectors, and obviously there has been a mistake in the calibration," Vettel rued.

For Webber, his World Championship charge was over when his brakes overheated and, despite a pit stop to clean the brake ducts, he crashed out when the brakes failed heading into Turn 1.

Button was also in brake trouble, significantly backing off his pace in the closing laps, but managing to finish ahead of his team-mate Barrichello and just one place behind Vettel. For Button's championship campaign, it was damage limitation… just as it was a case of damage limitation for the image of F1 and the Renault team thanks to the events 12 months previously.

TOP LEFT Cool heads were needed in a hot, humid climate for pit stops to run smoothly. This is Lewis Hamilton's

MIDDLE LEFT Timo Glock started sixth, benefited from the Alonso/Webber moment on lap 1 plus Rosberg's pit blunder, and raced on to finish second

LEFT Toyota's crew show their delight at Glock's result, giving the team its first points score since the Hungarian GP

SNAPSHOT FROM
SINGAPORE

CLOCKWISE FROM RIGHT No other circuit can offer a backdrop like this; Bernie Ecclestone offers advice to Red Bull's Christian Horner; finding a vantage point became a national sport; beauty in the east; Rubens Barrichello's Brawn is lifted clear after his accident curtailed Q3; ZZ Top dropped in to check out the action; a stunning sunset, but in Singapore this meant that the teams and drivers still had a great deal of work to do

WEEKEND NEWS

- The FIA World Motorsport Council announced a 19-race calendar for 2010 that would see the World Championship season kick off in Bahrain and come to a conclusion in Brazil. Included on the schedule for the first time was a grand prix on a new circuit in South Korea, pencilled in for October, and a welcome return for the Canadian GP in Montréal.

- F1 supremo Bernie Ecclestone expressed his desire to one day have a grand prix on the streets of New York. "Obviously, it would be Manhattan and it could happen. After all, we were told we couldn't do a race in Singapore."

- The Lotus name was set to return to Formula 1 in 2010, after a new team secured backing from the Malaysian government and a group of Malaysian entrepreneurs, including Air Asia's Tony Fernandes. The outfit employed the services of former Force India technical director Mike Gascoyne and would be based in Norfolk, while establishing a future R&D base close to the Sepang circuit in Malaysia. Lotus last raced in F1 in 1994.

- Bob Bell was appointed the new team principal of the Renault team, and Jean-Francois Caubet managing director, following the FIA World Council's decision to impose a lifetime ban on Flavio Briatore and a five-year ban on Pat Symonds for their involvement in the Renault 'Crashgate' saga.

- On the eve of the Singapore Grand Prix, Renault's main sponsor ING announced that it was terminating its sponsorship of the French marque with immediate effect, giving the team a long night while they removed all the ING logos from the cars and the pit garage.

- All the F1 teams met in Singapore and agreed in effect not to use the kinetic energy recovery systems (KERS) for the 2010 season, although it was understood that Williams was still pushing to use its unique flywheel system at some stage in the future.

- Jenson Button would have been crowned World Champion in Singapore, if Bernie Ecclestone's medal system (awarded to the three podium finishers at each race) had come into effect this year. Button would have had six 'golds' in comparison to Vettel's, Hamilton's and Barrichello's two apiece.

RACE RESULTS
SINGAPORE
MARINA BAY

RACE DATE September 27th
CIRCUIT LENGTH 3.148 miles
NO. OF LAPS 61
RACE DISTANCE 192.028 miles
WEATHER Dry and humid, 31°C
TRACK TEMP 34°C
ATTENDANCE 237,000
LAP RECORD Kimi Räikkönen,
1m45.599s, 107.358mph, 2008

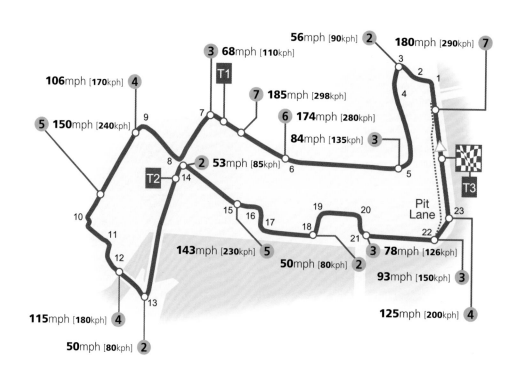

	PRACTICE 1		
	Driver	**Time**	**Laps**
1	R Barrichello	1m50.179s	19
2	J Button	1m50.356s	22
3	M Webber	1m50.416s	21
4	F Alonso	1m50.567s	16
5	S Vettel	1m50.614s	16
6	H Kovalainen	1m50.699s	21
7	L Hamilton	1m50.715s	17
8	R Kubica	1m50.815s	15
9	K Räikkönen	1m50.865s	19
10	K Nakajima	1m51.089s	25
11	N Rosberg	1m51.427s	23
12	A Sutil	1m51.544s	14
13	S Buemi	1m51.643s	28
14	N Heidfeld	1m51.656s	15
15	T Glock	1m52.083s	20
16	J Trulli	1m52.135s	20
17	G Fisichella	1m52.390s	24
18	V Liuzzi	1m52.905s	23
19	J Alguersuari	1m53.232s	25
20	R Grosjean	1m53.458s	9

	PRACTICE 2		
	Driver	**Time**	**Laps**
1	S Vettel	1m48.650s	31
2	F Alonso	1m48.924s	27
3	H Kovalainen	1m48.952s	30
4	N Heidfeld	1m49.098s	31
5	J Button	1m49.311s	34
6	M Webber	1m49.317s	14
7	N Rosberg	1m49.333s	33
8	T Glock	1m49.342s	30
9	L Hamilton	1m49.358s	28
10	R Kubica	1m49.609s	24
11	R Barrichello	1m49.616s	30
12	A Sutil	1m49.710s	31
13	J Trulli	1m49.795s	29
14	K Räikkönen	1m49.941s	29
15	K Nakajima	1m50.023s	34
16	G Fisichella	1m50.253s	31
17	S Buemi	1m50.527s	29
18	V Liuzzi	1m50.605s	28
19	R Grosjean	1m50.972s	17
20	J Alguersuari	1m51.423s	31

	PRACTICE 3		
	Driver	**Time**	**Laps**
1	L Hamilton	1m47.632s	15
2	S Vettel	1m47.909s	17
3	N Rosberg	1m48.332s	18
4	H Kovalainen	1m48.420s	14
5	R Kubica	1m48.501s	16
6	N Heidfeld	1m48.526s	13
7	R Barrichello	1m48.551s	16
8	T Glock	1m48.680s	17
9	S Buemi	1m48.754s	17
10	J Trulli	1m48.757s	12
11	K Nakajima	1m48.831s	17
12	K Räikkönen	1m48.864s	16
13	M Webber	1m48.876s	15
14	J Button	1m48.921s	17
15	F Alonso	1m49.032s	15
16	V Liuzzi	1m49.055s	16
17	A Sutil	1m49.122s	17
18	J Alguersuari	1m49.399s	17
19	R Grosjean	1m49.641s	16
20	G Fisichella	1m50.039s	21

	QUALIFYING 1	
	Driver	**Time**
1	L Hamilton	1m46.977s
2	J Button	1m47.180s
3	K Räikkönen	1m47.293s
4	N Heidfeld	1m47.347s
5	N Rosberg	1m47.390s
6	R Barrichello	1m47.397s
7	S Vettel	1m47.541s
8	H Kovalainen	1m47.542s
9	R Kubica	1m47.615s
10	K Nakajima	1m47.637s
11	M Webber	1m47.646s
12	S Buemi	1m47.677s
13	J Trulli	1m47.690s
14	F Alonso	1m47.757s
15	T Glock	1m47.770s
16	A Sutil	1m48.231s
17	J Alguersuari	1m48.340s
18	G Fisichella	1m48.350s
19	R Grosjean	1m48.544s
20	V Liuzzi	1m48.792s

	QUALIFYING 2	
	Driver	**Time**
1	N Rosberg	1m46.197s
2	M Webber	1m46.328s
3	S Vettel	1m46.362s
4	L Hamilton	1m46.657s
5	T Glock	1m46.707s
6	F Alonso	1m46.767s
7	R Barrichello	1m46.787s
8	R Kubica	1m46.813s
9	N Heidfeld	1m46.832s
10	H Kovalainen	1m46.842s
11	K Nakajima	1m47.013s
12	J Button	1m47.141s
13	K Räikkönen	1m47.177s
14	S Buemi	1m47.369s
15	J Trulli	1m47.413s

Best sectors – Practice			**Speed trap – Practice**		
Sec 1	L Hamilton	28.803s	1	A Sutil	179.327mph
Sec 2	H Kovalainen	41.842s	2	L Hamilton	179.203mph
Sec 3	S Vettel	36.741s	3	V Liuzzi	179.141mph

Best sectors – Qualifying			**Speed trap – Qualifying**		
Sec 1	L Hamilton	28.552s	1	L Hamilton	180.011mph
Sec 2	N Rosberg	41.108s	2	H Kovalainen	179.327mph
Sec 3	S Vettel	36.009s	3	A Sutil	179.265mph

IN 2008

F1's first visit to this street circuit was also its first night race and it produced a surprise winner: Renault's Fernando Alonso. He'd been right on the pace, then had a mechanical glitch that wrecked qualifying. Yet, he pitted early and found himself in the lead when the safety car came out after Piquet crashed, and he went on to win.

Lewis Hamilton

"I did have a little bit of pressure from Nico and the cars behind at the beginning, but I was just looking after my tyres and I think it paid dividends in the end."

Giancarlo Fisichella

"We brought my first stop forward to try and get me out of traffic, as I was stuck behind Sutil, but then with the safety car the move didn't give the result we'd hoped for."

Robert Kubica

"I was unlucky with the safety-car period. I lost a couple of places as I had refuelled before the safety car went out. On top of this, I had a lot of problems with rear degradation."

Fernando Alonso

"This was a great result, allowing us to put behind us the past few weeks. I had a good start and great pace throughout, and third came as a result of good strategy."

Jarno Trulli

"Not much went right for me. As soon as I got out of the traffic, the safety car came at the wrong moment; right when I was passing through the pits for my first stop."

Heikki Kovalainen

"I drove to the pace I could. I find it hard to maintain tyre performance and the car gets out of shape if I try to increase my pace, so I can't carry more speed in the corners."

Kimi Räikkönen

"I couldn't do any better. The car was sliding everywhere and I had no grip. In the final part, with the softer tyres, the situation improved a bit, but by then it was too late."

Nick Heidfeld

"It was Sutil's fault. He spun, then drove back onto the track and straight into my car. That's something you just can't do. I had no chance to avoid this accident."

Romain Grosjean

"We had brake problems that we hoped we'd solved before the race. I had a good start and a good first lap, when I felt my brakes failing, so the team asked me to retire."

Timo Glock

"It was vital to pass Alonso and I was annoyed I didn't do it at the start. I saw him fighting Mark, dived in and got by. It paid off, as after that our strategy worked well."

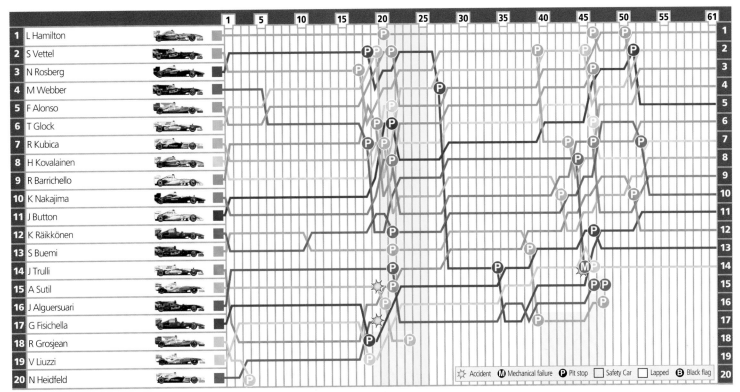

			1	5	10	15	20	25	30	35	40	45	50	55	61
1	L Hamilton														**1**
2	S Vettel														**2**
3	N Rosberg														**3**
4	M Webber														**4**
5	F Alonso														**5**
6	T Glock														**6**
7	R Kubica														**7**
8	H Kovalainen														**8**
9	R Barrichello														**9**
10	K Nakajima														**10**
11	J Button														**11**
12	K Räikkönen														**12**
13	S Buemi														**13**
14	J Trulli														**14**
15	A Sutil														**15**
16	J Alguersuari														**16**
17	G Fisichella														**17**
18	R Grosjean														**18**
19	V Liuzzi														**19**
20	N Heidfeld														**20**

☆ Accident Ⓜ Mechanical failure Ⓟ Pit stop ☐ Safety Car ☐ Lapped Ⓑ Black flag

QUALIFYING 3

	Driver	Time
1	L Hamilton	1m47.891s
2	S Vettel	1m48.204s
3	N Rosberg	1m48.348s
4	M Webber	1m48.722s
5	R Barrichello	1m48.828s
6	F Alonso	1m49.054s
7	T Glock	1m49.180s
8	N Heidfeld	1m49.307s
9	R Kubica	1m49.514s
10	H Kovalainen	1m49.778s

GRID

	Driver	Time
1	L Hamilton	1m47.891s
2	S Vettel	1m48.204s
3	N Rosberg	1m48.348s
4	M Webber	1m48.722s
5	F Alonso	1m49.054s
6	T Glock	1m49.180s
7	R Kubica	1m49.514s
8	H Kovalainen	1m49.778s
9*	R Barrichello	1m48.828s
10	K Nakajima	1m47.013s
11	J Button	1m47.141s
12	K Räikkönen	1m47.177s
13	S Buemi	1m47.369s
14	J Trulli	1m47.413s
15	A Sutil	1m48.231s
16	J Alguersuari	1m48.340s
17	G Fisichella	1m48.350s
18	R Grosjean	1m48.544s
19	V Liuzzi	1m48.792s
20^	N Heidfeld	1m49.307s

* 5-place grid penalty for gearbox change
^ Put to back as car underweight

RACE

	Driver	Car	Laps	Time	Avg. mph	Fastest	Stops
1	L Hamilton	*McLaren-Mercedes MP4-24	61	1h56m06.337s	99.323	1m48.345s	2
2	T Glock	Toyota TF109	61	1h56m15.971s	99.186	1m48.396s	2
3	F Alonso	Renault R29	61	1h56m22.961s	99.086	1m48.240s	2
4	S Vettel	Red Bull-Renault RB5	61	1h56m26.598s	99.035	1m48.398s	3
5	J Button	Brawn-Mercedes BGP 001	61	1h56m36.352s	98.897	1m48.369s	2
6	R Barrichello	Brawn-Mercedes BGP 001	61	1h56m38.195s	98.871	1m48.598s	2
7	H Kovalainen	*McLaren-Mercedes MP4-24	61	1h56m42.494s	98.810	1m49.283s	2
8	R Kubica	BMW Sauber F1.09	61	1h57m01.391s	98.544	1m48.847s	2
9	K Nakajima	Williams-Toyota FW31	61	1h57m02.391s	98.530	1m49.371s	2
10	K Räikkönen	*Ferrari F60	61	1h57m05.229s	98.490	1m48.391s	2
11	N Rosberg	Williams-Toyota FW31	61	1h57m06.114s	98.478	1m48.352s	3
12	J Trulli	Toyota TF109	61	1h57m19.346s	98.293	1m48.816s	2
13	G Fisichella	*Ferrari F60	61	1h57m26.227s	98.197	1m49.417s	2
14	V Liuzzi	Force India-Mercedes VJM02	61	1h57m39.839s	98.007	1m49.852s	2
R	J Alguersuari	Toro Rosso-Ferrari STR4	47	Brakes	-	1m52.483s	2
R	S Buemi	Toro Rosso-Ferrari STR4	47	Gearbox	-	1m50.636s	3
R	M Webber	Red Bull-Renault RB5	45	Brakes	-	1m49.319s	2
R	A Sutil	Force India-Mercedes VJM02	23	Brakes	-	1m52.623s	1
R	N Heidfeld	BMW Sauber F1.09	19	Accident	-	1m51.346s	0
R	R Grosjean	Renault R29	3	Brakes	-	1m57.192s	0

* Denotes car fitted with KERS

CHAMPIONSHIP

	Driver	Pts
1	J Button	84
2	R Barrichello	69
3	S Vettel	59
4	M Webber	51.5
5	K Räikkönen	40
6	L Hamilton	37
7	N Rosberg	30.5
8	F Alonso	26
9	T Glock	24
10	J Trulli	22.5
11	F Massa	22
12	H Kovalainen	22
13	N Heidfeld	12
14	R Kubica	9
15	G Fisichella	8
16	A Sutil	5
17	S Buemi	3
18	S Bourdais	2

	Constructor	Pts
1	Brawn-Mercedes	153
2	Red Bull-Renault	110.5
3	Ferrari	62
4	McLaren-Mercedes	59
5	Toyota	46.5
6	Williams-Toyota	30.5
7	Renault	26
8	BMW Sauber	21
9	Force India-Mercedes	13
10	Toro Rosso-Ferrari	5

Fastest lap
F Alonso 1m48.240s
(104.561mph) on lap 53

Fastest speed trap
K Räikkönen 181.502mph
Slowest speed trap
R Grosjean 173.859mph

Fastest pit stop
1 F Alonso 21.361s
2 T Glock 21.702s
3 J Trulli 22.055s

Jaime Alguersuari

"It would have been hard for me to do better, as conditions in terms of the track and the heat were tough. I ran my own pace, but was stopped with a brake problem."

Mark Webber

"We had a suspected brake problem, so when I came in for my stop, the guys made a check. It seemed reasonable to continue, but then we had the failure and I retired."

Nico Rosberg

"I made an unnecessary mistake by braking too late and running over the white line on the pitlane exit. Then the safety car came out at the worst possible moment."

Adrian Sutil

"I tried to pass Jaime, who was slow, but I was late on the brakes and spun. Then Nick came around the corner and hit my front wing. After that, I had a brake problem."

Jenson Button

"Getting ahead of Kazuki off the line was key. Then the safety car made it hard as I had fuel for a few more laps, so I had to put in some quick laps to close up to Rubens."

Sebastien Buemi

"We had a big problem at my second pit stop, as no fuel went in and I had to come in again. Finally, I had an issue with the gearbox which meant I had to stop."

Sebastian Vettel

"There's a questionmark as to why I got the drive-through. We knew we couldn't pass Lewis at the stop, as he was staying out longer, so I was surprised when I got the call."

Kazuki Nakajima

"There seemed to be a possibility of scoring a point in the last stint, as the car ahead was struggling with its tyres, but as well as attacking, I also had to defend from behind."

Vitantonio Liuzzi

"Having two cars with KERS in front of me didn't help. I couldn't pass Giancarlo even though I was faster on my first two stints. On the third, we started to have graining."

Rubens Barrichello

"I made up two places at the start, but I had a problem at my second stop when I couldn't get neutral and stalled which lost me the time needed to stay ahead of Jenson."

2009 FORMULA 1 FUJI TELEVISION JAPANESE GRAND PRIX
SUZUKA

VETTEL AIMS HIGH

Sebastian Vettel gave himself an outside chance of a shot at the world title by scoring a famous win at Suzuka as Jenson Button and Rubens Barrichello trailed home seventh and eighth

There is something very special about Suzuka. The other Japanese venue in the foothills of Mount Fuji was fine for a couple of years, but nothing quite beats the high-speed, snaking, unique figure-of-eight twist alongside a theme park in Japan's Mie region. It's also one of the most remote grand prix venues in the world, as the European-based F1 brigade has to cross hundreds of miles via mountainous, sometimes industrial, sometimes residential countryside, on the Shinkanen bullet train from Tokyo. Then there's the additional journey on the tight, single-lane roads by bus each morning. But then, as you near the track entrance and see the ferris wheel, the funfair and the multi-coloured clad queues of fans, all eagerly waving, you know you've arrived somewhere very special.

Most modern grand prix circuits have run-offs that extend into the next country, but good old Suzuka doesn't. It's a place that reminds you of Stirling Moss's classic phrase: "Anyone can walk a tightrope a foot off the ground, but very few can do it 500ft up, yet the skill is the same. It's the challenge that's different." At Suzuka, if you make a mistake, you will pay for it.

For a few drivers, it was their first visit to the circuit. And none were as vocal or as gushing in their praise for the track as the World Champion. And although Lewis Hamilton's McLaren MP4-24 didn't match the pace of the Red Bull RB5s, you still knew he was loving every single minute of driving at Suzuka.

"There's not a lot of room for error and, if you run just a little bit wide, you're in trouble and you can't stop the car," warned the British driver. "So, finding the limit and getting to the maximum and stepping over that limit is such a fine line. There's more margin for error in some corners, while in others there is certainly less margin for error." Hamilton, it should be noted on his first visit to Suzuka, found the limit, but didn't cross it. A few others did; and it wasn't just at one corner… Degner, Spoon, 130R and the final kink all caught drivers out over the course of the meeting.

Heavy rain on Friday limited running, so teams and drivers were chasing a set-up in Saturday morning practice: the occasion of the first big crash. Mark Webber lost it going into the quick, right Degner flick and damaged the steering column on his Red Bull. The tyre pressures had just been lowered, and it looked as though the reduced ride height didn't compute with

a bump, or the kerbs, and it sent his machine straight into the barriers. The Red Bull was the quickest car of the weekend, but the hapless Australian's race weekend was effectively over. The team spent the rest of the day replacing the tub, so he missed qualifying. Then, when Webber pitted just after the start, twice for a loose headrest to be taped back into position and then for a puncture, his race became an extended test session, in which he tried out different front wings on his lonely run to 17th and last place.

The next Red Bull-spec machine to go off at Degner was Sebastien Buemi's. He'd been setting very impressive times on Saturday morning and ended up second fastest overall to Jarno Trulli. Then he lost the Toro Rosso in Q1, but was able to get back to the pits for repairs. Impressively, the team got him out to compete in Q2 – before he crashed again (more of which later). His young rookie team-mate Jaime Alguersuari also crashed during Q2, which he had reached for the first time in his short F1 career. He carried too much speed into the first part of Degner, ran wide over the kerbs and the astro-turf that sits between the kerbs and the gravel, and had no way of stopping the car. It was a big impact, as he clattered

BELOW Jenson Button lost ground at the start and had to quickly fight his way back past Robert Kubica

OPPOSITE BMW Sauber's Nick Heidfeld started fourth and ended up a disappointed sixth

INSIDE LINE
JAIME ALGUERSUARI
SCUDERIA TORO ROSSO DRIVER

"This weekend felt like my first proper time in Formula 1. I had the pace and everything was easier in the car. We had a new floor, so more downforce, and I was faster as a result. I was more comfortable too, and everything felt improved, but it was still a tough race and I'm disappointed because it's not nice to finish a race by crashing.

I was pushing, as I had new tyres on and there were nine laps to go. It was the first day I felt F1 in my blood. But it's strange to understand what happened, as 130R is a flat-out corner, even in the wet, so maybe it was a tyre or something. I came into the corner flat-out in seventh gear and there was no way to catch it. At that speed, once it goes in the middle of the corner, you have no input and you just finish in the barrier.

I was fine and was really impressed with how safe and secure these cars are. You go off the track here and you hit the wall straight away. It's not nice to crash, but you do during your career and, as long as you understand why and you gain from the experience and learn, then it's alright.

It's been a good weekend, as I never expected to get into Q2 this year. But again it was a shame that I also crashed at Degner in qualifying, so I'm sorry for the mechanics and the team. It's a really fast corner and I took a bit of kerb and the car got unstable. Maybe they should change the kerbs there next year, as it's not one of the best tracks in the world for safety. You carry a lot more corner speed in these cars than you did in 2006 [Formula 1's last visit to Suzuka], and with the slick tyres it's crazy how fast you can be mid-corner and the fact there is no run-off, with the wall quite near to the track. I'm so impressed with how much speed you can carry into the corner, and I'm still not sufficiently used to the downforce of the car to be able to take the car to 100% of its potential. Also, it's difficult when I go back to racing in World Series by Renault, as that car and its Michelin tyres are completely different. But it's good for my experience."

into the tyre barrier on the outside, and he looked winded as he took a blow in the cockpit of the Toro Rosso STR4. The red flag was now out and, incredibly, it would make two more appearances in a little over an hour of chaotic qualifying.

The second stoppage, and a long delay, followed, as Timo Glock's Toyota speared into the retaining wall at the last corner on the exit of the chicane. There were initial thoughts that it was steering failure, but Glock, who had missed Friday's practice sessions because he was unwell, said it was simply his own mistake: "I had a bit of oversteer out of the chicane and tried to take as much speed as possible out of the last corner. I opened the steering wheel and at the last moment tried to turn back again, then I misjudged by around 50cm – I thought I was half a metre to the right, but I wasn't. Then I just touched the grass with the front-left wheel and then the car just took off and I had no chance," he rued.

The German suffered a 6cm gash under his left knee that required 14 stitches, caused by a piece of aluminium that is used on the front wing as ballast, which is something the rule-makers should address.

Heikki Kovalainen, also new to Suzuka, went off at Degner at the beginning of Q3 and brought out a third red flag. The damage necessitated a change of gearbox on his McLaren and so resulted in a five-place grid penalty for the race, leaving him 11th.

All of these stoppages caused anxiety for teams and drivers, as track time was limited and new tyres were being used up in aborted runs. As a result, it was hardly surprising that when Buemi crashed again during Q2, on the exit of Spoon, a number of drivers maintained pace under yellow flags through the debris. And so began a long night, as the stewards studied telemetry data and debated who would serve a penalty for speeding through the yellow-flag zone. As 10pm passed, there was still no grid. Officials

debated and calculated who should be where, but it wasn't until the morning that an official grid order was released. You had to feel sorry for some of the newspaper reporters who couldn't accurately give a starting grid for their papers back in Europe, for the race that had finished when most people came to read their stories over breakfast…

In all, nine drivers were out of position on the grid. Vitantonio Liuzzi and Kovalainen were both given five-place grid penalties for having their gearboxes changed. Webber had to start from the pitlane for using a new chassis, Glock was out altogether due to his injury, while Alonso, Sutil and the Brawns of Rubens Barrichello and Jenson Button were penalised for their speed under Buemi's yellow flag. The Toro Rosso man himself received a five-place penalty for impeding other drivers on his way back to the pits.

It was the worst possible news for Button as far as the title battle was concerned. He'd start 10th, four places behind Barrichello and nine behind pole-sitter Vettel. The Red Bull driver had been fastest throughout qualifying, taking just a single run towards the end of each session, thus avoiding the red flags and consequently also avoiding wasting tyres on aborted runs.

Come the race, Button made a poor start and was battling with Giancarlo Fisichella for 12th place into Turn 1. The Brawn muscled ahead of the Ferrari later in the lap, and dived down the inside of Kubica's BMW Sauber into the chicane on lap 3, but subsequent progress for the World Championship leader was more difficult. Indeed, it was a nervy few laps as the congested pack swarmed around Suzuka's twists. Slowly, they started to spread out, but at the front there was no contest. Vettel had the quickest car of the weekend and was able to drive with a degree of conservatism and still maintain a clear lead. His was an easy victory.

BELOW Kimi Räikkönen, Nico Rosberg and Nick Heidfeld fight over fourth place late in the race after the safety car withdrew

OPPOSITE Lewis Hamilton adored Suzuka and ran second until his car slowed when leaving its second pit stop, costing him a position

OPPOSITE BELOW Jarno Trulli atoned for a weak run in Singapore to battle past Lewis Hamilton and finish in second place for Toyota

TALKING POINT
TOYOTA'S FUTURE REMAINS IN FLUX

It was an unusual home grand prix for Toyota. First on the weekend agenda was Timo Glock, who rubbished rumours that he had been told his services would not be required for 2010. This was, remember, after he'd scored Toyota's fourth podium of the season in Singapore. Team President John Howett admitted that the driver market was "fluid" and said "he may well be out in the car next year," then added that the team was pushing with a big-money bid to snatch Robert Kubica from Renault's grasp, and even Kimi Räikkönen was on its shopping list.

Then, on Friday, it was announced at Suzuka that Kamui Kobayashi was to replace Glock for practice, as the German was feeling unwell. Howett was asked whether Glock had suffered from 'Kobayashi-fever?' His response was emphatic: "I just won't answer. It's a stupid question and it doesn't deserve an answer."

Glock was back in the car on Saturday, but crashed at the final corner, when he appeared to spear into the barriers. He was forced to have 14 stitches in his leg and was deemed unfit to race on Sunday.

Then, on Sunday, Jarno Trulli drove a magnificent race to eclipse Hamilton and finish second, thereby putting Toyota back into contention for third place in the constructors' championship. Toyota's big chiefs attended the race, but was the result enough to convince the board to stay in the sport despite eight years without a win? "It always helps, doesn't it? But I can't say that it's the fundamental issue," said Howett. "It's all down to Toyota's profit and loss situation. I think there are other teams that are the same, but the reality is that I'm sure that we will be on the grid next year." A board meeting on 15 November had been pencilled in to confirm their 2010 plans. So, while there were smiles at Suzuka, will they continue? Well, the smiles seemed to come from the bigwigs under the podium and not on it. Jarno Trulli had driven a great race, but seemed down. Was his future at stake too?

"You have to look over five years and, I don't wish to be tough, but we had a more competitive position leading the race at Spa, and we didn't deliver," added Howett… With a NASCAR test lined up, it looked as though Trulli's future was up in the air. An hour or so after the race, the Italian driver ran across the track, climbed the catch fencing and threw his cap into the crowd. It was a bizarre sight. Was this him saying goodbye to the loyal Japanese fans?

ABOVE Sebastian Vettel and his Red Bull were in a class of their own in qualifying and the race

RIGHT Adrian Sutil and Heikki Kovalainen came to blows and assisted Jenson Button's cause

Behind, Trulli made the most of a second stint in which he ran two laps longer than Hamilton and leapfrogged the McLaren during the stops. It was the major position change of a race that was notably devoid of action and overtaking.

As in Singapore, Sutil looked the most prepared to have a go, but once again it ended in tears. He dived inside Kovalainen for eighth place at the chicane, but the pair collided… This handed two places to Button, and he was hopeful of another one after the race, when the Williams team was summoned to see the stewards…

With nine laps to go, Alguersuari lost control and suffered an almighty impact by spinning into the inside of 130R. He was lucky to climb out unaided. The safety car appeared, just as Nico Rosberg was about to make his last stop. Modern electronic safety measures provide drivers with a target lap time when the safety car has been deployed – before it has time to pick up the lead driver – which is usually around 20% slower than normal racing speed. This target speed normally appears on the drivers' cockpit displays, but Rosberg's steering wheel simply read 'low fuel.' He tried to judge the correct pace, but

unfortunately he returned to the pits too quickly, although telemetry did prove that he backed off at the scene of the accident. After completing his stop, he rejoined in fifth place, ahead of both Brawns. After the race, Williams's Sam Michael was ordered up to race control.

There was then a nervous wait for the Brawn camp. If Rosberg was penalised, the team could open the champagne and celebrate the constructors' championship, here at Honda's home track of Suzuka, this just a little more than a year after the Japanese manufacturer pulled the plug on Ross Brawn and the team from Brackley…

Then the decision came. Rosberg retained fifth. It seemed akin to being stopped on the motorway, where you've broken the speed limit, having done 95mph. You backed off a little, but claimed that your car's speedometer was broken. "No worries, sir, that's fine, be on your way…"

Brawn's corks stayed in their champagne bottles. Heading to the penultimate race, in Brazil, Button led Barrichello by 14 points and was 16 ahead of race winner Vettel. Just half a point was needed for Brawn to take that constructors' crown.

SNAPSHOT FROM
JAPAN

CLOCKWISE FROM RIGHT Rain on Friday prevented the teams from finding the set-ups they sought; Jenson Button's girlfriend Jessica Michibata brightened up the paddock; ...or on the seats...; Jaime Alguersuari's wrecked Toro Rosso is recovered following his heavy impact at 130R; ...did you crash that car Alguersuari-san?; Suzuka's chequered start line; mechanics working with dry ice remains a favourite with the photographic professionals

WEEKEND NEWS

■ On the eve of the Japanese GP, Ferrari confirmed one of the worst-kept secrets by announcing that Fernando Alonso would switch to the Italian marque for three years from 2010 onwards. The team said that the Spanish driver would be replacing Kimi Räikkönen. "We wish to thank Kimi for everything he has done during his time with Ferrari," said team principal Stefano Domenicali.

■ In the week following the Japanese GP, Renault also made definite another key driver market move by confirming that Alonso's place would be taken by Polish ace Robert Kubica. "Ever since Robert made his grand prix debut in 2006, he has been on our radar as one of the most naturally talented drivers of his generation, and he has delivered on that promise, so it's great to have secured him in one of our cars for next season," said Renault team principal Bob Bell.

■ Germany's Hockenheim circuit confirmed that it had put a deal in place with Formula One Administration to secure its position as a grand prix venue for the foreseeable future. "A financial agreement will see co-operation on the business opportunities and risks of the event," said a statement. The track presently alternates hosting the German GP with the Nürburgring.

■ Toyota test and reserve driver Kamui Kobayashi made his grand prix debut at Suzuka, deputising for an unwell Timo Glock for Toyota during Friday's free practice sessions. The Japanese driver is the reigning GP2 Asia Series champion.

■ Lewis Hamilton spent the weekend eulogising about Suzuka on his first visit to the Japanese circuit. "This is the best circuit I've ever driven," beamed the McLaren driver after the first practice session. "It's very special. I've always wanted to drive here, there's such great history and I was at the chicane thinking 'wow this is where there was that famous incident between Prost and Senna'."

■ It was announced that former Cosworth Director of Motorsport Bernard Ferguson had been recruited by the new Team USF1 outfit ahead of their F1 debut in 2010.

■ Felipe Massa returned to Maranello in the days after the Japanese GP and made plans to return to the cockpit of a Ferrari later in the year. The Brazilian driver, who suffered a fractured skull in Hungary, was expected to test a 2007 Ferrari at Fiorano, but he ruled out a return for the season-ending Abu Dhabi GP.

RACE
RESULTS
JAPAN
SUZUKA

RACE DATE October 4th
CIRCUIT LENGTH 3.608 miles
NO. OF LAPS 53
RACE DISTANCE 191.126 miles
WEATHER Sunny and dry, 28°C
TRACK TEMP 43°C
ATTENDANCE 210,000
LAP RECORD Kimi Räikkönen,
1m31.540s, 141.904mph, 2005

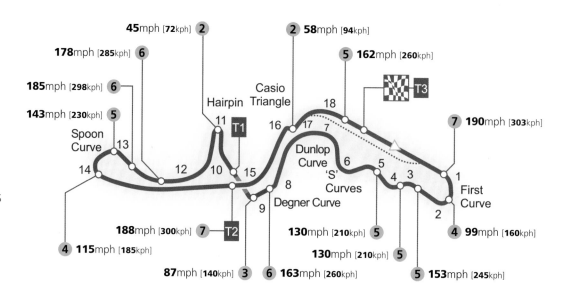

	PRACTICE 1		
	Driver	Time	Laps
1	H Kovalainen	1m40.356s	24
2	K Nakajima	1m40.648s	18
3	A Sutil	1m40.806s	14
4	G Fisichella	1m40.985s	27
5	S Buemi	1m41.421s	26
6	L Hamilton	1m41.443s	15
7	F Alonso	1m41.532s	22
8	K Räikkönen	1m41.577s	25
9	R Barrichello	1m41.821s	18
10	N Rosberg	1m42.188s	20
11	M Webber	1m42.332s	10
12	V Liuzzi	1m42.475s	15
13	J Trulli	1m42.657s	13
14	J Alguersuari	1m42.667s	27
15	R Kubica	1m42.833s	16
16	N Heidfeld	1m42.977s	14
17	S Vettel	1m43.218s	11
18	J Button	1m43.318s	17
19	K Kobayashi	1m43.407s	16
20	R Grosjean	1m43.572s	22

	PRACTICE 2		
	Driver	Time	Laps
1	A Sutil	1m47.261s	5
2	S Vettel	1m47.923s	6
3	V Liuzzi	1m47.931s	4
4	L Hamilton	1m47.983s	5
5	K Nakajima	1m48.058s	8
6	S Buemi	1m48.691s	9
7	F Alonso	1m48.693s	5
8	J Trulli	1m48.737s	6
9	J Alguersuari	1m48.802s	11
10	R Kubica	1m48.861s	6
11	K Räikkönen	1m48.886s	4
12	K Kobayashi	1m49.054s	7
13	M Webber	1m49.382s	7
14	R Grosjean	1m49.405s	6
15	G Fisichella	1m49.553s	5
16	N Rosberg	1m49.872s	7
17	N Heidfeld	1m50.179s	9
18	H Kovalainen	No time	0
19	J Button	No time	0
20	R Barrichello	No time	0

	PRACTICE 3		
	Driver	Time	Laps
1	J Trulli	1m31.709s	24
2	S Buemi	1m31.771s	26
3	N Rosberg	1m32.343s	28
4	S Vettel	1m32.414s	19
5	K Räikkönen	1m32.445s	26
6	A Sutil	1m32.467s	25
7	R Barrichello	1m32.488s	24
8	H Kovalainen	1m32.546s	22
9	J Button	1m32.668s	25
10	J Alguersuari	1m32.689s	20
11	R Grosjean	1m32.717s	25
12	N Heidfeld	1m32.736s	21
13	F Alonso	1m32.742s	21
14	T Glock	1m32.749s	26
15	K Nakajima	1m32.752s	23
16	L Hamilton	1m32.789s	19
17	R Kubica	1m32.848s	20
18	G Fisichella	1m32.878s	26
19	M Webber	1m32.930s	15
20	V Liuzzi	1m33.167s	18

	QUALIFYING 1	
	Driver	Time
1	S Vettel	1m30.883s
2	L Hamilton	1m30.917s
3	J Button	1m31.041s
4	J Trulli	1m31.063s
5	S Buemi	1m31.196s
6	K Räikkönen	1m31.228s
7	R Barrichello	1m31.272s
8	N Rosberg	1m31.286s
9	A Sutil	1m31.386s
10	F Alonso	1m31.401s
11	R Kubica	1m31.417s
12	H Kovalainen	1m31.499s
13	N Heidfeld	1m31.501s
14	T Glock	1m31.550s
15	J Alguersuari	1m31.571s
16	G Fisichella	1m31.704s
17	K Nakajima	1m31.718s
18	R Grosjean	1m32.073s
19	V Liuzzi	1m32.087s
20	M Webber	No time

	QUALIFYING 2	
	Driver	Time
1	S Vettel	1m30.341s
2	L Hamilton	1m30.627s
3	J Trulli	1m30.737s
4	J Button	1m30.880s
5	K Räikkönen	1m31.052s
6	R Barrichello	1m31.055s
7	S Buemi	1m31.103s
8	A Sutil	1m31.222s
9	H Kovalainen	1m31.223s
10	N Heidfeld	1m31.260s
11	N Rosberg	1m31.482s
12	F Alonso	1m31.638s
13	R Kubica	1m32.341s
14	T Glock	No time
15	J Alguersuari	No time

Best sectors – Practice			Speed trap – Practice			Best sectors – Qualifying			Speed trap – Qualifying		
Sec 1	S Buemi	32.214s	1	R Grosjean	192.749mph	Sec 1	N Heidfeld	31.704s	1	H Kovalainen	194.489mph
Sec 2	K Räikkönen	41.541s	2	L Hamilton	192.500mph	Sec 2	J Button	40.788s	2	L Hamilton	193.246mph
Sec 3	A Sutil	17.826s	3	S Buemi	192.438mph	Sec 3	J Button	17.539s	3	J Button	191.817mph

IN 2008

Fuji Speedway hosted Japan's 2008 grand prix and, unlike the 2007 race, the rain stayed away. Desperate to hold the lead into the first corner after being passed by Kimi Räikkönen, Lewis Hamilton pushed the front runners wide and, from sixth, Robert Kubica took the lead. However, he had no answer to Fernando Alonso.

Lewis Hamilton

"I went for the lead at the start, but couldn't do it. It was a good scrap with Jarno, but as I left the pits after my second stop, I had a gearbox problem, and coasted 100m."

Giancarlo Fisichella

"I had a better feel for the car, but it's a shame I lost a place in my battle with Kovalainen. Towards the end, I had to fight off Sutil who was very quick on the soft tyre."

Robert Kubica

"I wasn't able to show my pace in qualifying due to the red and yellow flags. Today I was stuck in traffic and lost time at the start with a heavy and understeering car."

Fernando Alonso

"My race was decided after qualifying as, though the car was competitive, it wasn't enough for points, so we must make sure we qualify well for the last two races."

Jarno Trulli

"Standing on the podium in the team's home race was fantastic. The new package has been really competitive, but Lewis got by and I spent the whole race fighting him."

Heikki Kovalainen

"Adrian tried to make a move, but only went halfway. When he tried to turn in, I was already on the kerb and I had no more room to avoid him, so I had to lean on him."

Kimi Räikkönen

"The car wasn't fast enough for a podium, but when I got on to the soft tyres, things improved. I managed to close on Heidfeld and pass him at the pit stop."

Nick Heidfeld

"I'm very disappointed, as fourth place was within reach, but several things went wrong, especially at the second pit stop when the rear-right wheel nut got stuck."

Romain Grosjean

"The car was very heavy on fuel and difficult to drive, as I had a lot of understeer. Suzuka was also new to me, but I did my best to finish the race with no problems."

Timo Glock

"Together with my physio I tried everything to be fit for the race, but it wasn't possible for me to race. It's a pity to miss Toyota's home race and I'm annoyed it happened."

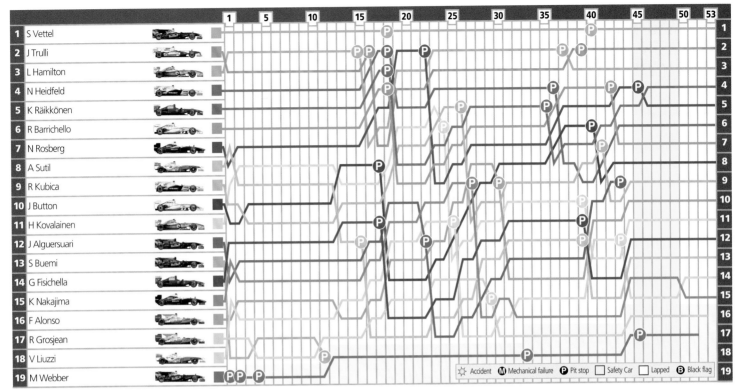

| | | Accident | (M) Mechanical failure | (P) Pit stop | Safety Car | Lapped | (B) Black flag |

Positions lap by lap chart, drivers 1–19:

1. S Vettel
2. J Trulli
3. L Hamilton
4. N Heidfeld
5. K Räikkönen
6. R Barrichello
7. N Rosberg
8. A Sutil
9. R Kubica
10. J Button
11. H Kovalainen
12. J Alguersuari
13. S Buemi
14. G Fisichella
15. K Nakajima
16. F Alonso
17. R Grosjean
18. V Liuzzi
19. M Webber

QUALIFYING 3

	Driver	Time
1	S Vettel	1m32.160s
2	J Trulli	1m32.220s
3	L Hamilton	1m32.395s
4	A Sutil	1m32.466s
5	R Barrichello	1m32.660s
6	N Heidfeld	1m32.945s
7	J Button	1m32.962s
8	K Räikkönen	1m32.980s
9	H Kovalainen	No time
10	S Buemi	No time

GRID

	Driver	Time
1	S Vettel	1m32.160s
2	J Trulli	1m32.220s
3	L Hamilton	1m32.395s
4	N Heidfeld	1m32.945s
5	K Räikkönen	1m32.980s
6*	R Barrichello	1m32.660s
7	N Rosberg	1m31.482s
8*	A Sutil	1m32.466s
9	R Kubica	1m32.341s
10*	J Button	1m32.962s
11^	H Kovalainen	No time
12	J Alguersuari	No time
13'	S Buemi	No time
14	G Fisichella	1m31.704s
15	K Nakajima	1m31.718s
16*	F Alonso	1m31.638s
17	R Grosjean	1m32.073s
18^	V Liuzzi	1m32.087s
19"	M Webber	No time

* Grid penalty for not slowing under yellow flag
^ 5-place penalty for gearbox change
' 5-place penalty for impeding other drivers
" New chassis so had to start from pits

RACE

	Driver	Car	Laps	Time	Avg. mph	Fastest	Stops
1	S Vettel	Red Bull-Renault RB5	53	1h28m20.443s	129.804	1m32.572s	2
2	J Trulli	Toyota TF109	53	1h28m25.320s	129.684	1m33.152s	2
3	L Hamilton	McLaren-Mercedes MP4-24*	53	1h28m26.915s	129.646	1m33.259s	2
4	K Räikkönen	Ferrari F60*	53	1h28m28.383s	129.610	1m32.999s	2
5	N Rosberg	Williams-Toyota FW31	53	1h28m29.236s	129.589	1m33.595s	2
6	N Heidfeld	BMW Sauber F1.09	53	1h28m29.952s	129.571	1m33.600s	2
7	R Barrichello	Brawn-Mercedes BGP 001	53	1h28m31.084s	129.544	1m33.910s	2
8	J Button	Brawn-Mercedes BGP 001	53	1h28m31.917s	129.523	1m33.251s	2
9	R Kubica	BMW Sauber F1.09	53	1h28m32.220s	129.516	1m33.334s	2
10	F Alonso	Renault R29	53	1h28m33.508s	129.485	1m33.946s	1
11	H Kovalainen	McLaren-Mercedes MP4-24*	53	1h28m34.178s	129.469	1m33.801s	2
12	G Fisichella	Ferrari F60*	53	1h28m35.039s	129.448	1m33.479s	2
13	A Sutil	Force India-Mercedes VJM02	53	1h28m35.402s	129.439	1m33.668s	2
14	V Liuzzi	Force India-Mercedes VJM02	53	1h28m36.177s	129.420	1m34.294s	2
15	K Nakajima	Williams-Toyota FW31	53	1h28m38.416s	129.366	1m34.783s	1
16	R Grosjean	Renault R29	52	1h28m39.798s	126.890	1m34.643s	1
17	M Webber	Red Bull-Renault RB5	51	1h28m42.682s	124.381	1m32.569s	5
R	J Alguersuari	Toro Rosso-Ferrari STR4	43	Accident	-	1m34.049s	2
R	S Buemi	Toro Rosso-Ferrari STR4	11	Clutch	-	1m35.392s	0
NS	T Glock	Toyota TF109	0	Leg injury	-	-	-

* Denotes car fitted with KERS

CHAMPIONSHIP

	Driver	Pts
1	J Button	85
2	R Barrichello	71
3	S Vettel	69
4	M Webber	51.5
5	K Räikkönen	45
6	L Hamilton	43
7	N Rosberg	34.5
8	J Trulli	30.5
9	F Alonso	26
10	T Glock	24
11	F Massa	22
12	H Kovalainen	22
13	N Heidfeld	15
14	R Kubica	9
15	G Fisichella	8
16	A Sutil	5
17	S Buemi	3
18	S Bourdais	2

Fastest lap
M Webber 1m32.569s
(140.326mph) on lap 50

Fastest speed trap
H Kovalainen 196.601mph
Slowest speed trap
N Heidfeld 186.411mph

Fastest pit stop
1	J Alguersuari	23.191s
2	V Liuzzi	23.210s
3	R Barrichello	23.449s

	Constructor	Pts
1	Brawn-Mercedes	156
2	Red Bull-Renault	120.5
3	Ferrari	67
4	McLaren-Mercedes	65
5	Toyota	54.5
6	Williams-Toyota	34.5
7	Renault	26
8	BMW Sauber	24
9	Force India-Mercedes	13
10	Toro Rosso-Ferrari	5

Jaime Alguersuari

"My accident came on the lap after my second stop, when I fitted the soft tyres. At 130R, which you take flat, I lost the rear and hit the wall, but I'm not sure why."

Mark Webber

"I had to make two stops in the first two laps, so it was all over. The headrest came loose. I went out again, but the same thing happened so we tested after that."

Nico Rosberg

"That was the best I could do. The car wasn't as quick as we wanted it to be, but we got the best out of it. I had a really good strategy that helped deliver this result."

Adrian Sutil

"The start was OK, but then I fell to ninth and was caught behind Kovalainen. I got past him at the chicane but he cut back across and I spun and lost a lot of time."

Jenson Button

"Today was about picking up points after an eventful qualifying, and that is what I did. Starting from 10th was going to make for a tough race but my pace was really good."

Sebastien Buemi

"I had a clutch problem from the start of the parade lap, when I couldn't get off the grid. We tried to fix it, but it didn't work for the start. After a few laps it failed."

Sebastian Vettel

"We were confident that I could defend pole, but it was close. After that, I was able to create a gap. We were two laps longer than Lewis in the first stint, so it all worked out."

Kazuki Nakajima

"It was a difficult race for me. I was on a one-stop strategy, but there was just too much traffic and the safety car came out so it didn't work out the way we had hoped."

Vitantonio Liuzzi

"Starting 18th, it was always going to be hard to score, but I had strong pace and never gave up as I enjoyed a good fight with Alonso, the Williams and the Toro Rossos."

Rubens Barrichello

"Qualifying proved crucial, as it put me ahead of Jenson. I was able to follow Kimi when we were on primes, but once he switched to options, he gained a lot of time."

FORMULA 1 GRANDE PREMIO
PETROBRAS DO BRASIL 2009
SÃO PAULO

BUTTON IS KING

Mark Webber stormed to victory for Red Bull, but all eyes were on Jenson Button's Brawn as he dived past car after car to advance from 14th to fifth to wrap up the title with a race to go

As the F1 world trudged through the murk on Saturday evening, one couldn't help thinking that the events of qualifying – Rubens Barrichello on pole position with rivals Jenson Button and Sebastian Vettel languishing 14th and 16th respectively – were nothing but an appetiser, a tantalising *amuse-bouche* for what might follow. Qualifying contained as much action as the rest of a normal F1 season, but this was Interlagos, where the rules are different: the paddock is cramped, the atmosphere electric and overtaking is possible. It's the one place where Sunday is always more exciting than Saturday afternoon.

Button left the circuit with a hang-dog look. "It was the first time in my career that I felt sick after qualifying," he admitted later. His disastrous grid slot was magnified by the brutal nature of the knockout system: in Q2, he and his team-mate had been 10th and 14th, and Barrichello was within a Kamui Kobayashi-half-spin whisker of being bumped to 11th. But he made it through and excelled in Q3, so a four-place gap became 13 grid spots, leaving Button a mountain to climb.

The next morning, the clouds had lifted both literally and metaphorically. The day dawned bright

INSIDE LINE
JENSON BUTTON
BRAWN GP DRIVER

"This was the best race I've driven in my life. Not just because of the emotion, but also because I knew what I had to do – and I did it. That is why I am sat up here now as World Champion.

It's weird, because I dreamt on Friday night that qualifying would be terrible and it was. I also dreamt that night that I would win the world title, so maybe there is some truth in dreams.

I thought qualifying would have gone very well because of the rain, and I enjoy the wet, but I saw the worst thing that could happen to me, which is my team-mate put it on pole... I felt sick after Q2, I really did.

However, we looked at the race strategy and it said I could be fifth or sixth. Then I went to see the boys, and everyone was positive. I headed home with my team of people, had a few drinks and knew I was ready for action. I went to bed very happy and was positive all morning.

It was an amazing race. I spent a long time behind Kobayashi – that guy is crazy! Everyone else was tough but fair. He was a bit crazy because he moves a lot in the braking zones. I had very good straightline speed but, when you have that, you don't have as much downforce as other people.

I had to fight the car in the last three corners of the lap to get close enough to challenge into Turn 1. Every time I overtook there, I was never on their tail, it was down to a late-braking move. You could call it risky, but I didn't think so: I knew that I had to get close to Rubens and he was running in second place, so I knew that I had to be fifth.

I gave a big 'woo-hoo' on the radio when I passed Kobayashi. Then the team came on the radio and told me that Hamilton was doing a one-stop and he was going to come out in front of me. I was like 'You're kidding me?' I'd fought my way through the field, overtaken five cars on track, then Hamilton and Vettel were going to get me at the stops.

I think Rubens was in third place and I was running in sixth late in the race, and that was all I needed. Then Hamilton overtook Rubens and he had the puncture. I think fifth place was all I could achieve today, but that was enough.

Ross Brawn deserves a medal. The team would not exist if Ross wasn't here, and I don't think any of us could have done it without him.

I don't know what else to say. I am World Champion!"

and Button wore that relaxed smile that can be both mask and truth. This day, though, was the chance to take control of his destiny. Ahead of him on the grid were Romain Grosjean, Jaime Alguersuari and Kobayashi: the kind of group that should come with a flashing warning when you're going for a title. Behind him, Vettel, and the KERS-boosted McLarens of Lewis Hamilton and Heikki Kovalainen. Metaphors about being caught between rocks and hard places flowed.

Button, though, ignored the lot. He went to the grid, surprised but not unnerved by the unusual experience of being humorously booed by the fans. After all, an Interlagos crowd is always a touch more football than F1. The start was clean, he negotiated the first-lap coming together between Sutil and Trulli and the subsequent safety-car period without trouble, and found himself running ninth as the AMG Mercedes peeled into the pitlane. It was time to get to work.

On lap 6, he made a brave move around the outside of Grosjean at Turn 6, Ferradura. By lap 7, he'd dispatched Nakajima and was latched on the rear wing of notable Toyota debutant Kobayashi, who'd qualified an impressive 11th. It took Button until lap 25 to get past and, in the meantime, he was on the radio protesting to the team. Perhaps it was the frustration of a championship leader with much to lose, or perhaps the determination of Button to use every possible lever to make things happen for himself. In any case, he made a move, then slithered wide and Kobayashi nipped back through. The next lap, Button made it stick and, finally, was free, in clear air with a title to win…

That pass happened at one-third distance and, by then, Interlagos had provided enough action to fill a short novel. As the red lights went out, everybody made a clean start, but things got tight as the cars funnelled into the downhill left-hander of Turn 1. Adrian Sutil and Kimi Räikkönen made light contact, but the Finn's KERS boost had put him ahead of the Force India and on the

tail of second-placed Mark Webber as they trailed leader Barrichello down the back straight. Räikkönen hit the KERS button again, and got a run on Webber who, as ever, defended robustly – jinking left once, then a second time. It was that second move that clipped Räikkönen's right-front wing, and left him limping back to the pits.

Behind, chaos was unleashed. Sutil braked late into Turn 4 and slightly locked his wheels, then found himself slowed by Räikkönen's hobbled Ferrari (why is it always Kimi?). Toyota's Jarno Trulli cut to the inside of Sutil, who blocked him, so Trulli used his momentum to run around the outside through Turn 5.

OPPOSITE Conditions were extremely wet on Saturday. Robert Kubica splashes his way around

ABOVE Rubens Barrichello dives into Turn 1 ahead of Kimi Räikkönen, Mark Webber and Adrian Sutil

BELOW Räikkönen's Ferrari is already damaged, as Sutil and Jarno Trulli bounce off each other behind

An unsighted Sutil took the racing line and left Trulli with nowhere to go, then his right wheels touched the grass. With snap oversteer to the left, Trulli hit Sutil's Force India and the two cars pinballed, Trulli to the left-hand barrier and Sutil across the wide grass up the hill to Ferradura. Trulli came to rest with a corner missing, while Sutil, unable to control his car, took out Fernando Alonso's Renault as he slewed across the circuit. Uncharacteristically, Trulli was apoplectic with rage, and ran to remonstrate with Sutil, echoing Nelson Piquet's famous Monza punch-up with Eliseo Salazar in 1988. The stewards later found nobody at fault, but fined Trulli $10,000 for his public remonstrations.

Meanwhile, the safety car emerged so that debris could be cleared, and some dashed for the pits; in Räikkönen's case, for a new front wing and a strategy swap; in the cases of Hamilton and Kovalainen, to switch to a one-stop strategy, having run the marginal super-soft tyre from the start, which meant that, in one lap, they'd fulfilled the obligation to run both types of tyre. Hamilton left the pit without problems but, as Kovalainen's car dropped from the jacks, the lollipop was lifted while the nozzle was still attached. The hose came away from the fuel rig, spraying fuel

BELOW Jenson Button dives past Kazuki Nakajima en route to the fifth place that clinched him the title

BOTTOM Kamui Kobayashi proved a harder nut to crack, but Button's patience was rewarded

OPPOSITE Mark Webber pitted after Rubens Barrichello and emerged ahead, going on to win

down the pitlane behind the McLaren and into the path of Räikkönen's Ferrari. The fuel ignited on the Ferrari's hot exhaust, causing a flash fire that scared the adjacent Renault pitwall, and left Räikkönen with stinging eyes for the rest of the race, as his visor had still been open after the stop. He even got fuel in his mouth during the incident: "I liked it," he joked with Kovalainen post-race. The McLaren driver stopped at the Brawn pit, where the crew obligingly removed the hose and sent him on his way. The incident gave the stewards more to look at: a $50,000 fine for McLaren and a 25s penalty for Kovalainen was the verdict.

As the race resumed, the order ran Barrichello, Webber, Nico Rosberg, Robert Kubica, Sebastien Buemi, Kobayashi, Kazuki Nakajima, Grosjean and Button. Kubica sliced inside Rosberg at the restart, which was the platform for an unobtrusive but mightily impressive drive to second place. Out in front, Barrichello needed to build a gap to Webber, who had a nominal three-lap advantage on fuel but, when Barrichello peeled into the pits on lap 21, he was less than 3s ahead. It transpired that Webber had been able to save two laps of fuel behind the safety car, while Barrichello, preoccupied with tyre warming to

TALKING POINT
ALL CHANGE AT THE FIA?

In the end, it wasn't even close: on Friday 23 October 2009, Jean Todt was elected FIA President by 135 votes to Ari Vatanen's 49. During a campaign that had, at times, veered towards dirty tricks, outgoing President (and Todt backer) Max Mosley had written to Prince Feisal of Jordan to say that Vatanen "will lose the election and lose badly." As so often, events proved that Mosley knew of what he spoke.

Just one week before the vote, during the grand prix weekend in Brazil, the respective campaigns of Todt and Vatanen had begun playing hardball. Neither candidate was present at Interlagos, but a flurry of claims and counter-claims, plus interventions from incumbent President Mosley, showed that what had been billed as a one-horse race had become very much a two-horse affair.

The weekend began amid accusations from the Todt camp that Vatanen had conducted 'personal attacks' and made 'false allegations' against Todt; a lengthy homily to Todt from his former driver Michael Schumacher followed. Over the course of the weekend, more endorsements hit the inboxes of the world's media, including a barbed series of comments from Vatanen's rallying colleagues and countrymen and, more bizarrely, a standalone quote of approval from Pelé.

The more serious background to this flurry of positive PR was Vatanen's decision to apply to a Paris court to impose measures to ensure the fairness of the election process. Unsurprisingly, this provoked a testy response from Mosley, who professed himself "at a loss to explain the purpose of the legal action", before asserting that "a large team of FIA personnel has worked continuously over recent months to ensure that the new FIA President is elected in a dignified and democratic way." Vatanen subsequently withdrew his court application following confirmation that a French Huissier de Justice would monitor proceedings and, similarly, that a private area for marking ballot papers would be available for candidates.

Ultimately, though, these skirmishes – no doubt intensified among the F1 press corps by the feverish atmosphere at the Brazilian GP – came to naught. The election followed type, and Todt was duly voted in; he immediately called on the FIA to unite after the divisive election process.

"The day the election is over, everybody must share the same goals, including those who did not support me," he said. "I am not closing the door to anybody."

TOP Heikki Kovalainen and fuel hose pull away from a pitstop, with Räikkönen about to get a surprise

ABOVE A clever strategy helped Lewis Hamilton to vault up the order to finish the race in third place

retain his lead at the restart, couldn't. Webber stopped on lap 26 and emerged 8s ahead of the Brazilian. So the race was, to all intents and purposes, his.

By then, Button – running longer than most drivers ahead of him – had vaulted up to second place before making his own stop on lap 29. He re-emerged 10th, then once again took his destiny into his own hands with a bold move on Buemi's Toro Rosso into Turn 1 on lap 34. There was a brief snap of oversteer as he reapplied the power, but Button made it stick and was up to seventh, thanks to other cars' pitstops. At half distance, the order ran Webber, Vettel (yet to stop), Kubica, Barrichello, Hamilton (yet to stop), Räikkönen (yet to stop), Button, Buemi. Good fortune had played a part, but Button had made things happen and was on course for a world title.

The remaining question was how things would shuffle out between Button and the long-fuelled Vettel, Hamilton and Räikkönen. Vettel made his first stop on lap 37, apparently taking on enough fuel to reach the finish but, crucially, putting the harder tyre back on, so he'd have to stop again. He emerged less than 1s behind Button. As for Hamilton, he'd put in a quiet but blemish-free drive, and spent the final part

of his long stint hounding Barrichello, He finally pitted on lap 42, one before Räikkönen, and re-emerged seventh. His battle with Barrichello wasn't over, merely paused. As for Räikkönen, he filtered back out 11th, which would become sixth place at the flag.

The second round of stops came and went without incident: Barrichello pitted on lap 50, Webber two laps later, while Button and Vettel stopped on laps 55 and 56 respectively. With 15 laps to run, this left Webber leading Kubica, from Barrichello, Hamilton, Vettel, Kovalainen (yet to stop) and Button – enough for Button to clinch the championship. But there was more drama to come – or what Ross Brawn referred to as Rubens's 'Brazilian curse'.

Barrichello had emerged from the pits around 2s ahead of Hamilton but, in spite of fresher tyres and a clear road, was unable to stretch that gap. If anything, the McLaren – with its KERS boost – was slightly faster, but Hamilton found himself stuck around 1s behind the Brazilian, yet hungry for a podium. On lap 61, Barrichello radioed his team that he was suffering from a severe vibration: a wheel weight had come loose on the right front. This backed him into Hamilton, who took advantage as they flashed past the pits on lap 62, slicing between Barrichello and the pitwall through the final left-hand sweep. As Barrichello closed the door, the tip of the McLaren's front wing endplate clipped the Brawn's left rear tyre, causing a slow puncture that forced Barrichello to pit again on lap 63. His title dream had been dashed.

As for Button, he cruised serenely to fifth place and the world title. It was the second time in two years that car 22, powered by a Mercedes engine, driven by an Englishman, had finished fifth at Interlagos to clinch the world title. This wasn't an evening for stats, though; it was a moment of compelling, visceral joy. "I am the World Champion," an ecstatic Button told the world. "I am not going to stop saying it!"

SNAPSHOT FROM
BRAZIL

CLOCKWISE FROM RIGHT This aerial view shows how the circuit is surrounded by suburbs; Kamui Kobayashi made a big splash on his debut; the crowd was as partisan as ever; future team-mates Fernando Alonso and Felipe Massa started their sparring for 2010; Mark Webber celebrates his second victory; the circuit celebrates the memories of one of Brazil' greats, Carlos Pace; more than a few champagne corks were popped in celebration of Jenson Button's World Championship title

WEEKEND NEWS

■ Felipe Massa returned to the F1 paddock for the first time since his crash in Hungary, insisting the experience hadn't changed him. "The recovery was pretty great," said the Brazilian, " and I can say I am the same as before." Massa even began needling future team-mate Fernando Alonso.

■ Bernie Ecclestone sounded a warning that "time is running out" for the sport's oldest race, the French GP, after 2009 marked the first time in World Championship history that the race hadn't been held. "It seems to be hard to put things in place in France," said Ecclestone. "It's going to get harder to find a place on the calendar. They need to act quickly, as time is short."

■ Disgraced former Renault boss Flavio Briatore announced during the Brazilian GP weekend that he would begin legal action against the FIA and his lifetime ban from F1. "The FIA has been used as a tool to exact vengeance on behalf of one man," said a statement on the Italian's behalf, which went on to list grounds for complaint including a lack of impartiality and the granting of selective immunities. "The decision is a legal absurdity."

■ While the stewards took no action over any of the on-track 'racing incidents' involving Trulli and Sutil, or Nakajima and Kobayashi, they did take action on a number of points after Sunday's race. McLaren and Kovalainen were penalised for the flash fire in the pitlane ($50,000 fine and a 25-second post-race penalty), while Trulli also had to cough up $10,000 for his behaviour when he furiously confronted Sutil following their tangle.

■ Toyota boss John Howett confirmed that the Japanese manufacturer had approached Kimi Räikkönen about driving for the team in 2010. "I think we could work well with him, give him a car that's quick," said Howett.

RACE RESULTS
BRAZIL
INTERLAGOS

Official Results © [2009]
Formula One Administration Limited,
6 Princes Gate, London, SW7 1QJ.
No reproduction without permission.
All copyright and database rights reserved.

RACE DATE October 18th
CIRCUIT LENGTH 2.677 miles
NO. OF LAPS 71
RACE DISTANCE 190.067 miles
WEATHER Hot but overcast, 23°C
TRACK TEMP 31°C
ATTENDANCE 130,000
LAP RECORD Juan Pablo Montoya,
1m11.473s, 134.837mph, 2004

#	PRACTICE 1 Driver	Time	Laps
1	M Webber	1m12.463s	29
2	R Barrichello	1m12.874s	32
3	S Vettel	1m12.932s	27
4	H Kovalainen	1m12.989s	25
5	L Hamilton	1m13.048s	25
6	K Nakajima	1m13.067s	21
7	J Button	1m13.141s	29
8	N Rosberg	1m13.147s	23
9	A Sutil	1m13.232s	23
10	K Räikkönen	1m13.321s	24
11	J Trulli	1m13.326s	26
12	N Heidfeld	1m13.464s	28
13	S Buemi	1m13.503s	24
14	R Kubica	1m13.563s	24
15	G Fisichella	1m13.619s	23
16	F Alonso	1m13.787s	28
17	V Liuzzi	1m13.829s	26
18	K Kobayashi	1m14.029s	27
19	J Alguersuari	1m14.040s	38
20	R Grosjean	1m14.173s	23

#	PRACTICE 2 Driver	Time	Laps
1	F Alonso	1m12.314s	27
2	S Buemi	1m12.357s	45
3	R Barrichello	1m12.459s	38
4	M Webber	1m12.514s	41
5	J Button	1m12.523s	45
6	J Trulli	1m12.605s	37
7	S Vettel	1m12.611s	45
8	N Rosberg	1m12.633s	42
9	A Sutil	1m12.720s	35
10	L Hamilton	1m12.749s	39
11	R Grosjean	1m12.806s	27
12	R Kubica	1m12.862s	39
13	K Kobayashi	1m12.869s	40
14	K Nakajima	1m12.929s	41
15	N Heidfeld	1m12.948s	38
16	V Liuzzi	1m12.950s	36
17	H Kovalainen	1m12.992s	39
18	K Räikkönen	1m13.026s	42
19	J Alguersuari	1m13.041s	40
20	G Fisichella	1m13.275s	38

#	PRACTICE 3 Driver	Time	Laps
1	N Rosberg	1m23.182s	9
2	K Nakajima	1m23.832s	7
3	J Button	1m24.122s	6
4	F Alonso	1m24.125s	5
5	A Sutil	1m24.149s	4
6	R Grosjean	1m24.389s	5
7	S Buemi	1m24.443s	5
8	J Trulli	1m24.859s	5
9	N Heidfeld	1m24.867s	5
10	M Webber	1m25.440s	5
11	K Räikkönen	1m25.508s	4
12	H Kovalainen	1m25.685s	5
13	J Alguersuari	1m26.224s	6
14	R Barrichello	1m26.530s	4
15	S Vettel	1m27.047s	4
16	V Liuzzi	1m27.341s	4
17	L Hamilton	1m27.798s	4
18	G Fisichella	1m29.285s	4
19	R Kubica	1m29.895s	3
20	K Kobayashi	1m30.259s	4

#	QUALIFYING 1 Driver	Time
1	N Rosberg	1m22.828s
2	K Räikkönen	1m23.047s
3	R Kubica	1m23.072s
4	K Nakajima	1m23.161s
5	R Barrichello	1m24.100s
6	J Button	1m24.297s
7	K Kobayashi	1m24.335s
8	R Grosjean	1m24.394s
9	A Sutil	1m24.447s
10	S Buemi	1m24.591s
11	J Trulli	1m24.621s
12	V Liuzzi	1m24.645s
13	M Webber	1m24.722s
14	J Alguersuari	1m24.773s
15	F Alonso	1m24.842s
16	S Vettel	1m25.009s
17	H Kovalainen	1m25.052s
18	L Hamilton	1m25.192s
19	N Heidfeld	1m25.515s
20	G Fisichella	1m40.703s

#	QUALIFYING 2 Driver	Time
1	N Rosberg	1m20.368s
2	K Nakajima	1m20.427s
3	J Trulli	1m20.635s
4	S Buemi	1m20.701s
5	A Sutil	1m20.753s
6	M Webber	1m20.803s
7	R Kubica	1m21.147s
8	K Räikkönen	1m21.378s
9	F Alonso	1m21.657s
10	R Barrichello	1m21.659s
11	K Kobayashi	1m21.960s
12	J Alguersuari	1m22.231s
13	R Grosjean	1m22.477s
14	J Button	1m22.504s
15	V Liuzzi	No time

Best sectors – Practice
Sec 1	R Grosjean	18.309s
Sec 2	J Trulli	36.420s
Sec 3	H Kovalainen	17.202s

Speed trap – Practice
1	K Räikkönen	193.246mph
	N Heidfeld	193.246mph
3	L Hamilton	192.749mph

Best sectors – Qualifying
Sec 1	R Barrichello	20.475s
Sec 2	R Barrichello	40.730s
Sec 3	K Räikkönen	18.153s

Speed trap – Qualifying
1	R Kubica	185.293mph
2	R Barrichello	183.366mph
3	S Buemi	182.559mph

IN 2008

The race of the century? This was pure drama from start to finish, with Felipe Massa knowing that he had to win to be World Champion and hope that Lewis Hamilton finished sixth or lower. Rain in the dying moments dropped Hamilton from fifth to sixth, but he passed Timo Glock at the last corner and so took the title.

Lewis Hamilton
"I was so far behind on the grid that I didn't expect to finish on the podium, but I kept pushing like crazy. It feels like a win when you come through fighting for places."

Giancarlo Fisichella
"My race was compromised by starting from the back. Then Heikki spun in front of me, which stopped me gaining a few places. On top of that, the KERS worked erratically."

Robert Kubica
"I was surprised at the beginning that it was quite easy to follow Rubens and Mark. But I had to reduce the revs after 15 laps, as the water temperature was too high."

Fernando Alonso
"It was a very busy first lap and I got caught up in it. I had a promising strategy, but unfortunately when Sutil and Trulli collided I was hit by the Force India as well."

Jarno Trulli
"Sutil was slow through Turn 4 as he was fighting Räikkönen. He was on the inside, so I took the outside, but he kept pushing me wider. In the end, I lost control."

Heikki Kovalainen
"I had a good race, but lost 6–7 laps of fuel with the fuel-hose incident. Without that, my first stint would've let me get in front of some of the cars ahead of me."

Kimi Räikkönen
"I was hit at Turn 1 then, when trying to pass Webber, I was hit and lost the front wing. At the pit stop, the fuel line stuck on Kovalainen's car and I was engulfed in flames."

Nick Heidfeld
"After my first pit stop, I wondered how quick the car was, and soon received the call to save fuel, then to save more fuel, but it was too late and the car ran dry in Turn 8."

Romain Grosjean
"I made a good start, but then found it hard to get heat into the tyres. I did my best and pushed hard throughout the race, but unluckily that wasn't enough."

Kamui Kobayashi
"As this was my grand prix debut, it felt like a really long race. My first target was to finish, but I was in a position to score points, so I'm a little disappointed that I didn't."

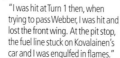

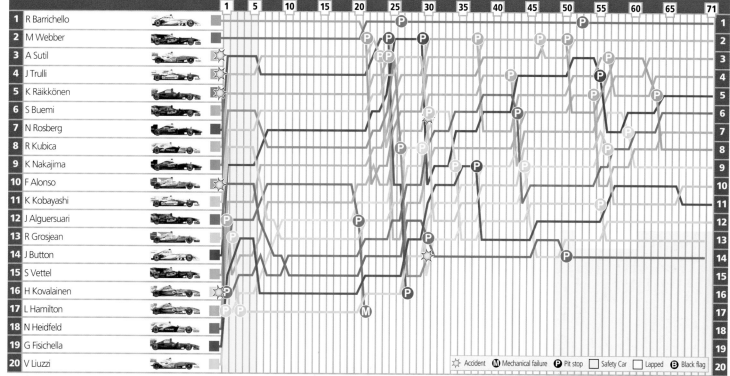

	Driver
1	R Barrichello
2	M Webber
3	A Sutil
4	J Trulli
5	K Räikkönen
6	S Buemi
7	N Rosberg
8	R Kubica
9	K Nakajima
10	F Alonso
11	K Kobayashi
12	J Alguersuari
13	R Grosjean
14	J Button
15	S Vettel
16	H Kovalainen
17	L Hamilton
18	N Heidfeld
19	G Fisichella
20	V Liuzzi

☆ Accident Ⓜ Mechanical failure Ⓟ Pit stop ☐ Safety Car ☐ Lapped Ⓑ Black flag

QUALIFYING 3

	Driver	Time
1	R Barrichello	1m19.576s
2	M Webber	1m19.668s
3	A Sutil	1m19.912s
4	J Trulli	1m20.097s
5	K Räikkönen	1m20.168s
6	S Buemi	1m20.250s
7	N Rosberg	1m20.326s
8	R Kubica	1m20.631s
9	K Nakajima	1m20.674s
10	F Alonso	1m21.422s

GRID

	Driver	Time
1	R Barrichello	1m19.576s
2	M Webber	1m19.668s
3	A Sutil	1m19.912s
4	J Trulli	1m20.097s
5	K Räikkönen	1m20.168s
6	S Buemi	1m20.250s
7	N Rosberg	1m20.326s
8	R Kubica	1m20.631s
9	K Nakajima	1m20.674s
10	F Alonso	1m21.422s
11	K Kobayashi	1m21.960s
12	J Alguersuari	1m22.231s
13	R Grosjean	1m22.477s
14	J Button	1m22.504s
15	S Vettel	1m25.009s
16	H Kovalainen	1m25.052s
17	L Hamilton	1m25.192s
18	N Heidfeld	1m25.515s
19	G Fisichella	1m40.703s
20*	V Liuzzi	No time

* 5-place penalty for gearbox change

RACE

	Driver	Car	Laps	Time	Avg. mph	Fastest	Stops
1	M Webber	Red Bull-Renault RB5	71	1h32m23.081s	123.451	1m13.733s	2
2	R Kubica	BMW Sauber F1.09	71	1h32m30.707s	123.281	1m14.155s	2
3	L Hamilton	*McLaren-Mercedes MP4-24	71	1h32m42.025s	123.030	1m14.345s	2
4	S Vettel	Red Bull-Renault RB5	71	1h32m42.733s	123.014	1m13.890s	2
5	J Button	Brawn-Mercedes BGP 001	71	1h32m52.086s	122.808	1m14.353s	2
6	K Räikkönen	*Ferrari F60	71	1h32m56.421s	122.712	1m14.558s	2
7	S Buemi	Toro Rosso-Ferrari STR4	71	1h32m59.072s	122.654	1m14.563s	2
8	R Barrichello	Brawn-Mercedes BGP 001	71	1h33m08.535s	122.447	1m13.950s	3
9	H Kovalainen	*McLaren-Mercedes MP4-24	71	1h33m26.405s	122.056	1m14.303s	3
10	K Kobayashi	Toyota TF109	71	1h33m33.746s	121.897	1m14.676s	2
11	G Fisichella	*Ferrari F60	71	1h33m34.469s	121.880	1m14.931s	1
12	V Liuzzi	Force India-Mercedes VJM02	71	1h33m36.580s**	121.835	1m14.990s	3
13	R Grosjean	Renault R29	70	1h32m24.926s	121.671	1m14.789s	2
14	J Alguersuari	Toro Rosso-Ferrari STR4	70	1h32m31.633s	121.524	1m14.861s	2
R	K Nakajima	Williams-Toyota FW31	30	Accident	-	1m15.073s	1
R	N Rosberg	Williams-Toyota FW31	27	Gearbox	-	1m14.370s	1
R	N Heidfeld	BMW Sauber F1.09	21	Out of fuel	-	1m14.988s	1
R	A Sutil	Force India-Mercedes VJM02	0	Accident	-	-	0
R	J Trulli	Toyota TF109	0	Accident	-	-	0
R	F Alonso	Renault R29	0	Accident	-	-	0

* Denotes car fitted with KERS ** Including 25s penalty for unsafe release from pit stop

CHAMPIONSHIP

	Driver	Pts
1	J Button	89
2	S Vettel	74
3	R Barrichello	72
4	M Webber	61.5
5	L Hamilton	49
6	K Räikkönen	48
7	N Rosberg	34.5
8	J Trulli	30.5
9	F Alonso	26
10	T Glock	24
11	F Massa	22
12	H Kovalainen	22
13	R Kubica	17
14	N Heidfeld	15
15	G Fisichella	8
16	A Sutil	5
17	S Buemi	5
18	S Bourdais	2

Fastest lap
M Webber 1m13.733s
(130.728mph) on lap 25

Fastest speed trap
R Kubica 195.732mph
Slowest speed trap
K Kobayashi 188.772mph

Fastest pit stop
1 V Liuzzi 22.889s
2 H Kovalainen 22.903s
3 S Vettel 22.974s

	Constructor	Pts
1	Brawn-Mercedes	161
2	Red Bull-Renault	135.5
3	McLaren-Mercedes	71
4	Ferrari	70
5	Toyota	54.5
6	Williams-Renault	34.5
7	BMW Sauber	32
8	Renault	26
9	Force India-Mercedes	13
10	Toro Rosso-Ferrari	7

Jaime Alguersuari
"I managed to get past Kobayashi at the start of the race, but I was on the wrong side of the track and other cars began going past me, as I was slow in a straight line."

Mark Webber
"I was a bit panicky in the second stint as Robert closed in, although my pace wasn't bad and I knew he was quite short. I was then able to control the gap and he backed off."

Nico Rosberg
"I was lying third, but then Kubica passed me when the safety car went in. Fourth was OK, as we had a strong strategy, so it was looking good until the gearbox problem."

Adrian Sutil
"I lost a place as Kimi passed me, but then Kimi hit Webber. I then got hit in the rear. Trulli tried to go round the outside. It was a stupid move as there was no space."

Jenson Button
"This was the race of my career. It has been a rollercoaster from the wins to the hard graft in the second half that has seen us grind out the results needed for the titles."

Sebastien Buemi
"I was sandwiched between Kubica and Rosberg at Turn 1, so they got past me. However, we didn't have strong pace, so we must try and understand why."

Sebastian Vettel
"It was a good race: starting from the back and finishing fourth. Without problems in qualifying, we could have won, but we didn't, so there's not much more to say."

Kazuki Nakajima
"I was lucky to gain places at the start and make progress after all the incidents. I was having a good race until the accident, so I'm disappointed it ended this way."

Vitantonio Liuzzi
"It was a long race, starting from last after a gearbox change. We changed to the soft tyres in the safety-car period, using them for a lap to get them out of the way."

Rubens Barrichello
"While I am disappointed with the result, it's been an amazing year. I'm pleased for Jenson as a friend. I fought really hard, but he really won it in the first half of the year."

2009 FORMULA 1 ETIHAD AIRWAYS ABU DHABI GRAND PRIX
YAS MARINA CIRCUIT

THREE IN A ROW

Red Bull made it three race wins in succession, with Sebastian Vettel heading home team-mate Webber and Button after mechanical failure cost Hamilton the first Abu Dhabi win

In the end, Sebastian Vettel made the first Abu Dhabi GP look like a twilight stroll along the harbourside. Judging by the weekend's form, and by the prodigious half-second fuel-corrected pole-position gap to the opposition, Lewis Hamilton should have had the pace to run away and hide. Instead, a rogue right-rear brake pad, exhibiting excessive wear, forced the McLaren back to the garage for Hamilton's first mechanical retirement of his F1 career. So, Vettel cruised to victory, ahead of team-mate Mark Webber, to complete Red Bull's fourth 1–2 of the year. Jenson Button was third, hounding Webber to the flag, to complete his season of seasons with one final trip to the podium. Abu Dhabi congratulated itself on a job well done, while the F1 world breathed a sigh of relief and headed into its long winter break.

The race was always going to hinge on the opening stint, and whether polesitter Hamilton could build the gap he needed to pit two laps earlier than Vettel (they were fuelled to laps 17 and 19 respectively) and emerge still in front. The McLaren excelled on the KERS-friendly straights of the second sector, where it was half a second quicker than the

INSIDE LINE
KAMUI KOBAYASHI
TOYOTA DRIVER

"Sixth place is a fantastic result for me and I'm extremely happy, as my target was to finish in the points. I certainly wasn't expecting to be racing in F1 this season and I want to thank Toyota for this opportunity.

I knew the Brazilian GP was going to be a big challenge for me, the biggest challenge I've had in motorsport, but there was no reason to be nervous. I really believe that if you're going to be successful in anything, you have to be confident, and so that was my approach. If you're not confident, you make mistakes.

The Brazilian GP was a tough race, but I learned a lot of things: it was physically demanding; the pit stops; the way the car behaviour evolves during the race; and how to manage the two different tyre compounds. It was good to finish in the top 10 on my debut, but I wanted to do better in Abu Dhabi.

It's a fantastic venue, and interesting to drive for the first time. It was the second time in two weeks that I had to learn a new circuit, so it was becoming a familiar experience.

Also, it was nice to have a lot of dry running, as that didn't happen in Brazil... We got a lot of data on Friday and I was confident we could make another step in qualifying.

This was my first qualifying session in dry conditions, so I needed a little bit of time to get used to it. I was hoping to get in the top 10 but, in the end, I was only a tenth of a second or so away, so it wasn't too bad. Even though I was starting 12th, I had focused on my race pace during practice, so I was positive I could fight for points.

In the end, the key was to overtake Räikkönen at the start: it would have been very difficult to finish in the top six if I had been behind him during the first stint. Once I got past, I was confident that I had the pace to fight for the points and my target was to be consistently fast.

I only did one pit stop and the team did a great job with the strategy. It played a big part in my finishing in the points. Points were the goal but, if I'm honest, I was surprised to finish in the top six."

Red Bull; then ceded its advantage through the twisting third sector, where Adrian Newey's RB5 returned the compliment. Hamilton eked out a lead, but by lap 10 the gap between the pair was just 1.7s.

Then came the first hint of trouble – Hamilton ran wide after locking the brakes into the tight Turn 17 in front of the Yas Marina Hotel. The gap was down to under a second, and Vettel, like a dog with a bone, just wouldn't let go. When Hamilton peeled into the pits, he was just 1.4s ahead. Vettel put in two blistering laps; the lead was his. "That was the key, pushing very hard when I had the two over-laps on Lewis," said Vettel. "It was quite exciting to leave the pits through the tunnel, because it was very slippery, and very easy to make a mistake, but I knew I was fighting for the lead and I had to push."

By then, Hamilton was back in the garage for good. His nascent brake problem had worsened, and the choice between risking an accident or parking an otherwise healthy car was no choice at all. He gave little more than a philosophical shrug of the shoulders, hoping better things await him in 2010. "I could hardly stop the car after about the third lap," said Hamilton. "I was really struggling and trying everything by changing the brake balance, but it was no good. The team called me in, as they felt it was too dangerous for me to continue."

Out front, the win was now Vettel's to lose: he had a 5.9s advantage over Webber after the first pit stops, and simply had to bring it home without losing concentration. Easier said than done when you're in the first day–night race in F1 history, of course, but it was something he accomplished with aplomb to win for the first time a race which he'd started from a grid position other than pole.

Behind Vettel, things were bubbling along nicely, although the circuit seemed to lend itself to a processional race, in spite of pre-race optimism that passing might be possible. After an orderly start, Webber had filed through Turn 1 behind Hamilton and Vettel, but swung across the bows of Barrichello, and ran over the Brazilian's front wing, putting the Australian into a slide on the exit of the corner. Button followed his team-mate for much of the first lap, but managed to slip by to complete lap 1 in fourth. Barrichello, Robert Kubica, Jarno Trulli and Nick Heidfeld rounded out the top eight. The first of the one-stoppers was Kamui Kobayashi in 11th, the Toyota driver having leapfrogged Kimi Räikkönen's Ferrari on the opening lap. That was to prove crucial.

The top 10 qualifiers all opted for a two-stop strategy, and the window opened on lap 16 for Barrichello and Kubica. Button went to lap 17, Webber to lap 18, and while the Red Bull emerged into clean air, the new World Champion found himself dicing with Kobayashi for what would become third place once the round of pit stops was over. Into Turn 8, at the end of the 1.2km back straight, Kobayashi outfumbled Button and slipped ahead. "I slightly outbraked myself, ran a bit wide and he got past," explained Button. "In reality, it didn't make a difference to my race, as

OPPOSITE McLaren's Lewis Hamilton set the pace all weekend, but retired with a brake-wear problem after leading from the start

BELOW Pole starter Hamilton leads the Red Bulls into Turn 1, with Rubens Barrichello about to have his nose wing bent by Mark Webber

BOTTOM Passing moves were rare, but Force India's Adrian Sutil attacked and passed Romain Grosjean on the penultimate lap

Webber, who in turn led Button by nearly 6s. But the gap immediately began to close: Button was on his favoured, softer option tyre, while the Red Bull team had inadvertently short-filled Webber at his final stop, forcing him into economy mode in order to make it to the finish. Button chased him down at between 0.5–1s a lap. With two laps to go, the Brawn was jinking in the braking zones to try and force Webber into a mistake, and powersliding on the exit of the slower corners as Button tried everything to find a way past. On the final lap, the mechanics in the Brawn garage were on their feet, willing their man on, and Button even nosed in front on the long straight towards Turn 8, then again before Turn 11. But, each time, Webber defended his position and kept him behind. "I just couldn't make the move stick," smiled Button. "We were clean but on the edge, so it was perfect."

Webber's view mirrored Button's: "I thought, 'Yeah, this is going to be quite tight at the end'," said the Australian. "I just had to make sure I was accurate with my braking points. We had a good, clean fight." It would have been the perfect finale for Button, a swashbuckling move for second place on the last lap of the last race, but it wasn't to be.

Behind the podium finishers, Barrichello completed the two-by-two Red Bull then Brawn finishing order, ceding second place in the final rankings to Vettel in the process. Heidfeld shadowed him, bringing BMW another points finish on their final F1 outing in their current guise. As often with Heidfeld, it was a strong but unobtrusive drive from eighth. His best lap was 0.3s faster than his team-mate Kubica, who fell from seventh to 10th after banging wheels with Sebastien Buemi at Turn 8 and coming out on the losing side.

Next past the line was Kobayashi, who headed his vastly experienced team-mate Trulli. The Italian had

ABOVE Toro Rosso's Sebastien Buemi enhanced his reputation by finishing in the points again, this time lifting a single point for eighth

BELOW Nick Heidfeld powers through the tricky pit exit tunnel *en route* to fifth place for BMW Sauber

OPPOSITE Kamui Kobayashi was best of the one-stoppers, finishing sixth for Toyota. Renault's Fernando Alonso is his shadow as night falls

he was quicker than me at that point." Over the course of the next 12 laps, until his pit stop on lap 30, Kobayashi extended his advantage over Button to 7.5s, and this would prove crucial. Kobayashi pitted for his only stop, swapped to the less-favoured option tyre, and emerged 9s clear of the next one-stopping driver, Heikki Kovalainen. That hard work before the pit stops, plus hard driving with a heavy fuel load immediately afterwards, put Kobayashi on course for his first F1 points.

Out front, the second round of pit stops came and went – trouble-free – on lap 41 for Webber, lap 42 for Vettel and Button. Vettel held a 7s lead over

TALKING POINT
A PLACE LIKE NO OTHER

The F1 circus arrived in Abu Dhabi to be greeted by the most expensive, and most high-tech, circuit ever constructed. "Monaco, Montréal and Singapore do different things fantastically," said Khaldoon al Mubarak, Chairman of the Yas Marina Circuit. "Our hope is that Abu Dhabi can take it to a whole new level."

Al Mubarak also heads Mubadala, the government's business development company, chairs the Abu Dhabi Executive Affairs Authority, and is Chaiman of Manchester City FC. "We wanted to bring the best event that's out there to Abu Dhabi and that's what we got," he said of F1. "We're helping the growth of F1 and we have built a circuit that is like nothing seen before."

The first ground was broken in February 2007, and what emerged from the desert is simply stunning.

It involved 1.6 million cubic metres of earthworks, and pouring 225,000 cubic metres of concrete – enough to fill nearly 300 Boeing 747s – while the area of asphalt (720,000 square metres) is enough to cover 100 football pitches. This work was carried out by a workforce of 14,000.

Reactions from the F1 community ranged from wide-eyed wonderment to bemusement at the scale and luxury of the facilities. While on paper, the layout offered plenty of intricate challenges and 'technical' corners, it didn't seem too promising. Initial driver impressions, though, were very positive, as new World Champion Jenson Button explained: "The Yas Marina circuit is certainly an interesting one. When you look at the layout, it doesn't seem that exciting, but when you drive it it's fantastic. The track has a bit of everything, with high- and low-speed corners, positive and negative camber, and the walls are pretty close most of the way round."

The circuit forms just one part of a vast social engineering project, entitled 'The Abu Dhabi Economic Vision 2030', which is designed to diversify the oil-rich Emirate's economy away from its dependence on 'black gold'. Yas Island will include the first Ferrari World theme park, plus the Yas Links golf course, a Warner Brothers theme park and a water park, to become the city's entertainment destination. Nearby Saadiyat Island will form Abu Dhabi's cultural hub, with outposts of the Louvre and Guggenheim, plus satellite campuses of the Sorbonne and New York University.

The government plans to invest a total of $100 billion on creating a premium tourist destination, to which it hopes to attract three million tourists by 2015. It's a vast, ambitious project, in which F1 is destined to play a small, but crucial, role by putting Abu Dhabi on the world map.

ABOVE Nico Rosberg failed to score on his last outing for Williams, but at least his car looked spectacular in F1's first day–night race

BELOW Team principal Christian Horner congratulates Sebastian Vettel after the German scored Red Bull Racing's sixth win of the year

started sixth, Kobayashi 12th, and Trulli notionally had the better strategy, two-stopping in order to keep his time on the less-favoured option tyre to a minimum. After the final stops, Trulli attempted to pile on the pressure, with a string of personal fastest laps as he attempted to close the 7s gap. By the penultimate lap, Kobayashi was still 5s ahead and his feisty three points were probably also worth a seat for 2010.

The final points-scoring position was claimed by Buemi, who started 10th and drove solidly to eighth for his second points finish in succession. He pushed to the flag and, on his final lap, even set the second-fastest race lap, just 0.05s off Vettel, and a quarter

of a second quicker than Webber. While Toro Rosso hardly scaled the momentous heights of Vettel's extraordinary performances in 2008, Buemi's late-season form was a hint of promise to come.

Behind the points positions, little of real consequence occurred. Kovalainen successfully out-raced Räikkönen to ensure McLaren retained third place in the constructors' championship by a solitary point, while Nico Rosberg (ninth) and Fernando Alonso (14th) brought their times with their respective teams to undistinguished conclusions. Giancarlo Fisichella could manage no better than 16th for Ferrari, making the swap with Luca Badoer ultimately, and literally, pointless. And Romain Grosjean brought the curtain down on his time with Renault with a lacklustre drive to 18th; his fastest lap was 1.5s slower than team-mate Alonso, who he briefly headed in the opening laps.

Post-race, the mood of the podium finishers was light-hearted; the end of term had clearly arrived. Webber and Vettel teased Button about his impending 'wedding', while the World Champion laughed it all off. "It's been a very competitive and challenging season for us all," said Button. "For all three of us to be up on the podium at the last race is very enjoyable, and it's a great way to round out the year. Now, I'm going to enjoy myself and celebrate what I've achieved this season."

As for Vettel, he conceded it was a case of too little, too late for Red Bull, but he wasn't reaching for excuses. "We can't change yesterday, we can change tomorrow," said the German. "We have learned already, but there is still a lot we can improve for the future, and hopefully we will do so and come back stronger next year."

As the drivers and teams headed home from Abu Dhabi, the clock was already ticking: 132 days to go until the 2010 season opener in Bahrain…

SNAPSHOT FROM
ABU DHABI

CLOCKWISE FROM RIGHT Abu Dhabi really pushed the boat out with the design of its circuit facilities; Jean Todt made his first race visit as the new FIA President; a Ferrari dashes under the hotel footbridge and dives into Turn 19; Red Bull's Webber and Vettel hug after their 1–2; Lewis Hamilton fans in the stands were to be disappointed; new circuit, new signposts; BMW Sauber's Mario Theissen leads the team's farewell before its final grand prix; Silvana Barrichello wishes Rubens good luck

WEEKEND NEWS

■ The new Lotus F1 team announced a flurry of appointments around the Abu Dhabi Grand Prix weekend. The most notable of these was the announcement of its new Chief Executive Officer, Riad Asmat, who was formerly general manager of Proton. The announcement was made by team principal (and Air Asia CEO) Tony Fernandes in a press conference at Malaysia's Sepang Circuit.

■ Renault sealed its first major sponsorship deal since the Singapore 'Crashgate' scandal, when it announced a tie-up with Dutch watchmaker TW Steel on the Wednesday before the race. The company's logos appeared on the nose, front-wing flaps and sidepods of the Renault cars in Abu Dhabi.

■ Timo Glock was ruled out of the Abu Dhabi GP owing to the injuries he suffered in his accident in qualifying at Suzuka, when he cracked a vertebra and suffered a cut to his leg. Toyota said it didn't want to take any risks with Glock, who was expected to leave the team at the end of the season, and handed a second start to Kamui Kobayashi – who may well be in contention for a seat in 2010.

■ During the weekend in Abu Dhabi, Sir Frank Williams confirmed officially that his team would use Cosworth engines in 2010. "We believe that, working together, we will develop not only a competitive racing car for 2010, but also a long-term partnership that can take on the best in Formula 1," said Williams.

■ Campos Meta 1 became the first of 2010's new teams to confirm a driver when it announced the signing of Bruno Senna, nephew of the three-time Brazilian World Champion Ayrton. "I'm absolutely delighted to fulfil a lifetime dream," said the Brazilian, who was GP2 runner-up in 2008. "It is an honour to be returning the name Senna to Formula 1," said Campos CEO Enrique Rodriguez de Castro.

RACE RESULTS
ABU DHABI
YAS ISLAND

Official Results © [2009]
Formula One Administration Limited,
6 Princes Gate, London, SW7 1QJ.
No reproduction without permission.
All copyright and database rights reserved.

RACE DATE November 1st
CIRCUIT LENGTH 3.451 miles
NO. OF LAPS 55
RACE DISTANCE 189.810 miles
WEATHER Hot and very dry, 31°C
TRACK TEMP 37°C
RACE DAY ATTENDANCE 42,000
LAP RECORD Sebastian Vettel,
1m40.279s, 123.893mph, 2009

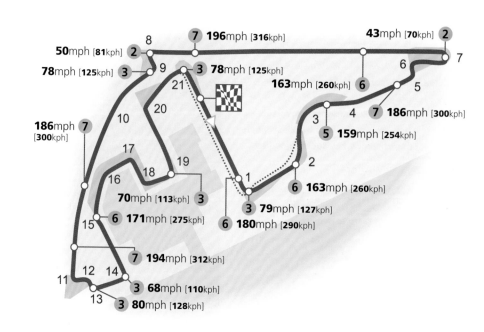

	PRACTICE 1		
	Driver	**Time**	**Laps**
1	L Hamilton	1m43.939s	18
2	J Button	1m44.035s	20
3	S Vettel	1m44.153s	28
4	R Barrichello	1m44.207s	23
5	N Heidfeld	1m44.667s	23
6	S Buemi	1m44.687s	32
7	A Sutil	1m44.688s	14
8	M Webber	1m44.805s	25
9	J Alguersuari	1m44.955s	33
10	J Trulli	1m44.958s	25
11	R Kubica	1m44.988s	22
12	H Kovalainen	1m45.123s	20
13	N Rosberg	1m45.649s	27
14	K Nakajima	1m45.679s	25
15	K Räikkönen	1m45.704s	27
16	F Alonso	1m45.865s	23
17	V Liuzzi	1m46.239s	22
18	G Fisichella	1m46.267s	26
19	K Kobayashi	1m46.364s	28
20	R Grosjean	1m46.411s	27

	PRACTICE 2		
	Driver	**Time**	**Laps**
1	H Kovalainen	1m41.307s	35
2	L Hamilton	1m41.504s	34
3	J Button	1m41.541s	39
4	S Vettel	1m41.591s	37
5	K Kobayashi	1m41.636s	34
6	S Buemi	1m41.683s	37
7	M Webber	1m41.684s	34
8	R Barrichello	1m41.831s	38
9	N Rosberg	1m41.931s	39
10	K Räikkönen	1m41.987s	39
11	A Sutil	1m42.180s	28
12	K Nakajima	1m42.245s	36
13	N Heidfeld	1m42.278s	36
14	J Trulli	1m42.409s	30
15	V Liuzzi	1m42.530s	33
16	F Alonso	1m42.782s	29
17	G Fisichella	1m42.932s	37
18	R Grosjean	1m43.021s	37
19	J Alguersuari	1m43.022s	39
20	R Kubica	1m43.708s	13

	PRACTICE 3		
	Driver	**Time**	**Laps**
1	J Button	1m40.625s	21
2	L Hamilton	1m40.627s	18
3	R Barrichello	1m40.907s	20
4	S Buemi	1m40.934s	22
5	N Heidfeld	1m41.241s	18
6	H Kovalainen	1m41.263s	20
7	J Trulli	1m41.310s	23
8	R Kubica	1m41.322s	20
9	A Sutil	1m41.372s	22
10	K Räikkönen	1m41.373s	23
11	S Vettel	1m41.403s	19
12	N Rosberg	1m41.478s	22
13	K Kobayashi	1m41.499s	24
14	V Liuzzi	1m41.675s	20
15	M Webber	1m41.682s	15
16	F Alonso	1m41.897s	19
17	K Nakajima	1m42.156s	21
18	R Grosjean	1m42.213s	19
19	G Fisichella	1m42.351s	23
20	J Alguersuari	No time	0

	QUALIFYING 1	
	Driver	**Time**
1	L Hamilton	1m39.873s
2	J Button	1m40.378s
3	J Trulli	1m40.517s
4	R Kubica	1m40.520s
5	N Heidfeld	1m40.558s
6	R Barrichello	1m40.574s
7	S Vettel	1m40.666s
8	M Webber	1m40.667s
9	H Kovalainen	1m40.808s
10	N Rosberg	1m40.842s
11	S Buemi	1m40.908s
12	K Kobayashi	1m41.035s
13	K Nakajima	1m41.096s
14	K Räikkönen	1m41.100s
15	J Alguersuari	1m41.503s
16	F Alonso	1m41.667s
17	V Liuzzi	1m41.701s
18	A Sutil	1m41.863s
19	R Grosjean	1m41.950s
20	G Fisichella	1m42.184s

	QUALIFYING 2	
	Driver	**Time**
1	L Hamilton	1m39.695s
2	S Vettel	1m39.984s
3	J Button	1m40.148s
4	M Webber	1m40.272s
5	J Trulli	1m40.373s
6	R Barrichello	1m40.421s
7	S Buemi	1m40.430s
8	R Kubica	1m40.545s
9	N Heidfeld	1m40.635s
10	N Rosberg	1m40.661s
11	K Räikkönen	1m40.726s
12	K Kobayashi	1m40.777s
13	H Kovalainen	1m40.983s
14	K Nakajima	1m41.148s
15	J Alguersuari	1m41.689s

Best sectors – Practice		
Sec 1	R Barrichello	17.632s
Sec 2	L Hamilton	42.482s
Sec 3	J Button	40.123s

Speed trap – Practice		
1	A Sutil	197.782mph
2	V Liuzzi	197.782mph
3	L Hamilton	196.601mph

Best sectors – Qualifying		
Sec 1	S Vettel	17.525s
Sec 2	L Hamilton	42.275s
Sec 3	S Vettel	39.709s

Speed trap – Qualifying		
1	J Button	198.031mph
2	A Sutil	197.285mph
3	V Liuzzi	196.601mph

IN 2008

There was no Abu Dhabi Grand Prix held in 2008, indeed the construction of the 3.5-mile Hermann Tilke-designed Yas Marina circuit was still progressing, the first ground having been broken in February 2007.

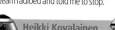

Lewis Hamilton

"After three laps, I had a problem with my right-rear brake pad, so I couldn't pull away from Sebastian. When the problem got worse, the team radioed and told me to stop."

Giancarlo Fisichella

"It was a shame about the drive-through penalty that compromised my second stint. I'm sorry that I wasn't able to contribute to the team in terms of points."

Robert Kubica

"My fight with Buemi was tough. We nearly touched into the chicane. He blocked the inside. When I moved to the right he pushed me over the inside kerb and I spun."

Fernando Alonso

"I'd have liked to finish on a high, especially as this was my last race with Renault. I would like to thank the entire team for everything that we have achieved together."

Jarno Trulli

"I made a good start and fought with the BMWs in the early laps, but I was struggling for traction. The rear tyres degraded, then braking consistency was an issue."

Heikki Kovalainen

"I got a really good start, but my car's performance wasn't as I would have liked, and the fuel load made it harder to make progress. After my pit stop, my KERS failed."

Kimi Räikkönen

"The track was a bit slippery at the start and that cost me a place to Kobayashi. When the Brawns were back ahead of me, after their first stop, our race was compromised."

Nick Heidfeld

"The strategy to go for a rather long stint paid off, and the track was even more fun when it had more rubber on it. It is a pleasing end to our last season together."

Romain Grosjean

"I made a good start, but was blocked several times. I also suffered some brake problems. Towards the end, I lost a place to Fisichella, which was a shame."

Kamui Kobayashi

"It was a really good race. I passed Räikkönen at the start, and that was vital as it would have been difficult to finish in the top six if I'd been behind him in the first stint."

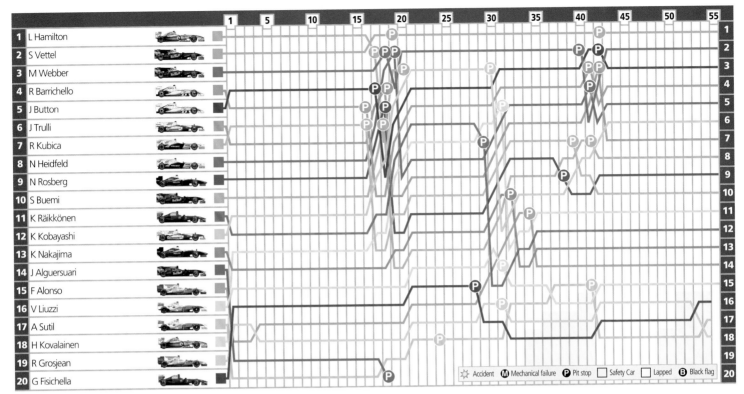

	Driver					
1	L Hamilton					
2	S Vettel					
3	M Webber					
4	R Barrichello					
5	J Button					
6	J Trulli					
7	R Kubica					
8	N Heidfeld					
9	N Rosberg					
10	S Buemi					
11	K Räikkönen					
12	K Kobayashi					
13	K Nakajima					
14	J Alguersuari					
15	F Alonso					
16	V Liuzzi					
17	A Sutil					
18	H Kovalainen					
19	R Grosjean					
20	G Fisichella					

☆ Accident Ⓜ Mechanical failure Ⓟ Pit stop ☐ Safety Car ☐ Lapped Ⓑ Black flag

QUALIFYING 3

	Driver	Time
1	L Hamilton	1m40.948s
2	S Vettel	1m41.615s
3	M Webber	1m41.726s
4	R Barrichello	1m41.786s
5	J Button	1m41.892s
6	J Trulli	1m41.897s
7	R Kubica	1m41.992s
8	N Heidfeld	1m42.343s
9	N Rosberg	1m42.583s
10	S Buemi	1m42.713s

GRID

	Driver	Time
1	L Hamilton	1m40.948s
2	S Vettel	1m41.615s
3	M Webber	1m41.726s
4	R Barrichello	1m41.786s
5	J Button	1m41.892s
6	J Trulli	1m41.897s
7	R Kubica	1m41.992s
8	N Heidfeld	1m42.343s
9	N Rosberg	1m42.583s
10	S Buemi	1m42.713s
11	K Räikkönen	1m40.726s
12	K Kobayashi	1m40.777s
13	K Nakajima	1m41.148s
14	J Alguersuari	1m41.689s
15	F Alonso	1m41.667s
16	V Liuzzi	1m41.701s
17	A Sutil	1m41.863s
18	H Kovalainen*	1m40.983s
19	R Grosjean	1m41.950s
20	G Fisichella	1m42.184s

* 5-place grid penalty for gearbox change

RACE

	Driver	Car	Laps	Time	Avg. mph	Fastest	Stops
1	S Vettel	Red Bull-Renault RB5	55	1h34m03.414s	121.036	1m40.279s	2
2	M Webber	Red Bull-Renault RB5	55	1h34m21.271s	120.655	1m40.571s	2
3	J Button	Brawn-Mercedes BGP 001	55	1h34m21.881s	120.641	1m40.642s	2
4	R Barrichello	Brawn-Mercedes BGP 001	55	1h34m26.149s	120.550	1m40.449s	2
5	N Heidfeld	BMW Sauber F1.09	55	1h34m29.667s	120.476	1m40.672s	2
6	K Kobayashi	Toyota TF109	55	1h34m31.757s	120.431	1m40.779s	1
7	J Trulli	Toyota TF109	55	1h34m37.780s	120.303	1m40.723s	2
8	S Buemi	Toro Rosso-Ferrari STR4	55	1h34m44.708s	120.157	1m40.326s	2
9	N Rosberg	Williams-Toyota FW31	55	1h34m49.355s	120.059	1m40.997s	2
10	R Kubica	BMW Sauber F1.09	55	1h34m51.594s	120.011	1m40.924s	2
11	H Kovalainen	*McLaren-Mercedes MP4-24	55	1h34m56.212s	119.914	1m41.316s	1
12	K Räikkönen	*Ferrari F60	55	1h34m57.731s	119.882	1m40.843s	1
13	K Nakajima	Williams-Toyota FW31	55	1h35m03.253s	119.766	1m40.754s	1
14	F Alonso	Renault R29	55	1h35m13.101s	119.560	1m40.757s	1
15	V Liuzzi	Force India-Mercedes VJM02	55	1h35m37.864s	119.044	1m41.277s	2
16	G Fisichella	*Ferrari F60	54	1h34m06.897s	118.761	1m41.132s	2
17	A Sutil	Force India-Mercedes VJM02	54	1h34m10.427s	118.687	1m40.904s	2
18	R Grosjean	Renault R29	54	1h34m11.396s	118.667	1m42.274s	2
R	L Hamilton	*McLaren-Mercedes MP4-24	20	Brakes	-	1m40.367s	1
R	J Alguersuari	Toro Rosso-Ferrari STR4	18	Gearbox	-	1m43.318s	0

* Denotes car fitted with KERS

CHAMPIONSHIP

	Driver	Pts
1	J Button	95
2	S Vettel	84
3	R Barrichello	77
4	M Webber	69.5
5	L Hamilton	49
6	K Räikkönen	48
7	N Rosberg	34.5
8	J Trulli	32.5
9	F Alonso	26
10	T Glock	24
11	F Massa	22
12	H Kovalainen	22
13	N Heidfeld	19
14	R Kubica	17
15	G Fisichella	8
16	S Buemi	6
17	A Sutil	5
18	K Kobayashi	3
19	S Bourdais	2

Fastest lap
S Vettel 1m40.279s
(123.893mph) on lap 54

Fastest speed trap
H Kovalainen 200.081mph
Slowest speed trap
R Grosjean 194.178mph

Fastest pit stop
1	J Button	22.369s
2	J Trulli	22.388s
3	N Heidfeld	22.603s

	Constructor	Pts
1	Brawn-Mercedes	172
2	Red Bull-Renault	153.5
3	McLaren-Mercedes	71
4	Ferrari	70
5	Toyota	59.5
6	BMW Sauber	36
7	Williams-Toyota	34.5
8	Renault	26
9	Force India-Mercedes	13
10	Toro Rosso-Ferrari	8

Jaime Alguersuari
"I had a gearbox problem, so pitted. But I came into the Red Bull pit next door, as my team wasn't expecting me. I drove out and had to retire when the gearbox broke."

Mark Webber
"Lewis struggled in the early laps and Seb and I were able to get closer than expected. Towards the end, Jenson closed the gap to me. We had a good fight on the limit."

Nico Rosberg
"It wasn't a terribly exciting race, as I just didn't have the pace to do any better. I'd have liked to help the team hold on to sixth place in the constructors' championship."

Adrian Sutil
"We had some problems at the start with the tyres, and had to stop earlier than expected for a new set. The two-stop strategy was the right one and the race went OK."

Jenson Button
"The last few laps were exciting and I was giving everything to take second place from Mark. I couldn't quite make the moves stick. He's a very difficult guy to overtake."

Sebastien Buemi
"I was having trouble matching Rosberg, but I picked up more and more speed as the race went on. I lost a bit of time behind Nakajima, but I think I did the best I could."

Sebastian Vettel
"The car was a dream. There was a lot of pressure, and I nearly went a bit wide in the pit entrance at my first stop, but it was enough to get past Lewis, who then had to retire."

Kazuki Nakajima
"It wasn't easy running a one-stop, and I didn't feel the first stint went well. The middle of the race was more affected by traffic, but there was nothing to do but plug away."

Vitantonio Liuzzi
"I had a brake problem more or less from the start, so couldn't fight for positions. I was behind the Williams at the start and then one of the Toyotas mid-race."

Rubens Barrichello
"Mark took a chunk of my wing at Turn 1. It lost me a lot of downforce which let Jenson past, but I was able to live with understeer so we decided not to change it."

CHAMPIONSHIP RESULTS

DRIVER RESULTS

	Driver	Nationality	Car	ROUND 1 March 29 AUSTRALIAN GP	ROUND 2 April 5 MALAYSIAN GP	ROUND 3 April 19 CHINESE GP	ROUND 4 April 26 BAHRAIN GP	ROUND 5 May 10 SPANISH GP
1	Jenson Button	GBR	Brawn-Mercedes BGP 001	1P	1PF	3	1	1P
2	Sebastian Vettel	GER	Red Bull-Renault RB5	13	15	1P	2	4
3	Rubens Barrichello	BRA	Brawn-Mercedes BGP 001	2	5	4F	5	2F
4	Mark Webber	AUS	Red Bull-Renault RB5	12	6	2	11	3
5	Lewis Hamilton	GBR	McLaren-Mercedes MP4-24	D4	7	6	4	9
6	Kimi Räikkönen	FIN	Ferrari F60	15	14	10	6	R
7	Nico Rosberg	GER	Williams-Toyota TF109	6F	8	15	9	8
8	Jarno Trulli	ITA	Toyota TF109	3	4	R	3PF	R
9	Fernando Alonso	SPA	Renault R29	5	11	9	8	5
10	Timo Glock	GER	Toyota TF109	4	3	7	7	10
11	Felipe Massa	BRA	Ferrari F60	R	9	R	14	6
12	Heikki Kovalainen	FIN	McLaren-Mercedes MP4-24	R	R	5	12	R
13	Nick Heidfeld	GER	BMW Sauber F1.09	10	2	12	19	7
14	Robert Kubica	POL	BMW Sauber F1.09	14	R	13	18	11
15	Giancarlo Fisichella	ITA	Force India-Mercedes VJM02	11	18	14	15	14
			Ferrari F60					
16	Sebastien Buemi	SWI	Toro Rosso-Ferrari STR4	7	16	8	17	R
17	Adrian Sutil	GER	Force India-Mercedes VJM02	9	17	17	16	R
18	Kamui Kobayashi	JAP	Toyota TF109					
19	Sebastien Bourdais	FRA	Toro Rosso-Ferrari STR4	8	10	11	13	R
20	Kazuki Nakajima	JAP	Williams-Toyota FW31	R	12	R	R	13
21	Nelson Piquet Jr	BRA	Renault R29	R	13	16	10	12
22	Vitantonio Liuzzi	ITA	Force India-Mercedes VJM02					
23	Romain Grosjean	FRA/SWI	Renault R29					
24	Jaime Alguersuari	SPA	Toro Rosso-Ferrari STR4					
25	Luca Badoer	ITA	Ferrari F60					

RACE SCORING

1st	10	POINTS
2nd	8	POINTS
3rd	6	POINTS
4th	5	POINTS
5th	4	POINTS
6th	3	POINTS
7th	2	POINTS
8th	1	POINT

DATA KEY

D	DISQUALIFIED
F	FASTEST LAP
NC	NON-CLASSIFIED
NS	NON-STARTER
P	POLE POSITION
R	RETIRED
W	WITHDRAWN

QUALIFYING HEAD-TO-HEAD

Brawn-Mercedes
Barrichello–Button **10–7**

Red Bull-Renault
Vettel–Webber **15–2**

McLaren-Mercedes
Hamilton–Kovalainen **12–5**

Ferrari
Räikkönen–Massa **6–4**
Räikkönen–Badoer **2–0**
Räikkönen–Fisichella **5–0**

Toyota
Trulli–Glock **11–4**
Trulli–Kobayashi **2–0**

BMW Sauber
Kubica–Heidfeld **10–7**

Williams-Toyota
Rosberg–Nakajima **15–2**

Renault
Alonso–Piquet Jr **9–1**
Alonso–Grosjean **7–0**

Force India-Mercedes
Sutil–Fisichella **6–6**
Sutil–Liuzzi **4–1**

Toro Rosso-Ferrari
Buemi–Bourdais **7–2**
Buemi–Alguersuari **8–0**

Race results for both drivers, ie, first and second listed as 1/2 with team's best result listed first.

CONSTRUCTOR RESULTS

1	Brawn-Mercedes
2	Red Bull-Renault
3	McLaren-Mercedes
4	Ferrari
5	Toyota
6	BMW Sauber
7	Williams-Toyota
8	Renault
9	Force India-Mercedes
10	Toro Rosso-Ferrari

Drivers (Rounds 6–17)

ROUND 6 MONACO GP (May 24)	ROUND 7 TURKISH GP (June 7)	ROUND 8 BRITISH GP (June 21)	ROUND 9 GERMAN GP (July 12)	ROUND 10 HUNGARIAN GP (July 26)	ROUND 11 EUROPEAN GP (August 23)	ROUND 12 BELGIAN GP (August 30)	ROUND 13 ITALIAN GP (September 13)	ROUND 14 SINGAPORE GP (September 27)	ROUND 15 JAPANESE GP (October 4)	ROUND 16 BRAZILIAN GP (October 18)	ROUND 17 ABU DHABI GP (November 1)	TOTAL POINTS
1P	1F	6	5	7	7	R	2	5	8	5	3	95
R	3P	1PF	2	R	R	3F	8	4	1P	4	1F	84
2	R	3	6	10	1	7	1	6	7	8P	4	77
5	2	2	1P	3F	9	9	R	R	17F	1F	2	69.5
12	13	16	18	1	2P	R	12P	1P	3	3	RP	49
3	9	8	R	2	3	1	3	10	4	6	12	48
6	5	5	4	4	5	8	16	11	5	R	9	34.5
13	4	7	17	8	13	R	11	12	2	R	7	32.5
7	10	14	7F	RP	6	R	5	3F	10	R	14	26
10	8	9	9	6	14F	10	14	2	NS			24
4	6	4	3	NS								22
R	14	R	8	5	4	6	6	7	11	12	11	22
11	11	15	10	11	11	5	7	R	6	R	5	19
R	7	13	14	13	8	4	R	8	9	2	10	17
9	R	10	11	14	12	2P						
							9	13	12	10	16	8
R	15	18	16	16	R	12	13	R	R	7	8	6
14	17	17	15	R	10	11	4F	R	13	R	17	5
									9	6		3
												2
8	18	R	R									
15	12	11	12	9	18	13	10	9	15	R	13	
R	16	12	13	12								
							R	14	14	11	15	
						15	R		16	13	18	
					15	R	R	R	R	14	R	
					17	14						

Constructors / Teams (Rounds 1–17)

ROUND 1 AUSTRALIAN GP (March 29)	ROUND 2 MALAYSIAN GP (April 5)	ROUND 3 CHINESE GP (April 19)	ROUND 4 BAHRAIN GP (April 26)	ROUND 5 SPANISH GP (May 10)	ROUND 6 MONACO GP (May 24)	ROUND 7 TURKISH GP (June 7)	ROUND 8 BRITISH GP (June 21)	ROUND 9 GERMAN GP (July 12)	ROUND 10 HUNGARIAN GP (July 26)	ROUND 11 EUROPEAN GP (August 23)	ROUND 12 BELGIAN GP (August 30)	ROUND 13 ITALIAN GP (September 13)	ROUND 14 SINGAPORE GP (September 27)	ROUND 15 JAPANESE GP (October 4)	ROUND 16 BRAZILIAN GP (October 18)	ROUND 17 ABU DHABI GP (November 1)	TOTAL POINTS
1/2	1/5	3/4	1/5	1/2	1/2	1/R	3/6	5/6	7/10	1/7	7/R	1/2	5/6	7/8	5/8	3/4	172
12/13	6/15	1/2	2/11	3/4	5/R	2/3	1/2	1/2	3/R	9/R	3/9	8/R	4/R	1/17	1/4	1/2	153.5
D/R	7/R	5/6	4/12	9/R	12/R	13/14	16/R	8/18	1/5	2/4	6/R	6/12	1/7	3/11	3/12	11/R	71
15/R	9/14	10/R	6/14	6/R	3/4	6/9	4/8	3/R	2/NS	3/17	1/14	3/9	10/13	4/12	6/10	12/16	70
3/4	3/4	7/R	3/7	10/R	10/13	4/8	7/9	9/17	6/8	13/14	10/R	11/14	2/12	2/NS	9/R	6/7	59.5
10/14	2/R	12/13	18/19	7/11	11/R	7/11	13/15	10/14	11/13	8/11	4/5	7/R	8/R	6/9	2/R	5/10	36
6/R	8/12	15/R	9/R	8/13	6/15	5/12	5/11	4/12	4/9	5/18	8/13	10/16	9/11	5/15	R/R	9/13	34.5
5/R	11/13	9/16	8/10	5/12	7/R	10/16	12/14	7/13	12/R	6/15	14/R	5/15	3/R	10/16	13/R	14/18	26
9/11	17/18	14/17	15/16	14/R	9/14	17/R	10/17	11/15	14/R	10/12	2/11	4/R	14/R	13/14	11/R	15/17	13
7/8	10/16	8/11	13/17	R/R	8/R	15/18	18/R	16/R	15/16	16/R	12/R	13/R	R/R	R/R	7/14	8/R	8

STARTS

286	Rubens Barrichello
256	Riccardo Patrese
250	Michael Schumacher
247	David Coulthard
230	Giancarlo Fisichella
218	Jarno Trulli
210	Gerhard Berger
208	Andrea de Cesaris
204	Nelson Piquet
201	Jean Alesi
199	Alain Prost
194	Michele Alboreto
187	Nigel Mansell
180	Ralf Schumacher
176	Graham Hill
175	Jacques Laffite
171	Jenson Button
	Niki Lauda
169	Nick Heidfeld
165	Jacques Villeneuve
163	Thierry Boutsen
162	Mika Häkkinen
	Johnny Herbert
161	Ayrton Senna
159	Heinz-Harald Frentzen
158	Martin Brundle
	Olivier Panis
157	Kimi Räikkönen
152	John Watson
149	René Arnoux
147	Eddie Irvine
	Derek Warwick
146	Carlos Reutemann
144	Emerson Fittipaldi
140	Fernando Alonso
139	Mark Webber
135	Jean-Pierre Jarier
132	Eddie Cheever
	Clay Regazzoni
128	Mario Andretti
126	Jack Brabham
123	Ronnie Peterson
119	Pierluigi Martini
116	Damon Hill
	Jacky Ickx
	Alan Jones
115	Felipe Massa
114	Keke Rosberg
	Patrick Tambay
112	Denny Hulme
	Jody Scheckter

OTHERS

70	Nico Rosberg
57	Robert Kubica
52	Lewis Hamilton
	Heikki Kovalainen
	Adrian Sutil
50	Luca Badoer
44	Vitantonio Liuzzi
43	Sebastian Vettel
36	Timo Glock
	Kazuki Nakajima

CONSTRUCTORS

793	Ferrari
666	McLaren
585	Williams
490	Lotus
418	Tyrrell
411	Toro Rosso (+ Minardi)
409	Prost (+ Ligier)
394	Brabham
383	Arrows
320	Force India (+ Jordan/Midland/Spyker)
317	Benetton (+ Toleman)
287	BMW Sauber
263	Renault
230	March
223	Red Bull (+ Stewart/Jaguar)

OTHERS

140	Toyota
105	Honda (+Brawn)

WINS

91	Michael Schumacher
51	Alain Prost
41	Ayrton Senna
31	Nigel Mansell
27	Jackie Stewart
25	Jim Clark
	Niki Lauda
24	Juan Manuel Fangio
23	Nelson Piquet
22	Damon Hill
21	Fernando Alonso
20	Mika Häkkinen
18	Kimi Räikkönen
16	Stirling Moss
14	Jack Brabham
	Emerson Fittipaldi
	Graham Hill
13	Alberto Ascari
	David Coulthard
12	Mario Andretti
	Alan Jones
	Carlos Reutemann
11	Rubens Barrichello
	Lewis Hamilton
	Felipe Massa
	Jacques Villeneuve
10	Gerhard Berger
	James Hunt
	Felipe Massa
	Ronnie Peterson
	Jody Scheckter

OTHERS

7	Jenson Button
5	Sebastian Vettel
3	Giancarlo Fisichella
2	Mark Webber
1	Heikki Kovalainen
	Robert Kubica
	Jarno Trulli

CONSTRUCTORS

210	Ferrari
164	McLaren
113	Williams
79	Lotus
35	Brabham
	Renault
27	Benetton
23	Tyrrell
17	BRM
16	Cooper
11	Brawn (+Honda)
10	Alfa Romeo
9	Ligier
	Maserati
	Matra
	Mercedes
	Vanwall
6	Red Bull
4	Jordan
3	March
	Wolf
1	BMW Sauber
	Eagle
	Hesketh
	Penske
	Porsche
	Toro Rosso
	Shadow
	Stewart

IN 2009

6	Jenson Button
4	Sebastian Vettel
2	Rubens Barrichello
	Lewis Hamilton
	Mark Webber
1	Kimi Räikkönen

CONSTRUCTORS

8	Brawn
6	Red Bull
2	McLaren
1	Ferrari

WINS IN ONE SEASON

13	Michael Schumacher	2004
11	Michael Schumacher	2002
9	Nigel Mansell	1992
	Michael Schumacher	1995
	Michael Schumacher	2000
	Michael Schumacher	2001
8	Mika Häkkinen	1998
	Damon Hill	1996
	Michael Schumacher	1994
	Ayrton Senna	1988
7	Fernando Alonso	2005
	Fernando Alonso	2006
	Jim Clark	1963
	Alain Prost	1984
	Alain Prost	1988
	Alain Prost	1993
	Kimi Räikkönen	2005
	Michael Schumacher	2006
	Ayrton Senna	1991
	Jacques Villeneuve	1997

CONSTRUCTORS

15	Ferrari	2002
	Ferrari	2004
	McLaren	1988
12	McLaren	1984
	Williams	1996
11	Benetton	1995
10	Ferrari	2000
	McLaren	1989
	McLaren	2005
	Williams	1992
	Williams	1993

POLE POSITIONS

68	Michael Schumacher
65	Ayrton Senna
33	Jim Clark
	Alain Prost
32	Nigel Mansell
29	Juan Manuel Fangio
26	Mika Häkkinen
24	Niki Lauda
	Nelson Piquet
20	Damon Hill
18	Mario Andretti
	René Arnoux
17	Lewis Hamilton
	Fernando Alonso
	Jackie Stewart
16	Stirling Moss
	Kimi Räikkönen
15	Felipe Massa
14	Alberto Ascari
	Rubens Barrichello
	James Hunt
	Ronnie Peterson
13	Jack Brabham
	Graham Hill
	Jacky Ickx
	Juan Pablo Montoya
	Jacques Villeneuve
12	Gerhard Berger
	David Coulthard

OTHERS

7	Jenson Button
5	Sebastian Vettel
4	Giancarlo Fisichella
	Jarno Trulli
1	Nick Heidfeld
	Heikki Kovalainen
	Robert Kubica
	Mark Webber

CONSTRUCTORS

203	Ferrari
145	McLaren
125	Williams
107	Lotus
51	Renault
39	Brabham
16	Benetton
14	Tyrrell
12	Alfa Romeo
11	BRM
	Cooper
10	Maserati
9	Prost (+ Ligier)
8	Brawn (+Honda)
	Mercedes
7	Vanwall
6	Red Bull (+Jaguar)
5	March
4	Matra
3	Force India (+Jordan)
	Shadow
	Toyota
2	Lancia
1	BAR
	BMW Sauber
	Toro Rosso

IN 2009

4	Jenson Button
	Sebastian Vettel
	Lewis Hamilton
1	Fernando Alonso
	Rubens Barrichello
	Giancarlo Fisichella
	Jarno Trulli
	Mark Webber

CONSTRUCTORS

5	Brawn
	Red Bull
4	McLaren
1	Force India
	Renault
	Toyota

FASTEST LAPS

75	Michael Schumacher
41	Alain Prost
35	Kimi Räikkönen
30	Nigel Mansell
28	Jim Clark
25	Mika Häkkinen
24	Niki Lauda
23	Juan Manuel Fangio
	Nelson Piquet
21	Gerhard Berger
19	Damon Hill
	Stirling Moss
	Ayrton Senna
18	David Coulthard
17	Rubens Barrichello
15	Clay Regazzoni
	Jackie Stewart
14	Jacky Ickx
13	Fernando Alonso
	Alberto Ascari
	Alan Jones
	Riccardo Patrese
12	René Arnoux
	Jack Brabham
	Felipe Massa
	Juan Pablo Montoya
11	John Surtees

OTHERS

3	Lewis Hamilton
	Mark Webber
	Sebastian Vettel
2	Jenson Button
	Giancarlo Fisichella
	Nick Heidfeld
	Heikki Kovalainen
	Nico Rosberg
1	Timo Glock
	Adrian Sutil
	Jarno Trulli

CONSTRUCTORS

218	Ferrari
137	McLaren
130	Williams
71	Lotus
40	Brabham
35	Benetton

OTHERS

29	Renault
6	Brawn (+Honda)
	Red Bull
3	Toyota
2	BMW Sauber
1	Force India

IN 2009

3	Sebastian Vettel
	Mark Webber
2	Fernando Alonso
	Rubens Barrichello
	Jenson Button
1	Timo Glock
	Felipe Massa
	Nico Rosberg
	Adrian Sutil
	Jarno Trulli

CONSTRUCTORS

6	Red Bull
4	Brawn
2	Renault
	Toyota
1	Ferrari
	Force India
	Williams

POINTS

(Figures given are for gross tally – ie, including scores that were later dropped.)

1369	Michael Schumacher
798.5	Alain Prost
614	Ayrton Senna
607	Rubens Barrichello
579	Kimi Räikkönen
567	Fernando Alonso
535	David Coulthard
485.5	Nelson Piquet
482	Nigel Mansell
420.5	Niki Lauda
420	Mika Häkkinen
385	Gerhard Berger
360	Damon Hill
	Jackie Stewart

OTHERS

326	Jenson Button
320	Felipe Massa
275	Giancarlo Fisichella
256	Lewis Hamilton
245.5	Jarno Trulli
220	Nick Heidfeld
169.5	Mark Webber
137	Robert Kubica
125	Sebastian Vettel
105	Heikki Kovalainen
75.5	Nico Rosberg

CONSTRUCTORS

4091.5	Ferrari
3372.5	McLaren
2606	Williams
1352	Lotus
1082	Renault
877.5	Benetton
854	Brabham
617	Tyrrell
504	BMW Sauber
439	BRM
424	Prost (+ Ligier)
344.5	Red Bull (+ Stewart/Jaguar)
333	Cooper
326	Brawn (+Honda)
301	Force India (+ Jordan/Midland/Spyker)
278.5	Toyota

OTHERS

94	Toro Rosso (+Minardi)

LAPS LED

5108	Michael Schumacher
2931	Ayrton Senna
2683	Alain Prost
2058	Nigel Mansell
1940	Jim Clark
1918	Jackie Stewart
1633	Nelson Piquet
1590	Niki Lauda
1490	Mika Häkkinen
1363	Damon Hill
1347	Juan Manuel Fangio
1237	Fernando Alonso

OTHERS

1040	Kimi Räikkönen
854	Rubens Barrichello
825	Felipe Massa
798	Lewis Hamilton
384	Jenson Button
264	Sebastian Vettel
213	Giancarlo Fisichella
163	Jarno Trulli
100	Mark Webber

IN 2009

280	Jenson Button
212	Sebastian Vettel
182	Lewis Hamilton
125	Rubens Barrichello
90	Mark Webber
43	Kimi Räikkönen
16	Nico Rosberg
15	Fernando Alonso
10	Timo Glock
6	Felipe Massa
4	Giancarlo Fisichella
3	Jarno Trulli
2	Heikki Kovalainen

CONSTRUCTORS

405	Brawn
302	Red Bull
184	McLaren
49	Ferrari
16	Williams
15	Renault
13	Toyota
4	Force India

MILES LED

14992	Michael Schumacher
8345	Ayrton Senna
7751	Alain Prost
6282	Jim Clark
5905	Nigel Mansell
5789	Juan Manuel Fangio
5692	Jackie Stewart
4820	Nelson Piquet
4475	Mika Häkkinen
4386	Niki Lauda
3958	Stirling Moss
3939	Damon Hill
3674	Fernando Alonso
3667	Alberto Ascari
3369	Kimi Räikkönen

OTHERS

2579	Rubens Barrichello
2455	Felipe Massa
2354	Lewis Hamilton
1145	Jenson Button
912	Sebastian Vettel
693	Giancarlo Fisichella
423	Jarno Trulli
289	Mark Webber
209	Robert Kubica
129	Heikki Kovalainen
91	Nico Rosberg
73	Nick Heidfeld
42	Timo Glock
40	Nelson Piquet Jr
9	Sebastien Bourdais

IN 2009

821	Jenson Button
727	Sebastian Vettel
570	Lewis Hamilton
394	Rubens Barrichello
261	Mark Webber
178	Kimi Räikkönen
56	Nico Rosberg
42	Fernando Alonso
34	Timo Glock
32	Felipe Massa
17	Giancarlo Fisichella
10	Jarno Trulli
6	Heikki Kovalainen

DRIVERS' TITLES

7	Michael Schumacher
5	Juan Manuel Fangio
4	Alain Prost
3	Jack Brabham
	Niki Lauda
	Nelson Piquet
	Ayrton Senna
	Jackie Stewart
2	Fernando Alonso
	Alberto Ascari
	Jim Clark
	Emerson Fittipaldi
	Mika Häkkinen
	Graham Hill
1	Mario Andretti
	Jenson Button
	Giuseppe Farina
	Lewis Hamilton
	Mike Hawthorn
	Damon Hill
	Phil Hill
	Denny Hulme
	James Hunt
	Alan Jones
	Nigel Mansell
	Kimi Räikkönen
	Jochen Rindt
	Keke Rosberg
	Jody Scheckter
	John Surtees
	Jacques Villeneuve

CONSTRUCTORS' TITLES

16	Ferrari
9	Williams
8	McLaren
7	Lotus
2	Brabham
	Cooper
	Renault
1	Benetton
	Brawn
	BRM
	Matra
	Tyrrell
	Vanwall

NB: Renault stats are based on the team that evolved from Benetton in 2002, and include the stats that have happened since plus those from Renault's first F1 spell from 1977–85. Likewise, Honda stats from the 1960s are combined with those from the 21st century team that evolved from BAR from the start of 2006.